CRIMINOLOGICAL THEORIES

Introduction, Evaluation, and Application

Fifth Edition

Ronald L. Akers
University of Florida

Christine S. Sellers
University of South Florida

New York   Oxford
OXFORD UNIVERSITY PRESS
2009

Oxford University Press, Inc., publishes works that further Oxford University's
objective of excellence in research, scholarship, and education.

Oxford   New York
Auckland   Cape Town   Dar es Salaam   Hong Kong   Karachi
Kuala Lumpur   Madrid   Melbourne   Mexico City   Nairobi
New Delhi   Shanghai   Taipei   Toronto

With offices in
Argentina   Austria   Brazil   Chile   Czech Republic   France   Greece
Guatemala   Hungary   Italy   Japan   Poland   Portugal   Singapore
South Korea   Switzerland   Thailand   Turkey   Ukraine   Vietnam

Published by Oxford University Press, Inc.
198 Madison Avenue, New York, New York 10016
http://www.oup.com

Library of Congress Cataloging-in-Publication Data

Akers, Ronald L.
   Criminological theories : introduction, evaluation, and application /
Ronald L. Akers, Christine S. Sellers.—5th ed.
      p. cm.
   Includes bibliographical references and index.
   ISBN 978-0-19-533252-0 (alk. paper)
   1. Criminology.   I. Sellers, Christine Sharon.   II. Title.
   HV6018.A38 2008
   364—dc22   2007050210

Printed in the United States of America
on acid-free paper

This book is dedicated
to the precious memory of my father

Charles E. Akers
(1920–1993)

and to my loving mother
Thelma Louise Akers

* * *

To my mother and father
Sharon Mary Sellers
and
Donald Orville Sellers

Contents

Chapter 1
Introduction to Criminological Theory

Chapter 2
Deterrence and Rational Choice Theories

Chapter 3
Biological Theories

Chapter 4
Psychological Theories

Chapter 5
Social Learning Theory

Chapter 6
Social Bonding and Control Theories

Chapter 7
Labeling and Reintegrative Shaming Theory

Chapter 8
Social Disorganization, Anomie, and Strain Theories

Chapter 9
Conflict Theory

Chapter 10
Marxist and Critical Theories

Chapter 11
Feminist Theories

Chapter 12
Integrating Criminological Theories

Preface to the Fifth Edition

The purposes of this book are to review the basic concepts and principles of criminological theories and to evaluate their adequacy as explanations of criminal and deviant behavior and/or explanations of the criminal law and justice system. Although not exhaustive, the coverage of theories is comprehensive. We have included all the major theories that have been and continue to be subjects of most theory-testing articles in the leading criminological journals, the main theories that are of interest in the history of criminology, and the principal newer theories that have received attention in the literature.

The first goal in presenting each theory is to give a concise and clear exposition of its central concepts, assertions, and hypotheses. The intent is to provide an accurate, understandable introduction for readers who are not familiar with the theory and a review for those who are. In each case, an effort has been made not only to present the classic or original statements of a theory but to show modifications and revisions of it, including the most recent and significant developments.

The second goal is to evaluate the theory. In chapter 1, we review the main criteria by which the merits of a theory can be judged: logical consistency, scope, parsimony, applicability to policy, testability, and empirical validity. All these are invoked at various points, but the central focus of the evaluation of each theory is the *empirical validity* of the theory. We review the research relevant to the theory and assess how well the findings support or contradict the main assertions of the theory. Before the empirical adequacy of a theory can be evaluated, of course, it must be testable, and a considerable amount of attention is given to questions of tautology and measurement.

The third goal is to extend this evaluation to the usefulness of each theory for guiding actions to control and prevent crime and delinquency. Classical and contemporary examples are given of how the theories have been or can be applied to policy and practice. Just as the empirical validity of a theory must be assessed by the research done to test it, its policy usefulness must be assessed by research on the effectiveness of programs related to it. Therefore, we report on relevant research and evidence to evaluate how well various programs work that explicitly or implicitly reflect identifiable theoretical principles.

Each chapter has been updated and substantially revised in light of recent research and important changes in the theories. More extensive revision and updating have been done on psychological, social learning, social bonding and self-control, labeling, anomie and strain, and feminist theories. The last chapter (chap. 12) is devoted to the topic of theoretical rivalry and integration, and it too has been substantially revised. Earlier and more recent examples of conceptual and propositional integration are reviewed and evaluated. An important feature of this edition is the addition of Table 12.1, which provides an overview of all of the major theories of criminal and deviant behavior showing in which chapter the presentation and evaluation of the theory can be found and brief entries on each theory's (1) major theorists or proponents, (2) main concepts, (3) main propositions, (4) level of empirical validity, and (5) main policy implications. This overview table is intended to provide a concise way of reviewing each theory and comparing the relative adequacy of the different theories.

The book is intended as the principal text in courses on theories of crime, delinquency, and deviance. It would also be useful as a supplemental text or one of several reading assignments in such courses or in general criminology, juvenile delinquency, deviance, criminal behavior, and similar courses.

Although writing with a student audience in mind, we have not hesitated to draw on the scholarly and research literature, and we have not shied away from addressing central issues and controversies in the field. The text citations to the theoretical and research literature and the list of references are thorough and extensive. Therefore, we believe that other readers will find some value in the book. It should be useful to criminal justice practitioners looking for validated theoretical principles and relevant literature on which to build or enhance programs and policy. Theoreticians and researchers will find some original analysis and insights that may be of interest.

Acknowledgments

We acknowledge the personal encouragement and highly competent help of Claude Teweles, former president and publisher of Roxbury Publishing Company, and his unfailing interest and attention to the project, from the first to the fifth edition. The transition to the new publisher was made smoother by the professional and diligent efforts of Sherith Pankratz of Oxford University Press. We thank Christine D'Antonio for her highly effective and efficient management of the setting and copyediting of the text and references. We thank Sherri DioGuardi and Jessica Shue Chiarizio, graduate students in criminology at the University of Florida, for help in library research, reference checking, proofing, and indexing.

We are grateful for the insights and suggestions for improvement from colleagues and students who have used the book. We want to thank an anonymous reviewer for the suggestion that was the impetus for constructing the overview Table 12.1. We are happy to recognize the contributions of all of these while absolving them of responsibility for any shortcomings of the book.

Acknowledgments by Ronald Akers

It is a joy to thank my family publicly for their unconditional love that always sustains me: my wife Caroline, Ron II, Tamara and Lee Phillips (and grandchildren William, Walker, and Caroline), and Levi and Marie Akers (and grandchildren Jair and Asia). The debt I owe Caroline and Levi extends to their specific contributions to this book. They collaborated on the concept and design of a prototype for the front cover of the book. In addition, Levi assisted me in compiling the indexes and performed various disc-checking, word-processing, and other tasks associated with submission of the text via electronic media in the first edition. The solid groundwork he did for that first edition has continued to be of benefit in preparation of subsequent editions.

Acknowledgments by Christine Sellers

I am deeply grateful to my family, friends, and colleagues (and especially to my co-author and publisher) for their patience while I completed the work on this edition of the book. My husband, Neil, has always been my staunchest supporter, and my daughter, Claire, is the light of my life.

Chapter 1
_____

Introduction to Criminological Theory

What Is Theory?
_____

To many students, criminal justice practitioners, and other people, theory has a bad name. In their minds, the word *theory* means an irrelevant antonym of *fact*. Facts are real, whereas theories seem to involve no more than impractical mental gymnastics. Theories are just fanciful ideas that have little to do with what truly motivates real people. This is a mistaken image of theory in social science in general and in criminology in particular. Theory, if developed properly, is about real situations, feelings, experience, and human behavior. An effective theory helps us to make sense of facts that we already know and can be tested against new facts. Theories are tentative answers to the commonly asked questions about events and behavior. Why? By what process? How does it work?

> In general, scientific theories make statements about the relationships between observable phenomena. (Vold, Bernard, and Snipes, 2002:4)

> Theories, then, are really generalizations of a sort; they explain how two or more events are related to each other and the conditions under which the relationship takes place. (Williams and McShane, 2004:2)

> A theory is a set of interconnected statements or propositions that explain how two or more events or factors are related to one another. (Curran and Renzetti, 2001:2)

Note that these and other definitions of theory (see Gibbs, 1990) refer to statements about relationships between actual events; about what is and what will be. They are not answers to questions of what ought to be, nor are they philosophical, religious, or metaphysical systems of beliefs and values about crime and society (see the section on theory and ideology, pp. 13–14).

1

Criminological theories are abstract, but they entail more than ivory-tower or armchair speculations. They are part of the broader social science endeavor to explain human behavior and society. Understanding why people conform to or deviate from social and legal norms is an integral part of a liberal education. Moreover, such understanding is vital for those who plan to pursue specialized careers in the law or criminal justice. Virtually every policy or action taken regarding crime is based on some underlying theory or theories of crime. It is essential, therefore, to comprehend and evaluate the major theories of criminology, not only for the academic or research criminologist, but also for the educated citizen and the legal or criminal justice professional.

Types of Criminological Theories

Edwin H. Sutherland (1947) defined criminology as the study of the entire process of law making, law breaking, and law enforcing. This definition provides us with a starting point for classifying criminological theories. One such major type of theory addresses the first and third parts of this process: the making and enforcing of the law. Theories of this kind attempt to account for why we have the laws we have and why the criminal justice system operates the way it does. Another major type of theory explains law breaking. Such theories account for criminal and delinquent behavior. They are usually extended to explain any deviant behavior that violates social norms, whether or not such behavior also violates the law.

There are not as many different theories of the first kind (theories of law and criminal justice) as there are of the second kind (theories of criminal and deviant behavior). Therefore, although both are important, more attention will be paid here to the second type of theory. Conflict, labeling, Marxist, and feminist theories are examples of theories that attempt to shed light on both criminal behavior and the law.

Theories of Making and Enforcing Criminal Law

Theories of making and enforcing criminal law (also herein referred to as theories of law and criminal justice) offer answers to questions of how or why certain behavior and people become defined and are dealt with as criminal in society. Why is a particular conduct considered illegal and what determines the kind of action to be taken when it occurs? How is it decided, and who makes the decision, that such conduct is criminal? And how are the resources of the public and state brought to bear against it? Theories try to answer these questions by proposing that social, political, and economic variables affect the legislation of law, administrative decisions and rules, and the implementation and operation of law in the criminal justice system.

Theories of Criminal and Deviant Behavior

Theories of criminal and deviant behavior try to answer the question of why social and legal norms are violated. This question has two interrelated parts: (1) Why are there variations in group rates of crime and deviance, and (2) why are some individuals more likely than others to commit criminal and deviant acts?

The first question poses the problem of trying to make sense of the differences in the location and proportion of deviant and criminal behavior in various groups and societies. For example, why does the United States have a higher rate of crime than Japan but a lower rate than some European countries? Why do males as a group commit so many more violent and criminal acts than females? How do we explain the differences in homicide and drug use among different classes and groups within the same society?

The second question raises the issue of explaining differences among individuals in committing or refraining from criminal acts. Why are some individuals more likely to break the law than others? By what process or under what circumstances do people typically, and not just in a specific, individual case, reach the point of obeying or violating the law? Why does one person commit a crime, given a certain opportunity, while another does not, given the same opportunity? Why are some people more likely than others to commit frequent crimes or pursue criminal careers?

The first set of questions focuses on societal and group patterns; the second on individual differences. A theory that addresses broader questions about differences across societies or major groups in society is called a "macro" theory. Conversely, one that focuses specifically on small group or individual differences is referred to as operating on the "micro" level of analysis (Alexander, Bernhard, Munch, and Smelser, 1987). Other terms have also been used to make a similar distinction between theories. Cressey (1960) referred to "epidemiology" (the prevalence and distribution of crime across groups and societies) and "individual conduct." Akers referred to such different theories as social structural or processual (Akers, 1968; 1985). These distinctions between macro and micro, structural and processual, refer not only to questions about groups and individual behavior, but also to the kinds of answers a theory offers. For example, a theory that tries to answer the question of the differences between male and female crime rates by relying on innate biological differences between men and women would still be operating on the micro level.

In actuality, the two major questions of group and individual behavior are really just subtypes of the same general question: Why do or do not people commit crime and deviance?

The dependent variable in macro-level theories is based ultimately on the same behavior that is the dependent variable in micro-level theories. Social structure and the crime rates are embodied in the actions and reactions of real people. Crime rates are summary statements of relative amounts of individual behavior in different groups or social categories (Akers, 1998:330).

This is why theories of criminal behavior are neither strictly structural nor processual, although each will emphasize one or the other. Theories emphasizing social structure propose that the proportion of crimes among groups, classes, communities, or societies differ because of variations in their social or cultural make-up. Most structural theories, however, also include implicit or explicit statements regarding the process by which these structural conditions produce high or low crime rates. Processual theories assert that an individual commits criminal acts because he or she has experienced a particular life history, possessed a particular set of individual characteristics, or encountered a particular situation. Such theories also consider the deviancy-producing structures that an individual must encounter in order to increase the probability of his or her committing a crime.

There are other ways to classify criminological theories (e.g., see Tittle and Paternoster, 2000; Bernard and Engel, 2001). One common way is to refer not just to micro or macro, but to several levels of explanation that ascend from the smallest to the largest unit of analysis. Such a classification typically categorizes the theories according to the general scientific discipline from which the explanatory variables are drawn. The most common classifications are biological theories that explain crime with one or more genetic, chemical, neurological, or physiological variables; psychological theories based on personality, emotional maladjustment, psychic disturbance, or psychological traits; social psychological theories that account for crime by reference to behavior, self, and cognitive variables in a group context; and sociological theories that explain crime with cultural, structural, and sociodemographic variables (see Jensen and Rojek, 1998; Vold et al., 2002; Liska and Messner, 1999).

Just as the categories of structure and process overlap to some extent, some theories will draw from two or more disciplines. For instance, contemporary biological theories do not rely exclusively on genetic or biochemical factors, but also draw from psychological or sociological variables as well. Other theories, such as social learning, are clearly social-psychological, utilizing both sociological and psychological variables.

The theories are arranged in the following chapters in an order that draws roughly from both the structure-process distinction and the classification of theories as biological, psychological, and sociological. Chapter 2 introduces the classical and contemporary statements of deterrence theory. Chapter 3 surveys early and recent biological theories. Psychological theories are surveyed in chapter 4. The remaining chapters review the major sociological theories of crime. Social learning theory (chap. 5), control theories (chap. 6), and labeling theory (chap. 7) are the more social-psychologically oriented of these sociological theories. Chapter 8 (anomie and strain theories), chapter 9 (conflict theory), chapter 10 (Marxist and critical theories), and chapter 11 (feminist theories) discuss those theories that draw the most heavily from social structure and culture. Labeling, conflict, Marxist, and feminist perspectives are theories both of criminal justice and theories of criminal behavior. The final chapter (chap. 12) examines the extent to which the differences and commonalities in theories can be reconciled and integrated. Whatever the classification of theory that may be used, there will be some kind of overlap, shortcomings, and loose ends. No special case will be made here for the order in which the various theories are presented. The focus here is not on how best to classify each theory but rather on introducing what each theory proposes and on evaluating its validity.

Criteria for Evaluating Theory

How do we know if a theory offers a sound explanation of crime or criminal justice? Commonalities across theories can be found, but the various theories that will be explored provide different, sometimes contradictory, explanations of crime. How do we judge which explanation is preferable over another or which is the best amongst several theories?

If criminological theories are to be scientific, then they must be judged by scientific criteria. The most important of these is empirical validity—the extent to which a theory can be verified or refuted with carefully gathered evidence. However, there are several other major criteria by which theories can be assessed. These include internal logical consistency, scope and parsimony, testability, empirical validity, and usefulness and policy implication. (For discussions of the criteria for evaluating criminological theories, see Gibbons, 1994; Barlow and Ferdinand, 1992; Tittle, 1995; Vold et al., 2002.)

Logical Consistency, Scope, and Parsimony

The basic prerequisite for a sound theory is that it has clearly defined concepts and that its propositions are logically stated and internally consistent (Budziszewski, 1997). For example, a theory that proposes that criminals are biologically deficient and that deficiency explains their criminal behavior cannot also claim that family socialization is the basic cause of criminal behavior.

The scope of a theory refers to the range of phenomena that it proposes to explain. For instance, a theory that accounts only for the crime of check forgery may be accurate, but it is obviously very limited in scope. A better theory is one that accounts for a wide range of offenses, including check forgery. A theory of juvenile delinquency that does not relate as well to adult criminality is more restricted than one that accounts for both juvenile delinquency and adult crime. A theory that explains only the age distribution of crime has a more limited scope than one that explains the age, race, sex, and class distributions of crime.

Parsimony, the conciseness and abstractness of a set of concepts and propositions, is also a desirable characteristic in a scientific theory. Scope and parsimony are interrelated in that a theory that explains a wide scope of events with a few succinct statements is scientifically preferable to one that relies on a complex set of propositions and variables that accounts for only a small range of events. The principle of parsimony is to use as few concepts and propositions as possible to explain the widest range of phenomena. For example, a theory that proposes that all crime and delinquency are caused by low self-control is much more parsimonious than a theory that requires a different set of multiple hypotheses to explain crime and delinquency, depending on the type of offense and the age, sex, or race of the offender.

Testability

A scientific theory must be testable by objective, repeatable evidence. If a theory cannot be tested against empirical findings, it has no scientific value. It is not enough for a theory to fit known facts about crime or empirical evidence consistent with its propositions. It must also be possible to subject the theory to empirical falsification; in other words, it must be open to evidence that may counter or disprove its hypotheses with negative findings. If it is not falsifiable in this sense, it is not testable (Stinchcombe, 1968).

A theory may be untestable because the definitions of its concepts and its propositions are stated as a tautology. A tautology is a statement or hypothesis that is true by definition or involves circular reasoning (Budziszewski, 1997). If, for example, one begins with the definition of low self-control as the failure to refrain from crime and then proposes low self-control as a cause of law violation, then one's proposition is tautological. Given the definition of low self-control, the proposition can never be proven false because self-control is defined by the very thing it is hypothesized to explain. It simply says that a person who has low self-control has low self-control, or that a person who violates the law violates the law. A variation on a tautology that is true by definition is seen in the practice of placing a label on some behavior, then using that label to explain the same behavior. For instance, one may label serial killers as psychopaths, then assert that people commit serial murders because they are psychopathic. Such a statement does no more than repeat the label. Similarly, we may observe that a person drinks excessively and has problems with alcohol, so we theorize that the person over drinks because he is an alcoholic. How do we know he is an alcoholic? We know because he drinks excessively and has problems with alcohol. We have come full circle.

Another way in which a theory may be untestable is that its propositions are so open-ended that any contradictory empirical evidence can be interpreted or reinterpreted to support the theory. For example, a theory may propose that males who rob banks are motivated by an irrational and unconscious impulse to resolve their guilt over their childhood sexual attraction towards their own mothers. This is a testable explanation of male bank robbery because it is not true by definition. If research finds enough bank robbers who fit this description, then the theory is supported. If research uncovers other cases where bank robbers claim their only motive is money and they have no such feelings toward their mothers, then that can be taken as falsifying the theory. However, the theory cannot be falsified if the claims of the latter bank robbers are dismissed by asserting that their very denial of these feelings in effect supports the theory because the same unconscious impulse that motivated them to rob banks also rendered them unconscious of their true motivations. Similarly, a theory may contend that criminal laws always serve the interests of the ruling capitalist elite. Even if laws are enacted to serve the interest of the working class, one could always reinterpret them with the argument that such laws only appear to serve the working class but in fact serve the ruling class. There is no way to falsify the theory. Hence, a theory that can never be proven wrong, regardless of the findings, is not a testable theory.

A theory may also be untestable because its concepts are not measurable by observable and reportable events. A theory's concepts and propositions identify the explanatory events or independent variables that account for variations in the dependent variables, which are events or behavior to be explained. Even a non-tautological theory cannot be tested if it is not possible to find observable events that can be taken as objective and repeatable measures of these concepts. Without such measures, the hypothesized relationships cannot be checked against actual events. If a theory proposes that people commit crimes because they are possessed by invisible demons, there is no way to prove whether such demons are responsible for the crime. If we cannot measure the existence of demons separately from the occurrence of criminal behavior, we may simply assume the existence of the demons from the existence of the crimes. We have a similar tautology if the dependent and independent variables are measured by the same events. For example, it is tautological to explain a high rate of delinquency as the result of social disorganization if one of the indicators of social disorganization is the delinquency rate itself. Both the events to be explained and the events used to explain them are the same thing. It is tautological to interpret an event as the cause of itself.

Not all concepts must be directly measurable for a theory to be testable, but one must be able to relate them in a logical and clear way to measurable phenomena. For instance, one part of social learning theory proposes that an individual's exposure to admired models who are involved in deviant or delinquent behavior will increase the chances that person will imitate those same behaviors. Imitation is defined as one engaging in acts after he or she has watched them being engaged in by others. It is quite possible to directly observe the behavior of adult or peer models whom adolescents are in a position to imitate, or to ask adolescents to report exposure to such models and then observe the extent to which their behavior matches that of the models. The concept of imitation refers to observable, measurable events; therefore, propositions about modeling are testable.

Empirical Validity

This is the most important criterion for judging a theory. Empirical validity simply means that a theory has been supported by research evidence. For a theory to be logical, parsimonious, and non-tautological means little if it turns out to be false. It is seldom the case, however, that a theory is found to be entirely true or entirely false. Falsifiable theories may encounter some negative evidence without being judged as wholly invalid. The question is, what degree of empirical support does the theory have? Do the findings of research provide weak or strong support? Does the preponderance of evidence support or undermine the theory? How does its empirical validity compare with that of other theories?

For instance, deterrence theory proposes in part that offenders will not repeat their crimes if they have been caught and given severe legal punishment. If research finds that this is true for only a small minority of offenders or that punished offenders are only slightly less likely to repeat crimes than unpunished offenders, then the theory has some, but not much, empirical validity. Labeling theory, on the other hand, proposes that the experience of being caught and processed by the criminal justice system labels offenders as criminal. This application of a stigmatizing label is hypothesized to promote their self-iden[...] criminals and makes them more likely, rather than less likely, to r[...] their crimes. If research finds that, other things being equal, apprehended offenders are more likely to recidivate than those who have not been caught, then labeling theory has more empirical validity than deterrence theory.

Concepts of Causality and Determinism. Notice the terms *more likely* and *less likely*. Empirical validity does not mean that a theory must identify variables that always cause criminal behavior to occur or always explain the decision to arrest an offender. The traditional concept of causality in science is that cause X must precede and produce effect Y. To be a cause, X must be both a "necessary condition," the absence of which means that Y will not occur, and a "sufficient condition," so that Y always occurs in the presence of X. No criminological theory can meet these two traditional causation criteria of necessary and sufficient conditions. But that makes little difference because a probabilistic concept of causality is more appropriate for assessing the empirical validity of criminological theories. The probabilistic concept of causation simply asserts that the presence of X renders the occurrence of Y more probable; that is, contemporaneous variations or changes in criminal behavior are associated or correlated with variations or changes in the explanatory variables identified in the theory. The presence of the variables specified in the theory precedes the occurrence of crime and delinquency, thereby predicting when they are more likely to occur or reoccur. The stronger the correlations and associations, the greater the theory's empirical validity.

Interpreting correlations as causation even in the probabilistic sense remains a problem because the direction of the relationship between two correlated variables may not be the same as specified in the theory. For instance, a theory may hypothesize that an adolescent engages in delinquent conduct as a result of associating with other adolescents who are already delinquent. Finding a correlation between one's own delinquent behavior and the delinquency of one's friends, therefore, could be taken as evidence in support of the theory. But the relationship may exist for converse reasons; that is, the adolescent first becomes delinquent and then seeks out delinquent associates. Thus, the association with other delinquents may be the dependent variable, resulting from one's own prior delinquency, rather than the independent variable that increases the probability that the adolescent will commit delinquency. Further research would be needed to find out in which direction the relationship typically runs.

The probabilistic concept of causality suggests that human behavior is neither completely determined by external forces nor completely an outcome of the unfettered exercise of free-will choices. Rather, behavior is best understood from the middle-ground perspective of "soft determinism" (Matza, 1964). Soft determinism allows for human agency and recognizes that various factors influence and limit actions but leave room for individual choices that cannot be completely predicted. Increasingly, criminological theorists have come to adopt this view (Gibbons, 1994; Akers, 1998; Walsh, 2002):

> Numerous theorists, however, have come to advance similar arguments in recent years. Versions of soft determinism or indeterminism are now advocated by control theorists, rational choice theorists, social learning theorists, conflict theorists, and others. ...[P]eople may transcend previous experience through reflective thought, altering their preferences and developing unexpected and sometimes novel strategies for acting on those preferences. (Agnew, 1995a:83, 88)

Quality of Empirical Tests of Theory. Not all empirical tests of theories are of equal methodological quality. The better studies do a good job of measuring the variables derived from the theory (or theories) being tested, correctly specify the hypotheses about the relationships expected or predicted by the theory, measure all of the main concepts, use more than one measure of each concept, and use measures that correctly and reliably reflect the meaning of the concepts in the theory (Carmines and Zeller, 1979). Such studies test the direct effect of the factors hypothesized by the theory to explain criminal behavior. But they also test, where appropriate, for indirect or interaction effects—that is, examine how much the independent variables affect the dependent variables when other factors are controlled or taken into account. For example, self-control theory proposes that those lower in self-control are more likely to commit crime when the opportunity for crime is high than when opportunity is low. The outcome of a study that allows for the interaction between self-control and opportunity (by testing the effects of low self-control taking into account the relative presence or absence of opportunities) carries greater weight than the outcome of a study that models only the combined effects of self-control and opportunity or ignores the effect of opportunity altogether. Other issues related to the quality of empirical tests include whether or not the appropriate causal order and the linear or nonlinear shape of the relationships specified in the theory have been carefully examined.

Further, the research should be done with well-selected samples of subjects, respondents, or informants to which the theory applies. For instance, a sample of lower class urban boys is appropriate, whereas a sample of adults would be inappropriate, for testing a theory that hypothesizes the existence of an urban delinquent subculture among lower class male adolescents. Similarly, good studies use the proper unit of analysis, that is, individuals or small groups for micro-level theories and communities, nations, or societies for macro-level theories.

Usefulness and Policy Implications

Finally, the value of a criminological theory can be further evaluated by its usefulness in providing guidelines for effective social and criminal justice policy and practice. Every criminological theory implies a therapy or a policy. The basic assumption in theory-guided practice is that the better the theory explains the problem, the better it is able to guide efforts to solve the problem.

All major criminological theories have implications for, and have indeed been utilized in, criminal justice policy and practice. Every therapy, treatment program, prison regimen, police policy, or criminal justice practice is based, either explicitly or implicitly, on some explanation of human nature in general or criminal behavior in particular (Barlow, 1995; Gibbs, 1995).

Every recommendation for changes in our legal and criminal justice system has been based on some underlying theory that explains why the laws have been enacted, why the system operates as it does, and why those who are in the system behave as they do.

The question, then, is not whether policy can be or should be based on theory—it already is guided by theory—but rather, how well is policy guided by theory and how good is the policy and the theory on which it is predicated? In most public discourse about criminal justice policy, the underlying theoretical notions are ill-stated and vaguely understood. A policy may be adopted for political, economic, or bureaucratic reasons; then a theoretical rationale is formulated or adopted to justify the policy. Typically, the theoretical underpinnings of a program are not a single coherent and tested theory, but rather a hybrid mixture of several, sometimes conflicting, theoretical strands (Wright and Dixon, 1978). This understandably results from the effort to try any number of things to see what works. Utility and effectiveness, not theoretical purity, are the standard in policy and practical application.

Criminological theory has implications not only for official public policy and programs, but also for what can be done informally in families, peer groups, neighborhoods, and communities. From a sociological perspective, this informal control system embedded in everyday life and interaction has more impact on behavior than formal criminal justice policy (Felson, 1998). Of course, there is an interdependence of formal and informal actions and activities to combat crime and delinquency. In either case, the policy should not rest solely on its t
or philosophical plausibility or simply conform to common s

as theories must be shown empirically to be valid, policy and practice must be shown empirically to work and produce the outcomes they are intended to have (prevention, control, or reduction of crime and delinquency). They must also meet ethical, legal, and moral standards of fairness, equity, due process, and appropriateness for a democratic society (Akers, 2005).

A clear, parsimonious, non-tautological, and empirically valid theory has even more to recommend it if it can also guide programs and practices. If a program guided by that theory is instituted and is successful in achieving its goals, we gain additional confidence in the validity of the theory. Evaluation research is often conducted to assess the degree to which a program achieves its goals. However, like empirical tests of theory, not all evaluations are of equal quality. "Outcome evaluations" that utilize experimental designs, with both pre- and post-intervention measures, and random assignment of subjects to treatment (experimental) and control conditions offer the most credible results. However, evaluations to verify a program's effectiveness, no matter how rigorous the design, may still produce an incomplete assessment of the program or policy. A "process evaluation" may also be done to see if the program has indeed been implemented in the proper manner and with the proper participants as specified by the theory and goals underlying the program. The program itself may be a poor adaptation of the theory's guiding principles. There may be practical or ethical roadblocks against carrying out the actions that the theory implies are needed to change criminal behavior, reduce recidivism, or make the system operate better.

The policy and program implications of some biological theories that involve chemical or surgical intrusion into a person's body are often seen as most objectionable and as involving the most severe ethical, moral, and constitutional problems. But the ethical, legal, and moral issues of fairness, equity, due process, and appropriateness are not qualitatively different from those faced by policy derived from any other theoretical perspective (Akers, 2005:30).

There may be political or economic factors that come into play to enhance or retard the effectiveness of the program that have nothing to do with the validity of the theory. Therefore, the success or failure of policies and programs cannot be used by themselves to test theory. This does not mean such outcomes are irrelevant to theory development and modification:

> The phrase "nothing is as practical as a good theory" is a twist of an older truth: Nothing improves theory more than its confrontation with practice. It is my belief that the development of applied social theory will do much good to basic theoretical sociology. This is obvious

enough as we deal with those parts of theoretical sociology that a
put to practical use; they become refined in the process. (Zetterberg,
1962:189)

Theory and Ideology

A theory to explain the existing operation of the criminal justice
system is not the same as a judgment about what kind of legal system
we should have. It is not a theoretical statement, for instance, to argue
that we should have a fair, just, and effective criminal justice system.
Such a statement offers desirable social goals about which the vast
majority of citizens may agree. Other statements, such as the desirability of completely disarming the civilian population, generate controversy. But neither provides a scientific explanation of law and criminal
justice. Arguments over the goals and purposes of the system—such as
whether it should focus on crime control to protect society rather than
due process to protect the rights of the accused or whether it should
simply punish law violators as their just deserts or should attempt to
rehabilitate them—are not theoretical arguments. Philosophical and
pragmatic debates over society's control of crime may be informed by
theory and have relevance to the application of theory, but they are not
themselves theoretical explanations of why laws are formulated and
enforced or why people commit crimes. Theories attempt to explain
the behavior of the participants in the legal system and the operation
of the system itself. They produce hypotheses about the factors that
account for legal and criminal justice actions and decisions. Theories
do not tell us what are the correct, proper, and desirable values that
should be exemplified in the system. Theories account for criminal
behavior. They do not tell us what should or should not be considered
criminal.

This is not to imply that those who are proponents of a particular
theory are unaffected by their philosophical and value judgments.
There is a relationship between theories of crime and criminal justice
and philosophies that defines the goals of a just, effective, and well-
managed criminal justice system. Such goals partially direct which
theories will be considered to be important, and those theories will
help to develop strategies to reach these goals.

For example, one of the reasons that conflict theory is important in
criminology is that its theoretical propositions about the operation of
the system are relevant to the political and moral debates over the just-
ness of that system. The goal of a just system is to treat everyone equita-
bly based on legally relevant factors such as the nature of the criminal
act and the laws relating to it. Conflict theory (see chap. 9) hypothesizes that actions taken in the criminal justice system may be decided

differentially based on such factors as the race, class, and gender of offenders, rather than on the type of crime. The decisions of a criminal justice system that relies more on such social characteristics than on the nature of the crime is not a just system. Therefore, the extent to which conflict theory is supported or refuted by research evidence is critical to the debate over the fairness of the criminal justice system.

Further, one's political, social, religious, or other philosophical leanings may influence preferences for different theoretical perspectives or vice versa. As an example of this, Walsh and Ellis (1999) surveyed criminologists at a national conference on their political ideologies, the theories they favored, and which conditions or factors they considered to be important causes of crime. The findings (based on a low response rate) showed that most academic criminologists consider themselves to be politically liberal (50%) or moderate (26%), but some identify themselves as conservatives (15.6%) or radicals (8.2%). Not surprising, this last group favored Marxist/radical (see chap. 10) or conflict theories (see chap. 9) and saw unjust economic conditions as the most important cause of crime. Criminologists who identify themselves as politically conservative tend to favor self-control (see chap. 6) and routine activities theory (see chap. 2) and to see lack of family supervision and unstable family life as the important causes of criminal and delinquent behavior. Political moderates tend to favor self-control and social control theories (see chap. 6), whereas liberals also endorse social control theory as well as differential association/social learning (see chap. 5), and to some extent conflict and feminist theory (chaps. 9 and 11). Thus, among this group of criminologists, one's theoretical stance is somewhat related to one's political philosophy. But the two are separable and incompletely related, as shown by the finding that some version of social or self-control theory is endorsed by conservatives, moderates, and liberals alike. Moreover, there are certain key theoretical issues over which there is little disagreement regardless of one's political ideology.

> Interestingly no significant disagreements were found among conservatives, moderates, liberals, or radicals regarding the importance of "lack of empathy," "peer influences," "impulsiveness," "alcohol abuse," and "drug abuse" as causes of serious and persistent offending. Criminologists of all political persuasions seem to consider these factors fairly important causes of criminal behavior. (Walsh and Ellis, 1999:14)

The adequacy of a theory cannot be properly judged by the political or partisan ideologies of its proponents. Valid explanations of crime and criminal justice may be used for liberal, conservative, or radical policies. The weakest reason for accepting or rejecting a theory of crime or criminal justice is how well it conforms to or defies one's own beliefs, ideologies, or preferred policies.

Emphasis on Empirical Validity and Application of Theories

The primary criterion for judging a theory is its verification or refutation by empirical research (Gibbs, 1990), and this will be emphasized in each of the following chapters. The policy implications and applications of theories are also important and will be highlighted. Reference will be made, where appropriate, to other criteria for evaluating criminological theories. But the emphasis in this book will be on the following: (1) introducing the central concepts and propositions of criminological theories, (2) evaluating their empirical validity, and (3) assessing their application to policies and programs.

Summary

Criminological theories are both theories of the making and enforcing of criminal law and theories of breaking the law. The former attempts to explain the content of the laws and the behavior of the criminal justice system; the latter tries to explain the commission, occurrence, and patterns of criminal and deviant behavior. Such theories best fit assumptions of probabilistic or soft determinism rather than strict determinism. Structural or macro theories focus on differences in group and societal rates of crime, whereas processual or micro theories address individual differences and social processes. The aim of criminological theory is to gain an understanding of crime and criminal justice. Theories are useful for addressing the issues of which policies are more or less likely to work, but they are not philosophical statements about what ought to be done. A theory may be evaluated, either on its own or by comparison with other theories, on the criteria of clarity and consistency, scope and parsimony, testability, practical usefulness, and empirical validity. Of these, the focus here will be on a theory's empirical validity and on its usefulness for guiding policy and practice.

6 characterstics

logical consistney

parsimony

testability

scope

usefulnesst

policy implications

empiracal support

|
U
P
P
t
e
s

Chapter 2

Deterrence and Rational Choice Theories

Classical Criminology and the Deterrence Doctrine

lassical criminology refers primarily to the 18th-century writings of Cesare Beccaria in Italy and Jeremy Bentham in England.[1] Both were utilitarian social philosophers who were primarily concerned with legal and penal reform rather than with formulating an explanation of criminal behavior. In doing so, however, they formulated a theory of crime that remains relevant to criminology today.[2]

The system of law, courts, and penalties of the day that the classical criminologists wanted to change was marred in most European countries by arbitrary, biased, and capricious judicial decisions. It was common to use torture to coerce confessions and to inflict cruel punishments, including whipping, public hanging, and mutilation. The classical criminologists were intent on providing a philosophical rationale for reforming the judicial and legal system to make it more rational and fair. Their ideas converged with the developing interests of the rising middle classes of merchants and the economic philosophy promoting trade, commerce, and industry. They promoted reforms that many of the leading intellectuals of the day were advocating. Their arguments also fit well with developing political movements seeking greater citizen participation and democratic control of government. Many of the law reforms proposed by classical utilitarian philosophers, such as doing away with cruel and unusual punishment and instituting the right to a speedy trial, were incorporated into the Constitution of the United States in its Bill of Rights amendments. Others, such as a legislatively fixed scale of punishment for each type and degree of crime, were incorporated into the new legal codes of France in 1791, following the French Revolution.

Deterrence: Certainty, Severity, and Celerity of Punishment

Severity and Fitting the Punishment to the Crime. The basic premise in classical criminology is that actions are taken and decisions are made by persons in the rational exercise of free will. All individuals choose to obey or violate the law by a rational calculation of the risk of pain versus potential pleasure derived from an act. In contemplating a criminal act, they take into account the probable legal penalties and the likelihood that they will be caught. If they believe that the legal penalty threatens more pain than the probable gain produced by the crime, then they will not commit the crime. Their calculation is based on their own experience with criminal punishment, their knowledge of what punishment is imposed by law, and their awareness of what punishment has been given to apprehended offenders in the past. (See the discussion of specific and general deterrence that follows.)

A legal system that is capricious and uncertain does not guarantee sufficient grounds for making such rational decisions. Such a system is not only unjust, it is also ineffective in controlling crime. To prevent crime, therefore, criminal law must provide reasonable penalties that are applied in a reasonable fashion to encourage citizens to obey rather than violate the law. The primary purpose of criminal law is deterrence. It should not be used simply to avenge the wrongs done to the state or the victim. The legislators enact laws that clearly define what is unlawful, prescribe punishment for law violation sufficient enough to offset the gain from crime, and thereby deter criminal acts by citizens. Judges should do no more than determine guilt or innocence and should use no discretion to alter penalties provided for by law. The punishment must "fit the crime." This may be interpreted as retribution: an eye for an eye, a tooth for a tooth. But to Bentham and Beccaria, fitting the punishment to the crime meant more than making the punishment proportional to the harm caused to society. It meant that the punishment must be tailored to be just severe enough to overcome the gain offered by crime. Punishment that is too severe is unjust, and punishment that is not severe enough will not deter.

The assumption behind this argument is that the amount of gain or pleasure derived from committing a particular crime is approximately the same for everyone. Therefore, making the punishment fit the crime stands in contrast to the punishment fitting the individual. The law should strictly apply the penalty called for a particular crime, and the penalty should not vary by the characteristics or circumstances of the offender. The argument also assumes that the more serious or harmful the crime, the more the individual stands to gain from it; therefore, the more serious the crime, the more severe the penalty should be to deter it. In classical criminology, this concept of proportionality meant that the legislature should enact an exact scale of crimes with an exact scale of threatened punishment, without regard to individual differences. This was later modified to consider that age and mental capacity may affect one's ability to reason rationally.

Certainty and Celerity of Punishment. The deterrence doctrine does not rest on the severity of legal penalties alone. It further determines that, to deter, punishment for crime must be swift and certain. Celerity refers to the swiftness with which criminal sanctions are applied after the commission of crime:

> The more immediately after the commission of a crime a punishment is inflicted, the more just and useful it will be.... An immediate punishment is more useful; because the smaller the interval of time between the punishment and the crime, the stronger and more lasting will be the association of the two ideas of crime and punishment. (Beccaria, 1972:18–19)

Certainty refers to the probability of apprehension and punishment for a crime. If the punishment for a crime is severe, certain, and swift, the citizenry will rationally calculate that more is to be lost than gained from crime and will be deterred from violating the law. Both Beccaria and Bentham saw a connection between certainty and severity of punishment. Certainty is more effective in deterring crime than severity of punishment. The more severe the punishment, the less likely it is to be applied; and the less certain the punishment, the more severe it must be to deter crime.

Specific and General Deterrence. There are two ways by which deterrence is intended to operate. First, apprehended and punished offenders will refrain from repeating crimes if they are certainly caught and severely punished. This is known as "specific deterrence" or "special deterrence." Second is "general deterrence" in which the state's punishment of offenders serves as an example to those in the general public who have not yet committed a crime, instilling in them enough fear of state punishment to deter them from crime (Zimring, 1971; Zimring and Hawkins, 1973).

Modern Deterrence Theory

Studies of Deterrence

The principles of certainty, severity, and celerity of punishment, proportionality, and specific and general deterrence remain at the heart

1. certainly
2. celerity
3. severity

of modern deterrence theory (Zimring and Hawkins, 1973; Gibbs, 1975; Wright, 1993b). Furthermore, the deterrence doctrine remains the philosophical foundation for modern Western criminal law and criminal justice systems. The policy implications of deterrence theory evolved from the interest in changing the judicial and penal policy of the 18th century, and the theory continues to attract many adherents today because of its direct applicability to policy on law enforcement, courts, and imprisonment. The most common policy reaction to crime problems is to call for increased penalties, more severe sentences, additions to the police force so more arrests can be made, and the increased certainty of conviction and sentencing. These trends are directly related to all the efforts by legislators to make criminal penalties more certain and severe, to reduce the recidivism of already punished offenders, and to deter new offenders. A policy of longer sentences, especially when selectively applied to habitual offenders, may also be based on the premise that imprisonment, even when it does not deter, will at least incapacitate offenders for a period of time (Blumstein, Cohen, and Nagin, 1978). But the deterrence potential is always behind the policy on all criminal sanctions, from the death penalty on down. (Next, see Deterrence and Criminal Justice Policy.)

Despite the long history and continuing importance of deterrence theory, empirical research designed to test it was rare until the late 1960s. Prior to that, most discussions of deterrence revolved around the humanitarian, philosophical, and moral implications of punishment rather than the empirical validity of the theory (Ball, 1955; Toby, 1964; Gibbs, 1975). Since 1970, however, deterrence has been one of the most frequently discussed and researched theories in criminology (see Gibbs, 1975; Tittle, 1980; Wright, 1993b). Although there have been fewer deterrence studies in the past decade, considerable research and policy interest in deterrence continues today (Pratt, Cullen, Blevins, Daigle, and Madensen., 2006; Webster, Doob, and Zimring, 2006).

The first studies on deterrence consisted primarily of comparisons between states that provided capital punishment for first-degree homicide and those that had no death penalty. The early studies also examined homicide rates in states before and after they abolished capital punishment. These studies found that the provision or absence of the death penalty in state statutes had no effect on the homicide rate (Sellin, 1959; Bedau, 1964). Most research since then has made similar findings, and there is a consensus among leading criminologists that the death penalty has little general deterrent effect on homicide (Radelet and Akers, 1996). Research by Gibbs (1968), Tittle (1969), and Chiricos and Waldo (1970) set the stage for many of the studies that followed and have continued to this day. Their studies moved beyond the effects of the death penalty to test the deterrent effect of certainty and severity

Objective vs. perceptual (handwritten annotation)

of punishment on a whole range of criminal and delinquent offenses. They did not include measures for celerity of punishment, however, and it has seldom been included in deterrence research ever since (see Nagin and Pogarsky, 2001).

Objective Measures of Deterrence. Deterrence research measures the severity and certainty of criminal penalties in two ways. The first approach is to use objective indicators from official criminal justice statistics. The certainty or risk of penalty, for instance, is measured by the arrest rate (the ratio of arrests to crimes known to the police) or by the proportion of arrested offenders who are prosecuted and convicted in court. The severity of punishment may be measured by the maximum sentence provided by law for an offense, by the average length of sentence for a particular crime, or by the proportion of convicted offenders sentenced to prison rather than to probation or some other non-incarceration program. Deterrence theory predicts an inverse or negative relationship between these official measures of legal penalties and the official crime rate measured by crimes known to the police. When the objective certainty and severity of criminal sanctions are high, according to the theory, official crime rates should be low (Gibbs, 1975; Tittle, 1980; Chiricos and Waldo, 1970; Ross, 1982; Pratt et al., 2006).

Perceptual Measures of Deterrence. The second approach is to measure individuals' subjective perceptions of legal penalties. The objective threat of legal punishment means nothing if citizens are not aware of the official sanctions or do not believe that there is any high risk of penalty if they were to commit a crime. There is evidence that one's perception of risk for violations are influenced somewhat by information regarding the objective certainty of sanction (Scheider, 2001). Most people, however, have a very limited knowledge of what the legal penalties actually are and often make very inaccurate estimations of the true odds of apprehension and incarceration. But a person's fear of punishment should have a deterrent effect on his or her decision to violate the law, even if that fear has no connection with objective reality. Ultimately, deterrence theory proposes that it is what people believe about the certainty, severity, and swiftness of punishment, regardless of its true risks, that determines their choice of conformity or crime.

Recognizing this crucial cognitive dimension of deterrence, researchers have utilized "subjective" measures of the risks and severity of legal penalties as perceived by individuals. This is measured, for example, by asking respondents on questionnaires or in interviews questions such as, "How likely is it that someone like you would be arrested if you committed X?" Most research on deterrence since the 1970s has used these perceptual measures, typically relating individuals' perceptions of risk and severity of penalties to their self-reported delinquency and crime.[3]

The higher the risks of apprehension and the stiffer the penalties for an offense perceived by individuals, the theory predicts, the less likely they are to commit that offense.

Do Criminal Sanctions Deter?

If there were no criminal justice system and no penalties provided by law for harmful acts against others and society, it would be obvious that laws prohibiting certain behavior would carry no threat for violation. The laws could maintain some moral suasion, and most people would probably still obey the law and refrain from predatory acts. But lawlessness would be more rampant than it is now. Indeed, a formal control system of laws and government is essential to social order in a modern political state. In this sense, the mere existence of a system that provides punishment for wrongdoing deters an unknown amount of crime. This effect of the chance of punishment versus no punishment at all has been referred to as *absolute deterrence* (see Zimring and Hawkins, 1973; Gibbs, 1975; see also Wright, 1993b).

However, absolute deterrence is not the relevant issue in deterrence research. Most people, most of the time and under most circumstances, conform to the law because they adhere to the same moral values as those embodied in the law, not because they are worried about imprisonment. We do not steal and kill primarily because we believe it is morally wrong. We have been educated and socialized to abhor these things. Our socialization comes from the family, church, school, and other groups and institutions in society; and partly from the educative effect of the law itself, simply by its formal condemnation of certain acts (Andenaes, 1971; see Gibbs, 1975, for a review of other preventive effects of law beyond deterrence). Therefore, the important question that research on deterrence attempts to answer is, does the actual or perceived threat of formally applied punishment by the state provide a significant marginal deterrent effect beyond that assured by the informal control system (Gibbs, 1975; Zimring and Hawkins, 1968)?

The best answer seems to be yes, but not very much. Studies of both objective and perceptual deterrence often do find negative correlations between certainty of criminal penalties and the rate or frequency of criminal behavior, but the correlations tend to be low (D'Alessio and Stolzenberg, 1998). Severity of punishment has an even weaker effect on crime, whether among the main body of criminal offenders (Smith and Akers, 1993) or among a special category such as those convicted of white-collar offenses (Weisburd, Waring, and Chayet, 1995). Celerity has little effect (Nagin and Pogarsky, 2001). With some exceptions (Cochran and Chamlin, 2000), neither the existence of capital punishment nor the certainty of the death penalty has been shown to have a

significant effect on the rate of homicides. Findings show t
some deterrent effect from the perceived certainty of crim
ties, but the empirical validity of deterrence theory is limite

This conclusion is supported, not only by the reports of sin
but also in "meta-analyses" of findings from many studies by Pratt et al.
(2006). They reported that "many of the variables specified in macro-
level tests of the deterrence perspective—such as increased police size/
police per capita, arrest ratios and clearance rates ... were consistently
among the weakest predictors of crime rates across virtually all levels of aggregation" (Pratt et al., 2006:368). Also, their meta-analysis of
studies that used perceptual measures found that, on average, there
is no significant deterrent effect of perceived severity of legal punishment. Further, the average deterrent effect of perceived certainty of
punishment, although statistically significant, is fairly weak. "[T]he
mean effect sizes of the relationships between crime/deviance and variables specified by deterrence theory are modest to negligible ... typically between zero and –.20 ... [and] much weaker than those found in
meta-analysis of the relationship between criminal/deviant behavior
and peer effects and self-control...." (Pratt et al., 2006:383).

Deterrence and Experiential Effects

Paternoster, Saltzman, Waldo, and Chiricos (1983) concluded from
their research that "the effect of prior behavior on current perceptions
of the certainty of arrest, the *experiential effect*, is stronger than the
effect of perceptions of certainty on subsequent behavior, the deterrent
effect" (Paternoster et al., 1983:471; emphasis added). Those respondents with "little prior experience in committing an offense have higher
estimates of the certainty of punishment than those with experience"
(Paternoster, 1985:429). In other words, the more frequently respondents have been involved in law violations in the past, the lower their
perceived risk of sanctions in the present. Paternoster et al. (1983) concluded that the relatively weak negative correlations between perceived
risks of punishment and criminal behavior reflect this experiential
effect of behavior on the perceptions of risk more than the deterrent
effect of perceived sanctions on behavior.

They failed to recognize, however, that their findings on the experiential effect may not in fact contradict the principle of specific deterrence. If respondents had previously committed offenses but had not
been punished for them, the principle of specific deterrence would predict a subsequently low level of perceived certainty. Individuals who
are involved in repeated crimes without suffering punishment should
have lower perceptions of risk because they have gotten away with it so
often. This in turn should be related to repeating offenses in the future

More criminal behavior

lower arrest prob. perceptions

(Stafford and Warr, 1993). Specific deterrence is supposed to operate based on persons getting caught and punished for criminal acts. If they are not, the theory argues, then they will come to believe that the certainty of punishment is low. In this sense, then, deterrence theory predicts the very experiential effect that Paternoster et al. found.

It would be contrary to the principle of specific deterrence if the research had found that respondents who reported frequent offenses followed by arrests in the past still had perceptions of a low risk of criminal sanctions. Paternoster et al. (1983) asked only about prior behavior. They did not measure past experience with arrest and punishment, so we do not know the extent to which their finding of an experiential effect contradicts deterrence theory.

If specific deterrence is based on being punished (or avoiding punishment), then general deterrence is based on the "vicarious" experience of seeing others punished (or avoiding punishment). Both of these should be related to offending and perceptions of risk (Stafford and Warr, 1993). This

> punishment avoidance acts as a negative reinforcer (i.e. the suspension of an unpleasant consequence, or punishment) which should increase the likelihood of future offending. Thus, when viewed in the context of the social learning perspective, the decision process underlying offending behavior is subject to an operant conditioning response (either a punisher or negative reinforcer), either through personal experience or the "modeling" behavior exhibited by others, which will influence individuals' future cost/benefit analyses for engaging in crime or deviance. (Pratt et al., 2006:372)

Piquero and Pogarsky (2002) found effects of both personal and vicarious punishment experience. However, in their study, experience with punishment had an "emboldening effect"; that is, it was positively related to future offending. This finding may be the result of more frequent offenders having a greater chance than non-offenders of being punished but, contrary to both deterrence and experiential hypotheses, having neither their offending nor perceptions affected by the direct or vicarious punishment experience. Rather, it may be that "prior experience with punishment serves to identify the most committed offenders, who then, not surprisingly, report a greater inclination toward future offending" (Piquero and Pogarsky, 2002:178).

Modifications and Expansions of Deterrence Concepts

Another aspect of the study by Paternoster (1985) points to the movement by many researchers to expand deterrence concepts beyond legal

penalties. Paternoster (1985) included variables from social l
theory (i.e., moral beliefs and attachment to parents and pee
social learning theory (i.e., the perceived risk of informal sanctions
from family and friends and association with offenders; see chaps. 5
and 6). When these other variables are taken into account, the already
weak relationship between the perceptions of risk of legal penalties and
offense behavior virtually disappears (see also Pratt et al., 2006).

The research by Paternoster (1985) followed up previous studies
(Akers et al., 1979; Grasmick and Green, 1980) in which the concept of
deterrence is expanded beyond the strictly legal or formal sanctions to
include "informal deterrence." Informal deterrence means the actual
or anticipated social sanctions and other consequences of crime and
deviance that prevent their occurrence or recurrence. This research
has found that the perceptions of informal sanctions, such as the disapproval of family and friends or one's own conscience and moral com-
mitments, do have deterrent effects. Indeed, they have more effect on
refraining from law violations than the perceived certainty of arrest or
severity of penalties (Green, 1989; Grasmick and Bursik, 1990; Pratt
et al., 2006).

Zimring and Hawkins (1973) have argued that formal punishment
may deter most effectively when it "sets off" or provokes these informal
social sanctions. An adolescent may refrain from delinquency, not only
out of fear of what the police will do, but of what his or her parents will
do once they learn of his or her arrest. Williams and Hawkins (1989)
expanded on this notion of the deterrent effects of informal sanctions
that may be triggered by the application of formal criminal justice sanctions. They found in their study that the arrest of an abusing husband
or boyfriend may have a deterrent effect, in part because of a concern
over the negative reactions of friends, family, neighbors, or employers
toward him based on their knowledge that he has been arrested. In this
instance, fear of arrest may be a deterrent, not only because of the negative experience of the arrest itself, but because of other negative consequences invoked by the arrest. These may include the informal costs
of severed relationships, damage to one's reputation, and the possible
loss of current or future employment. Williams and Hawkins argued
that the general concept of deterrence should be expanded to include
these informal negative sanctions. Subsequent research by Nagin and
Paternoster (1991b) does not support this argument, however, when it
is applied to delinquency. They find a very small deterrent effect from
the perceptions of formal sanctions, and this effect is not increased
at all as a result of informal costs that may be related to the formal
sanction. Instead, the informal sanctions have an independent effect
on delinquent behavior that is stronger than the effect of perceived
formal sanctions. Nagin and Pogarsky (2001) also find significant

deterrent effects from informal consequences of behavior and propose a model of general deterrence that includes "extra-legal" and legal consequences (along with the individual's "present orientation"). Pratt et al. (2006) also report that perceived certainty of "non-legal" sanctions had somewhat stronger deterrent effects than perceived certainty of legal sanctions.

That the informal sanction system may be more effective in controlling crime than legal sanctions should come as no surprise. But does research evidence that informal sanctions on criminal and delinquent behavior have a deterrent effect on crime increase the empirical validity of deterrence theory? In our opinion, it does not. Deterrence theory refers only to the threat of legal punishment:

> [T]he proper definition [of deterrence] … is narrow. In a legal context, the term "deterrence" refers to any instance in which an individual contemplates a criminal act but refrains entirely from or curtails the commission of such an act because he or she perceives some risk of legal punishment and fears the consequences. (Gibbs, 1986:325–336)

There is no room in deterrence theory for variations in the rewards for crime, the social consequences of actions, individual or group propensities toward crime, and the whole range of other variables. The question to be answered about deterrence theory is not whether punishment of any kind from any source deters, but whether the threat of punishment by law deters. The more the deterrence theory is expanded to include informal sanctions and other aspects of the social environment beyond the law, the less it remains a deterrence theory and the more it begins to resemble other theories that already include these variables. It is more appropriate, therefore, to interpret positive findings on informal sanctions, weakened social bonds, and similar variables as supporting the other theories (e.g., social learning and social bonding), from which the variables have been borrowed, than it is to conclude that such findings support an expanded deterrence theory that includes these borrowed variables.

Rational Choice Theory

Deterrence and Expected Utility

The expansion of the concept of deterrence has been most associated with the introduction into criminology in the 1980s of "rational choice" theory.[4] Rational choice theory is based on the "expected utility" principle in economic theory. The expected utility principle simply states

[handwritten annotations: "Expected Utility → ex Cost/benefit + perceptions"]

that people will make rational decisions based on the extent to which they expect the choice to maximize their profits or benefits and minimize the costs or losses. This is the same general assumption about human nature made in classical criminology.

The obvious affinity between deterrence and rational choice theories stems from the fact that they both grew out of the same utilitarian philosophy of the 18th century (see Gibbs, 1975). The former was applied to the law, and the latter to the economy. Despite this long historical connection, rational choice theory of crime has only recently been introduced in criminology. Except for the use of such concepts as "aleatory risk" in delinquency research by sociologists (Short and Strodtbeck, 1965), rational choice was introduced to criminology primarily through the analyses of crime by economists (see Becker, 1968; Heineke, 1978; Crouch, 1979). Gibbs (1975:203) noted that "shortly after the revival of interest in the deterrence question among sociologists, economists were drawn to the subject in large numbers."

Some criminologists, who had been conducting deterrence research for some time, began in the 1980s to refer to the economic model of rational choice as part of the movement to expand the deterrence doctrine beyond legal punishment. However, rational choice theorists claim much more than just an expansion of deterrence theory. The theory is proposed as a general, all-inclusive explanation of both the decision to commit a specific crime and the development of, or desistance from, a criminal career. The decisions are based on the offenders' expected effort and reward compared to the likelihood and severity of punishment and other costs of the crime (Cornish and Clarke, 1986; Newman, Clarke, and Shoham, 1997).

Research on Rational Choice Theory

Do offenders calculate before acting that the effort and costs of crime are less than the expected reward in the way predicted by rational choice theory? The answer depends on whether one believes this theory assumes that pure or partial rationality operates in crime. Does the theory hypothesize that each person approaches the commission of a crime with a highly rational calculation of pleasure versus pain before acting on or refraining from the crime? Does an offender choose to commit a crime with full knowledge and free will, taking into account only a carefully reasoned, objectively or subjectively determined, set of costs and benefits? If it is this kind of pure rationality that rational choice theory assumes, then the theory has virtually no empirical validity. The purely rational calculation of the probable consequences of an action is a rarity even among the general conforming public. Moreover, even offenders who pursue crime on a regular, business-like basis typically do not operate through a wholly rational decision-making process.

For instance, in a study of repeat property offenders, Tunnell (1990; 1992) found offenders thought that they would gain income from their crimes and would not be caught, or they believed that they would not serve much prison time if they did get caught. Furthermore, they were not afraid to serve time in prison because life in prison was not threatening to them. These findings would seem to be in line with rational choice theory because the expected benefits were perceived as outweighing the expected costs of the crime; hence, the decision was made to commit the crime. However, the process whereby offenders reached a decision to attempt another crime did not fit the model of a purely rational calculation of costs and benefits. They did try to avoid capture, but their actions and assessments of the risks were very unrealistic, even to some extent irrational. They were unable to make reasonable assessments of the risk of arrest, did little planning for the crime, and were uninformed about the legal penalties in the state where their crimes were committed. Moreover, all of the offenders in the study

> reported that they (and nearly every thief they knew) simply do not think about the possible legal consequences of their criminal actions before committing crimes.... Rather than thinking of possible negative consequences of their actions, those offenders reported thinking primarily of the anticipated positive consequences.... They simply believed that they would not be caught and refused to think beyond that point.

> The decision-making process appears not to be a matter of rational evaluation or calculation of the benefits and risks.... [R]isks (1) are thought about only rarely or (2) are considered minimally but are put out of their minds. (Tunnell, 1990:680–681)

Similarly, in an ethnographic study of burglars, Paul Cromwell and his associates found that "a completely rational model of decision making in residential burglary cannot be supported" (Cromwell, Olson, and Avary, 1991:43). Rather, professional burglars engage in only partially rational calculation of gains and risks before deciding to burglarize a house, and "research reporting that a high percentage of burglars make carefully planned, highly rational decisions based on a detailed evaluation of environmental cues may be in error" (Cromwell et al., 1991:42):

> Most of our burglar informants could design a textbook burglary.... [T]hey often described their past burglaries as though they were rationally conceived and executed. Yet on closer inspection, when their previous

burglaries were reconstructed, textbook procedures frequently gave way
to opportunity and situational factors. (Cromwell et al., 1991:42)

De Haan and Vos (2003) concluded from their interviews and focus
group sessions with street robbers that robbing is done for the "rational" reason of getting money, but other factors that one ordinarily
would not describe as elements of rationality ("release of tension,"
impulsivity, desperation, moral ambiguity, emotions) are equally
important motivations for the robbers. Dugan, LaFree, and Piquero
(2005) inferred some support for rational choice hypotheses from their
findings that a decrease in airplane hijackings is related to increased
certainty of apprehension and harsher punishment, but all of the relationships found in their study were relatively weak and few were statistically significant. Further, there was no measure of the actual rational
cognitive process assumed to underlie hijackers' decisions. Shover and
Hochstetler argued:

> [W]hite-collar criminals generally behave more rationally than street
> offenders; the latter routinely choose to offend in hedonistic contexts of
> street culture where drug consumption and the presence of other males
> clouds judgment and the ability to calculate beforehand. Many white-
> collar workers by contrast live and work in worlds that promote, monitor,
> and reward prudent decision making. (Shover and Hochstetler, 2005:3)

This remains an assumption because the empirical evidence is still
lacking as to how purely rational the decision-making process is for
white-collar offenders or whether the process is any more rational than
for other offenders.

The empirical validity of a purely rational explanation of crime may
not be important, however, because rational choice theorists seldom
put forth such pure models. Instead, they have developed models of partial rationality that incorporate limitations and constraints on choices
through lack of information, moral values, and other influences on
criminal behavior. Although rational choice theorists often refer to the
"reasoning criminal" and the "rational component" in crime, they go
to great lengths to point out how limited and circumscribed reasoning
and rationality are. The empirically verified models in the literature
are based on the assumptions of a fairly minimal level of rationality
(e.g., see De Haan and Vos, 2003; Matsueda, 2006).

Proponents often contrast rational choice theory with what they label
"traditional criminology," because, in their view, all other criminological theories assume that criminal behavior is irrational. But they are
mistaken about other criminological theories. In reality, except for psychoanalytic theory (see chap. 4) and some versions of biological theory

(see chap. 3), all other criminological theories assume no more or less rationality in crime than do those that are self-described as rational choice theory.

Furthermore, the rational choice models that have been supported by research evidence do not stick strictly with measures of expected utility. They incorporate various psychological and sociological background and situational variables taken from other theories to such an extent that there is little to set them apart from other theoretical models. In fact, some of the studies purporting to find evidence favoring rational choice theory actually test models that are indistinguishable from other, supposedly non-rational choice theories. The clearest example of this is the research by Paternoster (1989a; 1989b). He tested the effect on delinquent behavior of several variables in what he calls a "deterrence/rational choice" model. This model consists of the following variables: affective ties, costs of material deprivation, social groups and opportunities, informal social sanctions, perceptions of formal legal sanctions, and moral beliefs about specific delinquent acts. There is nothing in this set of variables that distinguishes it as a rational choice model. All the variables are taken from social learning and social bonding theories. Paternoster's finding that these variables are related to delinquent behavior, therefore, tells us little about the empirical validity of rational choice theory. However, it does tell us about the validity of social learning and social bonding theories (see chaps. 5 and 6).

The broadening of rational choice theory has the same consequence as the expansion of deterrence theory—it becomes a different theory. When rational choice theory is stated in its pure form, it does not provide an adequate explanation of criminal behavior (De Haan and Vos, 2003). It provides a more empirically verified explanation of crime when it is expanded to include variables beyond rationally expected utility. Opp (1997) said that the "narrow" rational choice model that assumes maximum rationality has been falsified by empirical research. He maintained criminal behavior is better explained by a "wide" model that assumes limited rationality and leaves room for "soft incentives" as well as tangible and intangible constraints found in informal social networks. However, when rational choice theory is modified in this way, the level of rationality it assumes is indistinguishable from that expected in other theories, and it incorporates explanatory variables from them. When the modifications reach this point, it is no longer appropriate to call the result rational choice theory (Akers, 1990).

Matsueda et al. (2006) found some empirical support for a model of adolescent theft and violence, which incorporates both "experiential learning" and "rational choice." Although they called this a rational choice model, they recognize that such modified models are quite similar to other social psychological theories:

[I]ndividuals begin with a *prior* subjective probability of an event, such as the risk of arrest, based on all the information they have accumulated to that point. They then collect or come into contact with new information—such as learning of a friend's arrest or being arrested themselves—which they use to update their probability estimates. . . . Such a process is consistent with general social learning theories of crime. (Matsueda et al., 2006:97–98; emphasis in original)

Deterrence and Criminal Justice Policy

Detection, apprehension, conviction, and punishment of offenders are all based on the theory that legal penalties are the chief deterrent to crime:

> The deterrence doctrine is an instructive example of a criminological theory that has immediate policy implications. It is not just that the doctrine identifies possible determinants of offending (individual offending, including recidivism, and the crime rate); additionally, *some* properties of legal punishments can be manipulated by officials. (Gibbs, 1995:74; emphasis in original)

Legislation and executive policy outlawing certain acts and providing punishment for committing those acts is based on the deterrence theory—that is, swift, certain, and severe sanctions for criminal acts will reduce crime in society through specific and general deterrence. Of these properties of punishment, most attention has been paid by policy makers to enhancing severity. The belief that the threat of more severe punishment produces a greater deterrent effect (along with retribution, just deserts, and incapacitation) is the primary justification given for a whole range of "get tough" criminal justice policies that have been enacted since the 1970s (Lynch and Sabol, 1997; Cullen, Fisher, and Applegate, 2000; Pratt et al., 2006; Webster, Doob, and Zimring, 2006). Examples of such policies are as follows: restoration of capital punishment; abolishment of parole and indeterminate sentencing; ending or restricting good time and gain time reductions in sentences for prison inmates; restriction of judicial sentencing discretion through sentencing guidelines and mandated sentences; longer prison sentences for drug and violent offenses; "three-strikes-and-you're-out" life sentences for habitual offenders; direct filing of juvenile offenders to criminal courts; and stricter intermediate sanctions such as home confinement, which controls offenders in the community more than traditional probation does.

The clearest effects of these policies has been the enormous increase in the number of prisons and the unprecedented growth in the number of Americans in prison and under criminal justice supervision. As of the end of 2005 there were over 2 million inmates in federal or state prisons and local jails, the highest incarceration rate (491 inmates per 100,000 population) in American history. The policies have greatly increased the proportion of prisoners who are African American and Hispanic (see Bureau of Justice Statistics at http://www.ojp.usdoj.gov/bjs/prisons.htm; Lynch and Sabol, 1997; Haney and Zimbardo, 1998).

The extent to which these policies have also increased marginal deterrence of crime in the United States is not yet known. During much of the past 25 to 30 years as these policies were instituted, the crime rate was not substantially reduced; it remained the same or increased. Beginning in the 1990s, the official crime rate has declined as the number of persons in prison has continued to increase. Although there have been recent increases in the national crime rate, it is still at the lowest levels since the 1960s. It is a plausible hypothesis, therefore, to attribute the reductions in the official crime rates to the type of policies outlined earlier. Some policy analysts (Reynolds, 1998) are convinced that the decrease in official crime rates is the direct result of the increased imprisonment and harsher penalties for both adult and juvenile offenders. Such analyses, however, rely only on observing recent trends in crime rates and imprisonment without controlled evaluations of outcomes of specific policies. The evaluations that have been done find insufficient evidence that the policies have had the intended effects of reducing recidivism and lowering the crime rate (Lynch and Sabol, 1997; Haney and Zimbardo, 1998). For instance, although some research found a deterrent effect following voter approval of a referendum providing for increased sentences for repeating certain offenses in California, subsequent research found that the rates for those crimes had already started to decline before, and actually increased in some of the years subsequent to, the policy being put into place (Webster et al., 2006; Levin, 2006).

It may be that the increases in actual or threatened criminal penalties have been sufficiently threatening over the years to deter criminal behavior and reduce crime. On the other hand, it may be that lower crime rates reflect other programs, policies, or social changes unrelated to increased severity of criminal penalties. The years that have seen increases in incarcerated populations have also seen large increases in the number of offenders who have been sentenced to probation, parole, community supervision, treatment, rehabilitation, and other alternatives to prisons that do not rely on the deterrent effects of punishment. Even within prisons there is a range of educational, vocational, drug/alcohol, behavior modification, and other group and individual rehabilitation programs. The larger number of prison inmates means that a larger number than in the past have participated in these programs. The goals of these programs are better reintegration ... the community and reduction in criminal offenses after release. Could the overall reductions in crime rate be attributed to the fact that the goals of these programs are being realized? Other social changes have taken place that may have reduced the crime rate. For instance, the proportion of young males (the most crime-prone demographic category) in the population has decreased. Moreover, the unemployment rate among this age group, particularly among minorities and in large cities, dramatically decreased over the last decade of the 20th century. Without well-controlled evaluation research, which of these criminal justice policies, which social changes, or which combination of factors are responsible for any demonstrated decreases in crime is unknown.

The limited evidence for the deterrent effects of the actual or perceived penalties for crime may result from the fact that the "main engine for creating deterrence ... has been the basic case-processing mechanisms of the criminal justice process" in which "most crimes are neither reported to nor observed by the police ... and the majority of crimes that are reported do not result in an arrest" (Kennedy, 1998:4). At the same time, there is some evidence that extra police patrols can reduce crime in certain "hot spots" in the city (Sherman et al., 1998). It may be that new criminal justice strategies that have specific targets such as gang violence by chronic offenders will enhance deterrence, but careful evaluation of such programs has not yet been done (Kennedy, 1998). Whereas other kinds of police crackdowns often do not work (Sherman et al., 1998), studies have shown that police crackdowns on drunk driving can have at least short-term deterrent effects (Ross, 1982). The longer-term reduction in alcohol-related automobile accidents seen in the past 3 decades may be due to more certain and severe penalties for drunk driving. It is just as likely, however, this downward trend is due to the public campaigns by groups such as Mothers Against Drunk Driving (MADD) to increase the moral abhorrence of drunk driving, designated driver programs, and other changes in public attitudes and behavior (Akers, 1992b). It should be noted, however, that these downward trends in offending, although relatively long-term, are not necessarily going to continue. What conclusions can be reached if the policies, to which crime reductions are credited, continue in effect while the crime rate begins to increase?

Scared Straight, Shock Incarceration, and Boot Camps

In 1978 a documentary film, *Scared Straight,* was shown that received cinematic awards and aroused enormous attention from the public and governmental officials. It appeared to offer a simple but highly effective way of deterring juvenile delinquency and preventing juveniles from pursuing adult criminal careers. The film was shot in Rahway Prison, New Jersey's toughest maximum security penitentiary. It featured 17 adolescent boys who were bused to the prison for 1 day to undergo an intensive confrontation by hardened Rahway prisoners. The prisoners yelled at the kids, physically confronted them, and laid out in graphic language the harsh realities and horrors of life in prison that are the consequences of crime. The point of the film was that such a reality shock would literally scare the youngsters straight. "Efforts to scare juveniles straight were firmly grounded in the deterrence approach to juvenile delinquency, especially the idea that fear of severe punishment suppresses delinquency" (Lundman, 1993:151).

The youth in the film were just a handful of the over 13,000 juveniles who took part in New Jersey's Juvenile Awareness Program. A success rate of 90% was claimed for the program, but a careful evaluation showed that most of the youth who visited prisons under the auspices of the program were recruited from the general school populations of middle-class communities. They were not at much risk of delinquency or crime anyway. Moreover, a follow-up study found that juveniles who took part in the program later committed four times as many offenses as a control group that did not participate (Finckenauer, 1982). It may be that the exposure to criminals by youth who otherwise would have no contact with them backfired with the unintended consequence of increasing rather than decreasing risk of delinquent behavior. Such programs in other states evaluated in the 1980s also showed no deterrent effect (Jensen and Rojek, 1998).

Meta-analyses of such scared straight and similar "juvenile awareness" programs confirm that they are "not effective as a stand-alone crime prevention strategy. More importantly, . . . these programs result in an increase in criminality in the experimental group when compared to the no-treatment control group" (Petrosino, Petrosino, and Buehler, 2006:98).

The scared straight theory also underlies "shock incarceration" or "shock probation" policies in which youthful and minor offenders first are given short prison time and then released to complete their sentence under probation supervision. Boot camps are based to a great extent on this shock incarceration model. These are military-style short-term institutions, some for juveniles and some for adult offenders, with a regimen of drills, strict discipline, and military decorum that is meant both to teach self-control and to produce a deterrent fear of incarceration. Boot camps became very popular in the 1980s and continue with the support of both federal and state correctional policy makers (Peters, Thomas, and Zamberian, 1997). But evaluations of their effectiveness have been disappointing. Boot camps seem able to maintain good discipline and behavior among their inmates under confinement, but are not able to reduce recidivism. In fact, boot camp releasees do not do as well as comparison groups in avoiding subsequent offending, arrest, and incarceration (MacKenzie and Piquero, 1994; MacKenzie and Souryal, 1994; Bourque, Han, and Hill, 1996; Jensen and Rojek, 1998; Zhang, 2000).

Routine Activities Theory

Felson and Cohen: Offenders, Targets, and Guardians

Elements of deterrence and rational choice are also found in routine activities theory.[5] For a personal or property crime to occur, there must be at the same time and place a perpetrator, a victim, or an object of property. The occurrence can be facilitated if there are other persons or circumstances in the situation that encourage it, or it can be prevented if the potential victim or another person is present who can take action to deter it. Lawrence Cohen and Marcus Felson (1979) took these basic elements of time, place, objects, and persons to develop a "routine activities" theory of crime events. They did so by placing these elements into three categories of variables that increase or decrease the likelihood that persons will be victims of "direct contact" predatory (personal or property) crime.

The three main categories of variables identified by Cohen and Felson (1979) are (1) motivated offenders, (2) suitable targets of criminal victimization, and (3) capable guardians of persons or property. The main proposition in the theory is that the rate of criminal victimization is increased when there is a "convergence in space and time of the three minimal elements of direct-contact predatory violations" (Cohen and Felson, 1979:589); that is, the likelihood of crime increases when there are one or more persons present who are motivated to commit a crime, a suitable target or potential victim that is available, and the absence of formal or informal guardians who could deter the potential offender. The relative presence or absence of these elements is variable, and "the risk of criminal victimization varies dramatically among the circumstances and locations in which people place themselves and their property" (Cohen and Felson, 1979:595). The theory derives its name from the fact that Cohen and Felson began with the assumption that the conjunction of these elements of crime are related to the normal, legal, and "routine" activities of potential victims and guardians. "[T]he spatial and temporal structure of routine legal activities should play an important role in determining the location, type, and quantity of illegal acts occurring in a given community or society" (Cohen and Felson, 1979:590).

Routine activities as defined by Cohen and Felson are "recurrent and prevalent activities that provide for basic population and individual needs ... formalized work, as well as the provision of standard food, shelter, sexual outlet, leisure, social interaction, learning, and childbearing" (Cohen and Felson, 1979:593). They hypothesized that changes in daily activities related to work, school, and leisure since World War II placed more people in particular places at particular times that both increased their accessibility as targets of crime and kept them away from home as guardians of their own possessions and property.

Felson (1994; 1998; 2002) continued over the years since his work with Cohen to develop and apply routine activities. He downplayed the significance of formal guardians because "crime is a private phenomenon largely impervious to state intervention." Rather, he emphasizes the crime prevention and deterrence that naturally occur in the informal control system, the "quiet and natural method by which people prevent crime in the course of daily life. This control occurs as people interact and bring out the best in one another" (Felson, 1994:xii–xiii). The police are not the only capable guardians. Indeed, guardians who prevent or deter crime are more likely to be ordinary citizens, oneself, friends, family, or even strangers. The vulnerability of property to theft is affected by a number of physical features, such as its weight and ease of mobility and how much physical "target hardening" (e.g., installing better locks) has been done. But sights and sounds, being in dangerous and risky places, routines of the family and household, and one's personal characteristics have an effect on the risk of victimization for both violent and property crime. Felson (1994; 1998; 2002) also extended the theory beyond predatory crimes to such offenses as illegal consumption and sale of drugs and alcohol and white-collar crime.

Felson's (1994; 1998; 2002) emphasis on the informal control system does not distinguish routine activities theory from the general sociological view (discussed earlier and in chap. 9) that conformity to the law comes more from the informal system of socialization and control than from the formal control system. This perspective has also been applied to drug use. "The general reduction in drug use in American society [from the late 1970s to the early 1990s] may be the result of changes in social norms and the informal control system unrelated to conscious and deliberate prevention, treatment, or law enforcement efforts" (Akers, 1992b:183). The validity of routine activities theory, therefore, does not rest on the relative importance of the informal and formal control systems in crime but on how well hypotheses about the effect of the three main elements (motivated offenders, suitable targets, and guardians) of the theory on crime are supported.

Felson's recent work (2006) focuses on the ecology of crin
ecosystem"), natural processes in crime, the adaptive i
"stimulus and response" between criminal activity and soc
to prevent crime. The ecological distribution of victims, crime opportunities, and motivated offenders has always been a concern of routine
activities theory. Moreover, Felson's (2006) discussion of crime targets,
crime reduction and prevention strategies, crime opportunities, relationship of crime to legal activities, environmentally designing crime
out (or in), and other issues have fairly obvious ties to routine activities
theory. However, he pays little direct attention to it, and it is unclear
how his perspective on "crime and nature" is or is not a restatement,
elaboration, or reformulation of, or otherwise linked to, routine activities theory. Rather, he refers to the early Chicago School of the sociology and ecology of the city (see chap. 8). *moderate*

Empirical Validity of Routine Activities Theory *Support*

The theory would predict that a change in any one of these main
elements would change the crime rates, but that the presence of all three
would produce a multiplier effect on crime rates. The early research
by Cohen and Felson (1979), however, focused on only two of the three
elements: suitable targets and the absence of capable guardians. They
presented data on trends in family activities, consumer products, and
businesses and found that these correlated with trends in the rates of
all major predatory violent and property crimes. They recognized that
these were not the direct measures of the concepts in the theory, but
concluded that the findings are consistent with the theory. They did
not rule out that the "routine activity approach might in the future be
applied to the analysis of offenders and their inclinations as well" (Cohen
and Felson, 1979:605). Nevertheless, the neglect of "motivated offender"
variables in the development, application, and testing of routine activities theory continues to this time (see Felson, 2002, and the review of
routine activities studies in Bernburg and Thorlindsson, 2001).

Cohen, Kluegel, and Land (1981) later presented the theory in a
more formalized fashion, renaming it "opportunity" theory and testing its propositions with data from the National Crime Victimization
Surveys. The formal theory refers to exposure, proximity, guardianship, and target attractiveness as variables that increase the risk of
criminal victimization. But these are not measured directly. They are
assumed from variations in age, race, income, household composition, labor force participation, and residence in different areas of the
city. Although inconclusive on some, their findings are consistent with
most of the hypotheses; consequently, they conclude that the theory is
supportable.

Messner and Tardiff (1985) used the routine activities approach to interpret their findings on the correlations between the social characteristics of Manhattan homicide victims, the time and location of the homicides, and the relationship between victims and offenders. They did not attempt to account for the rate or number of homicides, but only for the place and type of homicide. They contended that "sociodemographic and temporal characteristics structure routine activities and, in so doing, affect both the location of potential victims in physical space and the 'pool' of personal contacts from which offenders are ultimately drawn" (Messner and Tardiff, 1985:243). Messner and Tardiff found weak support for the expectations about family versus stranger homicides, but no relationship between time and location of homicides.

Sherman, Gartin, and Buerger (1989) also reported findings consistent with routine activities theory in their study of the "hot spots" of predatory crime. They noted that prior research on routine activities used data on the characteristics of individuals or households as measures of lifestyles that affect the convergence of victim, offender, and guardians. Their research focused on the "criminology of place" by using Minneapolis police "call data" (i.e., crimes reported to the police by telephone) to locate concentrations (i.e., hot spots) of such calls at certain addresses, intersections, parks, and hospitals. They found that most crime reports came from only 3% of all the locations in the city and that reports of each of the major types of predatory crime were concentrated only in a few locations. Sherman et al. do not know what it is about these places that makes them hot spots, but they believe that there is something about them that relates to the convergence of victims and offenders in the absence of guardians.

Kennedy and Forde (1990) also supported routine activities theory based on both property and violent crime data from a telephone victimization survey. They found that victimization varies by age, sex, and income, but also varies by the extent to which persons stay at home or go out at night to bars, work, or school. They believe that the routine activity of leaving home at this time renders these persons more vulnerable as victims and less capable as guardians over their property. Mustaine and Tewksbury (1998) reported similar findings in a sample of college students. Involvement in a number of legal activities (e.g., eating out frequently, leaving home frequently, not locking doors) and *illegal* activities increased the risks of both minor and serious theft victimization. However, these activities did not increase the risk very much, and many other routine activities included in the study were not related to victimization.

Findings from qualitative research on the responses of the formal and informal control systems to the devastation of Hurricane Andrew

in Florida in 1992 are generally consistent with routine a
The natural disaster temporarily increased the vulnerab
and property as crime targets. For a short time, there wa
plete loss of formal guardianship in the form of polic
some of the neighborhoods. Motivated offenders with pi
were attracted to the areas in the aftermath of the storm, ... some local
people took criminal advantage of the situation. However, there was little looting in the neighborhoods and crime rates actually went down
during the time when the community was most vulnerable (but then
increased again after the initial impact period). This was most likely the
result of stepping into the void by competent guardians in the form of
neighbors watching out for neighbors, citizens guarding their own and
others' property (sometimes with firearms), citizen patrols, and other
steps taken to aid one another in the absence of government and formal
control (Cromwell, Dunham, Akers, and Lanza-Kaduce, 1995).

The fact that some may be motivated to commit crime when targets
are made vulnerable by such events as natural disasters raises questions about the concept of the motivated offender. Does the concept of
motivated offender in routine activities theory refer only to someone
with a pre-existing set of crime-prone motivations or does it include
anyone who is enticed by the opportunity for quick gain itself, although
he or she may not have had any previously existing criminal intentions
or motivations? In the former case, the situation provokes motivation
to action but does not create it; in the latter, the situation both creates
and provokes the motivation (Wortley, 1997). Because all persons are
thus potentially motivated to commit crime, can the presence of a motivated offender simply be assumed from the presence of any person? If
so, how does the theory distinguish between circumstances in which
a motivated offender is present and those in which one is not? There is
ambiguity on this point in routine activities theory that has yet to be
clarified (Akers, Lanza-Kaduce, Cromwell, and Dunham, 1994).

Bernburg and Thorlindsson (2001) moved beyond the question of
situational motivations in their research on routine activities and
delinquency. Their hypothesis was that variables such as differential peer associations and social bonds (see chaps. 5 and 6) not only
account for the behavior of offenders, they also affect the patterns of
routine activities themselves. These social interactional variables condition what situations of targets and guardians are entered by motivated offenders (or that serve to motivate them to offend) and define
those situations as opportunities to commit delinquency. Therefore,
the many studies of routine activities that omit these variables are
"flawed" and do not adequately allow conclusions abut the empirical
validity of the theory. Their research revealed that the relationship
between measures of delinquency and routine activities is diminished

when conventional attachment (social bonding theory) is controlled, and the relationship essentially disappears when peer associations and attitudes favorable to delinquency (social learning theory) are controlled.

Jensen and Brownfield (1986) pointed out that studies of routine activities theory seldom take into account whether the activities that increase one's vulnerability to victimization are deviant or non-deviant. They found that the activities most strongly related to adolescents becoming victims of crime are not the normal conforming routine activities (dating, going out at night, shopping, or going to parties), but rather the deviant activity of committing offenses (see similar findings in Mustaine and Tewksbury, 1998, mentioned earlier). In other words, those who commit crimes are more likely to be victims of crime. Engaging in offense behavior itself, of course, does not fit the definition of "routine" activity. Therefore, Mustaine and Tewksbury's (1998) notion that even the commission of illegal acts by themselves constitutes a type of activity that can be categorized as "routine" stretches the concept of routine activity beyond recognition. If illegal acts are taken as measures of routine activities, then it becomes tautological to hypothesize that routine activities is one of the causes of illegal acts. Moreover, as Jensen and Brownfield (1986) pointed out, because criminal behavior is correlated with victimization, variables taken from theories that explain motivation for criminal behavior should also be correlated with victimization.

> In fact, most of the variables in the opportunity [routine activities] model of victimization have appeared in one form or another in traditional etiological theories of crime or delinquency. Exposure and proximity to offenders is central to differential association and social learning theories of criminality. Cohen et al. [1981] proposed that exposure and proximity to offenders increase the risk of victimization, while differential association and social learning theories propose that the same variables increase the chances of criminal behavior. In short, "victimogenic" variables have been introduced in earlier theories as "criminogenic." (Jensen and Brownfield, 1986:87)

Although it draws on etiological theories, routine activities theory is only indirectly a theory of the commission of criminal behavior. It is primarily a theory of criminal victimization. That is, it does not offer an explanation as to why some persons are motivated to develop a pattern of crime or commit a particular crime. It simply assumes that such persons exist and that they commit crimes in certain places and times at which the opportunities and potential victims are available. Routine activities theory does not explain why informal crime precautions may or may not be exercised by individuals in their homes or elsewhere, nor does it explain formal control exercised by law and the criminal justice system. It simply assumes that, if informal or formal guardians are not present or able to prevent crime, then crime will occur.

We have long known that vulnerability to criminal victimization is related to social characteristics such as age, sex, and race, and that unguarded or easily available property is more apt to be stolen or vandalized. Ordinary precautions, of course, decrease the chances of victimization. Common sense tells us that, if one is sitting at home watching television rather than out on the streets, one's home is not likely to be burglarized and one has a zero chance of being the victim of a street mugging. Possessing social characteristics correlated with a higher-risk lifestyle obviously makes one more vulnerable as a crime victim. But Felson (1994; 1998; 2002) has taken these common-sense and empirical realities and woven them into a coherent framework for understanding the variations in criminal victimization by time and place. The theory is well-stated, logically consistent, and has clear policy implications and powerful potential for understanding the impact of normal, even desirable, social structural changes on predatory crime.

Its empirical validity has not yet been well-established, however. As we have seen, several researchers have reported findings that are consistent with routine activities theory (see also Stahura and Sloan, 1988; Massey, Krohn, and Bonati, 1989; Miethe, Stafford, and Long, 1987; Cromwell et al., 1991). But that research has not really tested full models of the theory. With a few exceptions (Stahura and Sloan, 1988; Bernburg and Thorlindsson, 2001), researchers have not measured variations in the motivation for crime or variations in the presence of motivated offenders. Thus, at least one of the three major categories of variables in this theory is usually omitted. Even when included, offender motivation is not directly measured, but rather assumed from variations in the demographic correlates of crime.

A related difficulty in assessing the empirical support for the theory is introduced by the fact that the two other major categories in the theory—suitable targets of crime and absence of capable guardians—are usually are not directly measured either. The original research by Cohen, Felson, and associates used no direct measures of the routine activities of victims or suitable guardians. They were only assumed from labor force participation, household composition, and so on. In subsequent research, victim vulnerability and guardianship have usually been assumed from the social characteristics of victims, although some activities of victims (e.g., their presence at home or their going out at night) have been directly measured (Kennedy and Forde, 1990; Mustaine and Tewksbury, 1998). As Sherman et al. noted, "most tests

Operationalization

of routine activities theory lack independent measures of the lifestyles in question and substitute presumed demographic correlates for them" (Sherman et al., 1989:31). Smith, Frazee, and Davison (2000) used neighborhood-level indirect measures of motivated offenders (e.g., racial composition and distance from the central city), targets (number of stores and other commercial land use), and guardianship (number of owner-occupied homes). They find significant but fairly weak effects of all of these on street robberies reported to the police. The research on routine activities has reported numerous findings that are consistent with, and findings that are not consistent with, the assumptions in routine activities theory. More work needs to be done to devise direct empirical measures of its key concepts.

Routine Crime Prevention and Precautions

Marcus Felson (1998; 2002; Felson and Clarke, 1995) saw the policy implications of routine activities theory as building on long-standing "routine precautions taken against crime by individuals and organizations" such as locking doors, installing burglar alarms, locating in safe neighborhoods, avoiding dangerous places, and guarding and locking up valuables (Felson and Clarke, 1995:179–180). Many of the routine things that have been or can be done to prevent crime are common-sense practices among the general population, much as "folk remedies" have been used to combat illnesses. Felson and Clarke (1995) argued that many such remedies fail to reduce opportunities for crime and in some cases, such as purchasing guns for self-protection from criminals, may create more danger than safety. They believed routine activities theorists should propose policies that encourage people to take reasonable and prudent precautions, including the following: (1) formal social controls such as laws establishing juvenile curfews and closing hours for bars and liquor stores; (2) informal supervision through family and friends, keeping an eye out for each other, and reminding one another of precautions; (3) signage and instructions such as posting crime warnings in public places, reminding people to guard valuables, and giving information on safe areas and streets; (4) product design such as making cars with buzzers that activate when keys are left in them, self-closing doors, and providing easily remembered personal identification numbers; (5) improving natural surveillance through provision of public street lights, trimming of hedges, and putting up fences that do not obstruct visibility (Felson and Clarke, 1995).

Felson (2002) referred to "designing out crime" by individuals, neighborhoods, communities, and businesses. The patterns of movement of people, the design and siting of buildings, and other features of the everyday environment affect the decision-making process of

CPTED → "Defensible space"

potential offenders by providing cues about what is a good or poor set of conditions to commit a crime. Poor conditions for crime can be accomplished by recognizing the geographical distribution of crime in the city, constructing defensible spaces in public and private buildings, situating homes on lots that provide good visibility of neighbors' houses, placing fences and parking areas to maximize open exposure, reducing traffic flow through neighborhoods, and otherwise producing "local design" against crime. Money and clerks in convenience stores can be made less vulnerable to robbery and assault by putting cash registers in the front of the store, installing timed access safes, keeping little or no accessible cash on hand at any given time, and keeping the view from outside clear by keeping windows free of advertising posters and displays. He also notes that there is strength in numbers and even noise in defining situations where the cues are negative for crime to the potential offender. Anything that makes the situation more difficult, risky, or unrewarding for someone to steal, attack, or damage would seem to fit Felson's concept of routine activities crime prevention.

Such actions taken as precautions against crime include what has traditionally been known in criminology as "crime prevention through environmental design" (CPTED), constructing and locating buildings (especially in urban areas) in ways that "harden" crime targets, provide more "defensible space," and otherwise make it more difficult or less inviting for offenders (Newman, 1972; Jeffery, 1977). These and other techniques of "situational prevention" assume that offenders make rational choices before committing specific crimes (Newman et al., 1997). The theory is that offenders will choose not to commit a crime where safer streets are maintained in good condition, physical deterioration of houses, buildings, and property is controlled, and the physical environment has been modified to protect targets and victims better (Taylor and Harrell, 1996).

Certainly, the tangible steps recommended by Felson and others seem to be sound crime-resisting precautions. On the surface, at least, their thwarting of crime would seem to be self-evident. But, although Felson and Clarke (1995) recommended "clinical research" on the matter of effectiveness of these crime precautions, they do not report any research specifically evaluating the extent to which the recommended designs, siting, lighting, and other maneuvers protect victims and reduce the incidence of crime (see also Felson, 2002). However, Weisburd (1997) reported research showing that tactics such as access control, physical barriers, employee surveillance, street lighting, and property identification may counter crime without having a strong crime "displacement" effect. Nevertheless, he cautions that "the enthusiasm surrounding situational prevention must be tempered by the

may instead displace" crime

weakness of the methods used in most existing evaluation studies" (Weisburd, 1997:11).

Summary

Deterrence theory states that if legal penalties are certain, severe, and swift, crime will be deterred. In empirical studies severity is seldom found to have a deterrent effect on crime. Neither the existence of capital punishment nor the certainty of the death penalty has had an effect on the rate of homicides. A negative correlation between objective or perceived certainty and illegal behavior is a common research finding, but the correlation tends to be weak.

There is more empirical support when deterrence concepts are expanded to take into account the informal social processes of reward, punishment, and moral beliefs. Rational choice theory is another type of expansion or modification of deterrence theory. When rational choice theory is stated in its pure form, it does not stand up well to empirical evidence. However, when this theory is modified so that a relatively low level of rationality is assumed and explanatory variables from other theories are added, it is more likely to be upheld by the data. When deterrence and rational choice theories are so modified, they resemble more the modern social bonding or social learning theories than the classical deterrence or pure rational choice models. Therefore, positive research findings on these modified versions are more appropriately viewed as validating these other theories from which the more powerful explanatory variables are taken, rather than validating deterrence or rational choice theories alone.

The main proposition in routine activities theory is that the rate of criminal victimization is increased when there are one or more persons likely to commit a crime, a vulnerable target or victim is present, and formal or informal guardians to prevent the motivated offender are absent. Research has not tested full models of the theory, and the major variables are usually measured indirectly. Its empirical validity has not yet been firmly established, but most of the research done so far reports findings consistent with the theory.

The deterrence doctrine underlies the entire criminal justice system and is the main theory behind get-tough policy reforms. Programs such as "scared straight" and boot camps also rely heavily on deterrent effects of actual and threatened incarceration. The policy implications of routine activities theory revolve around taking practical and commonsense precautions against becoming victimized by crime. There is some evidence that they work, but evaluations of these policies and practices leave their crime-reduction effects uncertain.

Notes

1. For Beccaria's writings, see Beccaria (1963; 1972) and Monachesi (1972). For Bentham's writings, see Bentham (1948) and Geis (1972). For general discussions of the classical criminology of both, see Vold (1958), Vold et al. (2002), and Wright (1993b).

2. Piers Beirne (1991) argued that Beccaria's main purpose was neither legal reform nor a rational explanation of crime. Rather, it was to introduce a deterministic "science of man," which ran contrary to the assumptions of free-will, volitional acts. Therefore, his theory was just as positivistic as subsequent theories.

3. See, for instance, Jensen (1969), Waldo and Chiricos (1972), Anderson, Chiricos, and Waldo (1977), Jensen, Erickson, and Gibbs (1978), Tittle (1980), Paternoster et al. (1983), Klepper and Nagin (1989), Nagin and Paternoster (1994), Miller and Iovanni (1994), Scheider (2001), Nagin and Pogarsky (2001).

4. For general and specific rational choice models, many of which are basically expansions on deterrence theory, see Cornish and Clarke (1986), Piliavin, Thornton, Gartner, and Matsueda (1986), Klepper and Nagin (1989), Paternoster (1989a; 1989b), Williams and Hawkins (1989), Grasmick and Bursik (1990), Newman et al. (1997), Piquero and Rengert (1999). For general critiques of rational choice theory, see Akers (1990), and De Haan and Vos (2003).

5. Because routine activities theory stresses the ecological distribution of victims, crime opportunities, and motivated offenders, it could well be classified with social disorganization as an ecological theory of crime (see chap. 8). It is not rational choice or deterrence theory. However, the concept of guardianship includes formal actions by police to deter crime and incorporates elements of the deterrence doctrine. Also, it makes the assumption that motivated offenders choose to commit a crime after assessing the presence of guardians and the vulnerability of crime targets. Therefore, it is often interpreted as a rational choice theory. For these reasons, a discussion of it is included in this chapter.

Chapter 3

Biological Theories

Introduction

S ocial structural and social psychological theories, to be introduced and evaluated in later chapters, often either ignore or specifically exclude biological or psychological factors in crime. This is not because such theories assume that biological and psychological factors (see chap. 4) play no part in human behavior or that individuals are all the same. They focus on the social factors in crime with the assumption that biological and personality variations among individuals are more or less within the normal range. Little or no criminal behavior is considered to be directly caused by abnormal physiology. Traditional biological theories, on the other hand, take the opposite approach by focusing on anatomical, physiological, or genetic abnormalities within the individual that separate law-breakers into a distinctly different category of persons from the law-abiding majority. In turn, such theories ignore or downplay the effect of social environmental factors in crime. Much of the recent theorizing, however, emphasizes biological variations within the normal range and the interplay of biological, social, and psychological variables in crime and delinquency.

Lombroso and Early Biological Theories

The classical school of criminology retained a virtual monopoly on the study of crime until the latter part of the 19th century. By the 1870s, the classical theory, which upheld the belief that persons rationally calculate pleasure and pain during the exercise of free will to commit or refrain from crime, began to give way to biological "positivism." This new theory proposed that crime is not a rationally reasoned behavior that will occur unless prevented by the proper threat of punishment, but rather is the result of inborn abnormalities. An individual's physical traits index a bodily constitution with an associated mental and psychological makeup that causes one to violate the rules of modern

47

society. Rational decisions, the theory argues, have nothing to do with it. Although environmental conditions and situations can provoke or restrain criminal behavior, they do not cause the commission of a crime. Although some normal persons may on occasion succumb to temptations and pressures to commit a crime, the real criminal is born with criminal traits and will always be at odds with civilized society. The early biological criminologists viewed criminals as a distinct set of people who were biologically inferior to law-abiding citizens or inherently defective in some way.

Although society is certainly justified in punishing criminals for its own protection, the certainty or severity of punishment will have no effect on natural-born criminals because their crimes are caused by an innate biological makeup that no law can affect. Although the classical school of criminology was humanistic and focused on the crime itself, biological positivism was scientific and concentrated on the measurable characteristics of the individual criminal (see Wolfgang, 1972; Vold et al., 2002).

Lombroso's Theory of the Born Criminal

The most important of the early biological theories, the one from which nearly all other biological theories stem, was first introduced in 1876 by Cesare Lombroso in *The Criminal Man*. "Before Lombroso, the study of crime fell into the domain of metaphysicians, moralists, and penologists; Lombroso turned it into a biological science" (Rafter, 2006:39). Lombroso revised and enlarged this original publication through five editions and published separate volumes on the causes and remedies of crime and of the female criminal (Lombroso and Ferrero, 1912; Wolfgang, 1972; Rafter, 2006). Lombroso observed the physical characteristics (head, body, arms, and skin) of Italian prisoners and compared them to Italian soldiers. From these comparisons he concluded that criminals were physically different from law-abiding citizens and that these differences demonstrated the biological causes of criminal behavior.

Lombroso believed that certain physical features identified the convict in prison as a "born criminal." The born criminal comes into the world with a bodily constitution that causes him to violate the laws of modern society. The born criminal is an "atavism," Lombroso theorized, a throwback to an earlier stage of human evolution. He has the physical makeup, mental capabilities, and instincts of primitive man. The born criminal, therefore, is unsuited for life in civilized society and, unless specifically prevented, will inevitably violate its social and legal rules. Lombroso maintained that this born criminal can be identified by the possession of certain visible "stigmatas" for example, an asymmetry of the face or head, large monkey-like ears, large lips, receding chin, twisted nose, excessive cheek bones, long arms, excessive skin wrinkles, and extra fingers or toes. The male with five or more of these physical anomalies is marked as a born criminal, whereas the female-born criminal could be identified with as few as three anomalies. Measures of such anatomical features also became common for purposes of criminal identification by police and correctional authorities beginning in the 1870s until the second decade of the 20th century, by which time it had become supplanted by fingerprinting (see Cole, 2001).

Although Lombroso focused most of his attention on male offenders, he co-authored *The Female Offender* (1897/1958) with his son-in-law William Ferrero. Lombroso and Ferrero (1897/1958) explained the existence of a greater number of male than female born criminals by natural selection. They proposed that men are less likely to breed with physically deformed women, and therefore the degenerative traits in women would be less likely than such traits in men to survive over time.

In addition to the born criminal, Lombroso recognized two other types, the "insane criminal" and the "criminaloid." The insane criminal, with whom Lombroso included the idiot, imbecile, epileptic, and psychotic, is mentally unfit for society. These criminals are no more capable than born criminals of controlling their criminal tendency, but they do not possess the criminal stigmata of the evolutionary throwback. Criminaloids are motivated by passion or have an emotional makeup that compels them, under the right circumstances, to commit crime. Of these types, the born criminal is the true criminal type, the most seriously incorrigible and dangerous to society.

Lombroso originally viewed the great majority of criminals as born criminals, but later reduced the proportion to 35% of male and 14% of female criminals as he added more social, economic, and political conditions as factors in crime. Nevertheless, the concept of the born criminal remained the centerpiece of Lombrosian theory. This basic concept of innate criminality became the dominant perspective on crime and triggered an onslaught of biological theorizing about crime. Any theory that refers to inherited traits, physical abnormalities, the biological inferiority of certain races and categories of people, body type, feeblemindedness, biochemical imbalances, and biological defects and malfunctions that cause individuals to commit crime can be traced back to Lombroso's theory (see Vold et al., 2002). Indeed, Rafter (2006) maintains that Lombroso even anticipated important contemporary biological perspectives on criminal taxonomies as well as evolutionary and behavioral genetic theories of criminal behavior (see the following).

The Criminal as Biologically Inferior

Charles Goring, an English prison medical officer, published in 1913 *The English Convict*, a report of findings from a laborious study that took years to complete. Goring employed the most sophisticated physical measurements and statistical techniques of the day. Comparing prison inmates with university undergraduates, soldiers, professors, and hospital patients, his study found no statistically significant differences between inmates and each of these groups on 37 physical traits that included head sizes, color of eyes, and facial features. As a result, he concluded that Lombroso was wrong: There was no such thing as a physical criminal type. His findings provided no support at all for Lombroso's theory that criminals are clearly differentiated from law-abiding citizens by physical appearance and measurable stigmata.

Goring's study came to be viewed by many scholars as the definitive refutation of Lombrosian theory. In truth, although Goring rejected Lombroso's particular theory of the criminal as an evolutionary atavism, he accepted the Lombrosian notion that criminals are born with criminal traits. His own theory dismissed the effects of social factors on crime and proposed that criminals are inherently inferior to law-abiding citizens.

Of all of the measurements he took, Goring found statistically significant differences (even while controlling for social class and age) between prisoners and civilians on two characteristics, body stature and weight. The prisoners in his study were shorter and thinner than the civilians. They were also judged (by the researcher's impression rather than by IQ tests) to be of lower intelligence. Goring took these findings as evidence that criminals suffer innately from both a "defective physique" and "defective intelligence." He later added inherent "moral defectiveness" to include recidivists who did not appear to be physically or mentally defective. In one way or another, he concluded, all offenders have a general inherited inferiority to law-abiding citizens (Driver, 1972; Wilson and Herrnstein, 1985; Vold et al., 2002).

Subsequently, American anthropologist E. A. Hooton in *Crime and the Man* (1939) attacked Goring's methods and conclusions. Hooton conducted an elaborate study of 17,000 subjects in several states. The study included meticulous measurements of the physical characteristics of inmates in prisons, reformatories, county jails, and other correctional facilities. These were compared with measurements of the same characteristics in college students, hospital patients, mental patients, firemen, and policemen. This comparison of prisoners with civilians was made within one elaborate typology of racial and nationality groups and within another typology of criminal offenses.

Although he included "sociological gleanings" concerning prisoners, Hooton concluded that sociological factors were not important, because criminals are basically "organically inferior":

> [T]he real basis of the whole body of sociological, metric, and morphological deviations of criminals from civilians is the organic inferiority of the former.... [W]hatever the crime may be, it ordinarily arises from a deteriorated organism.... You may say that this is tantamount to a declaration that the primary cause of crime is biological inferiority and that is exactly what I mean.... Certainly the penitentiaries of our society are built upon the shifting sands and quaking bogs of inferior human organisms. (Hooton, 1939: 130)

Just as Hooton found Goring's techniques deficient, Hooton's work was itself criticized on several grounds. The differences he discovered between prisoners and non-prisoners were actually quite small. Furthermore, he did not take into account the fact that his civilian sample included a large proportion of firemen and policemen who had been selected for their jobs based on their size and physical qualities. In addition, there was more variation among the prisoners than there was between the prisoners and civilians. The prisoners may have been involved in many types of crime in the past, but only their most recent crime was recorded to identify the physical characteristics of types of offenders. Hooton began with the assumption of the biological inferiority of criminals and only interpreted the differences between prisoners and civilians (e.g., foreheads, nasal bridges, jaws, eye colors, eyebrows, tattoos, and ears) as the confirmation of that inferiority. No differences in measurements were interpreted as an indication of the superiority of the inmates, and similarities between the two groups were ignored altogether. Hooton's conclusion that criminals were biologically inferior to law-abiding citizens was clearly a case of the circular reasoning of tautology—that is, it was foreordained by the assumption with which he began. There was no possible way to falsify his theory, which was true because he assumed it to be true.

The Lombrosian notion of criminal inferiority promoted by Goring and Hooton is also found in theories of feeblemindedness, inherited criminal traits, endocrine imbalances, and body types, along with many similar explanations that flourished in the late 19th and early 20th centuries (see Vold et al., 2002). Social and non-biological factors were occasionally recognized by these early biological theorists, but environmental factors were seen as incidental when compared to the certain destiny of the physical criminal type. In all these theories the central proposition was that criminals, at least the most serious and dangerous ones, were born with a criminal "nature" rather than "nurtured" into criminality by their social environment. Criminals did not simply behave differently from ordinary people, it was proposed; they were inherently different with an inferior or defective biology that predetermined their criminal behavior (Rafter, 1992).

Recognizing the Inadequacies of Early Biological Theories

This single-minded biological determinism was later criticized by sociologists for ignoring or giving insufficient attention to social, economic, and environmental factors. The critics were very successful in pointing out the methodological flaws in the biological research, the tautological reasoning, and the fact that the empirical evidence did not really support the theories. By the 1950s, biological theories in criminology had been thoroughly discredited. Criminology and delinquency textbooks continued to discuss Lombroso and other biological theorists for their historical interest, but the authors were highly critical of biological theory. Journal articles proposing or testing the biological explanations of crime became virtually non-existent. Biological theory had by that time been regarded by criminologists as unfounded and inconsequential.

To some extent, the dismissal of biological theories was based on the disciplinary predilections of sociologists, the strongest critics of biological theory. Sociological approaches to crime were always treated more favorably in America and, by mid-century, sociologists dominated criminological theory and research. This sociological pre-eminence in American criminology persists, although it is not as pervasive as it once was (Akers, 1992a). C. Ray Jeffery (1979; 1980) and other modern proponents of biological theories of crime claim that even in recent times these theories are not only totally ignored, but are treated as a taboo subject and systematically suppressed by closed-minded, sociologically oriented criminologists (see Holzman, 1979; Gordon, 1980; Taylor, 1984; Walsh, 2000). This claim, however, seems to be highly questionable. Publications on biological theories in criminology have actually flourished in recent decades and continue to find a prominent place in scholarly journals (see the literature cited in this chapter; see also Fishbein, 1990; Walsh, 2000). Criminology textbooks today give much more space and favorable attention to biological theories than did earlier textbooks 30 years ago (Wright and Miller, 1998), and texts devoted to promoting biologically oriented theories in criminology continue to be produced by major publishers (see Fishbein, 2001; Rowe, 2002; Walsh, 2002). Attention continues to be paid to Hooton, and the impact he had on the "Harvard School" of biological criminology that persisted into the 1980s, as an important (albeit essentially wrong) figure in the history of American criminology (Rafter, 2004).

Proponents of biological theory should not mistake criticism and objection leveled at it as an expression of a disciplinary taboo. Although sociologists and other sociologically minded criminologists usually dismiss biological variables from their theories and remain the staunchest critics of biological theories, they are no less vehement critics of each other's sociological theories. Much of the objection to biological theory is based on its controversial implications for policy (see the following). But the major reason for the rejection of the earlier biological theories has in reality very little to do with disciplinary or policy issues. It is simply because the theories were found to be untestable, illogical, or wrong. They seldom withstood empirical tests and often espoused simplistic racist and sexist notions that easily crumbled under closer scrutiny. Even the strongest supporters of modern biological theories of crime and delinquency recognize that the discrediting of Lombrosian positivism was "due to the serious methodological flaws of these early studies and the weakness of their efforts to integrate their findings with sociological theory and data" (Mednick and Shoham, 1979:ix). They also recognize that traditional biological criminology was simplistic and unscientific (Fishbein, 1990) and often based on ideologically biased studies, including some from Nazi German (Mednick, 1987).

In light of this recognized history of the biological explanations for crime, is it any wonder that the modern resurgence of biological theories of crime and delinquency has been met with strong skepticism? Some of these modern proponents have not offered any new theories, but have simply resurrected many of the older biological explanations of crime, relied on the same old, flawed studies, and presented little evidence that could be any more convincing.[1]

Modern Biological and Biosocial Theories of Crime and Delinquency

For the most part, however, current biological theorists reject the kind of simplistic biological determinism characteristic of the theories of Lombroso, Goring, and Hooton. More recent biological explanations have been founded on newer discoveries and technical advances in genetics, brain functioning, neurology, and biochemistry. Because of this, biological explanations of crime have come to occupy a new place of respectability in criminology. Although they must still contend with methodological problems and questionable empirical validity (Fishbein, 2006), they are taken more seriously today than at any other time since the early part of the 20th century. The emphasis in biological theory has shifted from speculation over physical stigmata and constitutional makeup of the born criminal to *biochemistry* (e.g., nutrition, male and female hormonal balances, metabolism), *genetics* (e.g., heritability, IQ, evolution), and *neurophysiology* (e.g., brain, central and autonomic nervous systems, physiological arousal levels, neurotransmitters; Wright and Miller, 1998).[2]

Most of the modern theorists claim that they have no desire to dredge up old, meaningless debate over nature versus nurture or to resurrect the Lombrosian theory of the born criminal. Rather, they have taken a new course with the assumption that behavior, whether conforming or deviant, results from the interaction of the biological makeup of the human organism with the physical and social environment. "There is no nature versus nurture, there is only nature via nurture" (Walsh, 2000:1080). Therefore, no specific criminal behavior is inherited or physiologically preordained, nor is there is any single gene that produces criminal acts. Behavioral potentials and susceptibilities, they propose, can be triggered by biological factors. These potentialities have different probabilities of actual occurrence, depending on the environments the individual confronts over a period of time. Few biological factors in crime are viewed today as fixed and immutable. Rather, they interact with and may be affected by the physical and social environment (Rowe, 2002):[3]

> As a rule, what is inherited is not a behavior; rather it is the way in which an individual responds to the environment. It provides an orientation, predisposition, or tendency to behave in a certain fashion.... Findings of biological involvement in antisocial behavior have, in a few studies, disclosed measurable abnormalities, but in a number of studies, measurements do not reach pathologic levels. In other words ... the biological values do not necessarily exceed normal limits and would not alarm a practicing physician. (Fishbein, 1990:42, 54)

Although he gives primacy to biological causes (especially brain functioning) and is skeptical about the importance of social factors, C. Ray Jeffery (1977; 1979) proposed that criminal behavior results from the interaction of biology, behavior, and the environment. Lee Ellis and Anthony Walsh (Ellis, 1987a; 1987b; Ellis and Walsh, 1997; Walsh, 2000; 2002) pointed to the compatibility of modern biological explanations with "mainstream" criminological theories that rely on sociological and psychological factors. For these reasons Mednick, Ellis, and others prefer that their theories be known as "biosocial" rather than "biological"theories of crime. David C. Rowe (2002) argued for the "heterogeneity" of biological and social causes of crime. "The phrase 'gene for behavior' is really a metaphor. There are no genes for specific behaviors in humans...." (Rowe, 2002:105):

[T]he explanations for criminal behavior are likely to involve complex interplays among learning and genetic, hormonal, and neurochemical factors, all operating within a complex evolved social system." (Ellis and Walsh, 1997:259)

Genes are self-replicating slices of DNA that code for proteins, which code for hormonal and enzymatic processes.... Genes do ... make us differentially sensitive to environmental cues and modulate our responses to them.... Although there can be no gene(s) "for" crime, there are genes that, via a number of neurohormonal routes, lead to the development of different traits and characteristics that may increase the probability of criminal behavior in some environments and in some situations. (Walsh, 2000:1083)

IQ, Mental Functioning, and Delinquency

The theory that delinquents are inherently feebleminded or suffer disproportionately from "learning disabilities" has little empirical support (Murray, 1976). Childhood intelligence does not predict adolescent delinquency very well (McGloin, Pratt, and Maahs, 2004). Parental discipline, family cohesion, religious upbringing, and a child's exposure to delinquent peers are more effective predictors (Glueck and Glueck, 1959; McCord and McCord, 1959).

Nevertheless, research has consistently found a weak to moderate negative correlation between IQ (intelligence quotient) and delinquent behavior, even when class, race, and other factors are controlled (Gordon, 1987). The higher the IQ score, the lower the probability that the adolescent will commit delinquent acts. Gordon (1987), noting the frequency with which this IQ–delinquency relationship has been found in research literature, addressed the consistently lower average IQ score among Black youth compared to White youth. He attributed the differences in Black and White delinquency rates to differences in Black and White IQ scores. Hirschi and Hindelang (1977) showed that the relationship between delinquency and IQ scores, although not very strong, is at least as strong as that between delinquency and social class. But as shown in chapter 8, social class is itself a fairly weak predictor of delinquency, and other factors commonly reported in the literature such as peer associations and attitudes have considerably stronger effects (ranging from .10–.40) than IQ (ranging from .00–.17; Cullen, Gendreau, Jarjoura, and Wright, 1997).

Herrnstein and Murray (1994) proposed that persons with low IQ have a "cognitive disadvantage" (which they contend is up to 80% heritable) that disproportionately leads them to crime and other types of undesirable behavior. Therefore, although an IQ score may be slightly modified by a few points, the impact it has on behavior is highly resistant to the effects of nutrition, education, socioeconomic status, family, and other environmental factors throughout life. Herrnstein and Murray see the effects of this cognitive disadvantage as direct, powerful, and more important than other factors in crime such as social class or family. They base these conclusions mainly on analysis of data from a national survey in which they found that IQ is more strongly related than social class to both self-reported crime and being incarcerated in jail at the time of the survey interview. Cullen et al. (1997) reanalyzed the same data reported by Herrnstein and Murray and produced different results. They found that IQ and the other variables included in the Herrnstein and Murray analysis explained a very low percentage of the variance in self-reported crime (1.5%) and a modest amount of variance (9.6%) in being interviewed in jail. When they added other social variables, which Herrnstein and Murray had ignored, to the equation, such as urban residence, religious participation, and living with father, Cullen et al. (1997) found that the effect of IQ on incarceration was substantially weakened. The relationship between IQ and self-reported offenses disappeared.

Hirschi and Hindelang (1977) argued that the relationship between IQ and delinquency is an indirect one in which low intelligence negatively affects school performance and adjustment, which in turn increases the probability of delinquency. Gordon (1987) believed that IQ tests accurately tap an underlying "g" factor of innate intelligence, which measures of school achievement simply reflect.

Racial differences in intelligence are a highly controversial and unsettled issue, and the evidence of significant differences in average delinquent behavior between Black and White youth is inconsistent (see chap. 8). The notion of an IQ effect on delinquency is often rejected because it has racist and undemocratic policy implications. However, it is difficult to dismiss entirely the evidence of correlation (albeit one of low magnitude) between IQ scores and delinquency, which does not disappear when many other factors are controlled (Gordon, 1987). One the other hand, one must be careful not to make too much of the IQ-delinquency relationship because longitudinal studies have found that it does not hold over time; IQ measured at an earlier age does not predict future delinquency (McGloin et al., 2004).

The question is, assuming that one can establish a consistent correlation between delinquency and IQ , what theory does this correlation support? Too often, it has been concluded that the correlation demonstrates the impact of biological factors, a conclusion that holds true only if one begins with the assumption that intelligence is biologically innate and has a direct effect on delinquency. If one starts with the assumption that IQ is not immutable, is at least partly the result of socialization and education, or has an indirect impact on delinquency through school achievement, then the connection supports non-biological theories.

Terrie Moffitt and associates (Moffitt, Lyman, and Silva, 1994) proposed a neuropsychological model of male delinquency (arguing that it does not apply to female delinquency) that goes beyond IQ to incorporate other aspects of mental functioning, such as verbal ability, visual-motor integration, and mental flexibility. Such factors are proposed as predictors only of early onset "life-course-persistent" antisocial behavior–delinquencies that begin by age 13 and continue into later life stages. They are not proposed as factors in "adolescence-limited" delinquency—onset or acceleration of delinquency after age 13 that does not persist into adulthood (Moffitt, 1993; see chap. 12). The researchers report some support for the model for self-reported and official delinquency. But the delinquency at ages 15 and 18 consistently related only to verbal ability and memory at age 13. None of the neuropsychological measures at age 13 were strong predictors of later delinquency. Later research by Tibbetts and Piquero (1999) provided some evidence in favor of Moffitt's hypothesis regarding biological bases for the early involvement in delinquency by life-course persistent offenders. They found that for children reared in "disadvantaged environments" low birth weight (used as an indirect measure of "neuropsychological deficits") was a modest predictor of the early onset of delinquency in adolescence (but only for males).

Testosterone and Criminal Aggressiveness

Several researchers have pointed to a connection between testosterone (male hormone) levels and anti-social and aggressive behavior (Booth and Osgood, 1993; Walsh, 2002). Because testosterone is identified as a male hormone (although it occurs naturally in both males and females), one would expect the theory and research to be concentrated on the role that high levels of testosterone play in propensities toward male aggression and violence. However, the relationship between testosterone and a variety of other adolescent and adult behaviors, such as sexual behavior, substance use, smoking, and non-violent crime, has also been studied.

Research has found statistically significant relationships. However, except for the unsurprising finding that testosterone level is associated with increased sexual activity (Udry, 1988), the relationships appear to be weak. Further, what relationship there is may be the result of the same social environmental factors related to criminal behavior, such as participation in subcultures of violence, also having independent effects on testosterone levels (Walsh, 2002). No one has yet proposed a general theory of crime based on testosterone. "No reputable researcher ... claims that high levels of testosterone *cause* aggressive or sexual behaviors, only that they *facilitate* such behavior"(Walsh, 2002:192; emphasis in original). Nevertheless, the fact that the effects of testosterone level have been tested on so many different types of deviance would indicate that researchers are hypothesizing that higher levels of testosterone create a general propensity to violate social and legal norms.

Booth and Osgood (1993) presented a theory of adult male deviance that relies on the indirect effects of testosterone levels, mediated by the degree of social integration and prior adolescent delinquency. They were able to test this theory in part with a sample of Vietnam War veterans, measuring testosterone levels in blood specimens. Self-reported adult deviance (e.g., fighting, police arrests, and passing bad checks) and previous adolescent delinquency were also obtained from the veterans. Controlling for age and race, the researchers found a relationship between testosterone and adult deviance, but one that was reduced by introducing measures of social integration and, even more so, by measures of prior delinquency.

Booth and Osgood conclude that "we have firm evidence that there is a relationship between testosterone level and adult deviance. This relationship is strong enough to be of substantive interest, but it is not so strong that testosterone would qualify as the major determinant of adult deviance" (Booth and Osgood, 1993). This seems to be a modest conclusion, but it overstates the relationship found in their research. In fact, the initial relationship between testosterone levels is extremely weak (explaining close to 0% of the variance in adult deviance), and the relationship disappears when social integration and prior delinquency are taken into account.

Genetically Transmitted Criminal Susceptibility: Behavioral Genetics

Many of the factors discussed so far in this chapter and others included in biological theories are assumed to have genetic origins. David C. Rowe (2002) categorized those biological theories focusing on the "heritability" or genetic influences in individual criminality as either "behavioral genetics" or "evolutionary psychology" (sociobiology). Behavioral genetics studies the interplay of genetic and environmental influences on individual traits. Evolutionary psychology "focuses on universal behaviors, or on behaviors specific to males and females of a species over evolutionary time ... that affect the chances of survival and reproduction, such as aggression and altruism...." (Rowe, 2002:8). Rowe considered a number of predisposing mechanisms by which genetically transmitted susceptibilities interact with the environment to produce criminal behavior, such as levels of testosterone or serotonin. But he hypothesized that genetic factors most likely act through the prefrontal cortex of the brain to affect low attention span, sensation seeking, and low self-control and other traits that increase risk of criminal behavior. Whether these tendencies result in criminal or delinquent behavior depends on the individuals' exposure to "shared environments" (class, parents, religion) and "nonshared environments" (differences in family and siblings, peer groups, and teachers). Not only are the individuals' behavioral reactions to these environments influenced by their genetic predispositions, those same biological tendencies affect how they act on and partially create those environments. Walsh (2000) took a similar stance in his discussion of individual "agency" in behavioral genetics as a "biologically friendly environmental discipline"(Walsh, 2000:1076, 1080–81).

Harris (1998) also recognized the interaction of genetic heritability and socialization in the formation of behavior in adolescence and adulthood. But in Harris's view, the main effect of the family on this behavior and personality comes from genetic transmission of temperament and predispositions and not from the learning environment of the family. The social environments that count most are those outside the family of origin, especially peer groups (see chap. 5). Wright and Beaver (2005) found in a study following children from pre-school to the first grade that differences in parenting behavior have little impact on children's attention deficit hyperactivity disorder (ADHD). They concluded that their findings support Harris's theory that once genetic similarities in the family are controlled, parental socialization techniques have minimal effect on individual traits of their children. They see ADHD as an indicator of low self-control that is predictive of antisocial and delinquent behavior (see chap. 6). They theorized that low self-control results not from parenting practices or family socialization but from problems of the genetically heritable "executive control function" areas of the brain.

Of all the various biological explanations of crime that could be classified as behavioral genetics, the best known and most systematically stated and tested is the biosocial theory of Sarnoff Mednick and his associates (Mednick and Christiansen, 1977; Mednick and Shoham, 1979; Mednick, Volavka, Gabrielli, and Itil, 1981; Mednick, Moffitt, and Stack, 1987; Mednick, Gabrielli, and Hutchings, 1984; Brennan, Mednick, and Volavka, 1995; Rowe, 2002). Mednick's theory proposes that some genetic factor(s) related to commission of crime and delinquency is passed along from parent to offspring. Criminal or delinquent behavior is not directly inherited, the theory explains, nor does the genetic factor directly cause the behavior; rather, one inherits a greater susceptibility to succumb to criminogenic environments or to adapt to normal environments in a deviant way.

Mednick hypothesized that the susceptible individual inherits an autonomic nervous system (ANS) that is slower to be aroused or to react to stimuli. Those who inherit slow arousal potential learn to control aggressive or anti-social behavior slowly or not at all. Thus, they stand at greater risk of becoming law violators (Mednick, 1977):

> [ANS responsiveness] may play a role in the social learning of law-abiding behavior.... Briefly stated, this theory suggests that faster ANS recovery (or half recovery) should be associated with greater reinforcement and increased learning of the inhibition of antisocial tendencies. Slow ANS recovery, on the other hand should be associated with poor learning of the inhibition of antisocial responses. (Brennan et al., 1995:84–85)

Hans J. Eysenck proposed a similar biosocial "arousal" theory in which the inherent differences in individuals' levels of arousal affect their conditioning by the social environment. Those with low arousability are less likely to learn prosocial behavior and more likely to learn criminal and deviant behavior patterns (Eysenck and Gudjonsson, 1989). Similarly, Lee Ellis proposed that some people are more prone to crime, drug use, and other deviant behavior because they have a general tendency to engage in risk taking, thrill seeking, or impulsive behavior "primarily reflecting attempts to compensate for *suboptimal* arousal levels" (Ellis, 1987b:509; emphasis added); that is, those whose neurological arousal levels are low are more apt to seek out more stimulating and exciting situations and actions, such as breaking the law or social norms, and to avoid conforming behavior with low risk or stimulation. This does not explain, however, why individuals adapt to low arousal states by committing criminal acts rather than seeking other legal forms of behavior that are equally stimulating or risky (Rowe, 2002). In addition to positing the link between arousal levels and deviance, Ellis used the theory to explain the well-known negative relationship between religiosity and delinquency (see chap. 6). He hypothesized that those with a biological tendency toward low arousal avoid church because they find it boring while gravitating toward delinquency because it provides excitement (Ellis, 1987c).

The assumption that all attendance at worship services and involvement in church activities are unstimulating is itself questionable. But the theory can be indirectly tested by examining the interrelationships among measures of arousal, religion, and delinquency. This is the approach used by Cochran, Wood, and Arneklev (1994), who measured self-reported tendencies toward "sensation seeking" as a proxy for a direct physiological measure of suboptimal arousal. They found that, although not related to marijuana use, sensation-seeking tendencies are related to delinquency and mediate some of the relationship between religiosity and delinquency. Forthun, Bell, Peek, and Sun (1999) also measured self-reported sensation-seeking as an indirect indicator of arousal level. They found it was modestly related to alcohol use, but contrary to the theory, it was not related to marijuana use and did not mediate the effects of religiosity, religious denomination, or gender on substance use. Cochran, Wareham, Wood, and Arneklev (2002), however, did find that similar indirect measures of arousal attenuated the correlation between adolescents' attachment to school and some types of adolescent deviance. (See also Wood, Cochran, Pfefferbaum, and Arneklev, 1995, and the discussion of sensation seeking and social learning in chap. 5.)

The first study conducted by Mednick and colleagues in Copenhagen, Denmark, linked the criminality of biological fathers with the subsequent criminal behavior of their sons who had been adopted out and raised by adoptive parents. They found the highest rates of officially recorded criminal offenses among those sons whose biological and adoptive fathers both had criminal records, and the lowest rates when neither had criminal records. Those sons whose biological fathers had criminal records, but whose adoptive fathers did not, were more likely to be registered as criminals than those whose adoptive fathers, but not their biological fathers, had criminal records (Hutchings and Mednick, 1977c).

Later, the same type of study was conducted by Mednick on a larger sample of adopted sons from all parts of Denmark. Mednick interpreted the findings from this larger study as a replication and independent confirmation of the findings from the Copenhagen study. The larger study included the criminal background of both parents, biological and adoptive, and related that to the adoptees' criminal convictions. Again, Mednick reported verification of the theory. He found that those with only criminal biological parents were more likely than those with only criminal adoptive parents to have been convicted of offenses. The highest rate of convictions were found among persons whose biological and adoptive parents both had been convicted of crimes (Mednick et al., 1984).

These Danish studies are still among the most frequently cited in support of the heritability of criminal propensities. However, Gottfredson and Hirschi (1990:47–63) pointed to some serious flaws in this research, which has since raised doubts as to how much it actually validates the theory of inherited criminal potential. Gottfredson and Hirschi (1990) also showed that Swedish and American adoption research purporting to duplicate Mednick's findings has in fact found very small, insignificant differences in the criminality of offspring that could be attributed to inherited traits. They estimate that the correlation between biological fathers' and sons' criminality is about $r = .03$ and conclude that "the magnitude of the 'genetic effect' as determined by adoption studies is near zero" (Gottfredson and Hirschi, 1990:60).

Another approach to testing theories of genetic susceptibility is to study the behavior of twins. A central concept in twin research is known as "concordance." Concordance is a quantitative measure of the degree to which the observed behavior or attribute of one twin (or sibling) matches that of the other. Most studies of identical and fraternal twins, both those raised in the same family and those separated by adoption, have found higher concordance between the criminal and non-criminal behavior of identical twins than between fraternal twins. But these studies have not been successful in showing how much of this concordance is based solely on biological as opposed to social similarities (Hutchings and Mednick, 1977a; 1977b).

In the twin studies, the biological and social variables are seldom measured directly.[4] In the studies of adoptees, biological variables are indirectly measured by the degree of behavioral similarities between biological parent(s) and offspring when the biological parent(s) does not raise the child. Social variables are assumed to be operative when similarities are found in the behavior of adoptive parents and adoptees. Concordance in the behavior of twins reared apart is attributed to biological factors on the assumption that their social environments differ. Children reared together are assumed to have had similar social environments.

The assumptions in such studies hold only partially for social variables in the family environment and not at all for variables in other social environments. Moreover, the findings from family and twin studies fit other explanations as well as or better than genetic interpretations. For instance, Marshall Jones and Donald Jones interpret the research findings as pointing less to heritability and more to the "contagious nature of antisocial behavior." They defined *behavior* as "contagious if the risk to a given individual increases when someone in that person's vicinity, family, or social group becomes affected" (Jones and Jones, 2000:26). The finding that antisocial behavior of siblings is highly correlated and that identical twins tend to be more concordant for antisocial behavior than fraternal twins can be explained as well by contagion as by heredity. Moreover, other findings, such as the higher concordance between same-sex than between opposite-sex fraternal twins and siblings and in larger than in smaller families, can be explained by contagion but not by heredity (Jones and Jones, 2000).

Genetic explanations seem to be least applicable to adolescent delinquency. Based on findings from a mailed questionnaire study of twins, Rowe (1985; 1986) concluded that individual differences in self-reported delinquency were more the result of genetic factors than common or specific environmental factors. However, by adjusting for mutual sibling influence, he later reduced the estimates of the effect of heritability on delinquency from about two-thirds of the differences in delinquent behavior to about one-third (Rowe and Gulley, 1992; Rowe, 2002). Also, in a later analysis of the same data into which he included specific measures of family variables, Rowe concluded that delinquency is best explained by the combined effects of heredity and family environment. Similarly, Carey (1992) found in a study of Danish identical and fraternal twins that when imitation and other peer effects of sibling interaction are taken into account, the amount of variance attributed to genetic similarity is considerably reduced, in "... one case actually approaching 0.0" (Carey, 1992:21). Although twin studies of adult offenders often find substantial genetic effects at least for males (see Rushton, 1996), "twin studies of delinquency in adolescence show little genetic influence" (Rowe, 2002:30; see also Walsh, 2000; Iervolino et al., 2002). Research has found that the "concordance levels for juvenile delinquency are high and about the same for both dizygotic and monozygotic twins" (Jones and Jones, 2000:30):

> Genetic factors were less important for the peer delinquency dimension.... [P]eer-group similarity was comparable for MZ and DZ twins and full, half, and unrelated siblings. Accordingly, model-fitting results indicated negligible genetic (3 percent), moderate shared environmental (20 percent), and substantial nonshared environmental (77 percent) effects. Genetic factors did not influence adolescents' choice of delinquency-oriented peers. For this dimension, nonshared environment was the only significant contributor to individual differences. (Iervolino et al., 2002:168, 171)

Genetically Transmitted Criminal Susceptibility: Evolutionary Theory

Ellis and Walsh (1997) suggested that gene-based evolutionary theories can explain criminal behavior both in general and in specific types of crime. Such theories start with the assumption that evolutionary processes of natural selection have produced "reproductive niches for individuals and groups who victimize others" (Ellis and Walsh, 1997:229). Disposition to commit rape, as an example of a specific crime, is hypothesized to be evolutionarily selected because it provides a reproductive advantage; that is, it increases the chances that the genes of the rapists will be transmitted to the next generation. Because they have the least investment in raising those offspring, males (of both human and animal species) have more to gain genetically than do females from multiple sex partners, and sexual aggression is an effective technique for achieving that advantage. Rapists have more active sex lives and produce more pregnancies than males who rely only on voluntary sex. Not only rape but also criminal behavior of all kinds has evolved because of the advantage it affords in genetic reproduction. Some males have genetic make-ups that lean them in the direction of having very low involvement with offspring and very high involvement with as many reproductive partners as possible ("cads"), whereas others gain advantage through fewer sexual partners but with high investment in child rearing ("dads"). These reproductive strategies can be placed on an *r/K selection* continuum in which those at the *r* end of the continuum (quantitative, mating) reproduce often but invest very little in raising offspring. Those at the *K* end (qualitative, parenting) reproduce less often with fewer sexual partners but invest more time and energy in raising their offspring. The *K* strategy is manifested in altruism toward kin. Criminal and antisocial behavior is favored by *r* strategists who attempt to propagate their genes by producing many progeny and taking little interest in caring for them to help ensure their survival (see also Ellis, 1987a).

Ellis and Walsh generate several hypotheses from this theory that are consistent with known gender, ecological, and other variations in crime, but they acknowledge that those same variations are also consistent with non-genetic theories. Because the application to those known variations are *post hoc,* the genetic evolution theory of crime faces a problem of tautology that will not be solved until researchers devise indicators of reproduction strategy separate from the very behavior they are intended to explain. As of yet this has not been done in direct tests of evolutionary theory, and it remains weak on the criterion of testability (Rowe, 2002).

There has been some limited research using indirect measures of reproduction strategies. For instance, Griffin and Akins (2000) used high rates of twins in a population as an indirect indicator of high rates of *r* mating strategy (on the grounds that this strategy is intended to produce larger numbers of offspring). They found that racial groups with high rates of twinning also have high rates of crime. However, this evidence cannot be taken as supporting *r/K* selection theory of male mating strategies because, as Griffin and Akins pointed out, only the physiology of the mother determines whether a pregnancy will be single or multiple birth; the sexual behavior of the father is irrelevant. Rowe believed that evolutionary processes such as sexual mating strategies might account for cross-species differences and "the greater aggressiveness of males than females, but not how one male is more aggressive than another" Rowe (2002:58).

Empirical Validity of Biological Theories of Criminal Behavior

As shown earlier, modern biological explanations of crime have far surpassed the early biological theories of Lombroso, Goring, Hooton, and others. This is partly the result of greater theoretical sophistication, less reliance on immutable biological defects or destiny, and greater attention to interaction with social and psychological variables. It is also partly the result of more sophisticated methodology in biological studies and an expanded knowledge of genetics and neurological, hormonal, and other bodily systems.

Nevertheless, as indicated by findings reviewed in this chapter, such research has not yet established the empirical validity of biological theories. Tests of the theories continue to have problems with methodology, sampling, and measurement (Fishbein, 1990; 2001). Walters and White (1989) came to this conclusion based on their extensive review of research on the heritability of criminal behavior. They considered studies using four basic approaches: family studies, twin studies, adoption studies, and gene-environment interaction studies. Their review found that biological research on crime suffers from several methodological deficiencies, including the measurement of criminality, sample size, sampling bias, statistical procedures, and generalizability. Walters and White believed that genetic factors are correlated with some measures of criminal behavior, but they warned that

> [T]he large number of methodological flaws and limitations in the research should make one cautious in drawing any causal inferences at this point in time. Our review leads us to the inevitable conclusion that current genetic research on crime has been poorly designed, ambiguously reported, and exceedingly inadequate in addressing the relevant issues. (Walters and White, 1989:478)

Walters (1992) followed this up with a statistical "meta-analysis" (i.e., the recalculation of different measures of effect reported from different studies into a standard measure of effect that can be compared across studies). He found that the correlations reported from different studies were often statistically significant and usually in the expected direction. But the average overall effect of heredity on crime found in these studies was weak. The more recently and rigorously studies are conducted, the more likely they are to find the weaker effects of genetic factors on crime than did the older and more poorly designed studies. The strongest methodology, used in adoption studies, produces findings less favorable to the hypothesis of a genetic effect in crime than the weaker methodology in family and twin studies.

Thus far, newer biological explanations have garnered mixed and generally weak empirical support. Biological theories that posit crime-specific genetic or physiological defects have not been, and are not likely to be, accepted as sound explanations in criminology. The greater the extent to which a biological theory proposes to relate normal physiological and sensory processes to social and environmental variables in explaining criminal behavior, clearly the direction in which contemporary biological theories have gone, the more likely it will be empirically supported and accepted in criminology.

Rowe and Osgood (1984) argued that the operation of genetic factors can be integrated into current sociological theories of delinquency. Their stance was not that delinquency is the direct or inevitable outcome of genetic differences. Rather, they proposed that "causal sequences leading to delinquency are traceable to individual differences in genes, so any social causation entails either individual differences in reactions to social processes or differential social reactions to already differing individuals" (Rowe and Osgood, 1984:526). Similarly, Walsh (2000) maintained that individual differences in deviant or conforming response to social sources of strain can be accounted for by differences in genetically influenced predispositions.

There is little to disagree with in the assertion that biology interacts with the environment. The real question involves the nature of that interaction and the extent to which crime is influenced by biology or environment. If a theory proposes that biological defects or abnormalities are the direct cause of all or most criminal behavior, it is not likely to be supported by empirical evidence. It is also less likely to be supported if it contends that individual biological factors better explain the full range of crime and delinquency in general than do social or social-psychological factors.

Policy Implications of Biological Theories

What policies are implied by biological theories depends on whether they are based on the older theoretical style, which is highly deterministic, or on the newer theories that are less deterministic regarding the causes of crime. The more the theory views the biological causes as intractable and immutable, the more likely it is that biologically invasive or externally restrictive policies will be recommended. On the other hand, if the theory views biological factors as affecting criminal behavior only in interaction with social and psychological factors, it is likely that its policy implications will be ameliorative and rehabilitative (see Walsh, 2002). Policies based on the assumption of strong, direct, and essentially immutable effects of IQ will be different than those based on the assumption that IQ has weak effects on criminal behavior, whereas other, more malleable, variables have stronger effects (Cullen et al., 1997).

If biology is destiny, if crime and delinquency are innate in the individual, offenders will not be deterred by fear of punishment and cannot be rehabilitated through psychological counseling or changes in their social conditions. With this view, criminals can be changed only through medical, chemical, or surgical procedures to modify their brains or biochemical functions or they must be strictly controlled through long-term isolation, incarceration, and incapacitation. Thus, it would be possible to prevent criminal defects from being genetically transmitted by introduction of selective breeding or sterilization policies that prohibit individuals who carry the defective genes from reproducing (see Rafter, 1992).

This was the reasoning of the eugenics movement (based on social Darwinism of the late 19th and early 20th centuries) for involuntary sterilization and of the policies recommended by Hooton in 1939. Hooton rejected racism and participated in anti-Nazi campaigns, but he was a committed eugenicist who adhered to the doctrine that "criminals belong to the class of hereditary degenerates who are ruining our civilizations but can be brought under control through sterilization, euthanasia and cutbacks in welfare" (Rafter, 2004:761–762). He proposed both selective breeding and large-scale self-governing criminal reservations separating biologically inferior criminals from the rest of society:

> Of course, I think that habitual criminals who are hopeless constitutional inferiors should be permanently incarcerated and, on no account, should be allowed to breed. Nevertheless, they should be treated humanely, and, *if* they are to be kept alive should be allowed some opportunity for freedom and profitable occupation within their own severely restricted area. (Hooton, 1939:392; emphasis added)

> We can direct and control the progress of human evolution by breeding better types and by the ruthless elimination of inferior types, if only we are willing to found and to practice a science of human genetics. With sound and progressively evolving human organisms in the majority of our species, problems of human behavior will be minimized, and there will be improved educability. Crime can be eradicated, war can be forgotten. (Hooton, 1939:396–397)

Similar "invasive criminal justice policy ... from drug treatment and surgery to segregation and elimination through negative eugenics" (forced sterilization) and even death for those who could not be "cured" was supported by other early biological theorists (Lanier and Henry, 1998:108) including the developers of behavioral genetics (Rowe, 2002). But support for such policies by biological theorists has not been confined to the late 19th and early 20th centuries. Alterations in individuals' chemical or physiological structures and processes to change or prevent their criminal behavior have been made more recently.

For instance, Taylor (1984) suggested intrusion into the lives of persons diagnosed as genetically predisposed to crime (whether they have actually committed criminal acts) through isolation, ingestion of chemicals, lobotomies, and gene splicing. He also recommended intervention in the reproduction process through sterilization and abortion to forestall transmission of suspected criminal genes. Rowe (2002) strongly rejected involuntary genetic selection. However, he suggests a form of voluntary eugenics as one possible future application of behavioral genetics to the prevention of criminal behavior; parents, after genetic counseling and weighing other options, might choose to abort rather than give birth to a child genetically predisposed to criminality.

Various medical procedures were performed on small numbers of violent offenders from the 1950s to the late 1970s such as brain surgery, remote radio-controlled brain stimulation through implanted electrodes, and physical as well as chemical castration. These efforts were based on the assumption that the violent tendencies of the offenders could be stopped through alteration of "the internal milieu, by producing changes in the individual's physiology" (Moyer, 1979:32). In his review of the outcomes of these procedures, Moyer (1979) concluded that at least some instances of violent behavior are caused by brain lesions, hormonal imbalances, or other abnormal physiological processes. But he also reports that the medical procedures work with only a few individuals, their overall effectiveness has not been established, and they cannot deal with systematic or large-scale violence (Moyer, 1979). Because of their limited effectiveness, the irreversible physical damage to the individuals on which they are performed, and other ethical considerations, Moyer argued that these procedures should be used only as a last resort.

The reservations and caution shown by Moyer about biologically based crime control are more in line with the newer biological theories. Proponents of these theories are unlikely to hypothesize that criminal behavior is directly inherited through specific genes or caused by genetic abnormalities. Contemporary biological theorists support dietary therapy, genetic counseling, and drug therapies while opposing the invasive policies proposed by Hooton and others. They are also likely to recommend school or community programs and public health approaches to overcome biological risks (Pagani, Tremblay, Vitaro, and Parent, 1998; Fishbein, 2001; 2006). In addition, they are apt to suggest that "the environment of potential offenders can be manipulated to prevent their manifesting crime, including improving prenatal and perinatal care and, in the case of sensation seekers, providing alternatives that are less harmful but still exciting and challenging" (Lanier and Henry, 1998:109). As biological theories and research have changed over time, policy and practices based on them also have changed:

Contrary to popular belief, biological and genetic traits are not static and unchangeable: they can be altered in a social environment conducive to change. Thus, theoretically, large-scale social programs can lead to behavioral improvements even in cases where the propensities are genetically influenced by minimizing the impact of an environment that would otherwise be conducive to antisocial behavior ... Adverse interactions in the home ... association with peers promoting antisocial behavior [suggest that] ... The quality of interaction between the person having a particular biological disposition, and the social environment which determines the behavior ... should be the focus of interventions. (Fishbein, 2006:63)

Thus, some of the policy implications of contemporary social biologicalor bio-behavioral theories for prevention/treatment of delinquency look similar to those that would be derived from other theories— educational programs, teacher training, promotion of parenting skills, after school programs, drug treatment, and others (Fishbein, 2001).

Summary

Early biological positivism proposed that criminal behavior is directly determined by the person's biological makeup. This basic concept of innate criminality, of the criminal as a distinctly different type of person from law-abiding citizens, was proposed in theories of the born criminal, which listed physical abnormalities, biological inferiority, body type, biochemical imbalances, and biological defects as the primary causes of crime. This kind of biological theory has largely been discredited. Current biological theorizing tends to move beyond the simplistic determinism of early theories. The older biological theories have given way to theories relating crime and delinquency to measurable variations in inherited characteristics, brain functioning, central and autonomic nervous systems, nutrition, hormonal balances, metabolism, physiological arousal levels, biological processes in learning, and similar variables.

Modern biological theories propose the interaction of these factors with the social environment. However, they do not support the view that specific biological defects produce specific criminal behavior or that a single gene produces criminal acts. Biological factors are not regarded as fixed and immutable or as having any greater power over behavior than social or psychological variables. Rather, their effects are viewed as indirect and mediated by other factors. Proponents of more recent biological theories have moved away from the intrusive physical and isolation policies of the earlier theorists.

The newer biological explanations of crime have found greater acceptance in criminology, but they have been criticized for their dependence on research with serious methodological problems that produce questionable empirical validity. Research has provided some evidence in favor of the newer biological theories of criminal behavior, but problems with methodology, sampling, and measurement have resulted in mixed and generally weak empirical support.

Notes

1. See, for instance, the biological theorizing in Wilson and Herrnstein (1985) or Taylor (1984).
2. See the papers published in Mednick et al. (1987) and the review of various biological studies in Shah and Roth (1974), Vold et al. (2002), Walters and White (1989), Fishbein (1990), Wright and Miller (1998), and Andrews and Bonta (1998).
3. See Mednick and Christiansen (1977), Mednick and Shoham (1979), Jeffery (1977; 1979), Mednick et al. (1981), Mednick et al. (1987), Eysenck and Gudjonsson (1989), Fishbein (1990; 2001; 2006), Brennan et al. (1995), Walsh (2000; 2002), and Rowe (2002).
4. Some studies do directly measure these variables. See Mednick et al. (1981) and Rowe (1986). Also, social variables are seldom directly measured. See Rowe (1986; 2002).

Chapter 4

Psychological Theories

This chapter focuses on psychoanalytic and personality theories of criminal behavior. It should be noted these do not represent the broader range of psychological theories of criminal and deviant behavior such as behavioral, neuropsychological, developmental, and other psychological approaches that are not included in this chapter. However, concepts and variables from these other approaches can be found in other chapters. For instance, behavioral learning theory in psychology is part of the theoretical base for social learning theory presented in chapter 5. Developmental psychology has been applied in criminology either with a biological emphasis (chap. 2; see Andrews and Bonta, 2003) or with a focus on personality (see the I-level theory in this chapter). It is also part of some age-effect and life-course theories discussed in chapter 12. Psychoanalytic and personality theories recognize the effects of an individual's experiences, especially in early childhood, and environmental factors that may trigger criminal behavior, but they propose abnormal personality type/traits or emotional maladjustment as the primary causes of crime.

Psychoanalytic Theory

Psychoanalytic theory shares with biological theory the search for causes of crime within the makeup of the individual. Rather than seek the causes in biological processes or anomalies, it attempts to look deep into the mind of the individual. According to Kate Friedlander (1947), classical Freudian psychoanalytic explanations of delinquency focus on abnormalities or disturbances in the individual's emotional development from early childhood. The id is the unconscious seat of irrational, antisocial, and instinctual impulses that must be controlled and shaped for social adaptation to life in society. This is done through the development of the ego, or the conscious and rational part of the mind, and through the superego, or the conscience and moralizing part of the mind. Normally, a child's emotional maturation goes through developmental stages, each of which is rooted in sexuality: an oral phase as an infant, an anal phase up to about age three, a phallic phase up to about age five, a latency phase up to the time of puberty, then finally a mature genital phase of development as an adult.

The id is uncontrolled until the development of the ego gains control over the instincts at about age three. At the beginning of the phallic stage, the child wants to possess the parent of the opposite sex and perceives the same-sex parent as a rival for the affection of the other parent. These feelings are repressed, and an Oedipus complex (the unconscious love of the mother and hatred or fear of the father by the boy) or an Electra complex (the love of the father and hatred/fear of the mother by the girl) develops. The superego evolves by identifying with the same-sex parent and internalizing parental control; hence, the child gives up the desire to possess the opposite-sex parent. Any abnormal development during these stages, or any fixation at an infantile or childhood stage, leads to antisocial behavior by adolescence as the individual struggles with the unconscious guilt and pathology of this arrested development.

The basic premise of the psychoanalytic approach to crime is that delinquent or criminal behavior is in itself unimportant. It is only a symptom of the psychic conflict between the id, ego, and superego, arising from abnormal maturation or control of instincts, a poor early relationship with the mother or father, fixation at a stage of emotional development, or repressed sexuality or guilt. The most critical fixation is at the Oedipus/Electra stage. The adolescent is not consciously aware of these conflicts, because they all trace back to early childhood, the conscious memories of which are blocked by "infantile amnesia." Repressed guilt and conflict continue to be the "true" causes of delinquency, although other more visible factors may seem to be operating.

Other Freudian or neo-Freudian explanations of crime and delinquency emphasize the underdevelopment or disrupted development of the superego, due to the absence of parents or the presence of cruel, unloving parents. Some theorists stress that not only are the criminal acts themselves expressions of unresolved guilt, but criminals unconsciously seek to be caught and punished to expatiate this repressed guilt. Whatever the specific mechanism, psychoanalytic explanations rely heavily on irrational and unconscious motivations as the basic forces behind crime. In psychoanalytical theory, all criminal behavior is explained as expressions or symptoms of one or more underlying mental illnesses, emotional disorders, or psychic disturbances. Not only law violations but also various other types of deviant behavior, such as drug and alcohol abuse, are seen as dysfunctional attempts to deal with repressed guilt, feelings of hopelessness or helplessness, pent-up aggression, or other unresolved unconscious and emotional turmoil. Both adolescent delinquency and adult crime are believed to stem essentially from these irrational impulses or compulsions. Early childhood events are often seen as crucial, whereas current or anticipated environmental and social events are seen as irrelevant or important only as triggering events for the dysfunctional behavior.[1]

The empirical validity of psychoanalytic explanations of crime is difficult to assess. The language used is often strongly deterministic, claiming unequivocal empirical support for a psychiatric explanation of individual cases as the outcome of mental disorder. Flora Schreiber (1984) conducted interviews with Joseph Kallinger, a shoemaker who, along with his teenage son, committed a series of burglaries, robberies, and murders. Schreiber reached firm cause-and-effect conclusions about the connection between the elder Kallinger's criminal behavior and what she diagnoses as his psychosis caused by the psychological and physical abuse of him as a child by his adoptive parents. She concentrated especially on the time when Joseph was 4 years old and his parents told him that the hernia operation he had was really done to remove the demon from his penis. According to Schreiber, this and other statements made to the young boy about his penis produced "psychological castration" in Joseph. This was the primary cause of Kallinger's psychosis, which in his adult life "drives him to kill":

> Joseph Kallinger would never have become a killer without his psychosis. With it he had no other course.... [M]urder was the inevitable outcome of Kallinger's psychosis.... [H]e had become psychotic before he committed a single crime.... [T]he crimes sprang directly from the psychosis: from the delusional system and the hallucinations the psychosis had spawned.... One can, however, establish a cause and effect relationship between Joe Kallinger's murders and the psychological abuse of him as a child. (Schreiber, 1984:17, 390, 394)

Psychiatric studies rely heavily on clinical and case studies such as this, producing widely varying estimates of the proportions of offenders who have some diagnosable mental disorder or psychiatric problem. Such studies concentrate on individual cases or on small samples of the most serious offenders. Unfortunately, there are very few comparisons with samples of the general population or other offenders (Pallone and Hennessy, 1992).

Moreover, there may be no way to test psychoanalytic theory directly because the motivations are deeply hidden in the unconscious, unknown even to the offender. Therefore, it is only the interpretation of the therapist that determines when the independent variables of unconscious urges and impulses are present. Psychoanalytic interpretations, therefore, tend to be after the fact, tautological, and untestable (Shoham and

Seis, 1993). Typically, the "psychopathic deviation" assumed to be the cause of criminal behavior is determined by clinical judgment in which "habitual criminality" itself is a principal criterion for such a diagnosis. This procedure produces "a tautology of impressive proportions" (Pallone and Hennessy, 1992:56, 165). Various techniques of clinical measures, such as "projective" tests, are sometimes used to add to clinical judgment. But "both the paucity of studies and the instability of the interpretations preclude any valid generalizations based on projective test data" (Pallone and Hennessy, 1992:168). Although modifications and reformulations of Freudian-based theory continue in psychology, Andrews and Bonta (1998:102) "do not believe that classic psychoanalytic thought represents the current state of psychological knowledge," and psychoanalytic theory does not receive much attention in criminology today.

Personality Theory

In personality theory, the problem lies not in unconscious motivation, but in abnormal, inadequate, or specifically criminal personalities or personality traits that differentiate delinquents and criminals from law-abiding people. One version of personality theory explains criminal and delinquent behavior as an expression of such deviant personality traits as impulsiveness, aggressiveness, sensation seeking, rebelliousness, hostility, and so on. A related version claims that criminal and delinquent offenders differ from law-abiding persons in basic personality type. Conformity reflects normal personality. Serious criminal violations spring from an aberrant personality, variously labeled a psychopathic, antisocial, or sociopathic personality. These labels are applied to a self-centered person who has not been properly socialized into prosocial attitudes and values, who has developed no sense of right and wrong, who has no empathy with others, and who is incapable of feeling remorse or guilt for misconduct or harm to others. Personality-trait psychology has fairly broad scope from minor delinquency to serious criminal behavior, but because the list of deviance-producing traits is rather long, it is not parsimonious. Personality-type theory is more parsimonious in its postulating a single personality type (under which is subsumed a number of anti-social traits or characteristics) as the explanation of criminal behavior, but has more limited scope, applying mainly to the most serious and persistent offenders.

Personality Traits

Personality trait theories have been empirically tested with more rigorous methodology than psychoanalytic theories. The most common technique is to measure personality traits with a written personality inventory and compare mean responses on the inventory from adjudicated delinquents with mean responses from non-delinquents. The most commonly used personality tests are the Minnesota Multiphasic Personality Inventory (MMPI) and the California Psychological Inventory (CPI). The CPI is intended to measure variations in personality traits, such as dominance, tolerance, and sociability. The MMPI uses several scales to measure "abnormal" personality traits, such as depression, hysteria, paranoia, psychopathology, introversion/extroversion, and compulsiveness (Hathaway and Meehl, 1951).

The MMPI was originally designed by Starke Hathaway (1939) for the purpose of detecting deviant personality patterns in mentally ill adults. Using it to predict delinquency is based on the assumption that delinquency is symptomatic of mental illness similar to adult patterns of maladaptive behavior (Hathaway and Monachesi, 1953). Research has found that institutionalized delinquents score higher on the scales of asocial, amoral, and psychopathic behavior, whereas non-delinquents tend to be more introverted. However, attempts at predicting future delinquency from MMPI measures have only been partially successful. The strongest predictive scale from the MMPI, the "F Scale," does not measure any personality trait at all. Rather, it records any inconsistent or careless responses to the questions on the MMPI or any poor reading ability in completing the questionnaire (Hathaway and Monachesi, 1963).

Other research findings on the causative effects of personality traits on criminal and delinquent behavior are inconsistent. An early review of such studies concluded that only a minority of them found significant differences in personality between delinquents and non-delinquents (Schuessler and Cressey, 1950). A somewhat later review reported that a majority of the more carefully conducted studies found significant differences (Waldo and Dinitz, 1967), and later studies continued to find correlations of personality traits with self-report and other measures of delinquency and crime (Caspi et al., 1994). Some analyses have reported mixed findings in the research on personality and criminal behavior (see Sutherland, Cressey, and Luckenbill, 1992). Other more recent analyses have found that scores on at least some personality inventory scales are consistently, albeit weakly, correlated with criminal behavior (Andrews and Bonta, 2003).

Evaluating the empirical validity of personality trait theories is undermined to some extent by the fact that in studies using personality inventories the empirical measures of personality traits and delinquent behavior are, at least in part, tautological. For instance, in the MMPI, the main scale of personality correlated with delinquency includes items that ask about "trouble with the law," one of the very thing the scale is supposed to explain. The same tautology problem is found when personality or "conduct" disorder is proposed as a cause of criminal and delinquent behavior because the instruments used to diagnose the disorder itself includes items asking about law violations, fighting, destroying property, stealing, acts of cruelty, and use of weapons, again the same behavior that the theory is meant to explain. In effect, any conclusion about causation based on the empirical findings using these items amounts to saying that getting into trouble with the law is caused by getting into trouble with the law. Moffitt, Caspi, Rutter, and Silva (2001) showed, however, that this tautology problem can be avoided by treating conduct disorder itself as simply another label for, and not a cause of, deviant and criminal behavior. The research using personality inventories and other methods has provided some empirical support for personality trait theory, but thus far has not been able to produce strong findings that personality variables are major causes of criminal and delinquent behavior (Pallone and Hennessy, 1992; Sutherland et al., 1992; Vold et al., 2002; Shoemaker, 2004).

The Psychopathic Personality

The psychopathic criminal has been defined as an "asocial," self-centered, aggressive person with "a dangerously maladjusted personality," who craves excitement, feels little guilt, and is unable to form meaningful emotional attachments to others. "These last two traits, guiltlessness and lovelessness, conspicuously mark the psychopath as different from other men" (McCord and McCord, 1956:16).

Robert Hare is the chief proponent today of psychopathy as a theory of criminal behavior and author of both the original and revised Psychopathy Checklist (PCL-R), the most widely used instrument for the measurement of the psychopathic personality (Hare, 1965; 1999; 2003; Edens, Marcus, Lilienfeld, and Poythress, 2006). The 20-item checklist has also been slightly modified as the Psychopathy Checklist–Juvenile Versions (PCL-JV) for use with adolescent offenders (MacArthur Foundation, 2006). According to Hare, the psychopaths are entirely self-centered "social predators" who, although capable of being charming, manipulates others for their own purposes, and lack any conscience so that they feel no guilt, remorse or regret for their anti-social behavior or the harm they do to others. They "ruthlessly plow their way through life, leaving a broad trail of broken hearts, shattered expectations, and empty wallets" (Hare, 1999:xi). Hare preferred the term *psychopath* over *sociopath* because he believed that "psychological, biological, and genetic factors [beyond social forces] also contribute to development of the [psychopathic] syndrome" (Hare, 1999:23–240. He took the position that the psychopathic personality is formed through the "interplay between biological factors and social factors ... provided in part by nature and possibly by some unknown biological influences on the developing fetus and neonate" (Hare, 1999:173), and proposed that biological factors work against normal socialization and formation of conscience, whereas poor parenting and parental abuse affect the development of psychopathy.

The theory does not propose that all psychopaths are criminals or that all criminals are psychopaths. But Hare (1999:86–87) asserted that "psychopaths are well represented in our prison populations and are responsible for crime far out of proportion to their numbers: On average, about 20% of male and female prison inmate are psychopaths. Pyschopaths are responsible for more than 50% of the serious crimes committed." Further, "the violent recidivism rate of psychopaths is about triple that of other offenders" (Hare, 1999:96). To Hare (1999:34) "psychopathy is a *syndrome*—a cluster of related symptoms," but simply having these symptoms does not mean that one is a psychopath. Determining who does and does not have the syndrome sufficient to be diagnosed as a psychopath is a difficult and complex process and must be done *only* through proper use of the Psychopathy Checklist by highly trained professionals. The checklist is comprised of two sets of key psychopathic symptoms that identify "two facets—one depicting feelings and relationships, the other social deviance—[that together] provide a comprehensive picture of the psychopathic personality" (Hare, 1999:57). The first is made up of "emotional/interpersonal" psychopathic symptoms (e.g., being glib, superficial, and deceitful, lacking remorse, guilt, or empathy, and shallowness of emotions); later Hare divided this first facet of psychopathy into "interpersonal" and "affective" sub-dimensions. The second facet is defined as symptomatic of "social deviance" (e.g., impulsive behavior, need for stimulation, early behavior problems, and various kinds of deviant and offending behavior), later defined as comprised of "lifestyle" and "antisocial behavior" subdimensions (Hare, 1999; 2003; Edens et al., 2006). Although Hare proposed that psychopathy is a syndrome indicated by assessing variable scores along different dimensions, the traditional concept of psychopathy, and the one that continues to be espoused by many psychologists, holds that psychopaths are a "fundamentally distinct class of individuals who differ qualitatively from the rest of society." Recent research favors the contrary view supported by Hare and others that " psychopath" is simply a label for "a constellation or configuration of extreme levels of continuously distributed personality traits" (Edens et al., 2006:131).

There appears to be some empirical support for the theory because the psychopathic personality as measured by Hare's checklist "is associated with a number of real world criterion measures of considerable practical significance, such as increased risk for misconduct while institutionalized, community violence, and criminal recidivism following release from prison" (Edens et al., 2006:131). However, conclusions about the empirical validity of the theory (even with its scope restricted to the most serious and violent offenses) are limited by the fact that the measurement of psychopathic personality by the PCL–R produces problems of tautology when the dependent variable is criminal, delinquent, or deviant behavior. This raises questions about testability of the central hypothesis that individual differences in criminal behavior are explained by individual differences in psychopathy.

Some of the diagnostic items used to classify or score persons as psychopathic (especially on the social deviance dimensions) are measures of the individual's *prior* history of deviant, antisocial, delinquent, or criminal behavior. On both the adult and juvenile versions of the PCL, behavior items by which psychopathy is measured include early behavior problems, pathological lying, promiscuous sexual behavior, commission of deviant and delinquent behavior, criminal versatility, and even revocation (for violation) of parole, probation, or other conditional release programs (Hare, 2003; MacArthur Foundation, 2006). Thus, some of the very behavior (violation of social and legal norms) that is supposed to be explained by psychopathy is included in the definition and measurement of psychopathy. It is this pattern of involvement in flagrant and frequent offending, not occasional commission of minor deviance, that leads to the diagnosis of psychopathic personality. It is well known (Hare calls it a "maxim"), that past behavior predicts future behavior. This correlation between prior and current behavior cannot be taken as uniquely supportive of any theory of causation, and it is tautological for proponents of any theory, not just psychopathic personality theory, to claim that it is. The tautological issues would not be present if the checklist items measuring past delinquent, criminal, and deviant behavior were removed. The more the different facets of psychopathy are viewed as personal and behavioral characteristics that are measured separately from the behavior they are meant to explain, the less tautological will be hypotheses about psychopathy as a cause of crime and delinquency. However, this has not been done in any of the extant research, and Hare insists that a psychopath cannot be properly identified without measuring all dimensions (including the items creating the tautology problems) of the syndrome.

Psychological Counseling in Delinquency Prevention and Treatment

The treatment and policy implications of psychoanalytic theory are direct and obvious. According to this perspective, criminal and delinquent offenders should be treated as sick persons who are not responsible for their actions in any rational sense. Therefore, punishment of offenders will be ineffective and will only provoke more guilt and unhealthy psychological reactions. Delinquents and criminals, the theory contends, need treatment for underlying emotional disturbances. Cure that problem, and the problem of crime will be remedied. To deal with the criminal behavior, rather than the underlying illness or pent-up emotions of the offender, is to treat symptoms only and is likely to result in the substitution of another deviant symptom. The criminal must undergo psychoanalytic treatment to help him or her uncover the repressed causes of the behavior, which lie hidden in the unconscious. The objective is to reveal to the person's conscious mind the deep-seated unconscious motivations driving his or her deviant behavior. Once these are brought out into the open, they can be handled more rationally and resolved in a healthy way. Providing intensive, individual, in-depth therapeutic sessions is the ideal course to take, although other less intensive treatment is possible.

Personality theories share with the psychoanalytic approach the assumption that offending behavior is important primarily as a symptom of an underlying emotional or personality problem. Again, the implication is that individualized treatment, preferably intensive individual counseling and therapy, is needed to resolve the psychological problems to make a meaningful impact on the person's criminal or delinquent behavior. "Individual counseling focuses on the emotional and behavioral problems that presumably caused the ... crime" (Abrams, Kim, and Anderson-Nathe, 2005:8). These policy and practice implications of psychological theory were recognized long ago, and some of the major programs that have become classic examples of individualized treatment are described later. Since these pioneering efforts, programs that rely primarily on psychological treatment (although often incorporating other approaches as well) have been widely adopted in the criminal and juvenile justice system (Abrams et al., 2005). Virtually every residential and non-residential facility for delinquent and criminal offenders includes some form of individual counseling implicitly or explicitly guided by theories of emotional maladjustment or personality defects. There is promise in the approach, but the general effectiveness of such programs either for prevention or treatment of delinquency has not yet been sufficiently demonstrated.

Although psychological counseling may be offered in correctional or community settings for offenders diagnosed as psychopathic, Hare is pessimistic about the effectiveness of either individual or group therapies in the rehabilitation of psychopaths. He reviews the record of such efforts and concludes that essentially nothing makes a difference, and in fact, therapy with psychopaths may simply make them worse. "Virtually all of the evidence on the effectiveness of treatment for psychopaths is based on programs for people in prison or psychiatric facilities or in trouble with the law. Many of these programs are intensive, well thought out, and carried out under reasonably good conditions. And still they are ineffective" (Hare, 1999:201). Moreover, although the roots of psychopathy can be traced back to childhood, Hare cautions that early intervention programs are also not likely to work. He worries more about how family members, co-workers, acquaintances, and others can avoid victimization by the psychopaths with whom they may be in social interaction. He advises them to adopt a policy of "protect yourself" from entering into relationships with psychopaths and if that is unavoidable then "don't blame yourself," have a plan for "damage control" obtain "professional advice" and seek the help of "support groups." Edens et al. (2006) saw implications of classifying offenders as psychopaths for legal or correctional decisions made about them regarding close control of institution behavior and recidivism, but believed these will be mistaken if they rely on identifying them as possessing a distinct personality type qualitatively different from the rest of us. Researchers who have studied psychopathy in juveniles recognize that "their amenability to treatment is low" and also caution that the scales are not sufficiently validated to serve as the basis for making sound juvenile justice decisions about youthful offenders (MacArthur Foundation, 2006).

Wayne County Clinic. One of the first systematic attempts to apply intensive individual psychotherapy in the treatment of publicly identified delinquents was the Wayne County Clinic in Detroit (operating from the 1920s into the 1940s). This was a private clinic staffed with psychologists and psychiatrists who selectively accepted cases referred by the juvenile court. Although the clinic accepted only juveniles who were considered the most amenable to psychotherapy, the sessions apparently did not have the intended effect. Recidivism among the treated youth was not reduced, and the general level of delinquency in Detroit over the 2 decades of the clinic's operation was unaffected (Gibbons and Krohn, 1986). There have been few efforts since then to institute and evaluate this kind of specialized psychiatric clinic treatment of officially adjudicated delinquents.

Cambridge–Somerville Youth Study. The first large-scale, best-known, and most thoroughly evaluated delinquency prevention project based primarily on intensive individual counseling is the Cambridge–Somerville Youth Study in New Jersey (1937–1945). The subjects were 650 adolescent boys, one half of whom were nominated by teachers, police, and others as delinquency prone or "difficult"; one half of whom were nominated as "average" with no delinquent tendencies. Additional information was collected by social workers about the home and school situations, and medical examinations and personality tests were given to all participants. The Cambridge–Somerville project employed an experimental research design, with half of the boys randomly assigned to the "treatment group" and the other half to the "control group," and with follow-up measures to test the effectiveness of the project.

The boys assigned to the treatment group received intensive individual attention from adult caseworkers, who counseled the boys and worked to help them resolve whatever personality, emotional, or mental problems they may have had. The counselors also assisted the boys to improve their performance in school and counseled with them on family relationships. The counselors were mainly psychologically oriented social workers who were dedicated and committed to the goals of the project. They were instructed to establish themselves as friends of the youths and involve them in a number of activities and social services. But they were supposed to direct attention only to individual problems and to refrain from attempting change or interfering in the family, school, economic, or neighborhood environments. The boys in the control group received no special attention.

Few differences were found between the two groups of boys after leaving the program. They were essentially the same in school performance and in the number who had been picked up by the police for delinquent conduct. The treatment group boys were more likely (not less likely as expected) than those in the control group to have had more than one such contact with the police, to have committed more offenses, and to have appeared in juvenile court. But a slightly higher proportion of the control group boys were in the "most serious" offense category (Powers and Witmer, 1951).

Follow-up research later in the 1950s also found no difference in the two groups in the number of convictions for property, violent, or public order crimes committed as adults (McCord and McCord, 1959). Similar conclusions were reached from longer term follow-up studies (McCord, 1978; 2003). Those who had been part of the treatment group had positive memories of their experience in the program and recalled specific acts of kindness and friendship by the counselors. However, their adult criminal behavior did not differ from the behavior of those who had been in the control group. Indeed, the boys who had received the counseling attention as juveniles were more likely to be repeat offenders, to abuse alcohol, and to develop mental illness as adults (McCord, 1978; 2003).

The disappointing outcomes of this study may have resulted from difficulties encountered in carrying out the project. Although it was intended to be in operation for 10 years, it had to be cut short because of the outbreak of World War II. Before its completion, the project was disrupted because many of the counselors, and eventually some of the youths, had been drafted into the military and could not complete the project. There was attrition also because the boys in both groups who originally had been assessed as "average" without much risk of becoming delinquent dropped out in great numbers. For these and other reasons the amount of time actually spent in treatment was severely reduced from what originally had been planned. It may be that without these circumstances the project would have proven effective (Lundman, 1993).

Youth Consultation, Youth Board, and Maximum Benefits Projects. However, later projects designed to replicate the principles and practices of the Cambridge–Somerville Youth Study, but without its drop-out rate and other problems, also turned out not to be effective in preventing or curtailing delinquency. The New York Youth Consultation Service Project (1955–1960) was conducted with almost 400 students at a girls' vocational high school with a predominantly minority and lower class student body. In each of 4 years, a group of at-risk girls in the 10th grade was identified (based on low academic performance and misbehavior in school) and randomly assigned to a special program meant to prevent them from becoming delinquent. They were released during school hours for counseling sessions at a private social work agency that specialized in services for adolescent girls. The girls received both individual and group counseling directed toward the "individual member and her adjustment" (Lundman, 1993:51). Those randomly assigned to the control group attended school and did not receive any special counseling. The follow-up studies done at the end of the school year and at graduation found that those receiving the treatment services were slightly less likely to be suspended or expelled from school. However, there was no significant difference between the two groups in grades, honors, truancy, school attendance, personality test scores, sociometric patterns, or measures of self-concept. More important, for the goals of the program, there was no difference between the control and treatment groups in contact with the police or appearance in juvenile court (Lundman, 1993). In both the New York Youth Board Project (1952) and the Maximum Benefits Project in Washington, DC (1954–1957), adjudicated delinquent boys were randomly assigned either to a state institution (as the control group) or to an individual program in the community. There was little difference in recidivism between the two groups. In fact, in both projects the control group sent to the state facility did slightly better in avoiding future delinquency than the boys in the treatment group.

Pilot Intensive Counseling Organization (PICO) Project. The PICO project provided treatment within delinquency institutions for boys in California (1955–1960). The boys in the institutions were diagnosed as either "amenable" or "not amenable" to change through psychological counseling and then both types were randomly assigned to a treatment or control group. Those in the treatment groups (both amenables and non-amenables) received intensive individualized therapy by psychologists, psychiatrists, and social workers. The control groups received no special attention and simply participated in the usual institutional programs. The treatment went on for 2 years and the boys were followed up for 3 years after release from the institutions. Overall there was little difference in reinvolvement in the juvenile justice system between those who had been in the treatment groups in the institution and those who had been in the control groups. The amenable boys who received treatment did somewhat better than the non-amenable boys, but they, in turn, had a worse record at follow-up than the non-amenable boys in the control group (Adams, 1970).

Community Treatment Project: California's I-Level Program. Later, the Youth Authority of California instituted the Community Treatment Project (CTP; 1961–1969), a program utilizing individual counseling and intensive parole supervision in the community. The CTP was part of an overall effort carried out in state juvenile institutions, group homes, and other settings to apply the Interpersonal Maturity Level (I-level) theory of personality. The I-level theory posits "a sequence of personality (or character) integrations in normal childhood development" identified in "seven successive stages of interpersonal maturity [that] characterize psychological development" from the least mature to the most mature (Warren, 1970:422). Delinquents fall into subtypes of personality integration ranging from "asocial aggressive" subtypes at Level 2, to neurotic, acting-out delinquents, to "cultural identifier" delinquents at Level 4. The model calls for juveniles to be diagnosed according to I-level type and then assigned treatment, ranging from individual sessions for academic tutoring and psychological therapy to group counseling (Warren, 1970).

In the CTP, the treatment group consisted of adjudicated delinquents in three cities who were randomly assigned to specialized juvenile probation/parole caseloads. The counselors supervising these caseloads used group home placements, intensive supervision, counseling, educational programs, detention, or other community-based resources fitted to the particular needs and problems of the individual juvenile. The delinquents in the control group were committed to a state institution for 8 months and then released to the usual juvenile parole supervision in the community. Over the years of the project, more than 400 juveniles (80% male) were studied to test the effectiveness of the CTP.

The research did not demonstrate that the program achieved its goals. Those in the treatment group were less likely than those in the control group to have their parole status revoked for violation of parole rules. But the treatment group had three times as many new offenses recorded as did the control group. One cannot conclude from this that the treatment received created such a big difference, because the actual offense records of the two groups were probably not that different. Recall that the youth in the treatment group received more intensive, individual attention and had more frequent contact with their juvenile counselors. Thus, their misbehavior was more visible to authorities than was the misbehavior of those in the control group. The difference was likely more a matter of counselors knowing about and recording offenses than of treatment fostering more delinquency. The reason that the control group nevertheless had higher revocation rates was due mainly to the fact that the treatment counselors were much less likely to take action to revoke parole of the juveniles under their care. They wanted the program to succeed and were more reluctant to send their juveniles back to state institutions either for new offenses or violation of parole conditions. After discharge from the program, however, there was no difference between the two groups in rearrest for new offenses (Palmer, 1971; Gibbons and Krohn, 1986; Lundman, 1993).

Summary

Psychoanalytic, personality trait, and psychopathic personality theories are similar to biological theories in that they also concentrate on the causes of crime arising from within the individual, but the causes are not seen as inherited or biologically predetermined. Although biological predispositions are recognized, the chief causes are dysfunctional, abnormal emotional adjustment or deviant personality traits or disorders formed in early socialization and childhood development. Although empirical tests of personality-based theories have been hampered by tautological propositions and measures of key concepts, they are more testable than psychoanalytic theories. Empirical research on the theories has produced generally weak support for personality theories. The main programmatic implication of psychoanalytic and personality theories is that individualized counseling and therapy are needed to treat the emotional and personality problems causing crime and delinquency. Psychological counseling has been incorporated as the principal technique in several classic projects and in many criminal and juvenile justice programs, but it does not yet appear to be a very effective way of changing or preventing criminal and delinquent behavior. Proponents of psychopathic personality theory caution against programs for treatment or rehabilitation of psychopaths.

Note

1. See Lindner (1944), Aichhorn (1963), Halleck (1967), and the reviews of psychoanalytic theory in Shoemaker (2004), Pallone and Hennessy (1992), Shoham and Seis (1993), and Andrews and Bonta (2003).

Chapter 5

Social Learning Theory

Introduction

The designation of "social learning theory" has been used to refer to virtually any social behavioristic approach in social science, principally that of Albert Bandura and other psychologists (Bandura, 1977a; 1977b; Bandura and Walters, 1963; Miller and Dollard, 1941; Rotter, 1954; Patterson, 1975). As a general perspective emphasizing "reciprocal interaction between cognitive, behavioral and environmental determinants" (Bandura, 1977a:vii), variants of social learning can be found in a number of areas in psychology and sociology (see White, Bates, and Johnson, 1991). Gerald Patterson and his colleagues at the Oregon Social Learning Center have a long history of applying learning principles to the explanation, treatment, and prevention of delinquent and deviant behavior (Patterson, Reid, Jones, and Conger, 1975; Patterson, Reid, and Dishion, 1992; Patterson, 1995;2002; Patterson and Chamberlain, 1994). D. A. Andrews (1980; Andrews and Bonta, 2003) has offered a perspective on the explanation, treatment, and prevention of crime and delinquency that is grounded in social learning principles.

In the field of criminology, however, social learning theory refers primarily to the theory of crime and deviance developed by Ronald L. Akers. Akers's social learning theory was originally proposed in collaboration with Robert L. Burgess (Burgess and Akers, 1966b) as a behavioristic reformulation of Edwin H. Sutherland's differential association theory of crime. It is a general theory that has been applied to a wide range of deviant and criminal behavior. It is one of the most frequently tested (Stitt and Giacopassi, 1992) and endorsed theories of crime and delinquency among academic criminologists (Ellis and Walsh, 1999).

Sutherland's Differential Association Theory

The late Edwin H. Sutherland is widely recognized as the most important criminologist of the 20th century. Sutherland is known for pioneering sociological studies of professional theft (Sutherland, 1937) and white-collar crime (1940; 1949). He is best known for formulating a general sociological theory of crime and delinquency, the "differential association" theory.[1]

Sutherland was the author of a criminology textbook that was the leading text in the field for over 30 years. It was only in the pages of this text that he fully stated his theory, the final version of which was published in the 1947 edition. He proposed differential association theory as an explanation of individual criminal behavior and suggested that the theory was compatible with what he termed "differential social organization" as the cause of differences in group or societal crime rates. Sutherland gave only brief attention to differential social organization, however, and concentrated his efforts on fully explicating differential association theory, which is as follows (Sutherland, 1947:6–7):

1. Criminal behavior is learned.

2. Criminal behavior is learned in interaction with other persons in a process of communication.

3. The principal part of the learning of criminal behavior occurs within intimate personal groups.

4. When criminal behavior is learned, the learning includes (a) techniques of committing the crime, which are sometimes very complicated, sometimes very simple, and (b) the specific direction of motives, drives, rationalizations, and attitudes.

5. The specific direction of motives and drives is learned from definitions of the legal codes as favorable or unfavorable.

6. A person becomes delinquent because of an excess of definitions favorable to violation of law over definitions unfavorable to violation of law.

7. Differential associations may vary in frequency, duration, priority, and intensity.

8. The process of learning criminal behavior by association with criminal and anti-criminal patterns involves all of the mechanisms that are involved in any other learning.

9. Although criminal behavior is an expression of general needs and values, it is not explained by those general needs and values, because noncriminal behavior is an expression of the same needs and values.

The first proposition is that criminal behavior is learned, and the terms *learned* and *learning* are included in other statements.

Criminal behavior is learned in a process of symbolic interaction with others, mainly in primary or intimate groups. Although all nine statements constitute the theory, it is the sixth statement that Sutherland identified as the "principle of differential association." This is the principle that a person commits criminal acts because he or she has learned "definitions" (rationalizations and attitudes) favorable to violation of law in "excess" of the definitions unfavorable to violation of law.

The theory explains criminal behavior by the exposure to others' definitions favorable to criminal behavior, balanced against contact with conforming definitions. Although one expects that law-violating definitions are typically communicated by those who have violated the law, it is possible to learn law-abiding definitions from them, just as one can be exposed to deviant definitions from law-abiding people (Cressey, 1960:49). The seventh principle in the theory makes it clear that the process is not a simple matter of either criminal or noncriminal association, but one that varies according to what are called the "modalities" of association. That is, if persons are exposed first (priority), more frequently, for a longer time (duration), and with greater intensity (importance) to law-violating definitions than to law-abiding definitions, then they are more likely to deviate from the law.

After Sutherland's death, Donald R. Cressey revised *Principles of Criminology* from the 5th through the 10th editions (Sutherland and Cressey, 1978). Cressey became the major proponent of differential association, clarifying it and applying it to a number of different areas in criminology (see Akers and Matsueda, 1989), and on occasion included differential association as one of the concepts "related to general theories of *social learning*. ... The content of learning, not the process itself, is considered the significant element determining whether one becomes a criminal or non-criminal" (Sutherland and Cressey, 1960:58; emphasis added). In all of the revisions of the text, Cressey purposely left the original nine statements of differential association theory unchanged from the way Sutherland had them. After Cressey's death, David F. Luckenbill revised the text (Sutherland, Cressey, and Luckenbill, 1992), and he too changed nothing from the 1947 statement.

Both Cressey and Luckenbill were well aware of and discussed revisions and modifications of the theory made by others, but they preserved Sutherland's original statement. Others have proposed modification of differential association theory (see Glaser, 1956), but the most thorough and most tested revision of Sutherland's theory is found in Akers's social learning theory.

Akers's Social Learning Theory

Development of the Theory

Sutherland asserted in the eighth statement of his theory that all the mechanisms of learning are involved in criminal behavior. However, beyond a brief comment that more is involved than direct imitation (Tarde, 1912), he did not explain what the mechanisms of learning are. These learning mechanisms were specified by Burgess and Akers (1966b) in their "differential association-reinforcement" theory of criminal behavior. Burgess and Akers produced a full reformulation that retained the principles of differential association, combining them with, and restating them in terms of, the learning principles of operant and respondent conditioning that had been developed by behavioral psychologists.[2] Akers followed up his early work with Burgess to develop social learning theory, applying it to criminal, delinquent, and deviant behavior in general. He has modified the theory, provided a fully explicated presentation of its concepts, examined it in light of the critiques and research by others, and carried out his own research to test its central propositions (Akers, 1973; 1977; 1985; 1998).

Social learning theory is not competitive with differential association theory. Instead, it is a broader theory that retains all of the differential association processes in Sutherland's theory (albeit clarified and somewhat modified) and integrates it with differential reinforcement and other principles of behavioral acquisition, continuation, and cessation (Akers, 1985:41). Thus, research findings supportive of differential association also support the integrated theory. But social learning theory explains criminal and delinquent behavior more thoroughly than does the original differential association theory (see, for instance, Akers, Krohn, Lanza-Kaduce, and Radosevich, 1979; Warr and Stafford, 1991).

Burgess and Akers (1966b) explicitly identified the learning mechanisms as those found in modern behavioral theory. They retained the concepts of differential association and definitions from Sutherland's theory, but conceptualized them in more behavioral terms and added concepts from behavioral learning theory. These concepts include differential reinforcement, whereby "operant" behavior (the voluntary actions of the individual) is conditioned or shaped by rewards and punishments. They also contain classical or "respondent" conditioning (the conditioning of involuntary reflex behavior); discriminative stimuli (the environmental and internal stimuli that provide cues or signals for behavior); schedules of reinforcement (the rate and ratio in which rewards and punishments follow behavioral responses); and other principles of behavior modification.

Social learning theory retains a strong element of the symbolic interactionism found in the concepts of differential association and definitions from Sutherland's theory (Akers, 1985:39–70). Symbolic interactionism is the theory that social interaction is mainly the exchange of meaning and symbols; individuals have the cognitive capacity to imagine themselves in the roles of others and incorporate this into their conceptions of themselves (Sandstrom, Martin, and Fine, 2003). This, and the explicit inclusion of such concepts as imitation, anticipated reinforcement, and self-reinforcement, makes social learning "soft behaviorism" (Akers, 1985:65). It assumes human agency and soft determinism (see chap. 1). As a result, the theory is closer to cognitive learning theories, such as Albert Bandura's (1973; 1977a; 1986; Bandura and Walters, 1963), than to the radical or orthodox operant behaviorism of B. F. Skinner (1953; 1959), with which Burgess and Akers began.

The Central Concepts and Propositions of Social Learning Theory

The word *learning* should not be taken to mean that the theory is only about how novel criminal behavior is acquired. "Behavioral principles are not limited to learning but are fundamental principles of performance [that account for] ... the acquisition, maintenance, and modification of human behavior" (Andrews and Bonta, 1998:150; see also Horney, 2006). Social learning theory offers an explanation of crime and deviance that embraces variables that operate both to motivate and control criminal behavior, both to promote and undermine conformity. (See the discussion of questions of criminal motivations and inhibitors in chap. 6.) The probability of criminal or conforming behavior occurring is a function of the balance of these influences on behavior operative in one's learning history, at a given time, or in a given situation:

> The basic assumption in social learning theory is that the same learning process in a context of social structure, interaction, and situation, produces both conforming and deviant behavior. The difference lies in the direction ... [of] the balance of influences on behavior.
>
> The probability that persons will engage in criminal and deviant behavior is increased and the probability of their conforming to the norm is decreased when they differentially associate with others who commit criminal behavior and espouse definitions favorable to it, are relatively more exposed in-person or symbolically to salient criminal/deviant models, define it as desirable or justified in a situation discriminative for the behavior, and have received in the past and anticipate in

the current or future situation relatively greater reward than punishment for the behavior. (Akers, 1998:50)

As these quotations show, although referring to all aspects of the learning process, Akers's development of the theory has relied principally on four major concepts: *differential association, definitions, differential reinforcement,* and *imitation* (Akers et al., 1979; Akers, 1985; 1998).

Differential Association. Differential association has both behavioral-interactional and normative dimensions. The interactional dimension is the direct association and interaction with others who engage in certain kinds of behavior, as well as the indirect association and identification with more distant reference groups. The normative dimension is the different patterns of norms and values to which an individual is exposed through this association (see Clark, 1972).

The groups with which one is in differential association provide the major social contexts in which all the mechanisms of social learning operate. They not only expose one to definitions, but they also present one with models to imitate and with differential reinforcement (source, schedule, value, and amount) for criminal or conforming behavior. The most important of these groups are the primary ones of family and friends, although they may also be secondary and reference groups. Neighbors, churches, school teachers, physicians, the law and authority figures, and other individuals and groups in the community (as well as mass media and other more remote sources of attitudes and models) have varying degrees of effect on the individual's propensity to commit criminal and delinquent behavior. These may even be what Warr (2002) refers to as "virtual peer groups" formed through the internet, land and cell phones, movies, television, and other media. Those associations that occur earlier (priority), last longer and occupy more of one's time (duration), take place most often (frequency), and involve others with whom one has the more important or closer relationship (intensity) will have the greater effect on behavior.

Definitions. Definitions are one's own attitudes or meanings that one attaches to given behavior. That is, they are orientations, rationalizations, definitions of the situation, and other evaluative and moral attitudes that define the commission of an act as right or wrong, good or bad, desirable or undesirable, justified or unjustified.

In social learning theory, these definitions are both general and specific. General beliefs include religious, moral, and other conventional values and norms that are favorable to conforming behavior and unfavorable to committing any deviant or criminal acts. Specific definitions orient the person to particular acts or series of acts. Thus, one may believe that it is morally wrong to steal and that laws against theft should be obeyed, but at the same time one may see little wrong with smoking marijuana and rationalize that it is all right to violate laws against drug possession.

The greater the extent to which one holds attitudes that disapprove of certain acts, the less one is likely to engage in them. Conventional beliefs are negative toward criminal behavior. Conversely, the more one's own attitudes approve of a behavior, the greater the chances are that one will do it. Approving definitions favorable to the commission of criminal or deviant behavior are basically positive or neutralizing. Positive definitions are beliefs or attitudes that make the behavior morally desirable or wholly permissible. Neutralizing definitions favor the commission of a crime by justifying or excusing it. They view the act as something that is probably undesirable but, given the situation, is nonetheless all right, justified, excusable, necessary, or not really bad to do. The concept of neutralizing definitions in social learning theory incorporates the notions of verbalizations, rationalizations, techniques of neutralization, accounts, disclaimers, and moral disengagement (Cressey, 1953; Sykes and Matza, 1957; Lyman and Scott, 1970; Hewitt and Stokes, 1975; Bandura, 1990). (See the discussion of neutralizations in chap. 6.) Neutralizing attitudes include such beliefs as, "Everybody has a racket," "I can't help myself, I was born this way," "I am not at fault," "I am not responsible," "I was drunk and didn't know what I was doing," "I just blew my top," "They can afford it," "He deserved it," and other excuses and justification for committing deviant acts and victimizing others. These definitions favorable and unfavorable to criminal and delinquent behavior are developed through imitation and differential reinforcement. Cognitively, they provide a mind-set that makes one more willing to commit the act when the opportunity occurs. Behaviorally, they affect the commission of deviant or criminal behavior by acting as internal discriminative stimuli. Discriminative stimuli operate as cues or signals to the individual as to what responses are appropriate or expected in a given situation.

Some of the definitions favorable to deviance are so intensely held that they almost "require" one to violate the law. For instance, the radical ideologies of militant groups provide strong motivation for terrorist acts, just as the fervent moral stance of some anti-abortion groups justifies in their minds the need to engage in civil disobedience (Akers and Silverman, 2004). For the most part, however, definitions favorable to crime and delinquency do not directly motivate action in this sense. Rather, they are conventional beliefs so weakly held that they provide no restraint or are positive or neutralizing attitudes that facilitate law violation in the right set of circumstances.

Differential Reinforcement. Differential reinforcement refers to the balance of anticipated or actual rewards and punishments that follow or are consequences of behavior. Whether individuals will refrain from or commit a crime at any given time (and whether they will continue or desist from doing so in the future) depends on the past, present, and anticipated future rewards and punishments for their actions. The probability that an act will be committed or repeated is increased by rewarding outcomes or reactions to it (e.g., obtaining approval, money, food, or pleasant feelings)—positive reinforcement. The likelihood that an action will be taken is also enhanced when it allows the person to avoid or escape aversive or unpleasant events—negative reinforcement. Punishment may also be direct (positive) in which painful or unpleasant consequences are attached to a behavior, or indirect (negative) in which a reward or pleasant consequence is removed. Just as there are modalities of association, there are modalities of reinforcement—amount, frequency, and probability. The greater the value or amount of reinforcement for the person's behavior, the more frequently it is reinforced, and the higher the probability that it will be reinforced (as balanced against alternative behavior), the greater the likelihood that it will occur and be repeated. The reinforcement process does not operate in the social environment in a simple either/or fashion. Rather, it operates according to a "matching function" in which the occurrence of, and changes in, each of several different behaviors correlate with the probability and amount of, and changes in, the balance of reward and punishment attached to each behavior (Herrnstein, 1961; Hamblin, 1979; Conger and Simons, 1995).

Reinforcers and punishers can be nonsocial; for example, the direct physical effects of drugs and alcohol. Also, there may be a physiological basis for the tendency of some individuals (such as those prone to sensation-seeking) more than others to find certain forms of deviant behavior intrinsically rewarding (Wood et al., 1995; Brezina and Piquero, 2003). However, whether or not these effects are experienced positively or negatively is contingent on previously learned expectations. Social reinforcement, the peer or other social context in which the actions take place, one's learned moral attitudes, and other social variables affect how much one experiences the intrinsic effects of substance use or committing certain acts as pleasurable and enjoyable or as frightening and unpleasant. "Individual differences in the propensity to derive intrinsic pleasure and reward from substance use appear to be related to social learning factors in ways predicted by the theory" (Brezina and Piquero, 2003:284). Thus, the theory posits effects of nonsocial reinforcement, but proposes that these interact with other social learning variables. The prediction is that most of the learning in criminal and deviant behavior is the result of social exchange in which the words, responses, presence, and behavior of other persons directly reinforce behavior, provide the setting for reinforcement (discriminative stimuli), or serve as the conduit through which other social rewards and punishers are delivered or made available.

Individuals can learn behavior without contact, directly or indirectly, with social reinforcers and punishers. The concept of social reinforcement (and punishment), goes beyond the direct reactions of others present while an act is committed. It also includes the whole range of actual and anticipated, tangible and intangible rewards valued in society or subgroups. Social rewards can be highly symbolic. Their reinforcing effects can come from their fulfilling ideological, religious, political, or other goals. Even those rewards that we consider to be very tangible, such as money and material possessions, gain their reinforcing value from the prestige and approval value they have in society. Nonsocial reinforcement, therefore, is more narrowly confined to unconditioned physiological and physical stimuli. In self-reinforcement the individual exercises self-control, reinforcing or punishing one's own behavior by taking the role of others, even when alone.

Imitation. Imitation refers to the engagement in behavior after the observation of similar behavior in others. Whether the behavior modeled by others will be imitated is affected by the characteristics of the models, the behavior observed, and the observed consequences of the behavior (Bandura, 1977a). The observation of salient models in primary groups and in the media affects both prosocial and deviant behavior (Donnerstein and Linz, 1995). It is more important in the initial acquisition and performance of novel behavior than in the maintenance or cessation of behavioral patterns once established, but it continues to have some effect in maintaining behavior.

The Social Learning Process: Sequence and Feedback Effects

These social learning variables are all part of an underlying process that is operative in each individual's learning history and in the immediate situation in which an opportunity for a crime occurs. Akers stresses that social learning is a complex process with reciprocal and feedback effects. The reciprocal effects are not seen as equal, however. Akers hypothesizes a typical temporal sequence or process by which persons come to the point of violating the law or engaging in other deviant acts (Akers, 1998).

This process is one in which the balance of learned definitions, imitation of criminal or deviant models, and the anticipated balance of reinforcement produces the initial delinquent or deviant act. The facilitative effects of these variables continue in the repetition of acts, although imitation becomes less important than it was in the first commission of the act. After initiation, the actual social and non-social reinforcers and punishers affect whether or not the acts will be repeated and at what level of frequency. Not only the behavior itself, but also the definitions, are affected by the consequences of the initial act. Whether a deviant act will be committed in a situation that presents the opportunity depends on the learning history of the individual and the set of reinforcement contingencies in that situation:

> The actual social sanctions and other effects of engaging in the behavior may be perceived differently, but to the extent that they are more rewarding than alternative behavior, then the deviant behavior will be repeated under similar circumstances. Progression into more frequent or sustained patterns of deviant behavior is promoted [to the extent] that reinforcement, exposure to deviant models, and definitions are not offset by negative formal and informal sanctions and definitions. (Akers, 1985:60)

The theory does not hypothesize that definitions favorable to law violation only precede and are unaffected by the initiation of criminal acts. Acts in violation of the law can occur in the absence of any thought given to right and wrong. Furthermore, definitions may be applied by the individual retroactively to excuse or justify an act already committed. To the extent that such excuses successfully mitigate others' negative sanctions or one's self-punishment, however, they become cues for the repetition of deviant acts. At that point they precede the future commission of the acts.

Differential association with conforming and non-conforming others typically precedes the individual's committing the acts. Families are included in the differential association process, and it is obvious that association, reinforcement of conforming or deviant behavior, deviant or conforming modeling, and exposure to definitions favorable or unfavorable to deviance occurs within the family prior to the onset of delinquency. On the other hand, it can never be true that the onset of delinquency initiates interaction in the family (except in the unlikely case of the late-stage adoption of a child who is already delinquent who is drawn to and chosen by deviant parents). Parents supervise and control their children's selection of friends (Warr, 2005). However, behavioral similarity, including prior deviant behavior or tendencies, can play a role in the youth's friendship selection and initiation of interaction in peer groups. Even so, associations with peers and others are most often formed initially around attractions, friendships, and circumstances, such as neighborhood proximity, that have little to do directly with co-involvement in some deviant behavior. In either case, after the associations have been established and the reinforcing or punishing consequences of the interaction and the deviant or conforming behavior are experienced, both the continuation of old and the seeking of new peer associations (over which one has any choice) will themselves be affected "in proportion to the relative rate of positive reinforcement generated during interaction with each of those peers" (Snyder, 2002:109):

> Deviant peers reinforce each other for deviancy. Peers who maximize the child's immediate payoffs get selected as friends.... The selection of deviant peers insures the maintenance of deviant behaviors as well as the development of new forms of deviancy.... The findings show that antisocial boys are mutually reinforcing for rule-breaking talk, and that this talk predicts both later delinquency and later substance use. (Patterson, 2002:12–13)

One may choose further interaction with others based, in part, on whether they too are involved in similar deviant or criminal behavior, assuming the relationships are mutually reinforcing. But the theory proposes that the sequence of events in which deviant associations precede the onset of delinquent behavior, will occur more frequently than the sequence of events in which the onset of delinquency precedes the beginning of deviant associations.

This recognition of sequence and reciprocal effects through social interaction is another clear indication that social learning is *not*, as some critics (Gottfredson and Hirschi, 1990) claim that it is, simply a "cultural deviance" theory that assumes that violation of the rules of the larger society occurs only because individuals are conforming to the norms of deviant groups into which they have become completely socialized (see Akers, 1996; Sellers and Akers, 2006). One may learn deviant attitudes and behavior through exposure to street codes and deviant subcultures (Anderson, 1999; Benoit, Randolph, Dunlap , and Johnson, 2003) or immersion in criminal and illegitimate activities as a career criminal (Steffensmeier and Ulmer, 2005). Many offenders have come into association with somewhat older criminal "mentors" who go beyond being co-offenders to provide direct tutelage in criminal attitudes and behavior and help the younger offenders develop and enhance criminal careers (Morselli, Tremblay, and McCarthy, 2006). Benoit et al. (2003) identified the balance of social learning variables, including what they refer to as "inverse imitation," as the main mechanism by which the inner city social structure, neighborhood, and family affect young men's involvement in, and switching between, conforming and deviant norms and behavior such as drug use, trafficking, and violence (Benoit et al., 2003). However, the theory is not confined to delinquent, criminal, or deviant behavior acquired only through differential exposure to such deviant subcultures, environments, and individuals. It does not ignore, as Osgood and Anderson (2004:525) contend it does, "contextual and situational influences" and does not rest solely on "positing a causal role for peer culture that values delinquency." Their finding that delinquency is related to unstructured or unsupervised adolescent peer interaction fits precisely into the notion of differential peer association. The theory proposes that conforming and delinquent, criminal, or deviant behavior is learned through differential exposure to conforming and deviant patterns. This includes incomplete or failed socialization in conventional norms and values as well as countervailing processes of reinforcement, imitation, and exposure to deviant definitions or attitudes. (See Akers and Jensen, 2006, and Sellers and Akers, 2006, for a review of this and other common misinterpretations of social learning theory.)

Social Structure and Social Learning

Akers has proposed a social structure and social learning (SSSL) model in which social structural factors are hypothesized to have an indirect effect on the individual's conduct. They affect the social learning variables of differential association, differential reinforcement, definitions, and imitation that, in turn, have a direct impact on the individual's conduct. The social learning variables are proposed as the main ones in the process by which various aspects of the social structure influence individual behavior (see Figure 5.1):

> The social structural variables are indicators of the primary distal macro-level and meso-level causes of crime, while the social learning variables reflect the primary proximate causes of criminal behavior that mediate the relationship between social structure and crime rates. Some structural variables are not related to crime and do not explain the crime rate because they do not have a crime-relevant effect on the social learning variables. (Akers, 1998:322)

As shown in Figure 5.1, Akers (1998) identified four dimensions of social structure that provide the contexts within which social learning variables operate:

(I) *Differential Social Organization* refers to the structural correlates of crime in the community or society that affect the rates of crime and delinquency, including age composition, population density, and other attributes that lean societies, communities, and other social systems "toward relatively high or relatively low crime rates" (Akers, 1998:332).

(II) *Differential Location in the Social Structure* refers to sociodemographic characteristics of individuals and social groups that indicate their niches within the larger social structure. Class,

Figure 5.1

Figure 5.1

Social Structure and Social Learning				
Social Structure ➔ **Social Learning** ⟨ **Criminal Behavior** / ▲ **Conforming Behavior**				
I. Society Community IV. Family Peers School Others	II. Age Gender Class Race	III. Social Disorgani- zation Conflict	Differential Association Differential Reinforce- ment Definitions Imitation Other Learning Variables	Individual Behavior
		I. II. III. IV.	Differential Social Organization Differential Location in the Social Structure Theoretically Defined Structural Variables Differential Social Location in Groups	

(Adapted from Akers, 1998:331)

gender, race and ethnicity, marital status, and age locate the positions and standing of persons and their roles, groups, or social categories in the overall social structure.

(III) *Theoretically Defined Structural Variables* refer to anomie, class oppression, social disorganization, group conflict, patriarchy, and other concepts that have been used in one or more theories to identify criminogenic conditions of societies, communities, or groups (see chaps. 8–11).

(IV) *Differential Social Location in Groups* refers to individuals' membership in and relation to primary, secondary, and reference groups such as the family, friendship and peer groups, leisure groups, colleagues, and work groups.

The differential social organization of society and community, as well as the differential location of persons in the social class, race, gender, religion, and other structures in society, provides the general learning contexts for individuals that increase or decrease the likelihood of their committing crime. The differential location in family, peer, school, church, and other groups provides the more immediate contexts that promote or discourage the criminal behavior of the individual. Differences in the societal or group rates of criminal behavior are a function of the extent to which their cultural traditions, norms, and social control systems provide socialization, learning environments, and immediate situations conducive to conformity or deviance. The structural conditions identified in macro-level theories can affect one's exposure to criminal associations, models, definitions, and reinforcement to induce or retard criminal actions in individuals. It is possible, therefore, to integrate these structural theories with social learning. Although this has not yet been accomplished (see chap. 12), the SSSL model is a step in that direction.

Empirical Validity of Social Learning Theory

Research on Relationship of Criminal and Delinquent Behavior to Social Learning Variables

The great preponderance of research conducted on social learning theory has found strong relationships in the theoretically expected direction between social learning variables and criminal, delinquent, and deviant behavior. Many studies using direct measures of one or more of the social learning variables of differential association, imitation, definitions, and differential reinforcement find that the theory's hypotheses are upheld (Winfree, Sellers, and Clason, 1993; Winfree, Vigil-Backstrom, and Mays, 1994a; Winfree, Mays, and Vigil-Backstrom, 1994b; Mihalic and Elliott, 1997; Skinner and Fream, 1997; Esbensen and Deschenes, 1998; Batton and Ogle, 2003; Sellers, Cochran, and Winfree, 2003; Brezina and Piquero, 2003; Chappell and Piquero, 2004; McGloin et al., 2004; Osgood and Anderson, 2004; Triplett and Payne, 2004; Durkin, Wolfe, and Clark, 2005; Matsueda, Kreager, and Huizinga, 2006).[3] The relationships between the social learning variables and delinquent, criminal, and deviant behavior found in the research are typically strong to moderate and there has been very little negative evidence reported in the literature. Most of the research has been done in the United States, but social learning theory is well supported by research in other societies as well (Kandel and Adler, 1982; Lopez, Redondo, and Martin, 1989; Junger-Tas, 1992; Bruinsma, 1992; Zhang and Messner, 1995; Hwang and Akers, 2003; 2006; Wang and Jensen, 2003).

Pratt and Cullen's (2000) meta-analysis covering the findings of many studies found support for the impact of two social learning variables (differential association and definitions) on offending, but the effects of those variables were not stronger than measures of self-control

(Gottfredson and Hirschi's, 1990). However, when social learning theory is tested against other theories using the same data collected from the same samples, it is usually (but not always; see Hepburn, 1977) found to have greater support than the theories with which it is being compared (for instance, see McGee, 1992; Benda, 1994; Burton, Cullen, Evans, and Dunaway, 1994; Hwang and Akers, 2003; 2006; Rebellon, 2002; Preston, 2006; Neff and Waite, 2007). When social learning variables are included in integrated or combined models that incorporate variables from different theories, it is the measures of social learning concepts that have the strongest main and net effects (Elliott, Huizinga, and Ageton, 1985; Kaplan, Johnson, and Barley, 1987; Thornberry et al., 1994; Kaplan, 1996; Catalano et al., 1996; Huang et al., 2001; Jang, 2002).

Research on Social Learning in the Family and Delinquency

There is abundant evidence to show the significant impact on criminal and deviant behavior of differential association in primary groups, especially family and peers:

> Thus, the analysis confirmed social learning theory's prediction, and the findings from existing literature, that family and friends were important in understanding what was reinforcing for a particular person.... The analysis also showed that this measure of reinforcement worked in the way expected by social learning theory. (Triplett and Payne, 2004:628)

Family structure (two-parent vs. single-parent or no-parent families) and the larger social context of "the economy, the polity, the church, and the neighborhood or community ... necessarily influence the functioning and efficacy of families"(Simons, Simons, and Wallace, 2004:93–94). The family is a key primary group with which one is differentially associated, and the process of acquiring, persisting, or modifying conforming and deviant behavior in the family or family surrogate is a social learning process in which interaction in the family exposes the children to normative values, behavioral models and vicarious reinforcement, and differential reinforcement (Simons et al., 2004). The role of the family is usually as a conventional socializer against delinquency and crime. It provides anti-criminal definitions, conforming models, and the reinforcement of conformity through parental discipline; it promotes the development of self-control. But deviant behavior may be the outcome of internal family interaction (McCord, 1991b; Simons et al., 2004). It is directly affected by deviant parental models, ineffective and erratic parental supervision and discipline in the use of positive and negative sanctions, and the endorsement of values and attitudes favorable to deviance. Parents who remain very much in control of the children while also being highly supportive and sensitive to the children's needs have a better chance of raising prosocial, conforming, well-adjusted children, whereas problems of misconduct and delinquency are more likely to be found among children from permissive, neglectful, or too highly controlling families (Simons et al., 2004). Patterson and his colleagues at the Oregon Social Learning Center have shown that the operation of social learning mechanisms in parent–child interaction is a strong predictor of conforming and deviant behavior (Patterson, 1975; 1995; Snyder and Patterson, 1995; Reid, Patterson, and Snyder, 2002; Weisner, Capaldi, and Patterson, 2003). Ineffective disciplinary strategies by parents increase the chances that a child will learn behavior in the early years that is a precursor to his or her later delinquency. Children learn conforming responses when parents consistently make use of positive rewards for proper behavior and impose moderately negative consequences for misbehavior (Capaldi, Chamberlain, and Patterson, 1997; see also Ardelt and Day, 2002, for effects of parental discipline and supervision in early adolescence). The

> relative rate of reinforcement for child coercion during family conflict bouts ... also predicted the child's rates of deviancy observed one week later. If we then added how frequent conflicts or training trials occurred, we could account for over 60% of the variance in individual differences in deviancy. (Patterson, 2002:12)

In some cases, parents directly train their children to commit deviant behavior (Adler and Adler, 1978). And in general, parental deviance and criminality are predictive of the children's future delinquency and crime (McCord, 1991a). Moreover, youngsters with delinquent siblings (especially same-sex older siblings) in the family are more likely to be delinquent, even when parental and other family characteristics are taken into account (Rowe and Gulley, 1992; Lauritsen, 1993; Rowe and Farrington, 1997; Ardelt and Day, 2002). Of course, influence and effect on behavior in the parent–child relationship is mutual and not all one-way; the behavior and reactions of children affect parents and custodial adults and the way they carry out socialization in the family (Reid et al., 2002; Simons et al., 2004). Research on intra-family process in the etiology of sibling violence has found that:

> Of the three theoretical perspectives, social learning theory [compared to feminist and conflict theories] garnered the strongest, most consistent empirical support. Social learning theory directs attention to the behavioral consequences of interaction patterns in families, emphasizing that children tend to adopt behaviors they learn from their parents.... We find that witnessing arguments between parents and being

involved in verbal conflicts with parents and siblings is related to higher levels of sibling violence. (Hoffman, Kiecolt, and Edwards, 2005)

Research on Peers and Group Contexts in Crime and Delinquency

Among the range of actions and choices directly affected by families are the adolescent's choices of friends and peer associations. Sibling effects in part are peer effects, and delinquent tendencies learned in the family may be exacerbated, whereas prosocial influences of the family may be counteracted, by differential peer association (Lauritsen, 1993; Simons, Wu, Conger, and Lorenz, 1994; Simons et al., 2004). Harris's (1998) denial that socialization taking place in the family has any long-lasting effects on the children's behavior as adults, which is more permanently affected by socialization in groups (especially peer groups) outside the family, is very questionable. However, as one moves from childhood to adolescence family influences diminish, and peer groups play an increasing prominent role in learning conforming and deviant behavior. Jones and Jones (2000) saw the influence of peer groups as embedded in two types of social networks involved in the "contagious nature of antisocial behavior." One is a "cohesion" network in which there is direct communication in the network, and the other is a "structural equivalence" network that "consists of people who occupy the same niche in society." "[T]eenagers identify with one another in specific contrast to adults and especially with teenagers who are demographically, socially, or in their 'proclivities' like themselves. Because the members of a teenage group also communicate directly with one another, a teenage group *exemplifies both kinds of network* and can function in both ways as a conduit of antisocial socialization" (Jones and Jones, 2000:33; emphasis added).

Other than one's own prior deviant behavior, the best single predictor of the onset, continuance, or desistance of crime and delinquency is differential association with conforming or law-violating peers (Loeber and Dishion, 1987; Loeber and Stouthamer-Loeber, 1986; Liu, 2003). More frequent, longer-term, and closer association with peers who do not support deviant behavior is strongly correlated with conformity, whereas greater association with peers who commit and approve of delinquency is predictive of one's own delinquent behavior. It is in peer groups that the first availability and opportunity for delinquent acts are typically provided. Virtually every study that includes a peer association variable finds it to be significantly and usually most strongly related to delinquency, alcohol and drug use and abuse, adult crime, and other forms of deviant behavior (Warr, 2002). There is a sizable body of research literature that shows the importance of differential associations and definitions in explaining crime and delinquency.[4] The impact of differential peer association on delinquent behavior is among the most fully substantiated and replicated findings in criminology. Only the well-known relationships of crime rates to basic sociodemographic variables like age and sex are as consistently reported in the literature.

In fact, Mark Warr contended that there is no factor in criminal and delinquent behavior as powerful as peer associations:

> No characteristic of individuals known to criminologists is a better predictor of criminal behavior than the number of delinquent friends an individual has. The strong correlation between delinquent behavior and delinquent friends has been documented in scores of studies from the 1950s up to the present day ... using alternative kinds of criminological data (self-reports, official records, perceptual data) on participants and friends, alternative research designs, and data on a wide variety of criminal offenses. Few, if any, empirical regularities in criminology have been documented as often or over as long a period as the association between delinquency and delinquent friends. (Warr, 2002:40)

Warr (2002) documented these statements by reviewing the large body of research on the group character of, and the role of peers in, crime and delinquency in the United States and societies around the world. Peer influence is most noticeable and strongest in adolescence but is not restricted to the adolescent years. The vast majority of offenses by adolescents are committed in the company of others. These tend to be small groups and to be homogeneous by race, age, and gender. Warr (2002) argued that the mechanisms by which peers influence one toward delinquent behavior are not exactly known. But he proposes several probable mechanisms of peer influence: fear of ridicule, loyalty, status, anonymity, diffusion of responsibility, group excitement, reference group norms, dilution of moral responsibility, consensus, protection, and provision of deviant opportunities. One could argue that the specific means of peer influence listed by Warr are quite compatible with social learning concepts of differential reinforcement (e.g., ridicule as negative reinforcement and group status and excitement as positive reinforcement), imitation, and definitions (e.g., dilution of moral responsibility as neutralizing definitions).

In longitudinal research on friendship networks, Haynie (2002) found strong support for the social learning principle of the balance or ratio of association with delinquent and non-delinquent friends. The higher the proportion of one's friends who were delinquent, the greater the likelihood that he or she would become delinquent. Youth with only friends who had engaged in delinquency were twice as likely, and those with some delinquent friends were also much more likely, to commit delinquency acts than those youth who had only non-delinquent friends. This effect of the relative number of delinquent and non-delinquent friends remained strong even taking into account prior delinquency, time spent with peers, attachment to peers, and other characteristics of the network of friends.

One special context of peer association is participation in delinquent gangs. Although delinquent gangs account for only a portion of all group-related delinquency (Warr, 2002), delinquent gangs and subcultures have received a great deal of attention in criminology for a long time (see chap. 8). And research continues to find the strong influence of gang membership on serious delinquency. Curry, Decker, and Egley (2002) found that gang membership greatly increases involvement in both self-reported and official delinquency; even non-members who have only marginal association with gangs are more delinquent than youth who have no involvement at all with gang activities. Battin et al. (1998) found that, controlling for prior delinquency, adolescents with delinquent friends are more likely to engage in delinquent conduct and come before the juvenile court on delinquency charges, even if they are not part of a gang. But they are even more likely to do so if they and their friends are members of an identified delinquent gang. Whatever the frequency and seriousness of one's previous delinquency, joining a gang promotes an even higher level of his or her delinquent involvement, in large part because "group processes and norms favorable to violence and other delinquency within gangs subsequently encourage and reinforce participation in violent and delinquent behavior" (Battin et al., 1998:108).

These findings suggest that, compared to having one or more non-gang delinquent friends, gang membership produces more frequent, intense, and enduring association with delinquent friends, exposure to delinquent models and definitions, and reinforcement for delinquent behavior. Winfree et al. (1994a; 1994b) found that both gang membership itself and delinquency (gang-related as well as non-gang delinquency) are explained by social learning variables (attitudes, social reinforcers or punishers, and differential association). This is true even controlling for "personal-biographical characteristics, including ethnicity, gender, and place of residence" (Winfree et al., 1994a:167). The processes specified in social learning theory are

> nearly identical to those provided by qualitative gang research. Gang members reward certain behavior in their peers and punish others, employing goals and processes that are indistinguishable from those described by Akers. (Winfree et al., 1994a:149)

Esbensen and Deschenes (1998) found that although neither is especially strong, social learning models do a better job than social bonding models of distinguishing between gang and non-gang members among both boys and girls in the eighth grade.

Akers's Research on Social Learning Theory

In addition to the consistently positive findings by other researchers, support for the theory comes from research conducted by Akers and his associates in which all of the key social learning variables are measured (Akers, 1998). These include tests of social learning theory by itself and tests that directly compare its empirical validity with other theories. The first of these, conducted with Marvin D. Krohn, Lonn Lanza-Kaduce, and Marcia J. Radosevich, was a self-report questionnaire survey of adolescent substance abuse involving 3,000 students in Grades 7 through 12 in eight communities in three Midwestern states (Akers et al., 1979; Krohn, Akers, Radosevich, and Lanza-Kaduce, 1982; Krohn, Lanza-Kaduce, and Akers, 1984; Lanza-Kaduce, Akers, Krohn, and Radosevich, 1984; Akers and Cochran, 1985; Akers and Lee, 1999). The second, conducted with Marvin Krohn, Ronald Lauer, James Massey, William Skinner, and Sherilyn Spear, was a 5-year longitudinal study of smoking among 2,000 students in junior and senior high school in one Midwest community (Lauer, Akers, Massey, and Clarke, 1982; Krohn, Skinner, Massey, and Akers, 1985; Spear and Akers, 1988; Akers, 1992a; Akers and Lee, 1996). The third project, conducted with Anthony La Greca, John Cochran, and Christine S. Sellers, was a 4-year longitudinal study of conforming and deviant drinking among elderly populations (1,400 respondents) in four communities in Florida and New Jersey (Akers, La Greca, Cochran, and Sellers, 1989; Akers and La Greca, 1991; Akers, 1992a).

Other master's and doctoral research under Akers's supervision includes research on rape and sexual coercion among samples of college males (Boeringer, Shehan, and Akers, 1991), a study of substance use among adolescents in South Korea (Hwang and Akers, 2003; 2006), a study of terrorist violence (Akers and Silverman, 2004), and tests of the SSSL model on adolescent substance use (Lee, Akers, and Borg, 2004; Holland-Davis, 2006). The dependent variables in these studies have ranged from minor deviance to serious criminal behavior.

The findings in each of these studies demonstrate that the social learning variables of differential association, differential reinforcement, imitation, and definitions, singly and in combination, are strongly related to the various forms of deviant, delinquent, and criminal behavior studied. The social learning model produces high levels of explained variance, much more than other theoretical models with which it is compared. The combined effects of the social learning variables on adolescent alcohol and drug use and abuse are very strong.

High amounts (from 31% to 68%) of the variance in these variables are accounted for by the social learning variables. Social bonding models account for about 15% and anomie models account for less than 5% of the variance.

Similarly, adolescent cigarette smoking is highly correlated with the social learning variables. These variables also predict quite well the maintenance of smoking over a 3-year period. They fare less well, however, when predicting which of the initially abstinent youngsters will begin smoking in that same period. The social learning variables do a slightly better job of predicting the onset of smoking over a 5-year period. The sequencing and reciprocal effects of social learning variables and smoking behavior over the 5-year period are as predicted by the theory. The onset, frequency, and quantity of elderly drinking are highly correlated with social learning variables, and the theory also successfully accounts for problem drinking among the elderly.

The social learning variables of association, reinforcement, definitions, and imitation explain the self-perceived likelihood of using force to gain sexual contact or committing rape by college men (55% explained variance). They also account for the actual use of drugs or alcohol, non-physical coercion, and physical force by males to obtain sex (20% explained variance). Social bonding, self-control, and relative deprivation (strain) models account for less than 10% of the variance in these variables.

The research by Akers and others has also included some evidence on the hypothesized relationship between social structure and social learning. This research has found that the correlations of adolescent drug use and smoking, elderly alcohol abuse, and rape to sociodemographic variables of age, sex, race, and class are reduced toward zero when the social learning variables are taken into account. Also, differences in levels of marijuana and alcohol use among adolescents in four types of communities (farm, rural-nonfarm, suburban, and urban), and the differences in overall levels of drinking behavior among the elderly in four types of communities, are mediated by the social learning process. The same findings apply to the effects of family structure, gender, and other aspects of social structure on delinquency, violence, and binge drinking (Lee et al., 2004; Jensen, 2003; Bellair, Roscigno, and Velez, 2003; Lanza-Kaduce and Capece, 2003). Jensen and Akers (2003) found that social structural factors derivable from social learning principles accounted for 65% of the variance in homicide rates among 82 nations. These and findings from other research show some support for the SSSL theory (Warr, 1998; Mears, Ploeger, and Warr, 1998; Akers and Lee, 1996; Rebellon, 2002; Benoit et al., 2003; Haynie and South, 2005). There are good reasons to believe that the social learning principles provide a solid basis for the macro-level explanation of differences in crime rates across societies as well as structural varia-tions and changes in crime rates within the same society (Akers and Jensen, 2006). However, at this time there has not been enough research to confirm that social learning is the principal process mediating the relationship of social structure and crime as expected by the theory. And some research findings suggest the SSSL model may have to be modified to take into account not only the "mediating" of social struc-tural effects by the social learning variables but also "moderating," interacting with, the effects of social learning variables by social struc-tural variables, particularly gender (Holland-Davis, 2006; for informa-tion on the difference between mediating and moderating effects, see Baron and Kenney, 1986).

Research on Critiques of Social Learning Theory

The testability of the basic behavioral learning principles incor-porated in social learning theory has been challenged because they may be tautological. The way in which the principle of reinforcement is often stated by behavioral psychologists makes the proposition true by definition. They define reinforcement by stating that it occurs when behavior has been strengthened; that is, its rate of commission has been increased. If reinforcement is defined this way, then the state-ment "If behavior is reinforced, it will be strengthened" is tautological. If reinforcement means that behavior has been strengthened, then the hypothesis states simply, "If behavior is reinforced, it is reinforced." If the behavior is not strengthened, then by definition it has not been rein-forced; therefore, no instance of behavior that is not being strength-ened can be used to falsify the hypothesis.

Another criticism of social learning has to do with the temporal sequence of differential peer association and delinquency. Some have argued that youths become delinquent first, then seek out other delin-quent youths. Rather than delinquent associations causing delinquency, delinquency causes delinquent associations. If there is a relationship between one's own delinquency and one's association with delinquent peers, then it is simply a case of "birds of a feather flocking together" rather than a bird joining a flock and changing its feathers. Differential peer associations with delinquent friends are almost always a conse-quence rather than a cause of one's own behavior. Association with delinquent peers takes place only or mainly after peers have already independently established patterns of delinquent involvement. No deviance-relevant learning takes place in peer groups. From this point of view, any association with delinquent youths has no direct effect on an adolescent's delinquent behavior. Therefore, association with delinquent friends has an effect on neither the onset nor acceleration, the continuation nor cessation of delinquent behavior (Hirschi, 1969; Gottfredson and Hirschi, 1990; Sampson and Laub, 1993).

These criticisms, however, may be off the mark. Burgess and Akers (1966a) identified the tautology problem and offered one solution to it. They separated the definitions of reinforcement and other behavioral concepts from non-tautological, testable propositions in social learning theory and proposed criteria for falsifying those propositions. Others as well have proposed somewhat different solutions (Liska, 1969; Chadwick-Jones, 1976). More important, whatever circular reasoning there is in prior and classic statement of operant conditioning theory, social learning theory as first formulated and as developed to the present time does not contain any tautological propositions about the relationship between behavior and reinforcement. In addition, variables in the process of reinforcement are always measured separately (and hence non-tautologically) from measures of crime and deviance in research on social learning theory. No attempt is made to use a measure of any behavior hypothesized to result from differential reinforcement as the measure of differential reinforcement itself. The theory would be falsified if it is typically the case that positive social approval or other rewards for delinquency (that are not offset by punishment) more often reduce than increase its recurrence.

Also, as shown earlier, feedback effects are built into the reinforcement concept with both prior and anticipated reward/punishment influencing present behavior in a non-tautological way.

Furthermore, the reciprocal relationship between one's own conduct and one's definitions and association with friends is clearly recognized in social learning theory. Therefore, the fact that delinquent behavior may precede the association with delinquent peers does not contradict this theory. "Social learning admits that birds of a feather do flock together, but it also admits that if the birds are humans, they also will influence one another's behavior, in both conforming and deviant directions" (Akers, 1991:210). It would contradict the theory if research demonstrated that the onset of delinquency always or most often predates interaction with peers who have engaged in delinquent acts and/or have adhered to delinquency-favorable definitions. It would not support the theory if the research evidence showed that whatever level of delinquent behavioral involvement preceded association with delinquent peers stayed the same or decreased rather than increased after the association. Research has not yet found this to be the case. Instead, the findings from several studies favor the process proposed by social learning theory, which recognizes both direct and reciprocal effects. That is, a youngster associates differentially with peers who are deviant or tolerant of deviance, learns definitions favorable to delinquent behavior, is exposed to deviant models that reinforce delinquency, then initiates or increases involvement in that behavior, which then is expected to influence further associations and definitions (Kandel, 1978; Andrews and Kandel, 1979; Krohn et al., 1985; Sellers and Winfree, 1990; Kandel and Davies, 1991; Warr, 1993b; Esbensen and Huizinga, 1993; Thornberry et al., 1994; Menard and Elliott, 1994; Winfree et al., 1994a; Akers and Lee, 1996; Esbensen and Deschenes, 1998; Battin et al., 1998; Gordon et al., 2004).

Kandel and Davies (1991:442) noted that "although assortive pairing plays a role in similarity among friends observed at a single point in time, longitudinal research that we and others have carried out clearly documents the etiological importance of peers in the initiation and persistence of substance use." Warr (1993b) also referred to the considerable amount of research evidence showing that peer associations precede the development of deviant patterns (or increase the frequency and seriousness of deviant behavior once it has begun) more often than involvement in deviant behavior precedes associations with deviant peers. The reverse sequence also occurs and Warr proposed that the process is "...a more complex, sequential, reciprocal process: Adolescents are commonly introduced to delinquency by their friends and subsequently become more selective in their choices of friends. The 'feathering' and 'flocking' ... are not mutually exclusive and may instead be part of a unified process" (Warr, 1993b:39). This is, of course, completely consistent with the sequential and feedback effects in the social learning process spelled out earlier. Menard and Elliott (1990; 1994; Elliott and Menard, 1996) also supported the process as predicted by social learning theory. Reciprocal effects were found in their research, but

> in the typical sequence of initiation of delinquent bonding and illegal behavior, delinquent bonding (again, more specifically, association with delinquent friends) usually precedes illegal behavior for those individuals for whom one can ascertain the temporal order. ... [S]imilarly ... weakening of belief typically preceded the initiation of illegal behavior. (Menard and Elliott, 1994:174)

> These results are strong enough to indicate that serious forms of delinquent behavior such as index offending rarely, if ever, precede exposure to delinquent friends. Instead, in the vast majority of cases, exposure precedes index offending. (Elliott and Menard, 1996:43)

> We were *not* able to reject the learning theory hypothesis that the onset of exposure to delinquent others typically precedes the onset of delinquent behavior. Instead, we found that exposure to delinquent peers preceded minor delinquent behavior in a majority of cases, and serious delinquency in nearly all cases where some order could be determined.... Having delinquent friends and being involved in delinquent

behavior may influence one another, but the influence is not symmetric; the influence of exposure on delinquency begins earlier in the sequence, and remains stronger throughout the sequence, than the influence of delinquency on exposure. (Elliott and Menard, 1996:61–62)

Some research finds stronger effects of peer associations running in the other direction and some shows the relationship to be about equal depending on the measures and methods employed (Kandel, 1996; Krohn et al., 1996; Matsueda and Anderson, 1998; Gordon et al. 2004). However, the evidence is that delinquency is more probable for those in differential association with deviant peers, that whatever level of delinquent involvement already exists is increased through differential association with delinquent peers, and that, "Although many investigations offer evidence of reciprocal effects, no study yet has failed to show a significant effect of peers on current and/or subsequent delinquency" (Warr, 2002:42):

A peer "socialization" process and a peer "selection" process in deviant behavior are not mutually exclusive, but are simply the social learning process at different times. Arguments that ... any evidence of selective mechanisms in deviant interaction runs counter to social learning theory ... are wrong. (Akers, 1998:56)

Another criticism of the theory is that the strong relationship between self-reported delinquency and peer associations is entirely due to the fact that associations are often measured by the individual's report of the delinquency of his or her peers; they are the same thing measured twice. One is measuring the same underlying delinquent tendency, whether youngsters are asked about the delinquency of their friends or about their own delinquency. But research shows that the two are not the same and that the respondent's reports of friends' behavior is not simply a reflection of one's own delinquent behavior (Menard and Elliott, 1990; Agnew, 1991b; Warr, 1993b; Thornberry et al., 1994; Elliott and Menard, 1996; Bartusch, Lynam, Moffitt, and Silva, 1997). The major impact of differential peer association on the adolescent's own behavior, although not as strong, continues to be found in research that measures the proportion of delinquent friends by reports of delinquent behavior of the friends themselves, rather than relying on the adolescent's report or perception of friend's behavior (Haynie, 2002; Weerman and Smeenk, 2005). Although both are reasonable indicators of peer influence, the latter, perceptual, measure is more relevant and accurate for testing the theory because, "Even if peer behavior is misperceived as more (or less) delinquent than it actually is, the peer influence will still come through that perception" (Akers, 1998:119).

Warr contended that "... the generality of the theory has yet to be fully demonstrated. To be sure, the evidence for social learning is extensive and impressive ... but it is concentrated disproportionately on tobacco, alcohol, and other drug use, and on relatively minor forms of deviance ..." (Warr, 2002:78–79). Although the same criticism could be truthfully leveled against other major criminological theories, social learning theory claims the broadest scope of all the theories, except perhaps for self-control theory (see chap. 6), in accounting for all varieties of criminal and deviant conduct. Although, as we have seen in this chapter (see also Akers, 1998), the theory has been tested with a range of deviant and criminal behavior, more empirical evidence is needed on the scope of the theory. Future research on social learning theory should include as many different offenses as possible, from minor to the most serious.

Applications of Social Learning Theory in Prevention and Treatment Programs

If criminal and delinquent behavior is acquired and sustained through social learning processes in naturally occurring environments, then it should be possible to modify that behavior to the extent that one is able to manipulate those same processes or the environmental contingencies that impinge on them. This is the underlying assumption of prevention and treatment programs that have relied on the application of social learning principles. Reliance on one or more of the explanatory variables in social learning theory forms the implicit or explicit theoretical basis (often in combination with guidelines from other theories) for many types of group therapies and self-help programs, positive peer counseling programs, gang interventions, family and school programs, teenage drug, alcohol, and delinquency prevention and education programs, and other private and public programs. Behavior modification programs based on cognitive/behavioral learning principles, including both group and individually focused techniques for juveniles and adults, are operating in correctional, treatment, and community facilities and programs and in private practice (see Bandura, 1969; Stumphauzer, 1986; Morris and Braukmann, 1987; Akers, 1992b; Lundman, 1993; Ellis and Sowers, 2001; Pearson, Lipton, Cleland, and Yee, 2002; Andrews and Bonta, 2003; Hersen and Rosqvist, 2005). Some examples will serve to show how social learning principles have been put into practice.

Highfields and Essexfield

One of the first systematic uses of created prosocial peer groups to change delinquent behavior was in the Highfields project (Weeks,

1958). Highfields was an alternative treatment program for delinquent boys, who were allowed to go to school, work, and participate in other activities during the day and return to the Highfields residential facility at night. There was no education, vocational, or individual counseling program. The principal activity was regular participation in Guided Group Interaction (GGI) sessions. These were peer groups (guided by adult staff) in which common problems could be discussed in a group atmosphere that created and encouraged non-delinquent attitudes and behavior. At the end of the program, the boys had developed attitudes more favorable to obeying the law, and those who changed their attitudes the most were more likely to succeed and stay out of trouble later. However, the changes were not great and were more noticeable among the Black than the White youth in the program. The Highfields boys did somewhat better than a comparison group of boys, who had been committed to the state reformatory school (even when adjustments for in-program failures were made), in avoiding reinstitutionalization, but again this primarily was due to the differences observed among the Black youth. Essexfield later built on the Highfields experience, using similar peer group sessions to effect changes in delinquent behavior and attitudes, but in a nonresidential setting. The Essexfield boys were not more successful in staying out of future trouble than those who were either given regular probation supervision or assigned to the residential program at Highfields. But they did do somewhat better than the comparison group of those who had been sent to the state reform school.

The Provo and Silverlake Experiments

LaMar T. Empey's delinquency treatment experiment in Provo, Utah (Empey and Erickson, 1972), offered a semi-residential alternative to regular juvenile probation and to incarceration in a state training school for delinquent boys. Empey instituted a peer-group program with officially adjudicated delinquents in a group home facility known as Pinehills. He drew on differential association theory and applied techniques similar to the GGI of Highfields. With guidance from adult counselors, a prosocial, anti-delinquent peer culture was cultivated. The Pinehills boys had the responsibility and authority to form groups, orient new boys coming in, set standards and rules for behavior, determine punishment for rule violation, and decide when a boy was ready to be released from Pinehills. The boys gained recognition and status in the group for conforming rather than antisocial behavior. The intent was to use this peer-group interaction to foster the boys' definitions favorable to conforming behavior and peer influence to motivate them toward conformity and away from delinquency.

The Provo project was designed to have court-adjudicated delinquent boys randomly assigned to the Pinehills facility, to the secure-custody state training school, or to a regular juvenile probation caseload in the community. However, the experimental design did not last because the juvenile court judge began purposely assigning boys to Pinehills once he learned of the strong positive effects demonstrated by the program. The boys who had participated in the peer groups at Pinehills were very much less likely to be repeat offenders (27% recidivism among all the boys initially assigned and 16% recidivism among those completing the program) than those boys randomly committed to the state institution (60% recidivism) 6 months after release. Even 4 years later, recidivism of the Pinehills boys was still less than half that of a comparison group released from the state training school.

The Pinehills recidivism rate was also much better than the recidivism rate (about 45%) that had prevailed among delinquents placed on regular juvenile probation supervision prior to the Provo project. However, during the time the project was in operation, the boys assigned to the regular probation group experienced about the same level of recidivism as the Pinehills boys. This dramatic improvement over the pre-project recidivism may have resulted from the tendency of the regular probation officers, who knew their caseloads were being compared with Pinehills', to reduce revocations and to intensify their efforts with the boys under their supervision. The Provo project ended prematurely because it ran into opposition from county officials and received no additional public funding when its private funds ran out (Lundman, 1993).

The Teaching Family Model

Later community-based residential programs moved beyond the almost exclusive reliance on the peer group of the Highfields and Provo projects to create more of a family environment. They also explicitly applied the principle of differential reinforcement to modify behavior. The best examples are Achievement Place (in the 1960s) and its successor, the Teaching Family model (since the 1970s). The Teaching Family group homes became "perhaps the most systematic, and certainly the most long-lived and widely disseminated, application of the behavioral approach with juvenile offenders ..." (Braukmann and Wolf, 1987:135). The Teaching Family model involves a married couple ("teaching parents") and six to eight delinquent or "at-risk" youth living together as a family. A token economy is in effect in which the youth can earn reward points by proper behavior or have points taken away for improper behavior in the home or at school. The parents are responsible for teaching social, academic, and prevocational skills and maintaining mutually reinforcing relationships with the adolescents. But the youths in the home also operate a peer-oriented self-government system. Thus, in addition to the shaping of behavior by the teaching parents, the Teaching Family model promotes conforming behavior through exposure to a prosocial peer group.

Studies have shown this model works quite well to maintain good behavior and retard misconduct and delinquent behavior in the school and community while living with the teaching family. However, outcome evaluations in many states have found little difference in subsequent delinquent behavior between those who had been in the Teaching Family group homes and youth in control groups who had participated in other types of programs. The delinquency-inhibiting effects on the adolescents' behavior did not survive their release from the behavior modification system of the Teaching Family group homes back to their previous family and neighborhood environments (Braukmann and Wolf, 1987).

Oregon Social Learning Center (OSLC)

Gerald R. Patterson and his colleagues at the OSLC (Patterson, 1975; Patterson, Debaryshe, and Ramsey, 1989; Patterson, Capaldi, and Bank, 1991; Dishion, Patterson, and Kavanagh, 1992; Patterson and Chamberlain, 1994; Snyder and Patterson, 1995; Dishion, McCord, and Poulin, 1999; Reid et al., 2002) have long been conducting research on social learning theory and applying it in programs with families and peer groups. Their "coercive family" model proposes that the child's behavior and interaction with others are "learned in the family, and under more extreme conditions carries over to a child's interactions with others outside the family, including peers and teachers" (Dishion et al., 1992:254–255):

> [P]oor parent discipline practices increase the likelihood of child coercive responses, and high rates of child coercion impede parents' attempts to provide evenhanded, consistent, and effective discipline. It is in this sense that parental limit setting for behaviors such as lying, stealing, or fighting often fail in the quagmire of the child's arguments, excuses, and counteraccusations. (Dishion et al., 1992:258)

The OSLC Adolescent Transition Program (ATP) involves targeting family management skills in parent-focused and parent/teen groups as compared to teen-focused groups and self-directed change. In the parent groups, several sessions are held with a therapist to help parents develop monitoring, discipline, problem solving, and other effective socialization and disciplinary skills through instructions, discussion, and role playing. "Social learning parent training is a step-wise, skill-based approach for developing effective parenting skills and strategies for maintaining change" (Dishion et al., 1992:263). The teen-focused group and individual sessions are run for at-risk youth in the pre-teen and early adolescent years (ages 10–14). The goals of these sessions are to help develop and improve communication skills, self-control, pro-social attitudes, and prosocial peer associations. Evaluation research has shown improvements in parenting skills and reductions in antisocial behavior among the youth in the program (Dishion et al., 1992). However, intervention groups that include older delinquents can increase, rather than decrease, deviant behavior of the youths (Dishion et al., 1999).

Similar cognitive and behavioral principles are applied in another successful OSLC program, the Multidimensional Treatment Foster Care (MTFC), designed to change the behavior of youth who have been involved in chronic, high frequency, and serious delinquencies adjudicated by the juvenile court (Chamberlain, Fisher, and Moore, 2002; Eddy and Chamberlain, 2000). The adolescents in the treatment program are assigned to foster care families (1 or 2 per family) based on the court finding that, although the offenders are eligible for community rather than institutional placement, return of the youth to their own families is not feasible because their parents are no longer able to control them. Competent foster parents were recruited and trained to use "behavior management methods ... to implement and maintain a flexible and individualized behavior plan for each youth within the context of a three-level point system that made youth privileges contingent on compliance with program rules and general progress" (Eddy and Chamberlain, 2000:858). This training equips the foster parents "to notice and reinforce youngsters" for proper behavior in a positive way. In addition, each youth takes part in weekly sessions with behavioral therapists "focused on skill building in such areas as problem solving, social perspective taking, and nonaggressive methods of self-expression" (Chamberlain et al., 2002:205–206). The foster home placement, school attendance and homework, therapy sessions, and other aspects of the intervention are coordinated and supervised by case managers. After the youth completes the program they are returned to their biological or stepparents who also receive support and training in parenting skills.

Outcome evaluation has shown that the delinquents in the MTFC treatment group had lower rates of both official and self-reported delinquency than comparable youth placed in other community treatment programs. In a random-assignment study, boys in the MTFC were found to have significantly fewer arrests and self-reported delinquencies than boys assigned to Group Care (GC) homes 1 year after release from the programs and continued to have fewer arrests for up to

3 years later (Chamberlain et al., 2002). Research also shows that the treatment effects were mediated by family and peer association variables. That is, the reduction in and desistance from further delinquent behavior were achieved because the program "caused levels of family management skills [parental supervision, discipline, and positive reinforcement] to increase and deviant peer associations to decrease" (Eddy and Chamberlain, 2000:858)

Linking the Interests of Families and Teachers (LIFT) is an OSLC delinquency-prevention project utilizing social learning principles. This program is designed to affect troublesome childhood behavior that is often a precursor to delinquent and violent behavior in adolescence. Although high-risk areas of the community are targeted, the approach is a "universal strategy" that provides services to all first and fifth graders (as the transitional grades into elementary and middle schools respectively), their parents, and teachers in those areas rather than attempting to identify individual youth at risk and singling them out for preventive intervention. LIFT is focused on modifying the interaction of the children with their social environment at home, with peers, and in school. Theoretically, "the driving force in a child's conduct problems are the reinforcement processes that occur in his or her day-to-day relationships.... antisocial behavior develops as an interaction between the child's antisocial behavior and the reactions of those with whom he or she interacts on a daily basis" (Reid and Eddy, 2002:222). With the cooperation of the schools and voluntary involvement of the children and families, "the three major components of the LIFT are (a) classroom-based child social and problem skills training, (b) playground-based behavior modification, and (c) group-delivered parent training" (Eddy, Reid, and Fetrow, 2000:165).

The classroom interventions involves 30-min sessions twice a week for 10 weeks with lectures, group discussion, and practice of listening, cooperation, problem-solving, and other skills promoting prosocial behavior with peers (as well as study skills for the fifth graders). The approach on the playground following the classroom sessions is to have the children participate in a "good behavior" game with their behavior observed by project monitors. In this game, the children are rewarded by the monitors for good behavior (e.g., prosocial behavior, sharing, cooperation) and for refraining from aggressiveness or other antisocial acts toward peers. The reward points earned by accumulation of armbands, minus points deducted for observed displays of antisocial behavior, are later exchanged for group rewards. The parent training part of the program attempts to aid parents (through 6 weekly 1½-hr evening sessions held in school rooms with groups of 15 parents) to develop or strengthen "consistent and effective positive reinforcement, discipline, and monitoring skills" (Reid and Eddy, 2002:224). These sessions include video presentations and role playing with reading and practice at home. Group leaders monitored progress in the families weekly, and a voice messaging system was installed in the classrooms for daily communication between parents and teachers.

There were some modest to strong effects of the program almost immediately on reductions in physical aggression on the playground and improved behavior in the classrooms. Also, in the longer term, by the time the fifth graders were in middle school and the first years of high school, the LIFT participants had experienced significantly fewer police arrests, lower levels of self-reported drug use, and fewer associations with deviant peers (as observed by the teachers) than did the youth in the control group.

Andrews's Experiments and Model of Treatment and Prevention

Donald R. Cressey (1955) proposed that both juvenile and adult treatment and reformation groups, whether naturally occurring or deliberately organized as an intervention technique, are based on the process of differential association. The reformation process consists of some offenders joining with some non-criminals (staff or volunteers) to change the criminal behavior of other offenders in the group by reducing their exposure to definitions favorable to crime and enhancing exposure to prosocial definitions espoused by the group. Cressey proposed that the effects of such a process come from what he termed "retroflexive reformation." In retroflexive reformation, the offender affects his or her own balance of definitions favorable and unfavorable to criminal behavior more than he or she affects others' definitions. In agreeing to participate in the group to help reform others, the criminal comes to accept the prosocial purpose and values of the group while alienating himself or herself more from pro-criminal values.

Retroflexive reformation may have been operating along with other social learning processes in a pioneering prison and probation program designed and evaluated by D. A. Andrews (1980). Andrews applied three major principles in a program to change attitudes (definitions) and behavior of convicted adult offenders. These were (1) contingency (differential association and reinforcement in groups led by prosocial volunteers), (2) quality (modalities) of interpersonal relationships in those groups, and (3) self-management (a program of self-monitoring and self-reinforcement by the individual inmates). Manipulation of the associations and reinforcers produced significant changes toward less adherence to criminal definitions and greater acceptance of noncriminal definitions. Similarly, the more skilled the outside volunteers who worked with the groups were in creating cohesive groups (based on the principle of intensity of primary group relationships), the more likely the inmates were to develop anti-criminal attitudes. Adult probationers in the program developed greater respect for the law and were less likely to repeat criminal offenses. Prisoners assigned to self-management and prosocial–attitude groups also changed their own attitudes in a law-abiding direction and had lower recidivism rates.

Andrews has continued to emphasize the relationship and contingency principles in a more fully developed PIC–R ("personal-interpersonal, and community-reinforcement") model applied to treatment and prevention of criminal and deviant behavior. In this model, the Relationship Principle refers to the process whereby "interpersonal influence by way of antecedent and consequent processes is greatest in situations characterized by open, warm, and enthusiastic communication and by mutual respect and liking." The Contingency Principle refers to "the procriminal/anticriminal content of the messages communicated or by the procriminal/anticriminal nature of the behavior patterns that are modeled, rehearsed and subject to reinforcement and punishment contingencies" (Andrews and Bonta, 1998:273).

Andrews and his associates have carried out their own research and conducted a meta-analysis of the literature to gauge the effectiveness of behaviorally oriented models such as his as well as various other treatment and prevention strategies. They have found that social behavioral strategies utilizing the family and peers are the most effective, especially when targeted specifically to pro- or anti-criminal attitudes and behavior rather than general psychological states such as self-esteem. The "cognitive behavioral and social learning approaches" are more effective than "nondirective relationship-oriented counseling or psychodynamic insight-oriented counseling" and "behavioral treatments had a substantially greater average effect [mean effect size of .25] on recidivism than did non-behavioral treatments [mean effect size of .04]" (Andrews and Bonta, 1998:262–263, 267–268, 282–290). Other recent meta-analyses confirm the greater effectiveness of "cognitive-behavioral" drug abuse treatment programs in correctional facilities, which are consistent with "social learning theory [that] is broader than behavioral reinforcement theory because it includes as variables cognitions, verbalization, and social modeling to explain (and to change) behavior patterns" (Pearson et al., 2002:480; see also Lipsey and Landenberger, 2005; Gendreau, Smith, and French, 2006):

> The core criteria of successful programs in developmental prevention are similar to those in offender treatment. For example, such programs have a sound theoretical basis in social learning theory, follow a cognitive-behavioral approach, are well structured and address multiple risk and protective factors. (Losel, 2007:4)

[R]esearch on correctional programs supplies strong and consistent support for theories—such as differential association/social learning theory—that link offending to antisocial associations and to the internalization of antisocial values. A consistent finding across meta-analyses, including cross-cultural studies, is that "cognitive-behavioral" programs tend to achieve higher reductions in recidivism than other treatment modalities. (Cullen, Wright, Gendreau, and Andrews, 2003:353)

Other Prevention Programs

G.R.E.A.T. (Gang Resistance Education and Training) is a prevention program for school students with the goals of promoting anti-gang attitudes, reducing involvement in gangs, and increasing positive relations with law enforcement, with the expectation that achieving these goals among the students would prevent delinquent behavior in the community. The program originally consisted of nine sessions taught by police officers, including lessons on conflict resolution, resisting peer pressure, and the negative effect of gangs on quality of life in the community. It is entirely a cognitive-based program delivered in the classroom by uniformed police officers without any direct intervention in gang activity or any components for specific behavioral change. Quasi-experimental evaluation of G.R.E.A.T. found that youths in the program developed more positive attitudes toward police and more negative attitudes toward gangs, lower levels of victimization, less risk-taking behavior, and more association with peers in prosocial activities. However, the research also showed that gang membership was not prevented by participation in the program and that self-reported delinquent behavior was not lower among the youths taking part in the G.R.E.A.T. sessions than in control groups of youths not participating in the program (Esbensen et al., 2001).

These disappointing results led to revision of G.R.E.A.T. based on the advice of consultants with expertise in gangs and school-based prevention programs. There are now four "components" of the program: elementary school, middle school, and summer school curriculum components and a families component. The school components focus on teaching the students about gangs, violence, and drugs, attempting to foster prosocial attitudes and skills as well as "refusal skills" and other techniques of avoiding joining gangs and other deviant peer groups. In the family component, the officers attempt to teach good parental/family skills, effective parental discipline and monitoring, intra-family communication, prosocial role modeling, and control of access to television, movies, video games, and the internet. The revised program has not yet been evaluated (see the G.R.E.A.T. website: http://www.great-online.org/).

It appears that the designers of G.R.E.A.T. recognize that differential peer association has effects on delinquency and in particular assume that lowering frequency and intensity of association with deviant peers by reducing gang involvement will prevent delinquency that would be consistent, in part, with social learning theory. Also, the program attempts to undergird social skills and attitudes that could counteract gang-favorable and delinquency-favorable attitudes and that would appear to echo the concept of definitions in social learning theory. However, the original and revised program descriptions are vague about the theoretical assumptions on which they are based. Neither social learning nor any other theory is specifically delineated as providing the theoretical basis for the program activities. Some of it seems to be fashioned on social bonding theory (see chap. 6), and there are aspects of G.R.E.A.T. that do not follow from, or even run counter to, what one would expect from social learning theory. What social learning principles, for instance, would be the basis for projecting that police-led classroom curriculum (even after mid-stream revision in the program to involve teachers more and to move away from a strictly didactic approach in the classroom) and family sessions would have the desired outcomes? Social learning theory would predict that if the revised program does not reduce gang involvement or interaction with delinquent peers any more than the original program did, then it, too, is likely to have little preventive effect on delinquent behavior. Network analysis of gang membership and relationships suggests that a potentially more effective approach, perhaps in addition to or in conjunction with, classroom instruction would involve targeting direct intervention with individual gang members, especially those who occupy central "cut points" (sole connecting links between different individuals and groups) in the gang networks (McGloin, 2005; see also McGloin et al., 2004). These kinds of interventions would be more in line with social learning principles, but they are not part of the G.R.E.A.T. program.

Alcohol and drug education/prevention programs that employ various "social influence and skills" strategies and techniques reflect, to some extent, social learning assumptions. They are designed to teach about the influences of peers, media, and family that can affect drug-using and abstaining decisions, and how to deal with and resist these influences. Then, the effort is to help develop and improve the social skills needed to interact with and get along with others without using substances. Sometimes the programs are peer-oriented and involve youths in role-playing, socio-drama, and modeling drug-free behavior (Akers, 1992b; Botvin et al., 1995).

Participation in such programs has been shown to increase knowledge about drugs and alcohol and to change attitudes to some extent. The programs also appear to have modest effects on reducing or preventing drug behavior. The most effective are peer programs that focus on learning prosocial and life skills while discouraging drug-favorable attitudes (Tobler, 1986; Akers, 1992b; Botvin et al., 1995). Although they can claim some success, it should be noted that even the best programs have not had large effects. It has not been firmly established that they will produce long-term reductions in the prevalence of substance use, not only among White, middle class youth but also among lower class Black and Hispanic youth.

In their review of scientifically sound studies of crime prevention, Sherman et al. (1998) list a number of family and school programs under the category of "what works." They conclude that the most effective programs in the prevention of delinquency, drug use, and conduct problems are those designed for high-risk youths that rely on cognitive behavioral approaches. These include clarifying and communicating norms, reinforcement of positive behavior, and training in social competency, life skills, thinking skills, and self-control using behavior modification techniques.

Community and school-based programs directed toward families, children, and youth often draw on principles from both learning and bonding theories (see chap. 6) as well as from general strain theory (see chap. 8). These range from Head Start and other generalized children-oriented programs to early-intervention programs specifically geared to prevent misconduct and delinquency (Greenwood, 1998). They attempt to reduce the "risk factors" and promote "protective factors" in the family, school, and community by providing social, economic, and learning resources to school children and families, often in minority, disadvantaged, and high-risk neighborhoods (Jessor, 1996; Zigler, Tausig, and Black, 1996). The most notable program that melds learning and bonding theories is the Social Development Model (SDM) (Hawkins et al., 1992; Hawkins et al., 1999). The SDM is an early intervention, long-term project that has demonstrated some success in preventing adolescent delinquency and misconduct. The SDM and research evaluating it are described in the next chapter (chap. 6).

Summary

Akers's social learning theory combines Sutherland's original differential association theory of criminal behavior with general behavioral learning principles. The theory proposes that criminal and delinquent behavior is acquired, repeated, and changed by the same process as conforming behavior. While referring to all parts of the learning process, Akers's social learning theory in criminology has focused on the four major concepts of differential association, definitions, differential reinforcement, and imitation. That process will more likely produce behavior that violates social and legal norms than conforming behavior when persons differentially associate with those who expose them to deviant patterns, when the deviant behavior is differentially reinforced over conforming behavior, when individuals are more exposed to deviant than conforming models, and when their own definitions favorably dispose them to commit deviant acts.

This social learning explanation of crime and delinquency has been strongly supported by the research evidence. Research conducted over many years, including that by Akers and associates, has consistently found that social learning is empirically supported as an explanation of individual differences in delinquent and criminal behavior. The hypothesis that social learning processes mediate the effects of socio-demographic and community variables on behavior has been infrequently studied, but the evidence so far suggests that it will also be upheld. The behavioral, cognitive, and social interactional principles of social learning theory have been applied in a range of prevention and treatment programs, mainly with adolescent populations but also with adult offenders. The outcomes of these programs often have been disappointing. But there is also some evidence of success, and generally such programs are more effective than alternative approaches.

Notes

1. For detailed accounts of Sutherland's career and the way in which he developed this theory, see Cohen, Lindesmith, and Schuessler (1956), Gaylord and Galliher (1988), and Sutherland (1973). For further study of the development and revisions of differential association theory, see chapter 2 of Akers (1998).

2. For classic statements of behavioristic "operant conditioning" principles of learning, see Skinner (1953; 1959). See also the full statement of behavioral learning theory in Burgess and Akers (1966a). Prior to the full revision of differential association by Burgess and Akers, C. Ray Jeffery (1965) proposed to replace all of Sutherland's theory with a single statement of operant conditioning, essentially rejecting the theory. Burgess and Akers criticized Jeffery for doing this and retained all the major features of Sutherland's theory in their revision.

3. See also Conger (1976); Marcos, Bahr, and Johnson (1986); Matsueda and Heimer (1987); Burkett and Warren (1987); White, Pandina, and LaGrange (1987); Winfree, Griffiths, and Sellers (1989); Loeber, Stouthamer-Loeber, Van Kammen, and Farrington (1991); Agnew (1991a); Warr and Stafford (1991); Inciardi, Horowitz, and Pottiger (1993); Elliott (1994); Conger and Simons (1995); Simons et al. (1994); and Wood et al. (1995). Research on expanded deterrence models (see chap. 2), showing the strong effects of moral evaluations and actual or anticipated informal social sanctions on

an individual's commission of crime or delinquency, also provides support for social learning theory (Anderson et al., 1977; Meier and Johnson, 1977; Jensen et al., 1978; Tittle, 1980; Grasmick and Green, 1980; Paternoster et al., 1983; Paternoster, 1989a; Lanza-Kaduce, 1988; Stafford and Warr, 1993).

4. There is a very long list of supportive research on these variables both as part of the original differential association theory and the reformulated social learning theory that covers 5 decades going back to the pioneering studies by Short (1957) and continuing to the present time. For a review of this research, see Akers and Jensen (2003). See also the critiques of social learning theory and the SSSL model and a reply to them in the symposium edited by Robert Agnew in the November 1999 issue of *Theoretical Criminology* (Sampson, 1999; Morash, 1999; Krohn, 1999; Akers, 1999).

Chapter 6

Social Bonding and Control Theories

Introduction

Some proponents insist that control theory is entirely different from all other theories of crime because rather than trying to determine why some people deviate from social and legal norms, it asks: Why does anyone conform? Why don't we all violate the rules?

> In control theories, [this] question has never been adequately answered. The question remains, why *do* men obey the rules of society? Deviance is taken for granted; conformity must be explained. (Hirschi, 1969:10)

The answer offered by control theory is that we conform because social controls prevent us from committing crimes. Whenever these controls break down or weaken, deviance is likely to result (Reiss, 1951). Control theory argues that people are motivated to conform by social controls but need no special motivation to violate the law. That comes naturally in the absence of controls. This "natural motivation" assumption does not necessarily refer to inborn tendencies to crime. Rather, it refers to the assumption that there is no individual variation in motivations to commit crime; the impetus toward crime is uniform or evenly distributed across society (Agnew, 1993). Because of this uniform motivation to crime, we will all push up against the rules of society and break through them unless we are controlled. Thus, control theorists assert that their objective is not to explain crime; they assume everyone would violate the law if they could just get away with it. Instead, they set out to explain why we do *not* commit crime. For instance, Travis Hirschi, the leading control theorist stated:

> The question "Why do they do it?" is simply not the question the theory is designed to answer. The question is "Why *don't* we do it?"

There is much evidence that we would if we dared. (Hirschi, 1969:34; emphasis added)

Later statements by Hirschi and Michael Gottfredson have similarly drawn a sharp contrast between control theory and all other theories of criminal behavior, which they have referred to as "positivistic." They describe positivistic theories as having nothing to do with what prevents crime, but only with what factors positively motivate people to commit crimes. In their view, positivistic theories assume that everyone will conform in the absence of that motivation; whereas in contrast, control theories assume that crime will occur unless prevented by strong social and personal controls (Gottfredson and Hirschi, 1990). This assumption of universal motivation to crime has been incorporated into other recent theoretical models (see Wilcox, Land, and Hunt, 2003).

We disagree with this stark distinction between control theory versus positivist theory. It is true that all versions of control theory tend to focus more on social relationships that curb crime than on those that promote crime. However, different control theories vary considerably in the extent to which they limit or exclude the study of the positive motivations behind crime. Not all control theorists simply assume that everyone is equally motivated to deviate, nor do all confine themselves only to the problem of identifying influences toward conformity. Some control theorists have specifically incorporated the crime-motivating factors of personality, social environment, or situation into their own theories (Reckless, 1967; Briar and Piliavin, 1965).

F. Ivan Nye (1958) argued for a multicausal model that treats most crime as a result of the failure of social controls, but allows for the fact that "such 'positive' factors [personality or a delinquent subculture] sometimes combine with delinquent behavior as the product" (Nye, 1958:5). Hirschi himself rejected the assumption of an inherent impulse to delinquency. He proposed that the "natural motivation" assumption in control theory must be modified to recognize the fact that there are some inducements to delinquency, such as the approval of delinquent peers, that must be considered in addition to the inhibitors of delinquency (Hirschi, 1969). The assumption that everyone is naturally motivated to commit deviant acts is not crucial to any version of control theory. In fact, some control theories deliberately include factors that induce crime. Hirschi's social bonding theory and Gottfredson's and Hirschi's self-control theory have some motivational and positivistic elements in them (see Cochran et al., 1998; Wiebe, 2003).

Consequently, there is really not much difference between control theory and other theories in the type of questions about crime that each tries to answer. Whatever their other differences, all theories of crime, including control theory, ultimately propose to account for variations in criminal and delinquent behavior. They do not attempt, for example, to account for variation in occupational behavior, meritorious achievement, or prosocial contributions to the welfare of society. Thus, control theories have the same dependent variables (crime, delinquency, and deviance) as other criminological theories. Empirical tests of control theories measure these variables in exactly the same way (with official and self-report data) as do tests of other theories. If the concept and measurement of the dependent variable are essentially the same, what difference does it make whether one claims that the essential question involves committing a crime or that it involves refraining from a crime? In research on control and other theories, criminal or delinquent behavior is defined as the commission of some act(s) in violation of the law; conformity is defined as the absence of those acts. Conformity and crime are two sides of the same coin. It makes no meaningful difference which of the two a theory claims to explain, because to account for one accounts for the other. Theories vary in the extent to which they emphasize one side of the coin, whether it be the motivation for crime or the restraints on crime. It would be fair to contrast the stress on motivations to crime in some theories with the stress on inhibitors of crime in control theory (Agnew, 1993). But the difference is a matter of degree, not a qualitative difference. For this reason, it is difficult to divide explanations of crime into two mutually exclusive categories based on whether they try to explain either conformity or crime.

Early Control Theories

Reiss's and Nye's Theories of Internal and External Controls

The sociological concept of social control includes both socialization in which a person acquires self-control, and the control over the person's behavior through the external application of social sanctions, rewards for conformity, and punishments for deviance, with the understanding that the applications of sanctions is a major process by which socialization occurs. Albert J. Reiss (1951) provided one of the earliest applications of this concept to criminology by attributing the cause of delinquency to the failure of "personal" and "social" controls. Personal controls are internalized, whereas social controls operate through the external application of legal and informal social sanctions. Nye (1958) later expanded on this and identified three main categories of social control that prevent delinquency:

1. Direct control, by which punishment is imposed or threatened for misconduct and compliance is rewarded by parents.

2. Indirect control, by which a youth refrains from delinquency because his or her delinquent act might cause pain and disappointment for parents or others with whom one has close relationships.

3. Internal control, by which a youth's conscience or sense of guilt prevents him or her from engaging in delinquent acts.

Nye recognized that direct controls could be exercised through formal or legal sanctions, but he emphasized informal, indirect controls in the family. He also argued that the more adolescents' needs for affection, recognition, security, and new experiences are met within the family, the less they will turn to meeting those needs in unacceptable ways outside the family. It would seem, however, that Nye did not mean this to be a separate category of control. Rather, the insufficient satisfaction of youngsters' needs within the family, coupled with the fuller satisfaction of their needs outside the family, appears to be one of the factors that positively motivates them to commit delinquency. Therefore, this is one type of motivation toward delinquent behavior that must be counteracted by direct and indirect controls if delinquency is to be prevented.

Reckless's Containment Theory

At about the same time Nye was formulating his control theory, Walter Reckless (Reckless, Dinitz, and Murray, 1956; Reckless, 1961) proposed the "containment" theory of delinquency and crime. His containment theory was built on the same concept of internal and external control, which Reckless termed "inner" and "outer" containment. Reckless went beyond this, however, to include factors that motivate youth to commit delinquent acts (i.e., "pushes" and "pulls" toward delinquency). The basic proposition in containment theory is that these inner and outer pushes and pulls will produce delinquent behavior unless they are counteracted by inner and outer containment. When the motivations to deviance are strong and containment is weak, crime and delinquency are to be expected. Outer containment includes parental and school supervision and discipline, strong group cohesion, and a consistent moral front. Inner containment consists primarily of a strong conscience or a "good self-concept," which renders one less vulnerable to the pushes and pulls of a deviant environment, is the product of socialization in the family, and is essentially formed by age 12. This self-concept hypothesis is the only part of the containment theory that has been systematically tested. Reckless and his associates conducted research on boys' self-concepts in high-delinquency areas (Reckless et al., 1956; Scarpitti, Murray, Dinitz, and Reckless, 1960). They found, in support of the theory, that boys with good self-concepts at age 12 were less likely to be arrested or to exhibit delinquent behavior by age 16.

Sykes and Matza: Techniques of Neutralization and Drift

Gresham Sykes and David Matza proposed a theory in 1957 that explained delinquent behavior as the result of adolescents using "techniques of neutralization." These techniques are justifications and excuses for committing delinquent acts, which are essentially inappropriate extensions of commonly accepted rationalizations found in the general culture. Believing in these neutralizing definitions does not mean that delinquents totally reject the values of conventional society, or that they have a set of values that directly contradicts general cultural values. It is simply that they have a set of "subterranean values" that circumvent, and rationalize deviations from, conventional values (Matza and Sykes, 1961). In stating their theory, Sykes and Matza left no doubt that they considered techniques of neutralization to be types of "definitions favorable" to crime and delinquency, as referred to in Sutherland's differential association theory.[1] Nevertheless, Sykes and Matza's theory is viewed by many criminologists not as an extension of differential association theory, but as a type of control theory. This interpretation of Sykes and Matza came about principally because Matza (1964) later incorporated neutralization ideas into his "drift" theory of delinquency. Drift theory proposes that the techniques of neutralization are ways in which adolescents can get "episodic release" from conventional moral restraints. It is this periodic evasion of conventional morality that allows the adolescent to drift into and out of delinquency. If conventional beliefs are seen as controlling deviance, then neutralizing those beliefs represents a weakening of social control. It is probably for this reason that, although Matza (1964) made few references to internal or external controls, his drift theory and by extension his and Sykes's theory of the techniques of neutralization have usually been classified as control theory. Neutralization is not viewed as a form of definition favorable to delinquency as originally stated by Sykes and Matza, but as a weakening of inner containment (Ball, 1968) or as a breaking of the bonds to society (Minor, 1981).

This interpretation of techniques of neutralization as a type of control theory is not consistent with the way Hirschi viewed them in his original statement of social bonding theory. Hirschi (1969:199) recognized that the identification of the techniques of neutralization by Sykes and Matza was their "attempt to specify the content of the 'definitions favorable to violation of law,'" not an attempt to propose a control theory. Further, although Hirschi incorporated measures of techniques of neutralizations as indicators of "belief" (see the following) in testing his theory, he rejected Sykes and Matza's central concept that applying the techniques of neutralization is the delinquent's way of breaking the bond of strongly held conventional beliefs. Instead, he proposed that endorsement of the techniques of neutralization simply indicates that general beliefs are weakly held by delinquents in the first place.

Costello (2000) also viewed techniques of neutralization as different from control theory. She found that delinquents who endorse "police-related" neutralization score higher on measures of "self-esteem" (which she interprets as consistent with "neutralization theory"), but delinquents who use "general" neutralizing techniques do not have higher self-esteem (which she interprets as consistent with "control theory") (Costello, 2000:308). Maruna and Copes (2005) did not separate techniques of neutralizations from control theory. They pointed out the links between techniques of neutralization and such cognitive processes as attribution, locus of control, moral disengagement, and cognitive dissonance. Their references to basic cognitive processes underscored the links of techniques of neutralization to symbolic interactionism and definitions favorable to law violation.

In other research, adherence to neutralizing attitudes has been found to be moderately related to delinquent and criminal behavior, but again this seems to be because such attitudes favorably dispose individuals to violate the law rather than function to release them from the restraints of conventional or moral beliefs (Hindelang, 1970; 1973; Hollinger, 1991). In addition, Topalli (2005) demonstrated that neutralization can also mitigate guilt anticipated by "hardcore" offenders who violate their own code of the streets by snitching or refraining from retribution against an individual who victimized them.

Hirschi's Social Bonding Theory

All of the earlier control theories were superseded by the version proposed by Travis Hirschi (1969), who remains today the major control theorist. His control theory is usually referred to as social bonding theory. Hirschi's social bonding theory and his self-control theory proposed in collaboration with Gottfredson are what most criminologists today mean when they refer to control theory. Control theories are the most frequently tested of all criminological theories and are endorsed by higher proportions of academic criminologists (Ellis and Walsh, 1999) than any other type of criminological theory.

This position is well deserved. The full statement of Hirschi's control theory was published in *Causes of Delinquency* (1969). The theory presented in the book is an internally consistent, coherent, and parsimonious theory that is applicable to any type of criminal or deviant behavior, not only delinquency. Hirschi formulated a control theory that brought together elements from all previous control theories and offered new ways to account for delinquent behavior. He not only laid out the assumptions, concepts, and propositions in a lucid fashion, he provided clear empirical measures for each major concept. Then he reported systematic tests of the theory based on data from his own major study of self-reported delinquency, using a sample of the general adolescent population in Contra Costa County, California. His combination of theory construction, conceptualization, operationalization, and empirical testing was virtually unique in criminology at that time and stands as a model today.

The Central Concepts and Propositions of Social Bonding Theory

Hirschi's theory begins with the general proposition that "delinquent acts result when an individual's bond to society is weak or broken" (1969:16). There are four principal "elements" that make up this bond—attachment, commitment, involvement, and beliefs. The stronger these elements of social bonding with parents, adults, schoolteachers, and peers, the more the individual's behavior will be controlled in the direction of conformity. The weaker they are, the more likely it is that the individual will violate the law. These four elements are viewed by Hirschi as highly intercorrelated; the weakening of one will probably be accompanied by the weakening of another.

Attachment to Others. Attachment to others is the extent to which we have close affectional ties to others, admire them, and identify with them so that we care about their expectations. The more insensitive we are to others' opinions, the less we are constrained by the norms that we share with them; therefore, the more likely we are to violate these norms.

Although Hirschi later took a different position in presenting his and Gottfredson's self-control theory (see the following), in proposing social bonding theory, he argues that concepts such as self-control, internalization of norms, internal control, indirect control, personal control, and conscience are too subjective. They cannot be observed and measured. He contends that self-control was most often used by earlier control theorists in a tautological way; that is, they simply assumed that internal controls were weak when people committed criminal or delinquent behavior. Hirschi argued that attachment is a better concept than self-control, because it avoids the tautology problem and because all the concepts of internal self-control can be subsumed under the concept of attachment. "The essence of internalization of norms, conscience, or superego thus lies in the attachment of the individual to others" (Hirschi, 1969:18).

Hirschi emphasizes that attachment to parents and parental supervision are important in controlling delinquency and maintaining conformity. But he also stresses that attachment to peers can control delinquent tendencies. Although he often uses the phrase "attachment to conventional others," Hirschi maintained that it really does not matter to whom one is attached. It is the fact of attachment to other people, not the character of the people to whom one is attached, that determines adherence to or violation of conventional rules:

> [H]olding delinquency (or worthiness) of friends truly constant at any level, the more one respects or admires one's friends, the less likely one is to commit delinquent acts. We honor those we admire not by imitation, but by adherence to conventional standards. (Hirschi, 1969:152)

Therefore, according to social bonding theory, even for the juvenile attached to peers or friends who are delinquent, the stronger the attachment to those friends, the less likely he or she will tend to be delinquent. The delinquent tends to have "cold and brittle" relationships with everyone, to be socially isolated, and to be less attached to either conventional or delinquent friends than the non-delinquent (Hirschi, 1969:141). Similarly, the more adolescents are attached to parents, the less likely they are to be delinquent, even if the parents are themselves criminal or deviant.

Commitment. Commitment refers to the extent to which individuals have built up an investment in conventionality or a "stake in conformity" (Toby, 1957) that would be jeopardized or lost by engaging in law violation or other forms of deviance. Investment in conventional educational and occupational endeavors builds up this commitment. The greater the commitment, the more one risks losing by non-conformity. The cost of losing one's investment in conformity prevents one from norm violation. Commitment, therefore, refers to a more or less rational element in the decision to commit crime. (See the discussion of rational choice theory in chap. 2.)

Involvement. Involvement refers to one's engrossment in conventional activities, such as studying, spending time with the family, and participation in extracurricular activities. One is restrained from delinquent behavior because one is too busy, too preoccupied, or too consumed in conforming pursuits to become involved in non-conforming pursuits.

Belief. The concept of belief in social bonding theory is defined as the endorsement of general conventional values and norms, especially the belief that laws and society's rules in general are morally correct and should be obeyed. The concept does not necessarily refer to beliefs about specific laws or acts, nor does it mean that people hold deviant beliefs that "require" them to commit crime. In fact, Hirschi argued that, if deviant beliefs are present, then there is nothing to explain. What needs explaining is why people violate rules in which they already believe. Hirschi answered that their belief in the moral validity of norms and laws has been weakened. "...[T]he less a person believes he should obey the rules, the more likely he is to violate them" (Hirschi, 1969:26).

Measures of Social Bonding Concepts. Hirschi (1969) provided clear measures for the four principal elements of the social bond. Most research on this theory has since used Hirschi's or similar measures. A review of them will help us to understand the results of the research on social bonding theory.

An adolescent's attachment to parents is measured by close parental supervision and discipline, good communication and relationships of the adolescent with parents, and his or her affectional identification with parents (e.g., he or she would like to be the same kind of person as the parent). Academic achievement in school (as indicated by grades, test scores, and self-perception of scholastic ability) is taken as indicative of commitment, involvement, and belief, as well as attachment. Attachment to the school is directly measured by positive attitudes toward school, a concern for teachers' opinions of oneself, and an acceptance of the school's authority. Attachment to peers is measured by affectional identification with and respect for the opinions of best friends.

Adolescents' commitment to conventional lines of action refers to their desire and pursuit of conventional goals. Premature engagement in adult activities by adolescents, such as smoking, drinking, or owning a car, indicates a lack of commitment to the achievement of educational goals. Commitment to education is measured both by educational aspirations (e.g., completing more than a high school education) and achievement orientation. Commitment is also measured by occupational aspirations and expectations. Involvement in conventional activities is measured by asking about time spent with family and friends, doing homework, sports, recreation, hobbies, dating, and part-time work.

Belief is measured by reference to values relative to the law and the conventional value system. This includes the extent to which an adolescent has general respect for the police and the law, believes that the law should be obeyed, does not endorse the techniques of neutralization, and endorses values such as the importance of education.

Empirical Validity of Social Bonding Theory

Hirschi's own research generally showed support for the theory. He found that, except for involvement, the weaker the bonds, the higher the probability of delinquency. However, he found delinquency to be most strongly related to association with delinquent friends, a finding not anticipated by the theory. Similarly, later research has found that attachment to peers leads to conformity only when the peers are themselves conventional. Contrary to what Hirschi hypothesized, those who are strongly attached to delinquent friends are themselves more likely to be delinquent (Conger, 1976; Elliott et al., 1985; Junger-Tas, 1992; Warr, 2002), a finding more in line with social learning theory than with social bonding theory. Similarly, deviant youth have relationships with others that are no less intimate and stable than conforming youth (Kandel and Davies, 1991). Jensen and Brownfield (1983) also found evidence contrary to social bonding theory's hypothesis that attachment to parents inhibits delinquency regardless of parental behavior. For example, attachment to drug-free parents controls drug use by adolescents, whereas attachment to drug-using parents does not. Parental deviance provides deviant models and undermines social control in the family (Sampson and Laub, 1993:96). On the other hand, delinquency prediction studies have consistently shown that parental discipline, child-rearing practices, and other family variables affecting the young child, all of which are important in social bonding theory, are among the best predictors of subsequent delinquency (Glueck and Glueck, 1959; McCord and McCord, 1959; Loeber and Stouthamer-Loeber, 1986; Hill, Howell, Hawkins, and Battin-Pearson, 1999).

Krohn and Massey (1980) found that the social bonding variables of beliefs, attachment, and commitment/involvement (which they combined) are moderately related to delinquent behavior but more to minor than serious delinquency (see also McIntosh, Fitch, Wilson, and Nyberg, 1981). Agnew (1991a) found that attachment is not related and that commitment is only weakly related to minor delinquency and that social bonding variables have the expected, but weak, longitudinal effect on delinquency (Agnew, 1991b). Later, he reported findings that bonding variables are moderately related both to general and serious delinquency, but the relationships are mediated by strain and social learning variables (Agnew, 1993). Lasley (1988) found that some forms of adult crime (e.g., white-collar crime) are related to measures of social bonds. Akers and Cochran (1985) found attachment, commitment/involvement, and beliefs to be moderately related to adolescent marijuana use, but the effects of the bonding variables are much weaker than peer association and reinforcement or specific attitudes toward marijuana smoking. Attachment to both parents in an intact home is most preventive of delinquency, whereas children raised in single-parent families, even when they are attached to that parent, run a higher risk of delinquency (Rankin and Kern, 1994). Not only family structure, but parental supervision and other aspects of family relationships are related to delinquency and conformity in ways consistent with social bonding theory (Simons, Simons, Burt, Brody, and Cutrona, 2005). Attachment and commitment to school are negatively related to school misbehavior (Stewart, 2003) and to delinquency for both Black and White youth (Cernkovich and Giordano, 1992). Studies in other countries also report some support for social bonding theory (Junger-Tas, 1992).

Although Hirschi did not include religious beliefs in his original study, they are obviously representative of conventional values. Adherence to religious practices clearly indicates commitment to conventionality, involvement in conventional activities, and attachment to others. Therefore, the research findings reported by Hirschi and Stark (1969) that attachment to religion is unrelated to delinquency could be considered as evidence contrary to Hirschi's own social bonding theory. However, a large body of subsequent research has demonstrated consistently that the more adolescents hold to religious beliefs and practices, the less likely they are to engage in delinquency (see Cochran and Akers, 1989; Evans, Cullen, Dunaway, and Burton, 1995; Welch, Tittle, and Grasmick, 2006).

Baier and Wright (2001) conducted a meta-analysis of 60 studies of the impact of religion on delinquency and crime, including research that measured religiosity by behavioral measures (e.g., church attendance or prayer) and research that used attitudinal measures (e.g., belief in God, belief in Jesus, or importance of religion in one's life). All of the studies found that religious faith and activities were protective against delinquent behavior. The average negative correlation between religion and delinquency in these studies was moderate (–.11), but some were weak (–.05) and others were fairly strong (–.45). Baier and Wright (2001:14) conclude that "religious behavior and beliefs exert a significant, moderate deterrent effect on individuals' criminal behavior."

Similar conclusions are reached by Johnson, Spencer, Larson, and McCullough (2000) from a systematic review of 40 studies of religion and delinquency. All but one of the studies found the expected negative effect of religion on delinquency, and in all but five of the studies, the relationship was statistically significant; that is, the more faith and religious activities, the less delinquency. The more methodologically sound the study was, the more likely it was to have found that religious belief and observance operated as significant protective factors against delinquent involvement. The authors do not relate the findings to any specific theory but conclude that "future research on crime and delinquency may gain explanatory power by incorporating the effects of religious variables in theoretical models" (Johnson et al., 2000:46). However, it is clear that the counter-delinquency effects of religious beliefs and behavior are consistent with social bonding theory (beliefs and involvement in conventional lines of activity), and also with social learning theory (definitions unfavorable to deviance and differential associations with conforming groups).

On the whole, social bonding theory has received some verification from empirical research (see also Hindelang, 1973; Agnew, 1985a; Cernkovich and Giordano, 1992; Rankin and Kern, 1994; Costello and Vowell, 1999; Simons et al., 2004). However, the magnitude of the relationships between social bonding and deviant behavior has ranged from moderate to low. High correlations and levels of explained variance are seldom found in research literature on this theory. Although most of the findings on delinquent behavior and the social bonds that Hirschi found in his original research favor the theory, the relationships are fairly modest and some are in the opposite direction from that expected by the theory. Nevertheless, most social bonding research since then has produced similar supportive findings.

Gottfredson and Hirschi: Self-Control Theory

Low Self-Control as the Cause of Criminal Behavior

Hirschi later moved away from his classic social bonding formulation of control theory and collaborated with Michael Gottfredson (Gottfredson and Hirschi, 1990; Hirschi and Gottfredson, 1994) to propose a theory of crime based on one type of control only—self-control. Gottfredson and Hirschi present self-control theory as a general theory that explains all individual differences in the "propensity" to refrain from or to commit crime, including all acts of crimes and deviance, at all ages, and under all circumstances. Gottfredson and Hirschi began with this observation:

> [I]ndividual differences in the tendency to commit criminal acts ... *remain reasonably stable with change in the social location of individuals and change in their knowledge of the operation of sanction systems.* This is the problem of self-control, the differential tendency of people to avoid criminal acts whatever the circumstances in which they find themselves. Because this difference among people has attracted a wide variety of names, we begin by arguing the merits of the concept of self-control. (Gottfredson and Hirschi, 1990:87; emphasis in original)

The theory states that individuals with high self-control will be "substantially less likely at all periods of life to engage in criminal acts" (Gottfredson and Hirschi, 1990:89), whereas those with low self-control are highly likely to commit crime. Low self-control will lead to criminal behavior when opportunities are available, but it can be counteracted by circumstances and, therefore, does not "require crime." This means that the circumstances have to be right before the lack of self-control will produce crime. Gottfredson and Hirschi do not specify whether these circumstantial factors are external controls that make up for the lack of self-control, stronger positive motivations to commit the crime, or positive motivations to refrain from crime.

The source of low self-control is ineffective or incomplete socialization, especially ineffective child rearing. Parents who are attached to their children, supervise their children closely, recognize the lack of self-control in their children, and punish deviant acts will help to socialize children into self-control. Their children generally will not become delinquent as teenagers or engage in crime as adults. The explicit disapproval of parents or others about whom one cares is the most important negative sanction, and "the causes of low self-control are negative rather than positive" (Gottfredson and Hirschi, 1990:95). School and other social institutions contribute to socialization, but it is the family in which the most important socialization takes place.[2] Consequently, peer groups are relatively unimportant in the development of self-control and "taking up with delinquent peers is ... without causal significance" in the commission of delinquency or crime (Gottfredson and Hirschi, 1990:258). Once formed in childhood, the amount of self-control that a person has acquired remains relatively stable throughout life.

What Is the Relationship Between Self-Control Theory and Social Bonding Theory?

The concept of low self-control is similar to such concepts as vulnerable self-concept and internal controls in social control theories that predated Hirschi's. The concept of self-control is central to these earlier theories of crime and delinquency. However, as has been shown, there is no place for self-control as a separate element in Hirschi's (1969) social bonding version of control theory. Bonding theory rejects the self-control concept as unobservable and subsumes it under the concept of attachment. In contrast, the concept of self-control is absolutely central to Gottfredson and Hirschi's theory. Yet, the four key elements of social bonding theory (belief, attachment, commitment, and involvement) are virtually absent from Gottfredson and Hirschi's theory.

Gottfredson and Hirschi (1990) did not clarify how their self-control theory relates to Hirschi's (1969) social bonding theory and did not refer at all to the earlier control theories of Reckless, Nye, and Reiss. They offer no explanation of the neglect of the earlier theories or why they reversed Hirschi's position that self-control is subsumable under attachment to make self-control the only general control mechanism. Because of Gottfredson and Hirschi's initial and long-term silence on this issue and because social bonding theory contains concepts and propositions regarding "attachment" and "conscience" or "self-control" that are inconsistent with the later concept and claims of self-control theory, some researchers came to view the two as rival theories. "Hirschi's two control theories diverge, then, on a critical point. His second perspective [self-control] argues that *social bonds have no influence on criminal involvement*. Instead, the relationship between social bonds and crime is *spurious*. ... Therefore, attachment and delinquency are related only because both are caused by a third underlying factor—self-control" (Lilly, Cullen, and Ball, 2007:112). Sampson and Laub (1993; Laub and Sampson, 2003) interpreted their findings that enhanced social bonds is the main reason most delinquents discontinue law violations when they become adults as supportive of their "age-related informal social control" and contrary to the predictions of self-control theory. Wright, Caspi, Moffitt, and Silva (1999) pitted social bonding as a "causation" theory against self-control as a "selection" theory of crime. In a longitudinal study of a sample from birth to age 21, they found support for each theory but found greater support for a model incorporating both self-control and social bonding variables. However, measures of the social learning concept of adolescent peer associations used in the study (which Wright et al. confusingly listed as measures of social bonding) turned out to be the strongest predictors of crime at age 21, suggesting that learning processes may be a link between social bonds, self-control, and deviance.[3]

Other researchers proposed that the two theories be combined (Longshore et al., 2004). The authors of self-control theory have subsequently maintained that self-control and social control are one and the same, and as shown later, Hirschi (2004) recently suggested a modification of self-control theory that links it more closely to his earlier social bonding theory (see also Hirschi and Gottfredson, 2006).

Testability of Self-Control Theory

Low self-control not only explains crime but also explains what Gottfredson and Hirschi call "analogous behavior." Analogous behavior includes smoking, drinking, drug use, illicit sex, and even accidents. All are seen by Gottfredson and Hirschi as alternative "manifestations" of low self-control. In testing his original social bonding theory, Hirschi considered smoking and drinking as indicators of a lack of commitment to conventionality by adolescents, one of the elements of social bonding and a *cause* of delinquency, rather than as indicators of behavior *analogous* to delinquency caused by low self-control. Gottfredson and Hirschi stressed that there is great versatility in the types of crime and analogous behavior committed by persons with low self-control. Self-control, according to the theory, accounts for all variations by sex, culture, and circumstances and "explains all crime, at all times, and, for that matter many forms of behavior that are not sanctioned by the state" (Gottfredson and Hirschi, 1990:117), and is "for all intents and purposes, *the* individual-level cause of crime" (Gottfredson and Hirschi, 1990:232; emphasis in original). The theory hypothesizes that low self-control is the cause of the propensity toward criminal behavior. The testability of this explanation is put into question, however, by the fact that Gottfredson and Hirschi do not define self-control separately from this propensity. They use "low self-control" or "high self-control" simply as labels for this differential propensity to commit or refrain from crime. They do not identify operational measures of low self-control as separate from the very tendency to commit crime that low self-control is supposed to explain. Propensity toward crime and low self-control are treated by them as one and the same thing. This renders the theory, in the form stated by Gottfredson and Hirschi, an untestable tautology. The hypothesis is true by definition: Low self-control causes low self-control. To avoid this tautological problem, conceptual definitions or operational measures of self-control must be developed that are separate from measures of criminal behavior or propensity toward crime (Akers, 1991).

Research Indirectly and Directly Testing Self-Control Theory

Some researchers have attempted to take steps toward developing measures of self-control separately from the propensity toward crime. The research assumes low self-control from the commission of certain behavior or assumes low self-control from other indicators. For example, in a study of driving under the influence (DUI) offenses, Keane, Maxim, and Teevan (1993) assumed that offenders who reported drinking alcohol during the week prior to their drunk-driving arrests have low self-control. Not surprisingly, they reported that the drinking of alcohol is related to committing DUI offenses. But this simply relates one measure of alcohol behavior (frequency) with another measure of alcohol behavior (drinking and driving). It tells us nothing about self-control that is not already assumed by the fact of the DUI charge; it not only fails to solve the problem of tautology in the theory, it generates an additional empirical tautology.

Nonetheless, Hirschi and Gottfredson (1993; 1994) later argued that "the best indicators of self-control are *the acts we use self-control to explain:criminal, delinquent, and reckless acts*" (Hirschi and Gottfredson, 1993:49; emphasis added). They contended that the "behavioral" approach used by Keane et al. (i.e., taking the commission of deviant or "analogous" behavior as the measure of low self-control) is better than using measures of risk-taking and other attitudes such as Grasmick and others have used (see the following). And some later researchers have followed Hirschi and Gottfredson's advice. LaGrange and Silverman (1999), for example, used self-reported smoking and drinking by adolescents as one measure of low self-control and then measured other forms of self-reported delinquency as the dependent variable. However, using such behavioral measures of self-control only perpetuates the tautology problem. In the theory, crime, delinquency, and analogous behavior are *all* explained by the same underlying propensity, called low self-control. Therefore, all of these are measures of the dependent variable (criminal propensity) and none can be used as the measure of the independent variable (self-control). If both Y (crime, delinquency) and Z (analogous behavior, recklessness) are hypothesized to be caused by X (low self-control), then measures of neither Y nor Z can be taken as independent indicators of X. *Both* are supposed to be caused by low self-control. Either or both may be used as measures of hypothesized effects; neither may be taken as a measure of the hypothesized cause. To do so tautologically equates criminal propensity and self-control; it assumes the very causal relationship that one is testing. The same tautology problem is encountered when prior delinquent behavior is taken as a measure of self-control as the independent variable and then correlated with current or future delinquent behavior as the dependent variable (see Akers, 1998; Matsueda and Anderson, 1998).

One possibility is to locate behavior that is neither criminal nor analogous but can still somehow be seen as indicating low self-control such as not returning borrowed items or missing important appointments (see Marcus, 2003). However, in at least one instance where such measures of nondeviant "high risk" behavior were used, no relationships to criminal/analogous acts was found, undermining both the versatility hypothesis and the search for non-tautological behavior measures of low self-control (Jones and Quisenberry, 2004). The problem is that the use of *any* behavioral measure of the independent variable, based on the assumption that the behavior being measured is a manifestation of one's underlying low self-control, with *any* other behavioral measure, also assumed to be a manifestation of low self-control, as the dependent variable perpetuates an unavoidable measurement tautology.

Of course, the proposition that both crime and analogous behavior are manifestations of the same low self-control can itself be treated as a hypothesis from the theory that may or may not be empirically supported. This is the approach taken by Paternoster and Brame (1998). They fail to support the hypothesis because their measures of self-control did not account for the correlations between criminal offending and analogous behavior (e.g., smoking, drinking, and gambling).

Others have used different indirect measures of self-control, such as the extent to which there is persistence or change in individual tendencies toward delinquency and the extent to which this can be attributed to stable/changing individual characteristics or to stable/changing life circumstances. This research has produced mixed results (Nagin and Paternoster, 1991a; Nagin and Farrington, 1992a; 1992b; Benson and Moore, 1992; Creechan, 1994). According to the theory, self-control is stable; therefore, persons with low self-control will have a greater, and stable, tendency than persons with high self-control to commit deviance across all social circumstances and at all stages of life after childhood. The empirical evidence, however, shows both stability and change. From analysis of data in a long-term longitudinal study, Robert Sampson and John Laub (1993; Laub and Sampson, 1993) found some continuity from childhood antisocial behavior to adulthood crime, but changes in criminal propensity later in life were explained by changes in the person's family, employment, and social circumstances. Although some individuals involved in adolescent deviance persist in crime in adulthood, most delinquency is "adolescence-limited" rather than "life-course persistent" (Moffitt, 1993). Most antisocial children do not become antisocial adults; most adolescent delinquents do not become adult criminals (Sampson and Laub, 1993). Other researchers report that stability and change in social circumstances, rather than self-control or some other persistent individual characteristic, account for persistence and change in deviant behavior (Warr, 1996; Junger-Tas, 1992):

> Earlier involvement in minor offending (including minor forms of violence) has no significant effect on the subsequent onset of serious violence. This finding, together with earlier findings that used this model to predict involvement in minor delinquency,...does not offer much support for a causal interpretation of early aggression or delinquency leading to later serious violence; rather it suggests that the stability of aggressiveness-violence over the lifespan is due more to a stability in the nature of social relationships and social contextual factors than to some underlying individual predisposition. (Elliott, 1994:16–17)

Predicting delinquency from past delinquency provides neither a satisfying explanation nor a contribution to knowledge on the etiology of crime. Second, and more important, delinquency measures of self-control lack validity. At the present state of criminological knowledge, past delinquency may indicate low self-control, but is just as likely to indicate for example, an aggressive, hostile view of relationships, negative emotionality, or definitions favorable to deviant behavior. (Burt, Simons, and Simons, 2006:379–380)

Hay and Forrest (2006) found great stability of self-control from childhood into adolescence, but also found a small portion of their sample whose self-control underwent change. The central claim of stability of differences in self-control is called into question by other research findings that an individual's self-control and the differences in self-control between individuals sometimes increase and sometimes decline from childhood into adolescence and early adulthood and that offenders at times show higher self-control than non-offenders (Winfree, Taylor, He, and Esbensen, 2006; Turner and Piquero, 2002). Burt et al. (2006) found substantial instability in self-control from one point in time to another among a sample of African American children, with parenting, attachment to teacher, and differential peer associations explaining the changes in self-control

Michael L. Benson and Elizabeth Moore (1992) provided yet another (but still indirect) way of empirically testing self-control theory. They studied offenders charged with white-collar crimes, such as embezzlement and income tax violations, and compared them to offenders charged with "common" property and drug offenses who had been convicted in federal court. Gottfredson and Hirschi (1990) contended that there is no difference between white-collar offenders and other criminal offenders. All criminal offenders commit crimes because of low self-control, commit a wide variety of offenses with little specialization, and have the same propensity to engage in a number of other analogous deviant behaviors. Benson and Moore (1992) found that some white-collar offenders are similar to common crime offenders, but they do not have records of committing other offenses and do not engage in deviant behavior to nearly the extent that other offenders do. In short, contrary to the theory, white-collar offenders clearly differ from other types of offenders both in versatility and deviance proneness. Piquero et al. (1999) also tested the assertion by Gottfredson and Hirschi that offenders are versatile and do not specialize. They found versatility in offending but a tendency for offense specialization to increase with age. As expected by the theory versatility was related to early onset of deviant behavior, but contrary to the theory, the relationship disappeared when age was controlled. Sullivan et al. (2006) found a considerable amount of short-term offense specialization among a group of convicted felons.

Harold Grasmick et al. (1993) provided a more direct test of the theory, using non-tautological cognitive/attitudinal measures designed specifically to tap the different dimensions of self-control identified by Gottfredson and Hirschi (e.g., control of temper and risk-taking). Their research findings offered mixed support for the theory as an explanation of fraud and force. Burton et al. (1994) reported findings on a similar measure of self-control in a study of self-reported crime. They found that self-control (along with having law-violating friends and definitions favorable to crime) was strongly related to both utilitarian and non-utilitarian crimes. Longshore (1998) also used the Grasmick measures in a longitudinal test of the theory among a sample of serious adult offenders who had participated in a drug treatment program. He found that self-control and crime opportunity are related to recidivism in the way predicted by the theory, but they account for only 4% of the variance in repeated property and personal offenses. These findings are in line with other research showing that self-control variables account for 3% to 11% of the variance in criminal behavior.

Research by Vazsonyi, Pickering, Junger, and Hessing (2001), with samples in the United States and three European countries, found that measures of self-control account for 10% to 16% of the variance in various self-reported deviant acts (and an average of 20% of the variance in an overall index of deviance), indicating that self-control theory applies to some extent cross-culturally. Vazsonyi et al. (2001) also reported, in support of the theory, that the various measures of self-control cluster together as a single factor of self-control. Other research, however, has found, contrary to the theory, that the different measures of self-control do not hold together well as a single, unidimensional factor. Individual items such as risk-taking tendencies or impulsivity predict offending better than does the overall scale of self-control (Longshore, Turner, and Stein, 1996). Similar findings have been reported by Cochran et al. (1998) in a study of academic dishonesty among college students, by LaGrange and Silverman (1999) in a study of Canadian high school students, and by Arneklev, Grasmick, and Bursik et al. (1999) in samples of adults in the community and college students. Sellers (1999) found modest support for the theory in a study of intimate violence among university students. However, her finding that persons with high self-control took perceived rewards of violence into account more than those with low self-control contradicts a key proposition of the theory. Hay (2001a) tested that part of self-control theory that hypothesizes that low self-control results from ineffective monitoring, recognition, and punishment of deviant acts of their children by parents. He found weak to moderate relationships of these dimensions of parental control to adolescents' self-control and delinquent behavior. When Hay added other variables, excluded by Gottfredson and Hirschi but suggested by other theories, such as fairness of discipline and parental acceptance, he found that the strength of the relationships between parenting and delinquent behavior doubled.

Pratt and Cullen (2000) conducted a meta-analysis of 21 cross-sectional and longitudinal studies directly testing the relationship between low self-control and crime, some of which used attitudinal and others of which used behavioral measures of self-control. The analysis showed consistent effects in the expected direction, and on average self-control variables explained 19% of the variance in delinquent and criminal behavior. Similar findings come from research directly comparing cognitive with behavioral measures of low self-control in the same sample (Tittle et al., 2003; Tittle and Botchkovar, 2005). "Low self-control must be considered an important predictor of criminal behavior," but studies do not support the argument that self-control is the sole cause of crime or that the "perspective can claim the exalted status of being the general theory of crime" (Pratt and Cullen, 2000:953; see the same conclusion by Hay, 2001). In studies that add definitions favorable to crime and differential peer association in equations with measures of self-control, the amount of explained variance is doubled. Thus, "Gottfredson and Hirschi's claim that the variables from social learning theory should not contribute significantly to the amount of explained variation in crime after self-control has been held constant is unsupported by the data," and their argument that "the peer-delinquency relation was spurious and that no positive learning of antisocial attitudes was necessary for crime to occur" is contradicted by the results of the meta-analysis (Pratt and Cullen, 2000:948, 953). Nonetheless, they conclude that overall the findings provide "fairly impressive empirical support for Gottfredson and Hirschi's theory" (Pratt and Cullen, 2000:951).

Low self-control theory is logically consistent, is parsimonious, and has wide scope. It has generated enormous interest and attention in criminology and may have supplanted social bonding as the principal control theory. Thus far, the tautology issue has not been resolved, but the theory has been tested non-tautologically with Grasmick-type cognitive measures of self-control. Such measures are to be preferred over "behavioral measures" both because measuring "*attitudes* as causes and *behaviors* as effects...leaves no space for tautology" (Stylianou, 2002:537–538; emphasis in original) and because they are more faithful than are measures of overt behavior to Gottfredson and Hirschi's original concept of self-control as an unobserved, covert, internal, cognitive characteristic of individuals. Although some research reports contradict the theory, and the broad claims of being *the* explanation of criminal and deviant behavior cannot be sustained, on balance the empirical evidence supports the theory.

Hirschi's Social Bonding Modifications of Self-Control Theory

Hirschi (2004:543, 545) recently proposed what he called a "slightly revised" version of self-control theory by offering a "new definition of self-control." Hirschi asserted that "social control and self-control are the same thing" (see also Hirschi and Gottfredson, 2006) and stated:

> Redefined, self-control becomes the *tendency to consider the full range of potential costs of a particular act.* This moves the focus from the *long-term* implications of the act to its *broader* and often contemporaneous implications ... [emphasis in original]. ... Put another way, self-control is the set of inhibitions one carries with one wherever one happens to go. Their character may be initially described by going to the *elements of the bond identified by social control theory:* attachment, commitments, involvement, and beliefs. (Hirschi, 2004: 543–544; emphasis added)

As noted earlier, in his social bonding theory, Hirschi (1969) earlier had subsumed self-control under the concept of attachment. Now, this 2004 statement by Hirschi equated all of the elements of the social bond with, and perhaps subsumes them under, a new concept of self-control. Unlike the earlier concept of social bonds that pays little attention to behavioral consequences, the bonds are now seen as describing the true meaning of self-control—the extent to which the individual does or does not take into account all of the "broader" short-term and long-term consequences of the act. The focus on a latent trait characterized by impulsivity, short-term hedonism, and other elements in Gottfredson and Hirschi's (1990) concept of self-control is replaced in Hirschi's new concept of self-control by a focus on the person's consideration of the full range of anticipated costs of behavior.

Hirschi noted that his and Gottfredson's prior reactions to the question of tautology in self-control theory has had a "certain lawyerly quality about it" saying that "'yes' it is tautological, as it should be" and at the same time saying "'no,' it is not tautological." He believed that both answers are legitimate and that "the present effort [redefining self-control] should not be construed as an effort to deal with the tautology issue," (Hirschi, 2004:550). It may not be construed as resolving the tautology problem for the 1990 version of self-control theory or the tautology created by the behavioral measures of self-control in later research discussed earlier. However, if Hirschi's new definition of self-control by reference to the "broader" and "contemporaneous" (primarily negative) consequences of deviant acts is accepted as the proper one instead of the earlier Gottfredson and Hirschi definition, then that removes the conceptual tautology from the theory. Hirschi's new concept of self-control based on his old concept of social bonds renders the theory non-tautological because, unlike the

1990 concept, the new concept does not make self-control synonymous with criminal propensity or criminal behavior. Further, the new measures of self-control suggested by Hirschi, unlike the behavioral measures of self-control previously preferred by Gottfredson and him, are not themselves indicators of the dependent variable converted to measures of the independent variable. Thus, neither Hirschi's revised concept of self-control nor new measures of it (unlike the 1990 concept and behavioral measures of it) would seem to have any problem with tautology.

Unfortunately, the data Hirschi uses to test the reconceptualized theory do not contain any direct measures of the actual or perceived consequences of the acts as specified in the new definition of self-control. Therefore, as indirect measures of the revised concept he uses items originally designed as measures of social bonds (mainly attachment) in his 1969 theory and renames them "self-control responses" and "measures of the social bond/self-control." Piquero and Bouffard (2007) recognized the importance of Hirschi's new concept of self-control and the new focus on identifying and measuring "contemporaneous" behavioral consequences, but they rightly pointed out that he test was limited by using secondary data. They collected original data to directly measure expected consequences of behavior. They found that their respondents' self-reported likelihood of committing a drinking and driving offense and of engaging in sexual coercion were related to their measures of the new concept of self-control (including only inhibiting consequences).

Although he maintains that he is simply moving closer to the true meaning of self-control, Hirschi's new concept of self-control modifies both self-control and social bonding theories. In contrast to Gottfredson and Hirschi (1990), Hirschi's (2004) modified theory, by referring to attachment and other social bonds, goes a long way toward clarifying the link between social bonding theory and the self-control theory. In addition, unlike the original social bonding theory, his new version of self-control theory now explicitly includes differences in consequences of acts (albeit only or mainly negative consequences). This explicit reference to consequences of behavior was not found in the original social bonding theory but is found in the concept of differential reinforcement in social learning theory and moves control and social learning theories to even greater compatibility.

Policy Implications of Control Theories

Social Bonding Elements in the Social Development Model

As noted in chapter 5, many of the policy implications of social bonding theory are similar to those of social learning theory. The best known and most carefully done program predicated explicitly on both bonding and learning principles is the Social Development Model (SDM), implemented by J. David Hawkins, Richard Catalano, and their associates in Seattle in the Social Development Research Group (SDRG; Weis and Hawkins, 1981; Hawkins, Von Cleve, and Catalano, 1991; Hawkins et al., 1992; Hawkins et al., 1999; Brown et al., 2005). The SDM combines strengthening attachment and commitment (social bonding theory) with positive reinforcement, modeling, and learning prosocial attitudes and skills (social learning theory) in the school and family. The project aims to develop strong social bonds with family and school in childhood as preparation for learning prosocial skills, attitudes, and behavior as well as avoiding learning delinquent patterns in later childhood and early adolescence.

In the Seattle Social Development Project (SSDP) applying the SDM, students entering the first grade were randomly assigned to "intervention" or to "control" classrooms in eight Seattle schools. Thereafter, students were added to both groups as they entered grades one through four. By the time the initial cohort of students entered the fifth grade, the program had been expanded to include all fifth grade students in 18 elementary schools. The intervention was meant to enhance opportunities, develop social skills, and provide rewards for good behavior in the classroom and families.

The teachers in the intervention classrooms were trained to use "proactive classroom management" (e.g., reward desirable student behavior and control classroom disruptions), "interactive teaching" (e.g., state explicit learning objectives and model skills to be learned), "cooperative learning" (teams of students), and other innovative techniques to strengthen bonds to school and teach academic and social skills for interacting properly with others. These included interpersonal problem-solving and "refusal" skills to help the children recognize social influences on their behavior, identify consequences of behavior, and involve peers in conforming behavior.

At the same time, parenting skills training was offered on a voluntary basis to parents of students in grades one through three and grades five through six. This training involved parents' learning better to monitor their children's behavior, to teach normative expectations for the children, and to provide consistent discipline in applying positive reinforcement for desired behavior and negative consequences for undesirable behavior. Parents were also encouraged to increase shared family activities, involve their kids in family activities and times together, provide a positive home environment, and cooperate with teachers to develop the children's reading and math skills. From the beginning, the idea has been not only to teach parents who may not be skillful in doing these things but also to offer support for parents who are already doing them.

The program is ongoing and thus far it has been evaluated by comparing the intervention and control groups when they were in the fifth grade (Hawkins et al., 1992) and then again when they reached the age of 18 (Hawkins et al., 1999). Measures were taken of perceived opportunities, social skills, prosocial and antisocial attitudes, attachment and rewarding experiences in the family and school, academic performance, and peer interaction. Misbehavior and disciplinary actions at school, violent and non-violent delinquent activity (self-reported and official), sexual activity, and use of alcohol, tobacco, and other drugs were also measured. Instructional practices of the teachers, family disciplinary practices, and family involvement were also measured as well.

The findings on outcomes in the fifth grade show that the intervention group (20%) was somewhat less likely than the control group (27%) to have initiated alcohol. Also, relatively fewer (45%) students in the intervention group than in the control group (52%) had engaged in some other forms of misconduct or problem behavior. The intervention made the most difference for White boys, somewhat less difference for White and Black girls, and no difference for Black boys. The intervention group scored higher on commitment and attachment to school, but the control group actually did better on standardized academic achievement tests.

By age 18, those in the intervention group did better academically and were more attached to school than the controls. The two groups did not differ in self-reported non-violent delinquency, smoking, drinking, and use of other drugs or in official arrest and court charges. However, there were a number of other areas where the intervention was more successful. There were significant differences between intervention and control groups in self-reported violent delinquency (48.3% vs. 59.7%), heavy drinking (15.4% vs. 25.6%), and sexual activity (72.1% vs. 83%) with multiple partners (49.7% vs. 61.5%).

The SDM, "which integrates empirically supported aspects of social control, social learning, and differential association theories," has also been applied by the SDRG in the Raising Healthy Children (RHC) project (Brown et al., 2005:700). The project identified both "risk" and "protective" factors in childhood and adolescence that could be addressed to prevent substance use. The participants in the project were 959 students beginning in the first and second grades and followed through middle school and the early years of high school in a suburban school district in the Seattle area. The goals of the project were (1) to increase the probability of abstinence and reduce the probability of the onset of use of alcohol, marijuana, and tobacco; and (2) to reduce frequency or prevent escalation of use once it has been initiated among the students during the years when they were passing through Grades 6 through 10.

To accomplish these goals, principles of social learning and bonding were applied in interventions with teachers and their classroom management, with individual students, and with parents of the students. Five schools were randomly assigned to the intervention program and five schools to the control group receiving no intervention.

The teachers in the intervention schools were given training in teaching and classroom management strategies and techniques for developing positive learning, reading, social, and problem-solving skills during the times the students were in the elementary school and in the first year of middle school. Teachers were provided with "coaching sessions" and, beginning in the second year of the project, they were provided with monthly "booster sessions" to maintain their understanding and implementation of the RHC strategies to promote students' academic performance, bonding to school, and prosocial relationships. The approach to intervening with individual students was to make available, on a voluntary basis, after-school opportunities for academic tutoring, studying "clubs, " and other individual and group sessions to "(a) improve academic achievement, (b) increase students' bonding to school, (c) teach refusal skills, and (d) develop pro-social beliefs regarding healthy behaviors"(Brown et al., 2005:701). Interventions with families offered parents the opportunity to participate in after-school workshops on good child-rearing practices, techniques for handling internal family conflicts and problems, and ways of upholding norms supportive of healthy behavior and counteractive to risky misbehavior. These were held at school during the years when their children were in grades one to eight and in-home sessions with their children (guided by RHC staff) in their children's high school years. These interventions by RHC were intended to enhance bonding to school and family and association with prosocial peers while counteracting associations with substance-using peers and attitudes favorable to drug use.

Outcome data on prevalence (use vs. abstinence) and frequency of use of alcohol, marijuana, and tobacco were collected through self-reported questionnaires at school and telephone interviews with those youth not in school. The longitudinal analysis found that the RHC intervention seemed not to affect the youth's decision to remain abstinent or to use any of the substances. However, among the students in the intervention schools, there was significantly lower frequency of use of alcohol and marijuana (but not tobacco) than among those in the non-intervention schools during the middle school to high school years.

Policy Implications of Self-Control Theory

Self-control theory has not yet received this kind of explicit incorporation into a prevention program whose outcome has been evaluated.

However, the interventions of the SSDP and RHC are consistent with what Gottfredson and Hirschi propose as policy implications of their theory. Because the failure to exercise self-control is activated only by immediate gain, programs that are supposed to have an effect on longer term prospects by reducing social or economic inequality, providing better housing, enhancing job skills, and so on will not work. Neither can criminal propensity be changed by punishment, incapacitation, or rehabilitation. Therefore, because self-control is formed through childhood socialization in the family, only policies that take effect early in life and have a positive impact on families have much chance of reducing crime and delinquency:

> The interventions we have in mind would normally be regarded as prevention rather than treatment. They assume that trouble is likely unless something is done to train the child to forgo immediate gratification in the interest of long-term benefits. Such training must come from adults, but these adults need not be trained in one or another of the various academic treatment disciplines. Instead, they need only learn the requirements of early childhood socialization, namely to watch for and recognize signs of low self-control and to punish [this behavior]. (Gottfredson and Hirschi, 1990:269)

But Gottfredson and Hirschi did not spell out how this can be done in the future and did not identify what existing programs meet these requirements. Gibbs (1995) criticized their policy recommendations as unrealistic because "there is no feasible and demonstrably efficacious way to alter child rearing, particularly on a large scale" (Gibbs, 1995:72). However, it would seem that early intervention family programs such as SDM and other projects might have some promise for affecting socialization practices to buttress self-control or for controlling impulsive behavior.

Summary

Control theory takes motivations to commit crime and delinquency for granted and treats conformity as the real problem to be explained. In this sense, it differs from theories that concentrate on the motivations for crime, but the difference is a matter of degree and emphasis rather than irreconcilable and opposing assumptions. Ultimately, all theories of law-violating behavior address the same question of why people commit or refrain from committing crime and delinquency.

Reiss (1951) explained delinquency as resulting from the failure of "personal" and "social" controls. Nye (1958) identified direct and indirect family controls on delinquent behavior. The basic proposition in

Reckless's containment theory is that inner and outer "pushes" and "pulls" toward deviance will produce delinquent behavior, unless they are counteracted by inner and outer containment.

Sykes and Matza (1957) proposed that delinquents reduce the constraints on behavior produced by their initial beliefs in the conventional norms of society by utilizing "techniques of neutralization." Although there are methodological problems, findings are not consistent, and the relations are weak, each of these theories has received some support from empirical research.

Hirschi's (1969) social bonding theory proposes four types of bonding to others: attachment, commitment, involvement, and beliefs that control the individual in the direction of conformity.

Empirical research has produced moderate or weak evidence in favor of social bonding theory. In collaboration with Gottfredson, Hirschi moved away from his earlier social bonding theory to propose a general self-control theory that claims to explain all crimes and deviance under all circumstances. There are still unresolved problems of tautology in this theory and the way its concepts are measured to test it. Hirschi's most recent move to incorporate social bonding concepts into self-control theory may address some of these problems. Overall, the direct and indirect tests of self-control theory support it, albeit with weak to modest relations often reported. The SDM, a large-scale early intervention program that explicitly applies principles of both social bonding and social learning (and also seems consistent with self-control theory), has shown some success in preventing delinquency, substance abuse, and misbehavior.

Notes

1. See chapter 5 on social learning for a discussion of how techniques of neutralization fit into differential association theory and their current status in social learning theory.

2. Harris (1998) argued that although family genetics play a role, family socialization has little long-term influence on one's behavior and personality, whereas peer group socialization is more important. Wright and Beaver (2005) followed Harris and emphasized even more that genetic heritability is more important than both socialization in the family and self-control.

3. For a different way of reconciling social bonding and self-control theory, see Lab (1997). For additional evidence that social bonds and self-control are empirically related, see Polakowski (1994).

Chapter 7

Labeling and Reintegrative Shaming Theory

Introduction

Labeling theory is so named because of its focus on the informal and formal application of stigmatizing, deviant "labels" or tags by society on some of its members. The theory treats such labels as both a dependent variable (effect) and an independent variable (cause). It views labels as the *dependent* variable when it attempts to explain why certain behavior is socially defined as wrong and certain persons are selected for stigmatization and criminalization. It views labels as the *independent* variable when it hypothesizes that discrediting labels cause continuation and escalation of the criminal or delinquent behavior.

The most often quoted statement on labeling theory is Becker's assertion:

> *[S]ocial groups create deviance by making the rules whose infraction constitutes deviance,* and by applying those rules to particular people and labeling them as outsiders. From this point of view, deviance is *not* a quality of the act the person commits, but rather a consequence of the application by others of rules and sanctions to an "offender." The deviant is one to whom that label has successfully been applied; deviant behavior is behavior that people so label. (Becker, 1963:9; emphasis in original)

Thus, labeling theorists contend that the actual deviant behavior of those who are labeled is itself of secondary importance. The important question is, who applies the label to whom and what determines when the deviant labels will be assigned? What produces the stigmatizing label and determines the way in which it is applied, particularly by formal control agents, to different individuals and groups in society? The usual answer to this question that labeling theorists give is that the agents of control, who function on behalf of the powerful in society, impose the labels on the less powerful. The powerful in society decide which behavior will be banned or discredited as deviant or illegal. Moreover, the designation of an individual as criminal or deviant is not directly determined by whether or not he or she has actually violated the law or committed the deviant act. Even for the same law-violating behavior, individuals from less powerful groups are more likely to be officially labeled and punished than those from more powerful groups. Branding persons with stigmatized labels, therefore, results more from who they are than from what they have done.

The theory explains the differential application of official stigmatizing labels, then, as the result of the relative lack of power. Law and the criminal justice system represent the interests of the middle and upper classes and dominant groups in society over those of the lower-class and minority groups. The probability that one will be arrested, convicted, and imprisoned is determined by one's race, sex, age, social class, and other social characteristics that define one's status in society and one's membership in powerful or powerless groups. This is exactly the point that conflict theorists, whom we consider in chapter 9, are trying to make about the criminal justice system.

Labeling as a Process of Symbolic Social Interaction

Labeling theory as an explanation of criminal and deviant behavior is derived from general *symbolic interactionism* theory in sociology. In symbolic interactionism, an individual's identity and self-concept, cognitive processes, values, and attitudes are seen as existing only in the context of society acting, reacting, and changing in social interaction with others (Sandstrom et al., 2003). From the early writings of Charles Horton Cooley (1902) and George Herbert Mead (1934) to such later theorists as Herbert Blumer (1969), symbolic interactionism has emphasized the exchange of meanings communicated in face-to-face interaction through the language, verbal utterances, and gestures and the interplay of this interaction with an individual's self-identity. Thus, this emphasis leans toward "symbolic" dimensions, the meanings of words and actions to the actors in social interactions, rather than the concrete, behavioral, and objective aspects of such interactions.

One major concept in symbolic interactionism is the "looking-glass self" (Cooley, 1902) in which our own self-concepts are reflections of others' conceptions of us. We are or become what we think others think we are. If significant others interact with someone as if he or she were a certain type of person with certain characteristics, then a sort of self-fulfilling prophecy (Merton, 1957) may be set in motion, so that the person comes to take on those same characteristics. What others think we are is communicated in part by applying labels to us; thus, our self-concept and actions can be shaped by such societal labeling. Labeling theory proposes that the labeling in this process of symbolic interaction also applies to criminal and delinquent behavior. The theory treats the application of sanctions and stigmatizing labels, with such names as "criminal," "dope fiend," "crazy person," and "delinquent," as an *independent* variable fostering criminal and deviant behavior.

This aspect of labeling theory in which the application of socially stigmatizing labels is hypothesized to be an independent cause of criminal and delinquent behavior is what most clearly distinguishes it from other theoretical perspectives on crime and deviance. Whereas other theories may recognize that the enforcement of law meant to deter crime sometimes has the unintended consequence of fostering more crime, this notion is central to labeling theory.

The Label as an Independent Variable in Crime and Deviance

The basic symbolic interactionist proposition at the heart of labeling theory is that the formation of the individual's identity is a reflection of others' definition of him or her (Becker, 1963). The theory advances the thesis that individuals who are labeled or dramatically stigmatized (Goffman, 1963) as deviant are likely to take on a deviant self-identity and become more, rather than less, deviant than if they had not been so labeled. The label is attached to someone, informally or formally, in the process of reacting to and trying to prevent deviant behavior. It is intended to deter, not foster, deviance. An ironic, unintended consequence of labeling, therefore, is that the person becomes what the sanctioning process meant to prevent, even if he or she did not set out that way.

Labeling theorists do not see this as only a one-way deterministic process in which identity becomes fixed. Rather, self-concept is formed and reformed in an interactive process by which the individual is self-reflexive, role-playing, and negotiating his or her self-identity. People try to manage how others view them, as well as react to what others communicate to them. Proponents of labeling theory are right to object that the theory is sometimes misinterpreted as a simplistic, one-way causative model in which a deviant label inevitably produces a deviant way of life (see Paternoster and Iovanni, 1989). These objections notwithstanding, there is a clear deterministic element in labeling theory. It is not a distortion of the theory to say that it predicts that the identity a person takes on will be *profoundly* shaped by the way in which others identify and react to him or her. It is perfectly fair to say, therefore, that labeling theory hypothesizes that the person's subsequent deviant behavior is directly and significantly affected by the labeling experience.

We can also reasonably interpret labeling theory as proposing that deviance inducement is particularly likely to occur when those who are doing the labeling are formal agents of society, empowered to enforce its social and legal norms—the police, prosecutors, courts, prisons, and governmental officials. When confronted with a label applied by those with power and authority, the individual has little power to resist or negotiate his or her identification with it. Although there is frequent reference by labeling theorists to the informal, interactive process in deviance labeling, the emphasis remains on the strong effect of being labeled by the criminal justice system, mental health system, or other formal, norm-enforcing bureaucracies.

The earliest statements of latter-day labeling theory were made in the 1930s by Frank Tannenbaum (1938). The first systematic analysis stressing the effects of the social control system on the occurrence and form of deviant behavior and crime was formed by Edwin M. Lemert (1951; 1967). However, it was the publication of Howard S. Becker's book *Outsiders* in 1963 and his edited volume of articles in *The Other Side* in 1964 (as well as his editorship of the journal *Social Problems*) that brought this perspective to prominent attention and placed it at the center of theories of crime and deviance (see Ben-Yehuda et al., 1989).

The importance given to labeling as a cause of continuing deviance is very clear in the statements of labeling theory proponents:

> The first dramatization of the "evil" which separates the child out of his group...plays a greater role in making the criminal than perhaps any other experience....He now lives in a different world. He has been *tagged*....The person *becomes the thing he is described as being.* (Tannenbaum, 1938:21; emphasis added)

> One of the most crucial steps in the process of building a stable pattern of deviant behavior is likely to be the experience of *being caught and publicly labeled as a deviant. Whether a person takes this step or not depends not so much on what he does as on what other people do* ...being caught and branded as a deviant has important consequences for one's further social participation and self-image. (Becker, 1963:31; emphasis added)

> The *societal reaction to the deviant,* then, is vital to an understanding of the deviance itself and *a major element in—if not a cause of—the deviant behavior.* (Schur, 1965:4; emphasis added)

> The most pretentious claim for our point of view is that it opens the way to subsume deviation in a theory of social change. Even more

important, it gives a proper place to *social control* as a *dynamic factor or cause of deviation....* (Lemert, 1967:26; emphasis added)

These statements should not be mistaken to mean that labeling theorists claim that stigmatizing labels inevitably lead an individual to become more deviant. Indeed, Becker went to great lengths to make the point that the outcome was the result of an interaction process that could lead in other directions. Societal reaction to some deviance may actually prevent an individual from engaging in further deviant behavior. Applying a stigmatizing label and sanctions may sometimes have the intended consequence of deterring norm or law violation rather than the unintended consequence of fostering further violations.

Nevertheless, the core position taken in the quotations above from labeling theorists is unmistakable. The theory claims that labeling persons as deviant and applying social sanctions to them in the form of punishment or corrective treatment increases or "amplifies," rather than decreases, deviance (Wilkins, 1964). The central point of the labeling perspective, then, is that the disgrace suffered by people who are labeled as delinquent or criminal more often encourages than discourages future deviant behavior. The stigmatization of deviants puts them at high risk of behaving according to the label, playing out the role of a deviant, and developing deviant self-concepts as irrevocably deviant. In labeling theory, this deviant role and self-concept provide the principal link between the stigmatizing labels and future deviant behavior.

Prior to public labeling, according to labeling theory, deviants' violations of the law are believed to be unorganized, inconsistent, and infrequent. A very important, if not the most crucial, event that leads them toward more stable and frequent patterns of offending in a deviant or criminal "career" is the reaction of the larger society through agents of formal control, as well as the reaction of informal social audiences. For this reason, the labeling perspective is often referred to as the "societal reaction" perspective (Gove, 1980). Without this societal reaction, the deviance would most likely remain sporadic and unorganized. With the societal reaction, the deviance is likely to stabilize into a deviant career.

This commission of continuing deviance in a more coherent, organized fashion is one form of *secondary deviance* created by the societal reaction and by stigmatizing labels. The concept of secondary deviance "refers to a special class of socially defined responses which people make to problems created by the societal reaction to their deviance" (Lemert, 1967:40–41). Thus, secondary deviance is produced when deviants engage in additional deviant behavior, which they would not have otherwise done had they not been labeled as deviants.

The creation of secondary deviance can be caused not only by labeling individuals but by banning whole categories of behavior. For example, a boy labeled as delinquent may take on a more delinquent self-identity, join a delinquent gang, develop secondary deviant patterns to avoid future detection and sanction, become even tougher, and engage in a wider range of delinquent activities. Legally prohibiting gambling, drug use, and prostitution sets up conditions for a criminal black market to supply the demand for these products and services that otherwise would not have existed.

Becker (1973), Schur (1979), and Lemert (1974) later disavowed any intent to propose a theory of criminal and deviant behavior. They argued that this perspective was really meant to offer only "sensitizing" concepts, rather than a specific explanation of deviance or crime as such. Paternoster and Iovanni (1989) contend that critics of labeling theory misunderstand it and that the theory asserts no more than a minimal, highly variable effect of stigmatizing labels on secondary deviance. But, in fact, the theory does claim more than minor effects of the label. From its very beginning, the theory has maintained that persons take on deviant identities and play deviant roles because they are strongly influenced, if not overtly coerced, into doing so by the application of stigmatizing labels to them.[1]

Empirical Evidence on Labeling Theory

Although labeling theory gained widespread acceptance by both academics and practitioners, there were some who were highly critical of labeling theory from the start. The earliest critiques of labeling (Gibbs, 1966; Bordua, 1967; Akers, 1968) objected to the theory's disregard for the actual behavior of the deviant and the image of the deviant being coerced by the labeling process into a deviant identity and role. Even powerless people do not necessarily acquiesce to the application of a deviant label, allowing it to immediately define their self-identities. They fight back, reject, deny, and otherwise negotiate their identities (Rogers and Buffalo, 1974). Moreover, the label does not create the behavior in the first place. Other factors produce the initiation into deviance and can be expected to continue to have a major impact on the continuation of deviance, the maintenance of a deviant self-concept, and the stabilization of a deviant career. People often commit acts that violate the law or social norms for reasons that have nothing to do with labels that others apply to them. Labeling theory essentially ignores the continuing influence of these other variables after the deviant has been apprehended and labeled.

This inattention to other causes of behavior stems from labeling theory's focus on the power of official labelers to single out offenders against whom they invoke the labels and on the relative powerlessness of those being labeled to resist. Labeling theory pays little attention to the actual behavior of the person who is so labeled. The assumption is that what a person has actually done or not done is unimportant, or at least not as important as who the person is, in determining whether or not he or she will be labeled as deviant.

Akers (1968) argued that this assumption is incorrect. The labeling process is not arbitrary and unrelated to the behavior of those detected and labeled. Sometimes, errors are made, labels are falsely applied, and criteria extraneous to the deviant behavior are involved in tagging persons with deviant labels. But society does not identify, tag, and sanction individuals as deviant in a vacuum. The police do not arrest routinely without any probable cause and courts do not stigmatize with the label of criminal until they legally determine that criminal acts have been committed. People are labeled as delinquents, criminals, drug addicts, child molesters, and so on largely on the basis of overt acts they have committed or are believed to have committed. Therefore, the deviant behavior itself is prior to and forms the basis for the stigmatizing label. The behavior creates the label more than the label creates the behavior, and subsequent deviant behavior continues the label more than the label continues the behavior. Bordua (1967) criticized labeling theory for assuming that a deviant person is an "essentially empty organism" and for presenting a picture of "all societal response and no deviant stimulus" (Bordua, 1967:53).

Labeling theory has been criticized for a number of other shortcomings.[2] The most serious shortcoming of all is that it has little empirical validity. According to labeling theory, primary deviance is widespread, sporadic, unstable, and probably not very serious. Only some of those who commit such acts get detected and labeled. Those who do, especially if the labeling is done by official criminal justice agencies, have an increased chance of developing a deviant self-identity or self-concept. This self-concept, in turn, increases the likelihood that the labeled person will commit additional deviant acts and develop a stabilized career of secondary deviance. Conversely, if the detection and labeling can be avoided, then the deviant is not likely to develop a stabilized or serious criminal career. There are few findings from research on the official processing of offenders that fit this model.

This lack of empirical confirmation does not mean that labels and sanctions never have the unintended consequence of making future deviance more probable. It only means that this infrequently happens exclusively because of the label. Among those with the same level of primary deviance, the ones who escape detection and labeling are just as likely as those who are caught to repeat offenses and develop deviant careers. As noted in chapter 2, official sanctions have weak deterrent effect on criminal or deviant behavior. Nonetheless, the probability that offenders will desist is as high as, or higher than, the probability that they will persist in their deviant activities following official labeling. The deviance-enhancing effects of labeling do not occur as frequently as labeling theorists would propose.

This conclusion is supported by studies of the official processing of delinquents and criminals, the hospitalization of mental patients, the labeling of schoolchildren by teachers, the labeling of sexual behavior, and the labeling of other forms of crime and deviance. Although some research does report the deviance-enhancing effects of labels (Farrington, 1977; Hagan and Palloni, 1990), the effects are not strong. The preponderance of research finds no or very weak evidence of labeling effects. The more carefully the research keeps other factors constant, the less likely it is to find evidence that labeling has a significant independent effect on criminal or deviant behavior. The soundest conclusion is that official sanctions by themselves have neither a strong deterrent nor a substantial labeling effect. When prior offenses, personal propensities, social characteristics, and other non-labeling correlates of deviant behavior are held constant, official stigmatizing labels make little difference in either the continuation or cessation of deviant behavior, self-concept, or a deviant career.[3]

Implications of Labeling Theory: Juvenile Diversion Programs

Labeling theory was quickly adopted by sociologists, criminologists, and practitioners. It became almost an unquestioned assumption that the established social control system, rather than offering a solution, was making the crime problem worse. The best control system, then, is one that controls the least. The unintended consequence of a criminal black market for illegal drugs, for instance, was used to argue for repeal of drug control laws and to legalize all currently illicit drugs (Nadelman, 1989). The assumption that formal labeling of offenders motivates them to take on more serious criminal careers supports a policy of avoiding official processing of offenders whenever possible.

The major policy based on these assumptions is the juvenile *diversion* movement, which gained maximum attention in the 1970s in the United States. Diversion programs were first instituted to "divert" apprehended juvenile offenders away from further contact with the formal system. Lowering costs of juvenile justice was often the practical justification given for diversion, but from the beginning it was also justified by explicit reference to labeling theory. Proponents supported the policy on the grounds that diverting people from the system would avoid the stigma and deviance-enhancing effects of official labeling and thereby reduce recidivism. Although a great number of programs continue today, by the end of the 1980s the popularity of diversion waned as deterrence and retribution policies focused on keeping more offenders under custody for longer periods gained ascendancy.

One form of diversion is simply to remove juveniles from jails, detention facilities, and juvenile institutions. Federal legislation in 1974 mandated a nationwide *deinstitutionalization* of juvenile offenders. Not only were youth who were charged with "status offenses" (such as running away from home, truancy, curfew violations, and incorrigibility) removed from custody, laws were changed so that such status offenses were no longer classified as delinquent violations. They were removed entirely from the jurisdiction of the juvenile justice system. Even juveniles charged with felonies could not be held in adult jails, except for a brief time (under 6 hours) in non-secure booking areas or briefly detained out of sight and sound of adult offenders. Commitment to close-custody reform and training schools became less frequent, and the number of juveniles being held in them was drastically reduced (see Holden and Kapler, 1995; Jensen and Rojek, 1998).

From a labeling perspective, diversion from incarceration may occur too late in the process to avoid deviant labels. The major push of diversion advocates, therefore, was for local programs set up to avoid any further "penetration" into the system so that offenders could be diverted away from the juvenile court and institutions as early in the process as possible. Some labeling theorists urged a policy of "judicious non-intervention" (Lemert, 1981) or even "radical non-intervention" (Schur, 1973). Under these policies, it is deemed better for the community to tolerate the behavior of many minor offenders, rather than risk making the youth more serious deviants by formally labeling them.

Short of this strict non-intervention, "pure" diversion would simply get detected or apprehended offenders out of the system as soon as possible and pay no further official attention to them unless they commit new offenses. Very few diversion programs have actually been this pure. Rather, the common practice is to divert appropriate cases away from further processing at the point of police contact, referral to prosecutor, or initial court intake interview to some form of control, treatment, or supervision in the community. That is, rather than having no more attention paid to them, the diverted juveniles are placed on informal probation and required to participate in various programs in the community. In some communities, troublesome youth can be diverted to these programs by referral from other community agencies, schools, or parents even before police apprehension.

Typically the juvenile court retains control and can bring the youth back in for more severe disposition if he or she fails in the diversion program. Very often the diverted youth participate in exactly the same treatment, education, rehabilitation, and other programs in which the court has placed officially adjudicated delinquents as a condition of formal probation (Rojek, 1982; Jensen and Rojek, 1998; Lundman, 1993). So many different policies have been called "diversion" that the term has come to cover "policies as diverse as doing nothing to programs indistinguishable from existing juvenile justice practices" (Jensen and Rojek, 1998:439).

These policies have produced greater procedural justice for juveniles and reduced detained and institutionalized populations of juveniles. They have, by and large, taken status offenders out of the juvenile court system and placed them under the jurisdiction of state or local family services agencies. They have not, however, resulted in the intended behavioral changes in the diverted youth. Most research on diversion programs has found that they have not made much of a difference in reducing recidivism when compared to the usual juvenile justice process. Research in several states reveals that diversion is often effective in reducing the number in detention, but there is not much evidence to demonstrate that diverted youth are less likely to commit new offenses than non-diverted youth (Lundman, 1993; Jensen and Rojek, 1998).

Diversion programs have also had to face the problem of *net-widening*. Net-widening occurs when diversion has the unintended result of placing more, rather than fewer, youth under involuntary control in the community than would have been the case without a diversion policy in place. This occurs when many of the minor juvenile cases that, without a diversion program in place, would have simply been released without further official attention instead are assigned to supervision and remain accountable to the juvenile authorities. They are diverted to something, but not diverted from anything because they are the kind of minor offenders who would not have remained in the traditional juvenile justice system anyway. The community agencies to which diverted youth are referred may develop a vested interest in maintaining a flow of cases to remain in operation. The existence of such programs, then, may encourage more of an interventionist than a hands-off strategy as first envisioned by the diversion philosophy (Rojek, 1982).

Although diversion policies are geared primarily for juvenile delinquents, there are "pre-trial intervention" or "delayed adjudication" programs for first-time, non-violent adult offenders. In these programs, the accused agree to community supervision and certain conditions such as drug treatment, restitution, or payment of supervision costs in lieu of facing trial. Successful completion of the program avoids adjudication of guilt and a criminal record altogether. There has been little scientifically valid evaluation of the effectiveness of these adult programs.

Braithwaite's Reintegrative Shaming Theory

Some proponents of labeling theory dismiss the disconfirming empirical findings, because they believe that the theory has been misstated to such an extent that "the bulk of these studies do not constitute a valid test of labeling theory" (Paternoster and Iovanni, 1989:384). They suggested a less extreme, more complex model that hypothesizes modest labeling effects conditional on other factors. However, when Smith and Paternoster (1990) tested a more complex "deviance-amplification model" of labeling theory on juvenile court cases, they found the relationship between juvenile court appearance and the occurrence of future delinquency results from the fact that it is the juvenile with higher risk of recidivism in the first place who is more likely to be referred to juvenile court and thereby given the delinquency label. Juveniles who avoid the official delinquency label by being diverted from the court are lower-risk youth, those less likely to recidivate anyway. It is not the labeling that has the effect; the labeling is itself a function of the past and probable future behavior of the juveniles. The authors concluded that the "apparent labeling effect of court referral [on future delinquency] can instead be attributed to a selection artifact" (Smith and Paternoster, 1990:1128). The design and results of this study conform to most of the past research on labeling effects. Usually significant labeling effects have not been found.

Some labeling theorists accepted much of the criticism of the theory as valid and recognized that labeling theory needed revision to render it more empirically viable. Some of these revisions abandoned the hypothesis of labeling as deviance-causing and instead reemphasized the need to identify how the labeling process itself takes place (Goode, 1975; Hawkins and Tiedeman, 1975). Others moved toward placing the labeling process in the larger context of power and social conflict (Grimes and Turk, 1978). They view labeling as important only insofar as its effects are contingent on the broader context of social structure. Stigmatizing labels are viewed as an indirect cause of deviant behavior, so that the theoretical task now is to specify the other variables through which labeling has any effect. The most notable of these efforts in criminology is by John Braithwaite (1989).[4]

The key concept in Braithwaite's theory is "reintegrative shaming." Through this concept he set out to answer the question, when is a criminal label likely to have the effect of producing a criminal self-concept and future criminal behavior, and when is it likely to have the opposite effect of preventing crime? Shaming is defined by Braithwaite as social disapproval, which has the "intention or effect of invoking remorse in the person being shamed and/or condemnation by others who become aware of the shaming" (Braithwaite, 1989:100). This would seem at first to be just another term for stigmatization. However, Braithwaite reserves the term *stigmatization* for *disintegrative shaming,* which involves no attempt to reconcile the shamed offender with the community. It is with this type of disintegrative shaming that the effect predicted in past labeling theory is to be expected, namely provoking additional crime.

Reintegrative shaming, on the other hand, is that which is "followed by efforts to reintegrate the offender back into the community of law-abiding or respectable citizens through words or gestures of forgiveness or ceremonies to decertify the offender as deviant" (Braithwaite, 1989:100–101). The social disapproval of shaming works to control crime when it is embedded in relationships that are "overwhelmingly characterized by social approval" (Braithwaite, 1989:68). Thus, applying a criminal label under these conditions will not have a crime-enhancing effect. Reintegrative shaming tends to produce lower crime rates, whereas stigmatization fosters high crime rates, although only in an indirect way. To specify the indirect effects of labeling, Braithwaite drew on other theories, most notably social learning, anomie/strain, and social bonding. For instance, in his model, stigmatization renders participation in criminal groups (differential association) and taking advantage of illegitimate opportunities (strain) more attractive, which then increases the likelihood of repeating criminal behavior. (It should be noted that some of these indirect ways in which deviant labels can affect the stabilization of deviance were recognized by Becker in 1963.)

Braithwaite laid out 13 "facts a theory of crime ought to fit" (e.g., crime is disproportionately committed by young minority males, by unmarried people, by people with low educational aspirations, by those with criminal associates, in large cities, and so on) and maintains that his model fits them all. Thus far, few studies have been reported that claim to test directly the theory's central proposition that reintegrative shaming will reduce, whereas disintegrative shaming will increase, the likelihood of future offending. Makkai and Braithwaite (1994) studied changes in compliance with regulations by nursing homes in Australia. The findings from that test are supportive of the theory, in that the interaction of the inspectors' reintegrative ideology with disapproval of violations had an impact on future compliance by nursing home operators. Hay (2001b) studied the effects of perceived reintegrative shaming used in parental disciplining on self-reported delinquency in a sample of high school students in an American city. He found that reintegrative shaming in parental disciplining made little difference in self-projected likelihood of delinquent behavior. Moreover, he found "... that the low-integration/high-shaming category—what Braithwaite refers to as stigmatization—has a negative rather than a positive coefficient [which] is itself contradictory to RST [reintegrative shaming theory]"

(Hay, 2001b:144). Braithwaite, Ahmed, and Braithwaite (2006) referred to a relatively small but accumulating body of research on reintegrative shaming that provides fairly modest and mixed support for the theory. They reported, for instance, that some research finds evidence of the effects of stigmatization but not the reintegrative effects expected in the theory, whereas other research finds just the opposite.

Reintegrative Shaming, Restorative Justice, and Faith-Based Programs

Applications of Restorative Justice

Braithwaite (1995) argued that reintegrative shaming theory supports policies that facilitate the development of communitarianism at the neighborhood, community, and national levels. The goal is to find ways of shaming that are apt to create genuine remorse in offenders and then reintegrate them into the community. These policies advocated by Braithwaite and his theory of reintegrative shaming are a major impetus for, and remain a central part of, what has come to be called "restorative justice," although the term predates Braithwaite's first book and he did not himself explicitly link it to his theory until later (Van Ness and Strong, 2006; see also Bazemore and Day, 1996; Bazemore and Umbreit, 1998; Schiff, 1998; Bazemore and Schiff, 2001; Braithwaite, 2002; Braithwaite et al., 2006). The movement had its earliest advocates and is firmly embraced in Australia and New Zealand (Braithwaite, 2002), and it has taken hold in the United States and elsewhere around the world (Bazemore and Schiff, 2001; Van Ness and Strong, 2006).

Reintegrative shaming has been a motivating framework for only some restorative justice programs. However, the theory does specifically predict that this kind of intervention will reduce crime regardless of whether those implementing it have any discursive consciousness of the theory of reintegrative shaming. The theoretically relevant features of restorative justice are confrontation of the offender in a respectful way with the consequences of the crime (shaming without degradation), explicit efforts to avert stigmatization, (e.g., opportunities to counter accusations that the offender is a bad person with testimonials from loved ones that she is a good person) and explicit commitment to ritual reintegration (e.g., maximizing opportunities for repair, restoring relationships, apology and forgiveness that are viewed as sincere; Braithwaite et al., 2006:408).

A range of within-institution and community programs for juveniles and adults have been identified as restorative justice. These include programs with offenders performing community service, making direct apologies to victims, accepting responsibility for the harm caused, participating in conflict management/resolution training, joining affinity groups, and making restitution or "reparations" to victims and the community. They also involve victim advocacy, victim–offender mediation (VOM), "reparative probation," victim empathy groups, "peacemaker courts," "sentencing circles," and various forms of "restorative conferencing" such as moderated conferences of family members of victims and offenders (Bazemore and Umbreit, 1998; Schiff, 1998; Bazemore and Schiff, 2001; Braithwaite, 2002; Van Ness and Strong, 2006).

An example of community-based restorative justice is the state-wide Vermont Reparative Probation Program, which has been in place since 1995 and "represents the largest-scale restorative justice initiative in the United States" (Karp and Walther, 2001:214). In the Vermont system, offenders convicted of minor offenses may be sentenced by the judge to 90 days of "reparative probation" in lieu of a jail sentence or regular probation. The offender must appear before a Community Reparative Board composed of volunteers from the community (coordinated by probation officers) at the beginning, middle, and end of the probation period. The victims and their families harmed by the offender are invited to provide any information they want to the board and to be present at the board sessions (which are open to the public). The board meetings are non-adversarial and non-stigmatizing, with active participation by all parties in open-ended discussions and restorative decision-making. The purposes are for the offender to gain a concrete awareness of the harm he has caused in the community, decide on specific ways amends can be made by the offender to the victims and others, and "learn ways to avoid reoffending in the future" (Karp and Walther, 2001:201). The major outcome of these sessions is the negotiation of a "reparative contract" in which the offender agrees to take actions meant to restore the victims and take steps to help his reintegration into the community. Violations of the contract can result in serving the sentence under incarceration:

> Reparative strategies [in the reparative contracts] typically include letters of apology and community service, while reintegrative strategies often involve written statements or short papers by the offender that describe the impact of the crime, appearances before victim-impact panels, or participation in some form of competency development such as GED classes or driver safety courses. Boards often require a drug and alcohol screening in which the offender is assessed by a professional. (Karp and Walther, 2001:201)

Long-standing and recent "faith-based" prison and community programs also implicitly or explicitly reflect principles of restorative justice and reintegrative shaming, and advocates from faith-based backgrounds and organizations have been among the earliest and most persistent major proponents of the restorative justice movement (Van Ness and Strong, 2006). Prisons and correctional facilities in the United States have always provided chaplains and facilities to conduct religious services and provide spiritual guidance to inmates. In addition, religiously based rehabilitation and self-help programs run by inmate groups, local and national prison ministry organizations (such as Prison Fellowship and Justice Fellowship), and other groups have long flourished both inside the institutions and in the community (Johnson, Larson, and Pitts, 1997; Van Ness and Strong, 2006). They provide spiritual counseling, God-centered group sessions, Bible study, worship service, and other ways of helping and reforming prisoners by inculcating and strengthening faith and values of decency, kindness, honesty, responsibility, and consideration toward others. They teach spiritual growth, repentance, seeking forgiveness, and attempting to reconcile with those one has harmed. They also advocate a broader concern for fairness, rehabilitation, and reintegration in the community and help for victims and their families, as well as aiding the families of offenders:

> Prison Fellowship Ministries—the religiously based prison reform group—initiated the "Inner-Change Freedom Initiative" in a minimum-security prison (Jester III) located outside Houston under the auspices of the Texas Department of Correction. Based on a model used to reform and administer prisons in Brazil, this initiative sought to develop a faith-based prison community. The inmate participants had diverse criminal histories [although none had a history of violence or sex offenses] and were required to be within twenty-one to twenty-four months of parole or release from prison.... It is extensively programmed and relies heavily on church-based volunteers to serve as chaplains, lead small groups, mentor inmates, provide educational and artistic tutoring, facilitate family support groups, and coordinate the community service projects. (Cullen, Sundt, and Wozniak, 2001:281–282)

This program involves Biblical education, mentoring, peer group discussion, general education skills, life skills, employment skills, recreation, and short releases from incarceration to perform community service work during the day, evenings, or weekends. After serving 16 to 24 months in prison, the participants are released under parole supervision for 6 to 12 months, with local churches providing aftercare, support, help with employment and housing, continued Bible study, and involvement in church ministries and worship (Eisenberg and Trusty, 2002; see also http://www.ifiprison.org/). Similarly, programs of Bible study, faith-centered activities, spiritual guidance, and family and vocational counseling for ex-convicts through halfway houses and groups in the local community can be found all over the country (e.g., see Time for Freedom in Ocala, Florida at http://www.timeforfreedom .com/):

> All over the world churches and church members are stepping forward to help those coming back from prison toward reintegration. Halfway houses, job training and placement efforts, alcohol and other drug treatment programs, life-skills training, and mentoring are some of the ways churches are getting involved.... This positive association offers hope for reintegration for both victims and offenders.... (Van Ness and Strong, 2006:110)

Although the term *restorative justice* has come into common usage in the criminological literature only fairly recently, much of what is covered by the term has been in existence for a long time and does not represent innovative or radically different alternative policies or practices. Rather, the restorative justice movement attempts to bring together, under a single rubric, historical traditions of reconciliation and customary dispute resolution and a variety of activities such as victim advocacy, conflict resolution, mediation, and community service that have long been incorporated formally into criminal justice policies or practiced informally in the community (Van Ness and Strong, 2006). Although they contended that the movement represents a "new way of thinking" about justice, Bazemore and Schiff (2001:4) recognized that "indeed, some of the practices and agency policies now being called 'restorative justice' will be difficult to distinguish from long-standing offender diversion programs or alternative dispute resolution processes." Braithwaite (2002), in fact, claimed that restorative justice has held sway in traditional societies and throughout most of world history; it appears to be relatively new only because of its resurgence in the latter part of the 20th century after a period of decline in modernized societies. Although restorative justice programs have been heavily concentrated on juvenile offenders and minor offenses, Braithwaite (2002; Braithwaite and Drahos, 2002) persuasively argues that restorative justice applies as well to serious adult crime, organized crime, corporate crime, political crime, and even war crimes.

Theory and Philosophy of Restorative Justice: Reintegration and Rehabilitation

Reintegrative shaming theory remains the primary framework claimed for restorative justice, but many programs make no reference to theory, and the literature also refers to other theoretical concepts, structures, and processes (see Braithwaite, 1997; 2002; Braithwaite et al., 2006). Restorative justice is aimed toward repairing the damage done to victims and the community while providing reintegrative responses by the criminal justice system, victims, and other "stakeholders" in the community. Hopefully, this will provide the right amount of remorse in a context of community acceptance so offenders do not do harm in the future. This is where the theory of reintegrative shaming is most relevant to restorative justice policy, because the theory predicts that reintegrative societal responses will reduce the probability of repeat offenses, whereas disintegrative (stigmatizing) shaming will increase recidivism.

It is with regard to this goal of changing or rehabilitating offenders that other criminological theories also become relevant to restorative justice. Braithwaite (2002) said that reduction of recidivism, but not rehabilitation per se, is an expressed goal of restorative justice, although he believes that rehabilitation will occur as a natural outcome of restorative policies. This can occur through building motivation, mobilizing resources, fostering "responsivity" of offenders, and reinforcing "social cognitive principles that have been shown to be the hallmark of effective rehabilitation programs" (Braithwaite, 2002:97). However, "the role of rehabilitation in offender restoration is seldom discussed by restorative justice proponents" (Levrant, Cullen, Fulton, and Wozniak, 1999:13) and some proponents believe that many rehabilitative programs are not "truly restorative in nature" (Schiff, 1998:9).

Regardless of whether proponents recognize or deny it, Cullen et al. (2001) show that restorative justice programs have the same goal as all offender rehabilitation programs, namely to modify the attitudes, thinking, and behavior of offenders and to lower the chances they will return to crime after completing the program. The mechanisms by which restorative justice may affect values, beliefs, and behavior of offenders reflect the concepts, variables, and processes proposed in other criminological theories beyond reintegrative shaming. For instance, much of what takes place in restorative justice practices, including the faith-based prison programs, are efforts to socialize or re-socialize offenders to inculcate them with traditional, conventional, and religious values that support honesty, integrity, respect for others, kindness, and other moral virtues. If the restorative justice strategies actually induce internalization of these values and attitudes and bring to bear the positive influence of conventional groups in the community, the expectation is that the offender's criminal behavior patterns will be changed in the pro-social direction, thereby promoting restoration and reintegration. These assumptions fit not only reintegrative shaming but also social bonding (strengthening of social bonds through restoration of conventional beliefs), social learning (impact on definitions favorable and unfavorable and group influence), strain (reduction of strain), and other theories. The question is whether restorative justice programs actually induce these changes in offenders.

As is true for all policies and practices (see chap. 1), the restorative justice movement not only reflects theories of criminal and delinquent behavior, it is also grounded on political, religious, and moral philosophy. Restorative justice proponents contend that the morally right response to crime is to hold offenders responsible but work to restore both them and their victims to the community while protecting public safety (Schiff, 1998). It is a "value-based vision" of justice that seeks "to rebuild the capacity of citizens and community groups to mobilize informal social control and socialization processes." It downplays deterrence, incapacitation, retribution, treatment, and formal criminal justice efforts. There is a clear preference for informal, non-adversarial decision-making that holds "lawbreakers accountable for the harm caused . . . in ways that 'make things right' . . . to include victim, offender, and community in developing a plan for repairing this harm." (Bazemore and Schiff, 2001:4–8).

The philosophy of restorative justice is well stated by many, but Braithwaite's (1989; 1997; 2002; Braithwaite and Drahos, 2002; Braithwaite et al., 2006) rendering remains the most articulate and compelling. Braithwaite's philosophy, or as he prefers, "normative theory," is a form of "civic republicanism." The "master political value is republican freedom, or freedom as non-domination, liberty that is assured by legal, social and economic guarantees that those with greater power will have their ability to dominate us checked." But this must be accomplished by "virtuous control" that is exerted through the rule of law with "respect for the person, humility by the controller" (Braithwaite, 1997:89). Braithwaite's (2002) "republican normative theory" asserts limits on the use of punishment, but no limits on mercy, and does not accept retribution and "just deserts" as legitimate goals of criminal justice. Braithwaite rejected moral and cultural relativism by endorsing respect for universal human rights, dignity, good citizenship, political and religious freedom, and other values as expressed in the United Nations' and other declarations of rights and obligations that apply worldwide. These, along with respectful listening, mercy, apology, and forgiveness on the part of everyone, are central components of restorative justice philosophy. Braithwaite (2002) did not reject the judicious use of coercion and punishment in restorative justice because without the threat of force, law violators and those who do not endorse these values will not participate in any meaningful way in restorative processes. Persuasion and reasoning with corporate offenders, for instance, usually produce greater compliance with the law than monetary or jail penalties, but punishment is needed to back up the persuasion. He proposed a "pyramid" of appropriate responses to offenders who violate the law and refuse to reform that graduates from the most respectful, least costly, least coercive to the most coercive and costly sanctions, while avoiding an escalation of coercive enforcement (reminiscent of the "intermediate sanctions" movement of the 1980s and 1990s).

The philosophy and values expressed by Braithwaite and others also undergird the faith-based programs (Van Ness and Strong, 2006). But by definition, such programs add an emphasis on spiritual values, recognizing a just and loving God as the ultimate source of true justice, human rights, love, forgiveness, reconciliation, the inherent value of all persons, and the other positive values that have been claimed by the restorative justice movement. Programs such as the InnerChange Freedom Initiative (IFI) in Texas, described earlier, are "based on the belief that behavior is a reflection of values and worldview. For inmates, it is proposed that rehabilitation depends on a fundamental 'inner change' that reconciles the person with Christ. This sacred relationship then allows the offender to reconcile human relationships and to embark on genuine, long-term behavioral change" (Cullen et al., 2001:281–282). The program "teaches biblical standards of justice, principles of confession, repentance, forgiveness, and reconciliation, and provides offenders with a better understanding of the effects crime has on individual families and communities" (Eisenberg and Trusty, 2002:5). In the Christian faith, the best guidelines for relationships with others and all of the values of justice, reform, forgiveness, and restoration come from accepting a personal relationship with Christ and following His example. In one sense, one could argue that Braithwaite's normative theory is a secularized, political version of religious philosophy found in Judeo-Christian ("do unto others as you would have them do unto you," "love your neighbor as yourself," "treat kindly those who treat you spitefully") and other faith traditions.

In addition, the goals of rehabilitation and personal reform are often more explicit in faith-based programs than in other restorative justice programs (Cullen et al., 2001). It is this kind of fusion of the rehabilitative and restorative ideals that Cullen et al. (2001) believed provides a foundation for building what they call the "virtuous prison" in which "restorative rehabilitation" would be practiced. The virtuous prison (which Cullen et al. recognized would not be appropriate for all inmates) would strive to eliminate idleness, minimize the pains of imprisonment, engage prisoners in restorative activities, and enhance inmate contact with "virtuous people" from the community, "including those religiously-inspired...to mentor inmates, and to visit and socialize with inmates...[because] such volunteers are modeling the very kind of pro-social, virtuous behavior that we wish inmates to learn" (Cullen et al., 2001:279–280):

From our perspective, however, the InnerChange Freedom Initiative is instructive because the features incorporated into its prison community *besides religion* make it quite similar to the virtuous prison we have proposed. Thus, the Texas initiative largely embraces the dual principles of moral restoration and rehabilitation.... The Initiative is unabashed in expressing its desire not to inflict pain on inmates but to create a community of strong social bonds and love. Further it is committed to using an aftercare program to reintegrate offenders, upon their release, into a supportive religious community. (Cullen et al., 2001:282; emphasis in original)

Effectiveness of Restorative Justice Programs

Levrant et al. (1999) pointed to problems with restorative justice programs that may contribute to the "corruption of benevolence," and Braithwaite (2002) recognized that there are certain "worries about restorative justice." Among these actual or potential problems are: restoration for victims is often more symbolic than substantive; "net-widening" could occur similar to what happened with juvenile diversion programs; insufficient attention to due process and protection of legal rights in informal, non-adversarial decision-making; increased number of conditions of probation leading to greater risk of failure; confrontation with offenders in VOM or conferencing circles may increase victims' fears of re-victimization; and the assumption of a supportive and reintegrative community needed for reintegrative shaming may be more utopian than real in industrialized societies. Although one should pay attention to these issues in evaluating restorative justice programs, the key question is the same as for any program: Does restorative justice work? Knowing that a program is successful in achieving other goals of a program is not a trivial matter, but the most important question is, "Are the programs effective in reducing offenders' recidivism?" Reduction of crime and delinquency is a basic goal of and the gold standard by which all crime control, deterrence, prevention, treatment, and rehabilitation programs are judged.

Research so far has produced inconsistent and weak evidence that restorative justice techniques can reduce risks of re-offending, although one recent evaluation found that youthful offenders who successfully completed a restorative justice program (into which they had been diverted from court adjudication) had lower recidivism than offenders in other diversion programs (Rodriguez, 2005). Thus far, most evaluations of restorative justice policies and practices have not stressed crime reduction effects, but have tended to concentrate on evaluating success (with mixed findings) in such outcomes as "satisfaction" by the participants (victims, offenders, and other "stakeholders"), participants' sense of being treated fairly, the program's faithfulness to restorative justice philosophy, victim restoration, compliance by participants with program requirements, and other immediate and in-program processes and outcomes.

Although measures of recidivism are not often prominently featured in evaluations of restorative justice programs, reduction of recidivism is recognized as one of the goals of restorative justice (Schiff, 1998; Bazemore and Schiff, 2001; Braithwaite, 2002). As we have seen, Braithwaite (1989) specifically hypothesized that reintegrative shaming will reduce recidivism, and he believes that restorative justice programs can lessen the tendency to re-offend (Braithwaite, 2002). While reporting that there are few studies showing any restorative justice effects on recidivism, Braithwaite (2002:6) noted that "even badly managed restorative justice programs are most unlikely to make reoffending worse." Levrant et al. (1999:17, 22) argued that too often the assumption that restorative justice will produce reductions in recidivism is "based more on wishful thinking than on systematic understanding of how to change the conduct of offenders" and a clear "weakness of restorative justice is its failure to provide a plausible blueprint for how to control crime" (see also Cullen et al., 2001).

Levrant et al. (1999) recognized that this characterization does not apply to all restorative justice programs. Some of the faith-based programs, in particular, clearly include among their restorative and reintegrative goals of victim-offender and family reconciliation "the critical secular objective of reducing recidivism" (InnerChange Freedom Initiative, 2003:1). Cullen et al.'s (2001) argument for the fusion of restorative justice and rehabilitative ideals is directly linked to recidivism reduction. The religious programs, activities, and ministries are such a historical, integral part of correctional policy that they have been largely taken for granted or overlooked in the criminological literature on prison reform, rehabilitation, treatment, and policy evaluation studies. There is some research, however, which indicates that participation in systematic Bible study and faith-centered group sessions have lowered somewhat both in-prison disciplinary problems and post-prison recidivism after release (Johnson et al., 1997). Follow-up research on the IFI has found that the inmates who had been most active in the faith-based prison program with the highest frequency of participation in Bible study groups were significantly less likely than nonparticipants to be arrested during the first, second, and third years after release from prison. The differences in recidivism diminished thereafter so that by the eighth year following release there was no difference between the two groups in median time to re-arrest and re-imprisonment (Johnson, 2004). There is not yet a sufficient body of evidence to make firm conclusions about the effectiveness of faith-based or other types of restorative programs in modifying offender behavior, reducing recidivism, or achieving stated goals of restoration and reintegration. As Hall (2003:108–109) noted, "A cognitive-behavioral approach seems to be quite compatible with pastoral counseling and education aimed at treating criminal thinking patterns.…[C]ognitive therapy techniques and Christian ideas can be blended to provide an effective healing environment." The expectation is that "effective interventions [that] are rooted in behavioral or cognitive-behavioral models of treatment" will be more effective, and those programs that do not follow sound principles of rehabilitative intervention will "have a dismal success rate" (Levrant et al., 1999:18–19).

We can also predict, from a long history of evaluation research on programs of all kinds, that even the best will have moderate effects.

The Past and Future of Labeling Theory

At the center of labeling theory is the hypothesis that a stigmatizing label by itself, once applied, is very likely to cause further deviance (if it has already occurred) or create the deviance (if the label is falsely applied to someone who has not actually committed deviant acts). Indeed, this hypothesis is unique to labeling theory. Other theories recognize that social control techniques that result in publicly identifying and stigmatizing individuals can have unintended consequences. But it is only labeling theory that gives deviant social labels a central etiological role in the commission of future deviant or criminal behavior and the development of a deviant career.

In the 1960s, labeling theory captured the imagination of social science researchers, theorists, and practitioners alike. Its emphasis on the ironic twists in the self-fulfilling prophecy of deviant labels and its focus on the responsibility of the criminal justice system for the very criminal behavior it professes to deter resonated well within the academic and political climate of the time. The theory continued as a major but far less dominant theory in the 1970s. By the late 1970s, however, labeling theory was in decline and being criticized from several quarters. Many of its proponents moved on to other perspectives. After the mid-1970s, Becker himself essentially gave no further attention to the theory. Indeed, he claimed that he had been only "minimally" involved in the study of deviance and that he had never intended to create a labeling theory at all (see Ben-Yehuda et al., 1989).

There can be little doubt that the negative labeling, which occurs in the process of attempting to sanction and control deviance, does *on occasion* backfire and harden deviant tendencies, making matters worse with more rather than less crime. This kernel of truth has sustained labeling theory. Nevertheless, it is a truth that does little to distinguish labeling. If that is all there is to it, it adds very little to our knowledge. Labeling theory gained wide acceptance, partly because it was believed to have identified deviance enhancement as a frequently occurring outcome of social control efforts, offering a strong radical critique of the established system. But when the empirical research evidence failed to support the theory and its policy implications, it lost its radical luster and its influence waned. It no longer generates the interest, enthusiasm, research, and acceptance it once did as a dominant paradigm in criminology.

Revised labeling models, such as Braithwaite's, that incorporate these informal dimensions and the social characteristics of the community offer greater promise for empirical support than previous labeling theory models. The theory of reintegrative shaming has taken hold in criminology and its impact on public policy in the form of restorative justice will continue in the foreseeable future. Thus far, the theory has been slow to garner significant empirical verification and the policies informed by the theory still await consistent confirmation of effectiveness.

The symbolic interaction assumption that individuals' identities are shaped by social interaction and the reactions of others is a sound and empirically valid concept. Positive and negative labeling in social interaction has effects on self-identity or behavior. Further revisions and modifications that focus more on informal labeling by parents, peers, teachers, and others in the process of symbolic interaction, rather than the power-related formal labels of the criminal justice system, are more likely to receive empirical support. Studies using data from the National Youth Survey (see Elliott et al., 1985) have reported findings consistent with hypotheses about the delinquency-promoting effects of informal labeling by parents and others and, indeed, report some evidence that the label sometimes precedes the onset of primary deviance (Matsueda, 1992; Triplett and Jarjoura, 1994). However, much of the support for these hypotheses comes from the fact that informal labeling modifications incorporate variables from social bonding and social learning theory, such as attachments, attitudes and beliefs, and peer associations. Moreover, modifications such as those by Matsueda (1992) allow for the person's prior deviant behavior to have a significant effect on parents' and others' application of informal labels to the person. But this is contrary to the assumption in traditional labeling theory that the deviant behavior itself is not very important in determining to whom the labels are attached. Indeed, the finding in these studies, that the informal labels applied to youths fairly accurately reflect the actual level of their delinquent involvement, supports assertions by Akers and others that the label is more of a result than a cause of the person's deviant behavior.

Summary

Labeling theory expects differential application of stigmatizing labels to persons based on social characteristics such as class and race and explains the difference as the result of control agents selectively applying labels to the less powerful in society. The theory's basic proposition regarding these labels as independent variables is that those who are labeled as deviant are likely to take on a self-identity as a deviant and become more, rather than less, deviant than if they had not been so labeled. They tend to conform to the label, even if they did not set out that way. The delinquent or criminal identity is a very likely outcome of this labeling; subsequent behavior is caused by the person acting on the basis of the identity and engaging in various forms of secondary deviance.

The principal strength of labeling theory is that it calls attention to the unintended consequences of social control. Its principal weakness is that it essentially ignores primary deviance and seriously underestimates the influence that other variables have on behavior in the first place and continue to have on its future occurrence. The assumption that what a person has actually done or not done is of little importance in determining whether or not he or she will be labeled as deviant is incorrect. The behavior precedes and creates the label more than the label creates the behavior. This is the primary reason why the preponderance of research evidence shows that, when prior offenses, personal propensities, and social characteristics are held constant, official stigmatizing labels make little difference in the development of negative self-concept, a stabilized deviant career, or the continuation or cessation of deviant behavior. Labeling theory no longer generates the interest, enthusiasm, research, and acceptance it once did as a dominant paradigm in criminology and the sociology of deviance.

Efforts to revise labeling theory have viewed stigmatizing labels as only indirectly tied to criminal and deviant behavior and have shifted to focus more on informal labeling processes, rather than criminal justice processing, in producing self-identity and secondary deviance. Labeling is the principal theoretical underpinning for policies of deinstitutionalization and diversion programs. Although some of the goals of the policy have been achieved, there is not much empirical support for the expected reduction in recidivism through juvenile or adult diversion.

The key concept in Braithwaite's theory is "reintegrative shaming," in contrast to stigmatizing shaming. The application of criminal labels in reintegrative shaming tends to produce lower crime rates, whereas stigmatization fosters high crime rates. Restorative justice programs are undergirded to a considerable extent by reintegrative shaming theory, but also rely on other theories and moral philosophies. There is some evidence in support of these programs, but too little direct evaluation research has been done to confirm their effectiveness in reducing recidivism.

Notes

1. See Tannenbaum (1938), Lemert (1951; 1967), Becker (1963), Erikson (1964), Kitsuse (1964), Schur (1965; 1971; 1973; 1984).

2. See Hirschi (1973); Hagan (1973); Taylor, Walton, and Young (1973); Braithwaite (1989); Gibbons (1994); Curran and Renzetti (2001); and Vold et al. (2002).

3. See Mahoney (1974), Tittle (1975), Gove (1980; 1982), Thomas and Bishop (1984), Braithwaite (1989), Smith and Paternoster (1990), and Shoemaker (2004).

4. See also Link et al. (1989), Matsueda (1992), and Triplett and Jarjoura (1994).

Chapter 8

Social Disorganization, Anomie, and Strain Theories

Introduction

Social disorganization and anomie theories have evolved from different theoretical and research traditions, but they have a common theme. Both propose that social order, stability, and integration are conducive to conformity, whereas disorder and malintegration are conducive to crime and deviance. A social system (a society, community, or subsystem within a society) is described as socially organized and integrated if there is an internal consensus on its norms and values, a strong cohesion exists among its members, and social interaction proceeds in an orderly way. Conversely, the system is described as disorganized or anomic if there is a disruption in its social cohesion or integration, a breakdown in social control, or malalignment among its elements.

Both theories propose that the less there exists solidarity, cohesion, or integration within a group, community, or society, the higher will be the rate of crime and deviance. Each attempts to explain high rates of crime and delinquency in disadvantaged lower class and ethnic groups. At one time or another, both theories have focused specifically on delinquent or criminal gangs and subcultures.

Social Disorganization and the Urban Ecology of Crime and Delinquency

Social disorganization theory was first developed in the studies of urban crime and delinquency by sociologists at the University of Chicago and the Institute for Juvenile Research in Chicago in the 1920s and 1930s (Shaw and McKay, 1942; 1969). The Chicago studies plotted out the residential location of those youths who had been referred to juvenile court from different areas of the city. These studies showed that the distribution of delinquents around the city fits a systematic pattern. The rates of delinquency in the lower class neighborhoods were highest near the inner city and decreased outwardly toward the more affluent areas. The inner city neighborhoods maintained high rates of delinquency over decades, although the racial and ethnic makeup of the population in those areas underwent substantial change. The same pattern of declining rates of delinquency as the distance from the inner city neighborhood increased was found within each racial or ethnic group (Shaw and McKay, 1942; 1969).

These findings were explained by reference to a theory of urban ecology that viewed the city as analogous to the natural ecological communities of plants and animals (Park, Burgess, and McKenzie, 1928). The residential, commercial, and industrial pattern of urban settlement was described as developing an ecological pattern of concentric zones that spread from the center toward the outermost edge of the city. Directly adjacent to the commercial and business core of the city was a "zone in transition," which was changing from residential to commercial. It was in this area that the highest rates of delinquency were found.

This transition zone was characterized by physical decay, poor housing, incomplete and broken families, high rates of illegitimate births, and an unstable, heterogeneous population. The residents were at the bottom end of the socioeconomic scale, with low income, education, and occupations. In addition to high rates of delinquency, this area had high official rates of adult crime, drug addiction, alcoholism, prostitution, and mental illness. All these forms of deviance and lawlessness were interpreted as the outcome of social disorganization within this urban area. The Chicago sociologists emphasized that residents in this area were not biologically or psychologically abnormal. Rather, their crime and deviance were simply the normal responses of normal people to abnormal social conditions. Under these conditions, criminal and delinquent traditions developed and were culturally transmitted from one generation to the next. Industrialization, urbanization, and other social changes in modern society were seen by the Chicago sociologists as causing social disorganization by undermining social control exercised through traditional social order and values. This notion of social disorganization as the breakdown of social control at the local or neighborhood level has remained at the center of the theory through all subsequent restatements and revisions.

Restatements and Research on Social Disorganization

Since the pioneering studies of Shaw and McKay, a great deal of research has been done on the ecology of urban crime and delinquency.

Studies and research data on urban crime remain an important part of criminological research. Although some studies have been patterned closely after the social disorganization approach of the early Chicago studies, others only indirectly relate to it.[1] A trend in the migration of both White and Black middle class residents, as well as industry and business, out of the large cities into suburban communities has resulted in even more deprivation, decay, and other conditions of social disorganization within the urban centers. This trend has left a population of the "truly disadvantaged" (Wilson, 1987) or an "under class" with high rates of unemployment, welfare support, illegitimate births, single-parent families, drug use and abuse, and violence. Research continues to find that arrests, convictions, incarcerations, and other measures of official rates of crime and delinquency are alarmingly high among the residents in these neighborhoods.

However, to what degree crime in inner city areas is the result of social disorganization remains uncertain. It is difficult to judge whether the original Chicago research and subsequent research has verified social disorganization as an explanation of crime. Often the research does not carefully measure social disorganization. The very fact that crime and deviance are high within an area is itself sometimes used, tautologically, as an empirical indicator that the area is socially disorganized (see Bursik's 1988 review of this issue). Furthermore, even in those areas characterized as the most disorganized, only a minority of youths and even smaller minority of adults are involved in crime. There is also the question of how much concentration of official crime rates in these areas results from higher rates of criminal behavior among its residents or from race and class disparities in police practices (Warner and Pierce, 1993).

Moreover, exactly what physical, economic, population, or family conditions constitute social disorganization? Is it true that physical, economic, and population characteristics are objective indicators of disorganization, or does the term simply reflect a value judgment about lower class lifestyle and living conditions? By the 1940s, the term "differential social organization" (Sutherland, 1947) had been introduced to emphasize that these urban neighborhoods may not be so much *dis*organized as simply *organized* around different values and concerns. Edwin Sutherland's (1947) education and part of his academic career were at the University of Chicago, and he acknowledged the influence of the Chicago sociologists (Sutherland, 1973). His theory of "differential association" complements differential social organization by explaining crime as behavior learned through an exposure to different conforming and criminal patterns (see chap. 5 on social learning theory).

Social disorganization has received renewed theoretical attention through the work of Robert Bursik, Robert Sampson, and others who have reanalyzed the theory, related it to current theories, and addressed some of the criticisms of this theory (Sampson, 1995). Bursik (1988; Bursik and Grasmick, 1993) pointed out that Shaw and McKay were not trying to propose that urban ecology, economic conditions of urban neighborhoods, and rapid social changes are the direct causes of crime and delinquency. Rather, he argued, they were proposing that social disorganization undermines or hinders informal social controls within the community and neighborhood, thus allowing high rates of crime to occur. Therefore, the absence or breakdown of social control is a key component behind the concept of social disorganization that, Bursik contended, ties it to modern social control theory (see chap. 6). Bursik also links the assumptions of the ecological distribution of crime opportunities in routine activities theory (see chap. 2) to the social disorganization approach. Sampson and Groves (1989) pointed to the same problem identified by Bursik: Social disorganization theory does not propose that such factors as social class and the racial composition of a community are direct causes of crime and delinquency. Yet, these are the variables that have been used to measure social disorganization, rather than measuring the components of social disorganization itself. Therefore, Sampson and Groves (1989:775) concluded that, "while past researchers have examined Shaw and McKay's prediction concerning community change and extra-local influence on delinquency, no one has directly tested their theory of social disorganization."

Sampson and Groves (1989) proffered an empirical model of social disorganization that remedied this problem. Their model contains the usual measures of "external" factors affecting social disorganization, such as social class, residential mobility, and family disruption, but then goes beyond these variables to include the measures of three key components of the concept of social disorganization, namely little community supervision of teenage gangs, informal friendship networks, and participation in formal organizations. Their data from British communities supported this model. They found that most of the external factors were related to social disorganization, as predicted. The links in the model were completed by showing that the measures of social disorganization were good predictors of rates of crime victimization. Although not very adequately, the model also explained the rates of criminal offenses.

Most of the research since then has not followed the example set by Sampson and Groves of measuring social disorganization directly. Warner and Pierce (1993), for instance, reported strong relationships between rates of telephone calls to police (by victims of assaults, robbery, and burglary) and neighborhood poverty, racial heterogeneity, residential instability, family disruption, and high density of housing units as measures of social disorganization. Gottfredson, McNeil, and Gottfredson (1991) tested social disorganization theory by correlating census-block level data on disrupted families, poverty, unemployment, income, and education with individual-level self-reports of interpersonal aggression, theft and vandalism, and drug use. The independent variables accounted for individuals' delinquency, but the relationships were not strong and varied by type of delinquency and gender. Moreover, the adolescents' social bonds and peer associations mediated the effects of social disorganization on delinquency.

Silver (2000) acknowledged the points made by Sampson and Groves and by Bursik about the need to measure social disorganization directly if the theory is to be properly tested. Nevertheless, because direct measures cannot be found in census data, he continues to use indirect indicators of neighborhood disorganization such as disadvantage (e.g., poverty and unemployment) and mobility (e.g., average length of residence). In a study in Chicago, he found that these neighborhood level measures do have an effect on violence among former patients released from a psychiatric institute, but not as much as individual level variables such as impulsivity and prior history of violence. Similarly, Wikstrom and Loeber (2000) found that delinquent involvement begun in the latter teenage years, but not early onset delinquency, is related to neighborhood disadvantage and instability. Those adolescents at high risk (because of poor parental supervision, differential peer association, delinquent attitudes, and impulsivity) were more likely to be delinquent regardless of neighborhood context. Jang and Johnson (2001) do try to measure social disorganization directly with perceptions of neighborhood disorder and test its relationship to adolescent substance use. Their research did find a significant relationship but also found that the individual's religiosity acts as a protective factor for youth in neighborhoods perceived as disordered. However, substance use was more strongly affected by social bonding variables and most strongly by social learning variables. Having substance-using peers and adhering to pro-use attitudes mediated much of the neighborhood effects and virtually all of the buffering effects of religiosity.

These findings echo those of the earlier research by Gottfredson et al. (1991) and lend support to the theoretical proposition of Bursik (1988; Bursik and Grasmick, 1993), Sampson (Sampson and Groves, 1989), and others that social disorganization has an effect on crime and deviance because it affects informal social control in the community. Also, given the measures of informal social control used in these studies, one is led to the conclusion that what the researchers call informal social control affected by social disorganization operates through variables and processes referred to in theories of social learning (peer associations and attitudes), social bonding (family supervision and religiosity), and self-control (impulsivity).

Sampson more recently has proposed *collective efficacy* as the key "underlying social mechanism" in social organization/disorganization (Sampson, 2006) that accounts for higher or lower levels of crime in a community or neighborhood. He makes reference to the concept of "self-efficacy," which refers to self-appraisal of one's ability to accomplish a task, cope with a problem, or achieve a goal (Bandura, 1977b) and defines collective efficacy as the perceived ability of neighborhood residents to activate informal social control. There are two interrelated dimensions of collective efficacy; one is defined as social cohesion and mutual support and the other is defined "shared expectations for social control." Sampson maintains that social organization in urban areas in the form of collective efficacy may be built on social networks of "dense" ties, but actually is likely to be built on "weak" ties. High levels of collective efficacy are indicated by high likelihood that the residents will take action to exercise informal social control or invoke formal control (e.g., call the police) when confronted with acts of deviance or crime in the neighborhood. The prediction is that the higher the collective efficacy, the lower the crime rate.

Sampson and colleagues have conducted research to test a theoretical model in which structural characteristics of the community (concentrated poverty, residential mobility, density of social ties, family disruption) undermine collective efficacy that, in turn, allows for a higher level of violence. They measure collective efficacy by asking a sample of residents in urban neighborhoods how likely it is that "neighbors could be counted on to take action" in different hypothetical scenarios such as observing kids skipping school and hanging out on the corner, a fight taking place in front of their own house, youngsters acting disrespectfully to an adult, and spraying graffiti on a building in the neighborhood. The findings that lower collective efficacy is related to both the official homicide rate and levels of self-reported violence are consistent with the model. However, Warner (2007) found that social ties increased the likelihood of collective efficacy as indicated by willingness of residents to directly intervene in neighborhood trouble but not to collective efficacy as indicated by the readiness of residents to call in the police or other authorities.

Classic Anomie/Strain Theories

Merton's Theory of Social Structure and Anomie

Anomie/strain theories[2] provide an explanation of the concentration of crime not only in the lower class urban areas but also in lower class and minority groups in general, as well as the overall high crime rate in American society. This theory leans heavily on the work of Emile Durkheim, one of the founders of sociology. Durkheim (1897/1951) used the term *anomie* to refer to a state of normlessness or lack of social regulation in modern society as one condition that promotes higher rates of suicide. Robert Merton (1938; 1957) applied this Durkheimian approach to the condition of modern industrial societies, especially in the United States. To Merton, an integrated society maintains a balance between social structure (approved social means) and culture (approved goals). Anomie is the form that societal malintegration takes when there is a dissociation between valued cultural ends and legitimate societal means to those ends.

Merton argued that American society evinces this means-ends disjuncture in two basic ways. First, the strong cultural emphasis on success goals in America is not matched by an equally strong emphasis on socially approved means. Everyone, including the poorest and most deprived members of the lower class, is socialized to aspire toward high achievement and success. Competitiveness and success are glorified by public authorities, taught in the schools, glamorized in the media, and encouraged by the values that are passed along from generation to generation. Worth is judged by material and monetary success. The American Dream means that anyone can make it big.

Of course, this success is supposed to be achieved by an honest effort in legitimate educational, occupational, and economic endeavors. Societal norms regulate the approved ways of attaining this success, distinguishing them from illegitimate avenues to the same goal. However, Merton perceived American values to be more concerned with acquiring success, getting ahead, and getting the money at any cost, than with the right and proper way to do so. Although other industrial societies may have the same problem, American society is especially prone to stress achievement of the ends over utilization of approved means. When success goals are over-emphasized, the norms governing their achievement become weakened, producing what Durkheim conceived of as anomie.

Americans, then, are more likely than members of more integrated societies to do whatever it takes to achieve success, even if it means breaking the law, in part because legitimate efforts to succeed are not as highly valued in American culture. Hence, we have higher crime rates than other societies.

Second, there is a discrepancy between means and ends perpetuated by the class system in America and, to a lesser degree, other industrialized societies. The success ethic permeates all levels of the class structure and is embodied in the educational system to which persons of all social classes are exposed. The American dream promotes the ideal that equal opportunity for success is available to all. In reality, however, disadvantaged minority groups and the lower class do not have equal access to such legitimate opportunities. They are socialized to hold high aspirations, yet they are relatively blocked off from the conventional educational and occupational opportunities needed to realize those ambitions. This anomic condition produces *strain* or pressure on these groups to take advantage of whatever effective means to income and success they can find, even if these means are illegitimate or illegal.

Although Merton (1938) presented his discussion of the forces that create anomie in American society at the macro-structural level, he also proposed that individual behavior is affected by the culture and social structure. He identified five "logically possible, alternative modes of adjustment or adaptation *by individuals*" to the societal condition of anomie (Merton 1938:676; emphasis in original).

The first, "conformity," is the most common response: One simply accepts the state of affairs and continues to strive for success within the restricted conventional means available. The second type of adaptation, "innovation," is the most common deviant response: One maintains commitment to success goals but takes advantage of illegitimate means to attain them. Most crime and delinquency, especially income-producing offenses, would fit into this adaptive mode. Another deviant mode, "rebellion," rejects the system altogether, both means and ends, and replaces it with a new one, such as a violent overthrow of the system. Yet another, "retreatism," refers to an escapist response: One becomes a societal dropout, giving up on both the goals and the effort to achieve them. Merton placed alcoholics, drug addicts, vagrants, and the severely mentally ill in this mode. Finally, there is "ritualism" in which one gives up the struggle to get ahead and concentrates on retaining what little has been gained by adhering rigidly and zealously to the norms.

Innovation is the most frequently adapted non-conformist mode among members of the lower class. The high rate of crime in the lower class, therefore, is explained by its location in a society that subjects it to high levels of anomie-induced strain. This strain is produced by the disjuncture between society's dream of equality and success for all and the actual inequality in the distribution of opportunities to realize that dream. This inequity is most severe for members of the lower class, the disadvantaged, and minority groups. Relatively deprived of legitimate means, while still imbued with the American dream, they respond by resorting to illegitimate means.

Merton's theory was almost immediately embraced as a quintessential sociological theory of crime. Early social disorganization theorists such as Shaw and McKay (1942) quickly adopted the basic anomie concept of the disparity between success goals and access to legitimate means:

[C]hildren and young people in all areas, both rich and poor, are exposed to the luxury values and success patterns of our culture.... Among children and young people residing in low-income areas, interests in acquiring material goods and enhancing personal status are developed which are often difficult to realize by legitimate means because of limited access to the necessary facilities and opportunities. (Shaw and McKay, 1942, reprinted in Williams and McShane, 1998:66)

By the 1950s, Merton's theory was widely accepted and applied in modified form specifically to subcultural delinquency.

Cohen: Status Deprivation and the Delinquent Subculture

Albert K. Cohen (1955) followed Merton by emphasizing the structural sources of strain that lead to deviant adaptations by the lower class. But Cohen applied it specifically to the delinquent subculture found among lower class adolescent males. He recognized that the delinquent subculture has an effect on and plays a role in influencing individual lower class boys to become involved in delinquent behavior. But he denied any interest in the explanation of variations in individual behavior or why the delinquent subculture was maintained over a period of time. Instead, he wanted to explain why it existed in the first place.

Cohen's version of anomie/strain theory is in basic agreement with Merton's theory, because both perceive blocked goals as producing deviance-inducing strain. However, rather than the inability to gain material success, in Cohen's view, it is the inability to gain status and acceptance in conventional society that produces the strain. Status in conventional society is achieved by meeting society's standards of dress, behavior, scholastic abilities, and so on. The most pervasive of these standards, according to Cohen, are those of the middle class. Adolescents are most likely to be confronted by the middle class criteria of respectability and acceptance in the public schools. Middle class expectations are imposed by teachers and administrators on students from all class backgrounds. Such standards as good manners, appropriate demeanor, non-aggressive attitudes and behavior, attention to grades, studying, and active participation in school activities are among the ways that students gain status and approval.

Middle class adolescents, supported by middle class parents, are best able to meet these standards. They achieve recognition and gain status by measuring up to these standards, not only in the eyes of adults but to a large extent in the eyes of their peers. However, lower class youths, especially boys, cannot always meet these standards. They do not have the verbal and social skills to measure up to the yardstick of middle class values. As a result, their "status deprivation" produces "status frustration."

According to Cohen, the delinquent subculture is a collective response to this frustration, and the nature of its delinquent activities results from a "reaction formation." The criteria for acceptability found in this subculture can be met by lower class boys, who gain status in delinquent gangs by adhering to "malicious" and "negativistic" values in opposition to conventional standards. If non-aggression is acceptable in the middle class, then a reputation for aggressive toughness is the way to gain status in the delinquent subculture. If polite classroom behavior and making good grades will gain greater standing in the eyes of the teachers, then classroom disruption and disdain for academic achievement will gain greater standing in the delinquent subculture.

Cohen argued that Merton's image of deviants turning to illegitimate means because of the deprivation of legitimate means is too rationalistic to apply to the "non-utilitarian" delinquent subculture. For example, most of the property offenses committed by delinquent youths are really not intended to produce income or gain material success by illegal means. Rather, they are non-utilitarian responses to status frustration that also meet with the approval of delinquent peers.

Cloward and Ohlin: Differential Opportunity and Delinquent Subcultures

Shortly after Cohen's theory was published, Richard Cloward and Lloyd Ohlin (1960; Cloward, 1959) proposed a "differential opportunity" theory of delinquency. Their theory drew from the anomie theory of Merton and Cohen's subcultural theory on the one hand, and from Shaw and McKay's social disorganization and Sutherland's differential association theories on the other. Although the general propositions of their theory have subsequently been applied to a whole range of delinquent and criminal behavior, Cloward and Ohlin developed it specifically to account for types of, and participation in, delinquent subcultures.

In Cloward and Ohlin's view, Merton's anomie/strain theory incorrectly assumed that lower class persons, who are denied access to legitimate opportunities, automatically have access to illegitimate opportunities. They interpreted Sutherland, as well as Shaw and McKay, as focusing on the cultural transmission of delinquent values in lower class urban areas and implicitly demonstrating the importance of the availability of illegitimate opportunities. Their theory combines anomie, differential association, and social disorganization by proposing that deviant adaptations are explained by location in both the legitimate and illegitimate opportunity structures.

Motivation and the aspiration to succeed by themselves do not account for either conforming or deviant behavior, argue Cloward and Ohlin. The individual must be in deviant or conforming "learning environments" that allow one to learn and perform the requisite skills and abilities. Just because legitimate opportunities are blocked does not necessarily mean that illegitimate opportunities are freely available. Some illegitimate roles may be available, whereas others may not be at all. Just as there is unequal access to role models and opportunities to fulfill conforming roles, there is unequal access to illegitimate roles and opportunities.

Among adolescent boys, it is clear that deprivation of legitimate means produces a strain toward delinquent activities, but what kind of delinquent patterns they will become involved in depends on what illegitimate opportunities are available to them in their community. Boys from racial and ethnic minorities, especially those in the lower class neighborhoods of large urban centers, are most likely to be deprived of legitimate educational and occupational opportunities. Therefore, high rates of delinquency are to be expected among them. But the kind of subculture or gang delinquency they adopt depends on the nature of the illegitimate opportunities available to them. These opportunities are determined by the social organization of the neighborhoods or the areas of the city where they are raised.

Whereas Cohen posited a single delinquent subculture, Cloward and Ohlin saw several subcultures. Although they recognized that delinquent gangs carry on a variety of illegal activities, they argued that these gangs develop more or less specialized delinquent subcultures, depending on the illegitimate opportunities in their neighborhoods.

The first major type of specialized delinquent subculture, "criminal," is characterized by youth gangs organized primarily to commit income-producing offenses, such as theft, extortion, and fraud. Theirs is a more or less utilitarian choice of illegal means that corresponds with Merton's innovation adaptation. Such gangs are found in lower class ethnic neighborhoods organized around stable adult criminal patterns and values. Organized and successful criminals reside or operate openly in these neighborhoods, providing criminal role models and opportunities as alternatives to legitimate ones.

The second major type of delinquent subculture, "conflict," is expressed in fighting gangs. Status in these groups is gained by being tough, violent, and able to fight. They are found in the socially disorganized lower class neighborhoods with very few illegal opportunities to replace the legal opportunities that are denied them. There are few successful or emulated adult role models, either conventional or deviant. Youths become alienated from the adult world and view most of the adults they encounter as "weak." They are unable to develop the skills, either legitimate or illegal, to achieve economic success and see no way to gain conventional or criminal status. In frustration they turn to gangs in which the only status to be gained is by fearlessness and violence.

The third major type of delinquent subculture, "retreatist," is primarily focused on the consumption of drugs and alcohol. Retreatist gang members have given up on both goals and means, whether conventional or illegal. Cloward and Ohlin did not specify the type of neighborhood in which retreatist gangs are found, but they described their members as "double failures." Double failures not only perform poorly in school and have little or no occupational prospects, they are neither good crooks nor good fighters. They escape into a different world in which the only goal is the "kick" and being "cool." Whereas most sustain themselves by one type or another of a non-violent "hustle," status and admiration can be gained only within the gang by getting high and maintaining a drug habit.

Miller: Focal Concerns of Lower Class Culture

Walter B. Miller (1958a), following Cohen and Cloward and Ohlin, concentrated on the delinquency of lower class male gangs (or, in Miller's terms, "street corner groups") in economically deprived neighborhoods. He also agreed with anomie/strain theorists that the commission of delinquent behavior is motivated by the attempt to gain desired ends. But rather than positing a distinct delinquent subculture(s) adapted to the availability of legitimate or illegitimate opportunities, Miller proposed that delinquent behavior is a youthful adaptation to a distinct lower class culture. Delinquency is one way of achieving or gaining acceptance according to the expectations of this lower class culture. Lower class youth learn and act according to the central values or "focal concerns" of lower class adults, but the delinquent adolescents express and carry out these values in an exaggerated way. These values are: *trouble* (revolving around getting away with law violations), *toughness* (showing physical power and fearlessness), *smartness* (ability to con or dupe others), *excitement* (seeking thrills, risk-taking, danger), *fatalism* (being lucky or unlucky), and *autonomy* (freedom from authority, independence). By demonstrating toughness, smartness, autonomy, and the other characteristics implied in the focal concerns, lower class males achieve status and belonging in the street corner groups. These qualities can be demonstrated and the valued ends achieved by fighting and other forms of illegal and deviant behavior.[3]

Research on Classic Anomie/Strain Theories

Because Merton's theory of social structure and anomie offers explanations of both macro- and micro-level processes, empirical studies conducted on his theory and the theories of Cohen and Cloward and Ohlin have utilized both individuals and larger groups as units of analysis. The extant research on these classic anomie/strain theories has addressed a number of different questions.

Are Crime and Delinquency Concentrated in the Lower Class and Minority Groups?

In both theory and practice, anomie/strain theories emphasize the predominance of crime and delinquency among the lower class and minority populations, the most deprived of legitimate opportunities. All varieties of this theory discussed so far have predicted an inverse relationship between social class and law breaking, and by extension of the assumptions and logic of anomie, one is also led to expect higher rates of crime and delinquency in disadvantaged minority groups.

As we have already seen, early urban research based on official statistics found a disproportionate amount of crime and delinquency in the lower class and minority groups. Studies of self-reported delinquent behavior that began in the 1950s, however, raised serious questions about the class distribution of delinquency (Nye, 1958; Akers, 1964). By the 1970s, nearly all of the self-reported delinquency studies, as well as the few self-report studies of adult crime, found little difference in the levels of delinquent behavior by socioeconomic status (SES; Tittle and Villemez, 1977). Studies using official measures of crime and delinquency continued to find more offenders in the lower class than in the middle and upper classes, but even in these studies the correlations were not high (Tittle, Villemez, and Smith, 1978). The effects of class and race were stronger in longitudinal studies of official arrest histories from delinquency to adult crime (Wolfgang, Figlio, and Sellin, 1972; Wolfgang, Thornberry, and Figlio, 1987).

Some researchers have argued that, if self-report studies would utilize more effective measures of illegal behavior, then they too would find crime and delinquency to be related to both social class and race (Hindelang, Hirschi, and Weis, 1979). They contended that self-report studies only measure the more trivial offenses and do not include high-frequency offenders, whereas official measures pick up the more serious, frequent, and chronic offenders. Their conclusion, then, was that there may be little difference by class and race in low-frequency, minor offenses, but there are considerable class and race differences in the most frequent and serious offenses. Some self-report studies that include high-frequency and serious offenses have found them most likely to occur in the lower class, as is found in studies using official measures (Hindelang et al., 1980; Elliott and Ageton, 1980; Thornberry and Farnworth, 1982). Up to now, however, "overall … recent analyses concerning the strength of an SES–delinquency relation, as revealed by officially recorded measures relative to self-report measures, show mixed results" (Tittle and Meier, 1990).

Other researchers have concluded that, although there is no relationship between class and delinquency or crime in general, there is a relationship under some conditions. Some argue that a correlation exists when social class is dichotomized and the most disadvantaged underclass is compared with every other class level. Others maintain that the relationship is stronger among Blacks than Whites and among males than females. It has also been suggested that the relationship will hold true for urban centers but not for suburban communities, and for lower class youths in middle or upper class communities but not for those in predominantly lower class neighborhoods. However, research evidence does not clearly support a class–crime relationship under these conditions. Research by Dunaway, Cullen, Burton, and Evans (2000) on self-reported crime among urban adults uncovered little direct effect of social class on criminal behavior regardless of how class is measured.

It is possible that the relationship between class-related access to legitimate opportunities and the official crime rate is different for Blacks and Whites. LaFree, Drass, and O'Day (1992), for example, found that the burglary, homicide, and robbery arrest rates in the United States since 1957 were related in the expected direction to indicators of economic well-being among White males but not among Black males. The unemployed are expected to experience the greatest strain of blocked opportunities and are more likely to commit crime than the gainfully employed. There is mixed support for this hypothesis. It is also proposed that offenders who are apprehended and imprisoned are more likely to come from the ranks of the unemployed (Chiricos, 1991). However, there is little evidence that unemployment motivates people to commit criminal acts (Kleck and Chiricos, 2002). Moreover, crime is as likely to affect unemployment as vice versa (Thornberry and Christenson, 1984; Cantor and Land, 1985).

Self-report studies find class and race variations in criminal and delinquent behavior, but they are not as great as the class and race differences in officially arrested, convicted, or imprisoned populations. This may result, in part, from disparities in criminal justice decisions. But it may also result from a tendency for relatively small numbers of serious, chronic offenders who commit a large number of offenses, and who are the most likely to be caught up in the criminal justice system, to come from lower class and minority groups (see chap. 9).

Social Structural Correlates of Crime Rates

Correlating crime with social class as a test of anomie conforms to Messner's (1988) argument that Merton's anomie theory is a theory of social organization, not a theory of individuals' criminal motivations. Therefore, the proper test of the empirical validity of anomie theory is to determine the social structural correlates of rates of crime. Bernard (1987) also contended that anomie theory is a structural theory that makes no direct predictions about individual criminal behavior, and anomie theory cannot be verified or falsified by individual-level tests (see also Burton and Cullen, 1992; Bernard and Snipes, 1995). There have been a number of macro-level studies testing the effects on city, region, and state crime rates of such structural factors such as class, poverty, inequality, unemployment, family instability, and racial heterogeneity. Although there are inconsistent findings in these studies, some have found fairly strong effects of these structural variables on both property and violent crime rates (see Land, McCall, and Cohen, 1990).

Much of this research is not presented as a test of anomie theory, and none of it provides a direct measure of anomie as malintegration of cultural goals and societal means. In this sense, no structural version of anomie theory has yet received substantial empirical support. Nevertheless, it is reasonable to infer anomie from conditions of inequality (and perhaps other structural variables). Thus, the findings on structural correlates of crime can be viewed as consistent with anomie theory. They are also consistent with social disorganization theory, because the variables included in the research are very similar to those measured at the local community or neighborhood level in research on social disorganization theory.

Gangs and Delinquent Subcultures

There can be little doubt that gang delinquency continues to be concentrated in the lower class, Black and Hispanic neighborhoods of Los Angeles, Chicago, Detroit, New York, and other large cities. Yet, there is considerable doubt as to how closely these urban gangs fit the theoretical specifications of Cohen and of Cloward and Ohlin (see Schrag, 1962). Lower class and non-White gang boys perceive more limited legitimate and more available illegitimate opportunities than middle class, nongang White boys. But whether these perceptions precede or result from gang membership is not clear (Short and Strodtbeck, 1965). Moreover, neither gang members nor other delinquents sustain a distinct subculture that promotes values and norms directly contrary to conventional culture. They are more likely to agree in general with conventional values and to "neutralize" or excuse their behavior that violates those values. Such excuses themselves come from the general culture and are conceptually linked to the concept of definitions in social learning (Sykes and Matza, 1957; Matza and Sykes, 1961; see chap. 5).

As yet, researchers have been unable to verify Cloward and Ohlin's three major types of delinquent subcultures located in specific kinds of neighborhood opportunity structures. Research shows that there is some tendency for offense specialization by delinquent groups (Warr, 1996). However, this specialization does not conform closely to the types of subcultures identified in differential opportunity theory. Delinquent gangs can be very versatile, committing a wide range of violent, criminal, and drug offenses. Although some gangs and gang members are heavily involved in drug trafficking, there do not appear to be any "retreatist" gangs as described by Cloward and Ohlin, organized around the need for drugs. Drug use is high among all gangs, but then so is fighting and theft. (See Short and Strodtbeck, 1965; Spergel, 1964; see also Empey, 1967; Huff, 1990.)

School Dropout and Delinquency

According to anomie/strain theory, particularly Cohen's (1955) version, the school is an important arena in which lower class youths are confronted with the failure to live up to the conventional standards for status. It is there that they continually face the realities of their academic and social liabilities. The school experience, therefore, is often filled with failure and a strain toward delinquency. If this is true, then dropping out of school would reduce the strain and the motivation to commit illegal acts. Elliott and Voss (1974) found some support for this hypothesis by comparing officially detected crime (up to age 19) for high school graduates with that of youngsters who had dropped out of school. The school dropouts had fairly high rates of delinquency while in school, but they reduced their offenses considerably after dropping out. However, the dropouts still had higher rates than the school graduates. It is also unclear how much of the decline in their delinquency resulted from leaving a stressful school situation and how much stemmed from the tendency for law violations to decline after age 17 among all groups.

Thornberry, Moore, and Christenson (1985) found that arrests among school dropouts increased the year after leaving school and remained higher than the arrest rate for high-school graduates through age 25. Controlling for social class and race does not seem to change the findings (Thornberry et al., 1985). A later study with a national sample of adolescents found that dropping out of school sometimes increases delinquent involvement and sometimes lowers it. The effects of dropping out of school depend on the reasons for doing so and other factors such as race, age, and gender. When these other variables are controlled, most of the relationships between dropping out of school and delinquent behavior become statistically non-significant (Jarjoura and Junger-Tas, 1993).

Perceived Discrepancy Between Aspirations and Expectations

The gap between the cultural ends and social means proposed by anomie theory at the structural level implies that individuals in anomic situations may perceive this discrepancy, thereby experiencing strain. At the social psychological level, strain can be directly measured by the difference between an individual's aspirations and expectations. Aspirations refer to what one hopes to achieve in life, economically, educationally, or occupationally (e.g., how much schooling one would like to complete). Expectations refer to what one believes is realistically possible to achieve (e.g., how much education one would expect to get). Anomie/strain theory would hypothesize that the greater the discrepancy between aspirations and expectations, the higher the probability of that an individual will engage in law violation.

There is not much empirical support for this hypothesis, however. The delinquent behavior of those youths who perceive a great discrepancy between their educational or occupational aspirations and their expectations does not differ much from the delinquency of those who perceive little or no gap between their aspirations and expectations. A bigger difference in delinquent behavior is found between those who have low aspirations and those who have high aspirations, regardless of the level of their expectations (Hirschi, 1969; Liska, 1971; Elliott et al., 1985; Burton and Cullen, 1992). Strain theory receives less empirical support than either social learning or social bonding when all three theories are directly compared (Akers and Cochran, 1985; McGee, 1992; Benda, 1994; Burton et al., 1994).

A number of researchers have questioned the manner in which the disjunction between aspirations and expectations has been measured. Farnworth and Leiber (1989) claimed that these studies do not correctly measure strain because they concentrate on gauging the difference between *educational* aspirations and expectations and between *occupational* aspirations and expectations. They proposed that a better indicator would be the "disjunction between economic goals [the desire to make lots of money] and educational expectations [the means to achieve the goal]" (Farnworth and Leiber, 1989:265). Their research found that the discrepancy between economic goals and educational expectations was a better predictor of delinquency than economic aspirations alone or the gap between the two. Contrary to their argument, however, the best predictor in the study was educational aspirations alone, without regard to expectations.

Agnew et al. (1996) argued that the disjunction between aspirations and expectations provides only an indirect measure of strain because dissatisfaction with that gap is merely assumed. When strain is measured directly as dissatisfaction with one's monetary status, it is significantly, although modestly, related to both drug use and income-generating crime. In contrast, Wright, Cullen, Agnew, and Brezina (2001) examined the effect of adolescents' economic resources on delinquent involvement and drug use and found a *positive* relationship between money obtained from jobs or allowance and both delinquency and drug use. Wright et al. (2001:241) reasoned that, although their results refute strain theory's individual-level proposition that "access to money alleviates deprivation and thus reduces criminal behavior," their findings supported a proposition drawn from the macro-structural version of the theory that possession of money only serves to fuel an appetite for more of the same, leading to deviant or criminal conduct.

Contemporary Anomie/Strain Theories

Despite anomie/strain theory's wide acceptance in the 1950s and 1960s, research on the theory, particularly that demonstrating only weak effects of the disjunction between aspirations and expectations, led some critics in the 1970s to reject the theory as a viable explanation of criminal behavior (e.g., see Kornhauser, 1978). However, Merton's theory saw a revival in the 1980s when theorists began to take a fresh look at the original theoretical statement and the manner in which the theory had been tested in the extant empirical literature (Messner, 1988; Agnew, 1985b). This revival of anomie/strain theory has taken two distinct paths. The first, known as institutional-anomie theory (Messner and Rosenfeld, 1994; 2001a), approaches Merton's anomie theory from a strictly macro-structural perspective and extends the analysis to a variety of institutions in the social structure. The second, known as general strain theory (Agnew, 1992; 2006a), takes a social psychological approach and expands on the connection between sources of strain, strain-induced negative emotion, and individual criminal behavior.

Messner and Rosenfeld's Institutional-Anomie Theory

Steven Messner and Richard Rosenfeld (1994; 2001a) used Merton's theory of social structure and anomie as the framework on which their institutional-anomie theory rests. Specifically, they utilize Merton's discussion of culture to articulate their vision of the "American dream," which, they argued, contains at least four value orientations conducive to criminal behavior. First, a strong *achievement orientation* creates a culture in which people are valued ultimately on the basis of what they have achieved or possess. Failure to achieve is equated with failure to contribute meaningfully to society, and "the cultural pressures to achieve at any cost are thus very intense" (Messner and Rosenfeld, 2001a:62). Second, *individualism* encourages people to "make it on their own," pitting individual against individual in a competitive rather than a cooperative stance. Third, a strong emphasis on *universalism* creates the normative expectation that all members of American society must desire and strive toward the same success goal. Finally, the *"fetishism" of money* designates the accumulation of monetary wealth as an end in itself, valued above even the possessions it can buy or the power it can wield. Money itself is the sole "metric of success" (Messner and Rosenfeld, 2001a:63). What makes the accumulation of money conducive to crime is its infinite nature. "Monetary success is inherently open-ended. It is always possible in principle to have more money.... The pressure to accumulate money is therefore relentless, which entices people to pursue their goals by any means necessary" (Messner and Rosenfeld, 2001a:63–64).

Although Messner and Rosenfeld borrow heavily from Merton's depiction of American culture, they find Merton's conception of social structure to be too narrowly focused on the class system:

> The function of social structure, for Merton, is to distribute opportunities to achieve cultural goals. However, ... [s]ocial structure also functions to place limits on certain cultural imperatives so that they do not dominate and ultimately destroy others. This is the specific role of social institutions. (Messner and Rosenfeld, 2001a:57)

Institutional-anomie theory thus extends Merton's theory to consider the roles played by a variety of institutions. Messner and Rosenfeld focused, in particular, on the economic, political, family, and educational institutions. They recognized that the cultural values embodied in the American dream give preeminence to the economic institution. The dominance of the economy in this "institutional balance of power" results from three interrelated forces. First, the functions of non-economic institutions become "devalued." For example, within the family, the homemaker or caregiver enjoys less social esteem than the breadwinner; within the educational institution, schools are often underfunded and educators underpaid. Second, non-economic institutions must "accommodate" the requirements of the economy. Family life often revolves around work schedules, schools tailor their curricula to the needs of business, and governments regularly accede to corporate interests. Finally, economic norms begin to "penetrate" non-economic institutions. Education is increasingly depicted as a commodity and students as consumers of knowledge, and schools, governments, and even families to some degree are pressured to adopt corporate models of operation and management.

Messner and Rosenfeld argued that economic dominance in the institutional balance of power weakens the social control functions of non-economic institutions. When combined with cultural values that "stimulate" criminal motivations, criminal behavior is simply a natural outcome of the social organization of American society. Because the economic institution does not strongly caution against the use of illegitimate but highly effective means to monetary success, it becomes even more necessary for non-economic institutions such as families and schools to step in and foster these beliefs and values. However, when these institutions are devalued, forced to accommodate, and penetrated by the economy, their capacity to exert normative control is diminished. These weakened non-economic institutions also lose their ability to impose external controls on behavior. Families forced to place work requirements above the needs of the family, or schools overcrowded from lack of funding, may be unable to provide adequate supervision and consistent discipline of children. Finally, the cultural imperative of "competitive individualism" encourages people to challenge and resist weak non-economic institutions. The universal expectation to compete and win requires that success be reached with a minimum of interference:

> Anomic societies will inevitably find it difficult and costly to exert social control over the behavior of people who feel free to use whatever means prove most effective in reaching personal goals. Hence, the very sociocultural dynamics that make American institutions weak also enable and entitle Americans to defy institutional controls. If Americans are exceptionally resistant to control—and therefore exceptionally vulnerable to criminal temptations—the resistance occurs because they live in a society that enshrines the unfettered pursuit of individual material success above all other values. In the United States, anomie is considered a virtue. (Messner and Rosenfeld, 2001a:79)

In a restatement of institutional-anomie theory, Messner and Rosenfeld (2001b:155; emphasis in original) broaden their theoretical claims beyond American society asserting that "institutional imbalance *per se,* and not simply dominance of the economy, produces high rates of criminal activity." Societies characterized by different forms of institutional dominance produce different forms of crime. Economically dominant societies produce "anomic" crimes, which involve material gain. Politically dominant societies produce a "moral cynicism" that diminishes personal responsibility for the well-being of others and invites corruption. Societies dominated by kinship or religion tend to develop an "extreme moral vigilance" that produces "crimes in defense of the moral order" such as vigilantism or hate crimes (Messner and Rosenfeld 2001b:155–156).

Research investigating the empirical validity of institutional-anomie theory is scarce. Chamlin and Cochran (1995:415) provided partial support for the hypothesis that "the effect of economic conditions on instrumental crime rates will depend on the vitality of non-economic institutions." They found that the effect of poverty (as an indicator of economic inequality) on state rates of property crime is dependent in part on levels of church membership, divorce rates, and percentage of voters participating in elections (as indicators of strength of non-economic institutions). Messner and Rosenfeld (1997) hypothesized that crime rates should be lower when a society can buffer its members from market forces by providing for their social welfare, making them less dependent on the economy for their survival and diminishing economic dominance in the institutional balance of power. This social protection is also known as the "decommodification" of labor. Using a sample of 45 nations, they found that the quantity and quality of social welfare in a society is inversely related to the rate of homicide, even when controlling for economic inequality. Savolainen (2000) extended Messner and Rosenfeld's (1997) analysis by examining the interaction effects of income inequality measures and decommodification on homicide rates in the same sample. His analysis failed to demonstrate the expected negative interaction effect predicted by institutional-anomie theory. However, in a supplemental sample that included several Eastern European nations with emerging market economies (i.e., less decommodified), he did ascertain that the effect of income inequality on homicide was lower in societies that provided greater protection of its members from the market. Batton and Jensen (2002) also found the expected effects of decommodification on homicide rates in the earlier part but not the latter part of 20th century in the United States. These studies examine only the effects of economic dominance on crime, but none makes a direct comparison between American society as the exemplar of this type of institutional imbalance and all other societies. No research has yet been published that investigates the effects of other forms of institutional imbalance on other types of crime.

Messner and Rosenfeld (2006) listed several studies that they saw as supportive of the theory and several that they see as providing mixed or no support. They point out that the least researched aspect of the theory, and the one that has received the least empirical support, is "the claim of American cultural exceptionalism" (Messner and Rosenfeld, 2006:141). Lilly et al. (2007) agreed with this and concluded that the empirical validity of the theory is weak and uncertain. They pointed out that there is little or no empirical evidence that Americans are more likely to focus on success goals and devalue the socially approved means of achieving success than citizens of other countries. Further, they recognize that it is very difficult to measure the key explanatory concept of institutional imbalance.

Although American crime rates were generally higher than the rates in other societies from the 1930s through the 1980s, since then American crime rates have declined, whereas those in many other societies have remained stable or increased. Today, the property crime rates in the United States are similar to or lower than the rates in other societies around the world. For instance, according to recent United Nations victimization surveys, the rate of car theft in the United States is lower than Australia, England and Wales, France, Poland, Sweden, and Japan and its rates of burglary, robbery, personal theft, and assault are the lowest or nearly the lowest among these countries (Broadhurst, 2006). Although the American homicide rate is still higher than in other industrialized countries, it is at the lowest level since the 1950s, and rates of other violent offenses such as robbery are very much lower than the rates in some European nations and at a level similar to other industrialized nations (Messner and Rosenfeld, 2007). These trends run counter to the assumption in both Merton's original version and the later institutional-anomie version that anomic conditions are much more acute in the United States than anywhere else. If anomie is a strong macro-level predictor of crime, then the changes in crime rates would indicate a dramatic decline of anomic conditions in American society and an increase in anomie in some other societies. But there has been no research that directly measures different levels of anomie, as the cause of these different levels of crime, across societies or changes in anomie in the same society. Messner and Rosenfeld (2007) recognized that these changes in crime trends in American, European, and other societies run counter to the basic premise in their theory that the United States has the highest crime rates, hypothesized to reflect the highest level of anomie and institutional imbalance, in the world. Therefore, they have moved away from the focus on high crime rates and now argue that American "exceptionalism" is reflected less in the crime rate and more in the very high rates of imprisonment in the United States, which are the highest among industrialized democracies.

Agnew's General Strain Theory of Crime and Delinquency

In contrast to the macro-structural approach to the revision of anomie/strain theory taken by Messner and Rosenfeld, Robert Agnew (1985b; 1992) approached the revision from a micro-level, social psychological perspective. His approach was primarily to broaden the concept of strain beyond that produced by the discrepancy between aspirations and expectations, to encompass several sources of stress or strain. According to Agnew's theory, crime and delinquency are an adaptation to stress, whatever the source of that stress. He identified three major types of deviance-producing strain: the failure to achieve an individual's goals, the removal of positive or desired stimuli from the individual, and the confrontation of the individual with negative stimuli.

Failure to Achieve Positively Valued Goals. Included within this are three subtypes. First is the traditional concept of strain as the disjuncture between aspirations and expectations. Agnew expanded this slightly to include not only ideal or future goals but more immediate goals. He also included failure based not only on blocked opportunities but also on individual inadequacies in abilities and skills. Second is the gap between expectations and actual achievements, which leads to anger, resentment, and disappointment. The third subtype results from a discrepancy between what one views as a fair or just outcome and the actual outcome. In this subtype, the positive consequences of an activity or relationship are not perceived as comparable to the amount of effort put into it and are viewed as unfair when compared to others' efforts.

Removal of Positively Valued Stimuli. This source of strain refers primarily to the individual's experience with the stressful life events that can befall adolescents, such as the loss of something or someone of great worth. The loss of a girlfriend or boyfriend, the death or illness of a friend or family member, suspension from school, or changing schools can all produce anomic feelings.

Confrontation With Negative Stimuli. This type refers to another set of stressful life events that involve the individual's confrontation with negative actions by others. An adolescent may have been exposed to child abuse, victimization, adverse school experiences, and other "noxious stimuli." Because adolescents cannot legally escape from family and school, legitimate ways to avoid stress from parents or teachers are blocked. This motivates the individual to react in a deviant way.

Deviant actions may be taken to deal with stress by getting around it, seeking vengeance against the perceived source of the strain, or retreating into drug use. Deviance is most likely to occur when the response to strain is *anger*. Anger results when one blames the system or others, rather than oneself, for the adverse experiences (see also Bernard, 1990).

As in previous strain theories, Agnew's general strain theory views crime and delinquency as only one of several possible adaptations to strain. Whether a conforming or deviant mode is adopted depends on a number of internal and external constraints on the individual. These constraints, such as peer associations, beliefs, attributions of causes, self-control, and self-efficacy, affect the individual's predisposition to select a delinquent response to strain.

Agnew's theory represents a significant advancement beyond traditional strain theory. He has given more viability to strain theory, which should better facilitate its purpose to explain crime and delinquency than earlier anomie/strain theories. Its focus remains primarily on negative pressures toward deviance, which, Agnew claimed, clearly distinguishes it from social bonding and social learning theories. Moreover, because the various strains are experienced by individuals in any class or race, there is no need for strain theory to be tied only to class or race differences in delinquent behavior. Because strain is not confined only to the disjunctures between means and ends, a number of other measures beyond the discrepancy between aspirations and expectations can now be used. In specifying the types of strain (especially the second and third) and outlining factors that influence each adaptation, Agnew moves strain theory closer to social bonding and social learning theories, thereby incorporating a number of explanatory variables from those theories.

A number of studies have demonstrated a direct link between various measures of strain and delinquency (Agnew and White, 1992; Paternoster and Mazerolle, 1994; Hoffman and Miller, 1998; Hoffman and Cerbone, 1999; Mazerolle et al., 2000; Piquero and Sealock, 2000), but not all sources of strain have been significantly related to delinquency or the intention to deviate (Mazerolle, 1998; Mazerolle and Piquero, 1998; Broidy, 2001; Agnew, Brezina, Wright, and Cullen, 2002).

In his recent modifications of general strain theory, Agnew (2001a; 2001b; 2006a; 2006b) more clearly specified what types of strain are most likely to lead to criminal or delinquent coping. These are strains that are seen as unjust, are high in magnitude, emanate from situations in which social control is undermined, and pressure the individual into criminal or delinquent associations. Agnew recommended measuring types of strain that meet these criteria, including, but not limited to, parental rejection, negative school experiences, abusive peers, and criminal victimization. He has expanded the concept to include not just objective and subjective strains of the past and present but also "vicarious" and "anticipated" strain and proposes ways in which general strain theory can explain gender, class, and race/ethnic, community, and societal differences in offending, crime over the life course, and situational variations in crime. In Agnew's model, strain mediates the effects of these factors in crime and delinquency, but the effects of strain themselves operate through learning, control, and personality variables. Strain induces negative emotions such as anger, depression, fear, envy, and frustration, which have both a direct effect on crime and an indirect effect on crime through reduced ability to cope with strain legally, as well as (at least temporarily) reducing levels of social control and fostering social learning of crime and delinquency (Agnew 2006a; 2006b).

In addition to these links to other theories, many sources of strain measured in previous research, as well as those recommended by

Agnew for future research, may be interpreted as variables measuring concepts from other theories, especially social learning and social bonding theories. Agnew (1995b) contended that although many theories share similar or even identical variables predictive of delinquency, they can be distinguished by their "motivational processes." In general strain theory, strain leads to delinquency because negative emotions, especially anger, intervene between the experience of strain and criminal coping. The role of anger in general strain theory has received relatively little attention in the empirical literature, but the scant research has provided little support for anger as an intervening mechanism between strain and delinquency. Those studies that have examined this variable have generally found that some (although not all) types of strain produce anger (Brezina, 1996; Mazerolle and Piquero, 1998; Broidy, 2001), but the impact of anger on delinquency is questionable. Broidy (2001) found anger and other negative emotions to be related to general crime among college students, but others have found such a relationship to be relatively weak and limited only to violent or aggressive acts (Mazerolle and Piquero, 1998; Piquero and Sealock, 2000). Mazerolle et al. (2000) demonstrated no direct link at all between anger and violent delinquency, drug use, or school deviance. Despite general strain theory's hypothesis that strain produces delinquency only when anger is high, Mazerolle and Piquero (1998) produced no evidence that anger mediated the effect of strain on the intention to deviate, and Mazerolle et al. (2000) actually found that strain mediated the effect of anger, and not the reverse, on violent delinquency. These results must be viewed with some caution, however, because the anger variables in these studies measure "trait" anger, a general disposition to be chronically angry, rather than "state" anger, a situation-specific measure of negative emotion more consistent with general strain theory's predictions (Spielberger, Jacobs, Russell, and Crane, 1983).

Broidy and Agnew (1997) pointed out that the processes in general strain theory may be different for males and females. They hypothesized that perceptions of "strainful" situations, types of emotional responses (e.g., anger vs. depression or anxiety), and availability of legitimate and illegitimate coping mechanisms may all vary by gender. Few studies have examined the role of gender in general strain theory. Thus far, no test of the theory has observed any gender differences in levels of strain or anger. Both males and females experience equal levels of strain and are equally angry in response to strain. Neither Hoffman and Su (1997) nor Mazerolle (1998) found gender differences in the predictive power of strain variables on various forms of delinquency or drug use. However, neither study included measures of negative emotion nor legitimate coping strategies, both thought to be crucial to explaining gender differences in crime within the context of general strain theory.

Broidy (2001), however, found that although males and females had similar levels of strain and anger, women were more likely than men to respond to strain with other emotions such as depression, insecurity, or resentment rather than anger, and were more able than men to utilize strategies such as downplaying the importance of the strain, avoidance, or talking to others rather than crime to cope with strain and negative emotions (see similar findings in Neff and Waite, 2007).

Most problematic for general strain theory is its specification that other theoretical variables "condition" or moderate the effects of strain on delinquency. As Lilly et al. (2007:67–68; emphasis in original) noted: "...general strain theory contends that ... [learning and control variables] increase criminal behavior only when they occur in *conjunction with strain*. ...But another possibility is that the conditioning variables identified by Agnew mainly have direct effects on criminal behavior rather than coming into play mainly when a person is under strain."

Although a few studies have demonstrated that strain is more likely to result in delinquency when exposure to delinquent peers is high and social bonds are weak (Mazerolle et al., 2000; Mazerolle and Maahs, 2000), many studies have failed to demonstrate the sort of conditioning effects predicted by the theory (Paternoster and Mazerolle, 1994; Hoffman and Miller, 1998; Mazerolle and Piquero, 1998; Hoffman and Cerbone, 1999). Neff and Waite (2007) found a relationship between strain and substance abuse, but their measures of social learning variables, rather than conditioning the effects of strain, had the strongest direct effects. Agnew et al. (2002) investigated the ability of a composite personality trait, negative emotionality/constraint, to condition the strain–delinquency relationship. They found that adolescents who are "high in negative emotionality and low in constraint are much more likely than others to react to strain with delinquency," (Agnew et al., 2002:60) but the conditioning effect is still weak. Although general strain theory fares better empirically than the more limited strain theories of the past, the articulation between general strain and other theoretical explanations needs clarification, and better measures of key concepts must be included in empirical assessments of the theory.

Community Projects Based on Theories of Social Disorganization, Anomie, and Delinquent Subcultures

The ultimate policy implication of any structural theory is that basic social changes need to be fostered to remove the criminogenic features of economic, political, and social institutions of society. The clear implication of anomie theory, for instance, is to promote the integration of cultural goals and socially approved means, and the redistribution of opportunities in the class system. Short of this kind of broad-scale social transformation, however, there are many ameliorative, control, and preventive policies that can be linked to social disorganization, anomie, and subcultural theories. The most prominent are community or neighborhood organization, working with delinquent gangs, enhancement of economic opportunities, and training programs. The classic models of such programs were instituted in large American cities in the 1930s (Chicago Area Projects), 1950s (Boston's Mid-City Project), and 1960s (New York's Mobilization for Youth). Although they all met with difficulties and limited success (usually for reasons that had little to do with the theory), they have inspired similar job, youth opportunity, and gang programs up to the present time.

The Chicago Area Projects. The Chicago sociologists, Shaw and McKay, were directly concerned with using social disorganization theory and research for the control and prevention of crime and delinquency. In the 1930s, they developed the first large-scale urban delinquency prevention program, known as the Chicago Area Projects (CAP), in several of the lower class, high-delinquency neighborhoods of Chicago. One major objective was to mobilize local informal social organization and social control among the law-abiding residents. If properly done, such local organization could counteract the effects of social disorganization and work against criminal values and norms to which Shaw and McKay believed many subscribed in the high crime areas of the city. Another related objective was to overcome the influence of delinquent peers and criminal adults in the neighborhoods by providing more opportunities for association with conventional adults and peers. Efforts were also directed toward improved sanitation, traffic control, and physical restoration of dilapidated private and public properties. Neighborhood organization was attempted through formation of local groups and clubs run by pro-social adults in the community. These conventional adults were engaged to establish and run recreational programs, summer camps, athletic teams, and other groups and activities. They were to cooperate with the police, the juvenile court, churches, social work agencies, lodges, political organizations, and other community groups to work directly with neighborhood youths. Delinquent gangs were identified and "detached" social workers were assigned to make contact with them on the streets and try to involve them in alternative, non-delinquent behavior (Kobrin, 1959; Schlossman and Sedlak, 1983; Finestone, 1976; see also Lundman, 1993).

Long-term assessments after 25 years (Kobrin, 1959), 30 years (Finestone, 1976), and 50 years (Schlossman and Sedlak, 1983;

Schlossman et al., 1984) indicated that CAP met with mixed success. Capable and willing lower class adults committed to conventional values were located and enlisted even in areas that were deemed the most disorganized with the highest rates of crime and delinquency. Various parts of the overall plan were successfully implemented in many neighborhood areas. But there was a good deal of variation from neighborhood to neighborhood in how well organized the programs were and how much support and cooperation they received from the residents. Professional social workers in the areas often were critical of the amateur volunteerism that characterized CAP. Some community leaders and residents at the time argued that the organized intervention with delinquent youth and gangs served only to encourage delinquency and undermine the authority of the schools, churches, and parents.

Although delinquency rates were in fact reduced in some neighborhoods with strong CAP committees (Finestone, 1976), it is difficult to show that the area projects were the main reason for the reduction, and some areas showed no decline or even an increase in delinquency over the years. Schlossman and his associates rated six CAP areas from low to high in terms of how much delinquency would be expected in each area, based on its demographic and economic characteristics. They found that two of these areas had experienced higher official rates of delinquency than expected, but in four of the areas the delinquency rates were lower than expected. These findings provide some evidence for success. But the measures of neighborhood organization and delinquency were not good, and differences in delinquency rate among the neighborhoods could not be tied directly to the activities and organizations of the CAP programs (Schlossman et al., 1984).

Bursik and Grasmick (1995) proposed a newer formulation of social disorganization that they believe will provide better guidelines for anti-crime actions in the community. They focused on differences in neighborhood capacity to control the deviant behavior of its residents. The level of control is a function of how cohesively organized the neighborhood is through its social networks of friends, family, and voluntary organizations, its population characteristics, and its level of economic well-being. These private and local levels of control are linked to political, social, and economic forces and the "public level of systemic control" exercised by the law and justice system. Linking different levels of social control may improve crime control in the local community, but some policies could make things worse. For instance, although a state-level imprisonment policy that removes large numbers of offenders from the local neighborhoods reduces the crime threat there, it also may undermine community cohesiveness and reduce effectiveness of informal social control (Rose and Clear, 1998).

The Boston Mid-City Project. The Mid-City Project was based explicitly on Miller's (1958b; 1962) lower class culture theory but incorporated some central features of the CAP. It was conceived as an all-out, coordinated community effort to combat delinquency and illicit activities among street-corner gangs in the central city. The project had three facets: (1) direct social work services to families with delinquent children or families experiencing other kinds of problems that placed their children at risk of delinquency, (2) a community neighborhood program, and (3) a detached worker (graduate students in sociology, anthropology, and social work) program with juvenile gangs. Of these, only the detached worker program was actually put into operation. The project was never completed primarily because of the conflict over goals, ideologies, and strategies among the various community agencies that were enlisted in the project.

There was considerable hostility directed toward the detached workers from members of the community who thought that it was not right to pay so much special attention to delinquent gangs. Despite this opposition, the detached workers identified and reached a fairly sizable number of gangs and street-corner groups. They provided conventional role models and personal persuasion in an effort to move gang activities away from violence and delinquency. They were able to get the gang members involved in athletic and sports activities, regular clubs, fundraising, and volunteer community service. They made arrangements for trips, reserved local gyms, located ball fields, and secured participation in sports leagues.

Were they successful in reducing gang-related or individual delinquent behavior in the community? Because conflicts among community agencies disrupted the project in midstream, and because it was not fully implemented, it is difficult to tell. But data collected by the project staff themselves showed little reduction of deviant and law-violating behavior among the gang members on the street. The number of appearances in court by gang members actually increased during the time of the project. Also, there was no difference when the contacted gangs were compared to a group of corner boys who were not included in the new clubs and affiliations established by the detached workers. Actually, having a detached worker may have become something of a status symbol among the boys. An unintended consequence of the program, then, may have been to make the gangs more cohesive and more inclined to carry out delinquent activities to gain the attention of a detached worker (Miller, 1958b; 1962; Lundman, 1993).

Mobilization for Youth. The policy guidelines provided by anomie theory are clear. If blocked legitimate opportunities motivate persons to achieve through criminal activity, then that activity can be countered by the changes to society that offer greater access to legitimate opportunities for those groups that have been relatively deprived of that access. The expansion of opportunities in the society as a whole can come about through promotion of economic prosperity, creation of new jobs, and lowering the unemployment rate through trade, economic, and tax policies. The individual's ability to take advantage of legitimate opportunities and perception that such opportunities realistically are available can be enhanced through educational and job-training programs. If delinquent gangs form in the city because of unequal opportunity and the availability of delinquent subcultures and opportunities, then the objective should be to provide legitimate opportunities and to counter the influence of delinquent subcultures.

This was the theoretical rationale, derived specifically from Cloward and Ohlin's differential opportunity theory, for the Mobilization for Youth project in New York's lower east side in the early 1960s. The project was organized to increase the ability of lower class youths to gain access to legitimate means of success through job opportunities, education, and skill training. In addition, just as in the CAP and Mid-City projects, detached workers were hired to interact directly with youth on the street. Again the goal was to redirect gang members away from delinquent activities and values and toward participation in conventional activities, sports, and community service.

As with the earlier community projects, Mobilization for Youth faced political opposition and conflict among community agencies. There also was a growing gap between what the theory called for and what was actually put into practice. The program ignored the key part of Cloward and Ohlin's theory that linked three different types of delinquent subcultures to different types of neighborhoods. Also, as in previous programs, there may have been some gangs attempting to show they were more seriously delinquent than others to get a detached worker assigned to them.

Mobilization for Youth did provide something of a prototype for community action programs funded by the federal anti-poverty initiatives of the later 1960s, such as the Job Corps and Office of Economic Opportunity, as well as for local equal-opportunity and job-training programs for school dropouts and lower class youths. But its success in preventing delinquency could not be adequately judged because opposition and problems resulted in its early termination. Neither it nor similar programs that followed were able to achieve the ambitious goals of changing the social structure of communities, modifying the behavior of delinquent gangs, and preventing delinquency (Hackler, 1966; Arnold, 1970; Short, 1975; Bynum and Thompson, 1992).

Policy Implications of Contemporary Anomie/Strain Theories

Unlike the recommendations arising from earlier anomie/strain theories, Messner and Rosenfeld (2001a) emphasized that enhancing legitimate opportunities for all is likely to backfire because it simply fuels the desire for greater monetary wealth and ultimately increases the pressure to succeed at any cost. They recommended instead the strengthening of non-economic institutions in the American social structure to create a balance among its institutions. This restoration of the institutional balance of power can be accomplished by (1) implementing pro-family economic policies such as family leave, "flex time," and on-site child care facilities at the place of employment; (2) loosening the strong ties between academic performance and future economic prospects, so that even those who cannot achieve in school can count on economic survival; (3) limiting the costs of crime control through the use of intermediate sanctions in the community; and (4) creating broader social and civic participation through national service programs such as AmeriCorps. These policy recommendations may also be derived from social bonding theory, which, like institutional-anomie theory, recognizes the regulatory forces inherent in family, religion, and educational settings.

Agnew (1995c; 2006b) identified some prevention programs that are consistent with general strain theory but that also draw heavily from learning and bonding theories. "The most promising programs focus on the family and involve parent management training and functional family therapy" (Agnew, 1995c:48). But they also include in-school, peer, and individual interventions. Agnew advocates family and school interventions to (1) reduce the adversity of the youth's social environment and train parents in parenting skills for better supervision and discipline of their children, including more consistent and effective use of rewards and punishment; (2) provide social skills training for children and youth to reduce the individual's tendency to do or say things that provoke negative reactions from others; (3) increase social support for youth through counseling, mediation, and advocacy programs; (4) increase the adolescent's ability to cope with negative stimuli in a non-delinquent way through training in anger control, problem-solving, social skills, and stress management. Although applied programs may not explicitly rely on these implications of general strain theory, Agnew noted that many applied efforts, especially restorative justice programs, are compatible the theory (Agnew, 2006b).

Summary

Anomie/strain and social disorganization theories hypothesize that social order, stability, and integration are conducive to conformity, whereas disorder and malintegration are conducive to crime and deviance. Anomie is the form that societal malintegration takes when there is a dissociation between valued cultural ends and legitimate societal means to those ends.

The more disorganized or anomic the group, community, or society, the higher the rate of crime and deviance. Merton proposed that anomie characterizes American society in general and is especially high in the lower classes because they are more blocked off from legitimate opportunities. High levels of anomie and social disorganization in lower class and disadvantaged ethnic groups, therefore, are hypothesized to be the cause of the high rates of crime and delinquency in these groups. At the individual level, the strain produced by discrepancies between the educational and occupational goals toward which one aspires and the achievements actually expected are hypothesized to increase the chances that one will engage in criminal or delinquent behavior. Research provides some support for these hypotheses in regard to class and race, but the relationships are usually not strong. Other structural variables are more strongly related to crime rates. Self-perceived aspirations/expectations discrepancy seems to be only weakly related to delinquency.

Cohen, and Cloward and Ohlin, modified Merton's theory to apply anomie to lower class delinquent gangs. Miller theorized that the delinquency of street corner groups expresses the focal concerns of lower class culture. Research shows clearly that gang delinquency continues to be concentrated in the lower class and minority neighborhoods of large cities. But research has not verified that urban gangs fit very well into the theoretical specifications of Cohen, Cloward and Ohlin, and other subcultural versions of anomie theory. Social disorganization and anomie theory have been applied in community programs to enhance neighborhood social organization and legitimate opportunities for youth. Due, in part, to political opposition, these programs have been hampered in implementation and effectiveness.

Messner and Rosenfeld suggested in institutional-anomie theory that the high crime rate (later modified to include the high rate of imprisonment) in American society can be explained by a distinctively American emphasis on monetary success and an institutional imbalance of power in which the economy dominates the social structure. There has not been enough research done as yet to assess the theory's empirical validity, but a variety of ways to strengthen non-economic institutions through social welfare programs are recommended.

Agnew has proposed a modification of anomie/strain theory, primarily by broadening the concept of strain to encompass several sources of strain, failure to achieve goals, removal of positive or desired stimuli from the individual, and exposure to negative stimuli and by including negative emotions as the mechanism by which some types of strain lead to delinquency. Research offers some support for his general strain theory, but the process by which strain operates through anger and variables derived from other theories to influence delinquency has not been demonstrated. Agnew recommends applications of general strain theory in family and school interventions that resemble those based on social learning and social bonding theories.

Notes

1. See the studies in Lander (1954), Shaw and McKay (1969), Voss and Petersen (1971), Wilson (1987), and Simcha-Fagan and Schwartz (1986). For reviews of theoretical issues and research on social disorganization that address and offer solutions to some of the problems in earlier theory, see Bursik (1988), Sampson and Groves (1989), and Warner and Pierce (1993).

2. The terms *anomie* and *strain* are often used interchangeably when referring to Merton's theory and subsequent theories influenced by his perspective. However, some theorists (Messner, 1988; see also Cullen, 1983) distinguish "strain theory," which refers to a micro-level process in which goal frustration leads to individual criminal behavior, from "anomie theory," referring to a weakening of society's ability, at the macro-level, to regulate the behavior of its members. Messner and Rosenfeld (2001a:45) observed, however, that macro-level explanations, including Merton's, routinely refer to individual behavior, and thus a "hybrid" approach is most useful; hence, they recommended "anomie/strain" as the most appropriate label for theories emanating from Merton's theoretical framework.

3. Others have used the concept of subculture as a specific explanation of violence. Wolfgang and Ferracuti (1982) relate the violence of lower class, young, and disproportionately Black males to a subculture of violence. Others have attempted to explain the high rates of homicide in the South by referring to a southern regional subculture of violence. Research casts doubt on the subculture of violence thesis of both the regional and class types (Erlanger, 1974; 1976).

Chapter 9

Conflict Theory

Introduction

Conflict theory begins with the assumption that society is not held together by agreement and consensus on major values but rather is

> a congeries of groups held together in a dynamic equilibrium of opposing group interests and efforts. Conflict is viewed, therefore, as one of the principal and essential social processes upon which the continuing on-going society depends. (Vold, 1958:204)

Power is the principal determinant of the outcome of this conflict. The most powerful groups control the law, so that their values are adopted as the legal standards for behavior. The members of less powerful groups, although they suffer legislative and judicial defeats, continue to act in accordance with their internal group norms, which means violating the law. Thus, conflict theory offers both an explanation of law and criminal justice and an explanation of criminal and deviant behavior. In the first part of this chapter, conflict theory is contrasted with consensus/functionalist theory as an explanation of law and criminal justice. In the second part, the theory that crime is produced by group and culture conflict is presented and evaluated.

Law Is a Type of Social Control

Social control consists of a normative system with rules about the way people should and should not behave and a system of formal and informal mechanisms used to control deviation from, and promote conformity to, these rules. Informal social control exists in the family, friendship groups, churches, neighborhoods, and other groups in the community. Formal social control includes law and the criminal justice system in which the rules are officially promulgated and enforced by legally authorized agents.

These two forms of social control are viewed by some theorists as inversely related. A breakdown in informal control brings about an increase in formal control, and informal controls grow out of the need to fill gaps left by the disintegration of formal control. Donald Black hypothesized the following:

> Law is stronger where other social control is weaker. *Law varies inversely with other social control.* ... Thus, it varies across the centuries, growing as every kind of social control dies away—not only in the family but in the village, church, work place, and neighborhood. (Black, 1976:107–109; emphasis in original)

Social control relies in large measure on socialization. Socialization is the process of teaching and learning values, norms, and customs through example and the application of positive and negative social sanctions. Conventional morality and values are acquired through socialization within the family, church, and other social institutions. An important outcome of this socialization process is the individual's internalization of societal norms and the development of self-control. To the extent that the law contains the same values and norms that individuals have learned and now adhere to, they will constrain their own behavior in conformity with the law. The fact that most members of a society, most of the time, conform to social expectations rests primarily on the strength of this self-control. However, no informal or formal social control system depends entirely on internal control. External sanctions are applied both directly and indirectly, not only in the socialization of children, but in the informal interaction and socialization that continues through adulthood in society. The giving or withholding of affection, praise or ridicule, acceptance or rejection, and other forms of social sanctions all help to maintain compliance with social norms (Akers, 1985).

Law differs from other types of social control, however, in that it relies primarily on the external application of formal negative sanctions in the form of punishment for wrongdoing. The main feature of law that differentiates it from other forms of social control in modern society is the fact that its sanctions are supported by the legitimized and authoritative coercion of the state (Akers, 1965). Law is the system of rules promulgated and enforced by the sovereign political state that exercises authority over a territory and recognizes no higher secular authority (see the definitions in Davis, 1962:41; Akers and Hawkins, 1975:5–16):

> Every normative system induces or coerces activity. The normative system we have defined as "law" uses state power to this end. (Chambliss and Seidman, 1971:10)

This definition encompasses both the substantive law on the books and the law in action. There are two major perspectives on the enactment and enforcement of the law by the political state. The first views the law as developing out of a widespread normative *consensus* in society and reflecting the common interests of society as a whole. The second views law as the product of a *conflict* between group interests and the exercise of power in society. The law on the books and in action endorses and protects the narrow interests of those groups as they wield economic, social, and political power (Quinney, 1969; 1970; Chambliss and Seidman, 1971; 1982; Bernard, 1983). Consensus and conflict theorists agree that the law is both shaped by and has an impact on the social structure. However, they differ on their basic image of society (Sutherland et al., 1992; Ritzer, 1992).

Consensus and Functionalist Theories of Law

Until the 1960s, the major sociological approach to law and social control was based on some form of *consensus* theory, which views the formal system of laws and enforcement as incorporating those norms in society on which there is the greatest normative consensus. This approach is represented principally by the writings of late 19th- and early 20th-century sociologists (Sumner, 1906; Ross, 1901; Durkheim, 1893/1964; Weber, 1921/1954).

Emile Durkheim (1893/1964) theorized that the content and general nature of the law evolves from the type of "solidarity" that characterizes the society. His thesis was that in those less complex societies with "mechanical solidarity," whose members are integrated by their common values and beliefs, the law is especially "repressive" or punitive. In complex and diverse societies that are integrated more by functional interdependence, "organic solidarity," than by cultural sameness, the criminal law moves from harsh and brutal forms of punishment to deprivation of liberty through incarceration as the main penalty for crime. The law is aimed more toward restitution than severe punishment and geared primarily toward civil and constitutional law. Max Weber (1921/1954) proposed that, as the social organization of economically advanced societies becomes more rational, the law also becomes more rational. The rationality of law is based on adherence to the rule of law characterized by due process and fair procedure determined by established legal principles and rules ("formal rationality") rather than on the fairness of the actual outcome of the process judged according to the interests or ideology of particular individuals or groups ("substantive rationality").

Although E. A. Ross (1901) and other early sociologists espoused similar views, the classic statement of consensus theory of law was given by William Graham Sumner (1906). To Sumner, the content of the law is developed primarily by the formal codification, through legislation and court rulings, of the prevailing "folkways and mores." These are unorganized, intuitive principles of right and wrong that have gradually evolved over a long period of time and to which all segments of society subscribe. Although not immutable, folkways and mores are persistent and slow to change. When laws are passed, they express these underlying mores. Legislation cannot create new mores, nor does law readily change existing mores. Sumner should be interpreted to mean that legislation cannot modify the mores quickly or easily, rather than that all law flows directly from the mores or that it cannot induce any social change (Ball and Simpson, 1962). Nevertheless, Sumner's main emphasis was on how the law is shaped by the customs of society. He dismissed attempts to alter custom through law as futile exercises in social engineering. (For a good review of Weber's, Durkheim's, and Sumner's theories of law, see Trevino, 1996.)

This type of consensus model was more dominant in the early part of the 20th century. However, its importance declined, and no major theorist since the 1950s has considered this to be the best model of the law. To the extent that assumptions or hypotheses about consensus theory were given credence in theories of law, they were most apt to be found in "mutualist" models, "the mutually reinforcing potential of laws and norms" (Schwartz, 1986:65), or in some type of conflict model.

The same can be said of *functionalist* theory that "underscores the consensual norms and values of society, the social system's orderly state of *equilibrium,* and the law's ultimate function of social *integration*" (Trevino, 1996:333; emphasis in original). Functionalism overlaps with, and may be considered to be a variant of, consensus theory. It views the law as functioning for the greater public welfare. By the orderly settlement of disputes, regulation of disruptive behavior, and control of crime, the law serves the interests of everyone in society and not just the special interests of certain powerful groups. This should not be taken to mean that the emphasis in functionalism is only on the effectiveness of the law in controlling deviance in society. The theory also recognizes that laws serve *symbolic* functions for society and officially condemn certain behavior, whether or not they actually deter it. Although functionalist explanations of law have had more recent adherents than the traditional consensus model (Davis, 1966; Friedman, 1975), neither have many proponents today. However, functionalist and consensus notions have not been dropped entirely. They have been recast and retained in pluralistic conflict theory.

Conflict Theory of Law and Criminal Justice

Conflict theory began to challenge consensus and functional models in sociology in the 1950s. Although discussions of conflict theory often refer to Karl Marx, this approach is more directly traced back to the European sociologist Georg Simmel (1950), who viewed conflict as a fundamental social process. Its chief proponent in criminology at that time was George Vold (1958), who, in his classic *Theoretical Criminology*, proposed that group conflict explains not only criminal law and justice but criminal behavior as well:

> [T]he whole political process of law making, law breaking, and law enforcement becomes a direct reflection of deep-seated and fundamental conflicts between interest groups and their more general struggles for the control of the police power of the state. Those who produce legislative majorities win control over the police power and dominate the policies that decide who is likely to be involved in violation of the law. (Vold, 1958:208–209)

In subsequent revisions of Vold's book, Thomas Bernard and Jeffrey Snipes (Vold and Bernard, 1986; Vold et al., 2002) repeated and expanded on the theory.

In the 1960s, several criminologists, most notably Richard Quinney (1964; 1969; 1970), William Chambliss (1964; 1969), and Austin Turk (1964; 1966; 1969a) further developed the conflict approach and placed it at the forefront of criminological theory. They argued that criminological theory had for too long focused almost exclusively on explaining criminal behavior, and that theoretical attention needed to be shifted toward the explanation of criminal law. Turk (1964;1969a) maintained that the central task of criminological theory was not to untangle the causes of criminal behavior but to explain criminality, the process by which certain behavior and individuals are formally designated as criminal. Chambliss (1975:i–ii) agreed: "Instead of asking, 'Why do some people commit crimes and others do not?' we ask, 'Why are some acts defined as criminal while others are not?'" Conflict theory answers that question: Both the formulation and enforcement of the law directly and indirectly are more likely to serve the interests of the more powerful groups in society.[1]

Even the early consensus theorists observed that the law on the books and the law in action often favor the interests of special groups (Ball and Simpson, 1962; Sumner, 1906:39, 55, 169). But this observation is not at the heart of consensus theory; it is central to conflict theory. Diversity and lack of uniformity, not commonality of values, are the hallmarks of modern society. Conflict theory portrays society in a more or less continuing state of conflict among groups (Ritzer, 1992). Social structure is comprised of the working arrangements, coalitions, and balancing forces "in a shifting but dynamic equilibrium of opposing group interests and efforts" (Vold, 1958:204).

The values and interests of various groups conflict with one another to the degree that what is considered normal in one group may be considered deviant in another. The dominant groups can see to it that their particular definitions of normality or deviance will become enacted as law, ensconced in public policy, and protected by the operation of the criminal justice system. When the behavior of members from subordinate groups clashes with the law, they are less able to resist official apprehension, prosecution, conviction, and incarceration for criminal charges. The theory is succinctly stated by Quinney:

> (Formulation of Criminal Definitions): Criminal definitions [laws] describe behavior that conflicts with the interests of the segments of society that have the power to shape public policy. (Quinney, 1970:16)

> (Application of Criminal Definitions): Criminal definitions are applied by the segments of society that have the power to shape the enforcement and administration of criminal law. (Quinney, 1970:18)

Class, race, sex, age, ethnicity, and other characteristics that denote social position in society determine who gets apprehended and punished. Thus, the economically and socially disadvantaged groups of lower class, minorities, youth, women, and others will be similarly disadvantaged and differentially processed through the criminal justice system.

The theory developed by Quinney, Chambliss, Turk, and others emphasized power and coercion in the formulation and administration of law, but it left some room for consensus and the protection of the interests of the less powerful by the law:

> In many cases there is no conflict whatsoever between those in power and those not. For most crimes against the person, such as murder, assault, and rape, there is consensus throughout society as to the desirability of imposing legal sanctions for persons who commit these acts. It is also true that laws are passed which reflect the interests of the general population and which are antithetical to the interests of those in power. (Chambliss, 1969:10)

Although consensus is recognized, law and criminal justice are explained primarily by reference to power and group conflict. Law is both the result of, and a weapon to be used in, group conflict (Turk, 1976). Although some groups or alliances maintain considerable power over a period of time and on many issues, no single group or interest is all-powerful. There are the social, economic, and political elites that may have overlapping interests but do not constitute a monolithic, all-powerful class that perpetually gets its way in the law, economy, and society.

Quinney (1970) and other conflict theorists rejected "pluralism" because they believed it views the political state as nothing more than a fair and neutral arena for the expression and adjudication of competing interests. This disdain for pluralism is also found in the radical, critical, and Marxist theories to which many of the conflict theorists of the 1960s came to subscribe in the 1970s[2] (see chap. 10). Nevertheless, their earlier statements of conflict theory are clearly pluralistic in the sense that they recognize several power centers, rather than one all-encompassing power elite, and admit that criminal law does indeed embody some common values. These are the central features of the *pluralistic conflict* model explicated by Akers (Akers and Hawkins, 1975; Akers, 1985).

Theoretical efforts, such as the "integrative conflict model" of McGarrell and Castellano (1991), continued to develop the pluralistic conflict model of criminal law. McGarrell and Castellano proposed three levels of factors that come into play in the process of crime legislation and policy making. At the highest level are the fundamental social-structural conflicts generated by heterogeneity and inequality and the symbolic cultural conflicts in public perceptions and "myths" about crime. At the mid-level are rates of victimization, fear of crime, and persistent public demands for the punishment of criminals. At the third level are the more immediate events and activities that trigger legislative action to change policy, such as media reports on crime problems, interest-group activities, reform campaigns, and political events.

Development of the pluralistic conflict model continues to reject the image of the system as tightly controlled by a small, powerful elite at the top. Instead, it is characterized as a decentralized, "loosely coupled" system into which multiple elites and competing groups interject their influence, but which responds to institutional, economic, and political changes (Hagan, 1989c; Wright, 1993a; McGarrell, 1993; Walker, Spohn, and DeLone, 2007):

> Policies gradually emerge through a complex process of negotiation, bargaining, and compromise. Implemented policies seldom resemble the initial proposals of particular interest groups; rather, goals and solutions are twisted, amended, watered-down, combined, and distorted, so that while most parties are appeased, few are fully satisfied. (Wright, 1993a:145)

The pluralistic conflict model applies to democratic societies in which competing interest groups attempt to uphold their values through the legislature and government. Competing interests need not exist only in distinct, organized pressure groups with headquarters, budgets, and registered lobbyists. They can also be found in large-scale social movements and in broadly defined economic, political, social, regional, religious, gender, ethnic, racial, age, and other divisions and segments of society. There is an underlying agreement among all groups on the legitimacy of the political system, which no group will use its power to overthrow. Within this system and process, however, the groups with the most power and resources, best organization, or greatest numbers will be the winners. Highly organized political pressure groups actively seek the protection of their values and interests by legislation and try to influence the actions of governmental officials and bureaucrats in administering the laws. Pressure groups also try to influence executive appointments and the legislative confirmation of judges to appellate and supreme courts in an effort to ensure appointments of those who share their views and special interests. These interest groups need not take any direct action to have their influence felt. Many lawmakers, judges, police officers, and government executives require virtually no direct pressure to act according to the best interests of the groups with which they identify.

It should also be noted that the interests threatened or defended by criminal law may be as much symbolic as material. Laws against prostitution, drugs, and certain kinds of sexual behavior, for instance, will be staunchly defended and actively promoted by certain groups, because such laws formally endorse a moral stance against such behavior, although these groups have no economic or political stake in the laws and know that they may be ineffective in controlling such behavior.

Although politically dominant subgroups and segments of society may be successful in imposing their interests on public policy, the law also reflects the general interests of society as a whole. Not all legislation and administration of laws stem from compromises and victories by identifiable group interests. The core of criminal law—prohibitions of and sanctions for personal violence, destruction of property, fraud, and other predatory crimes—mirrors and protects the interests of the entire society. This core outlaws offenses that are *mala in se*, wrong in themselves, and that would be abhorred by society even if not condemned by the law. On the other hand, there is likely to be more conflict and less consensus on offenses that are seen as *mala prohibita*, wrong only because they have been prohibited by law. Laws on sexual behavior, drugs, alcohol, business activities, and other areas usually generate more conflict in the process of their passage and enforcement. Even for mala in se offenses, there remains considerable conflict over what the proper legal sanctions should be. All condemn murder, for instance, but not all agree on what behavior or circumstances constitute murder or what moral grounds justify the death penalty (see Cullen et al., 2000, for a review of public opinion on the death penalty).

Furthermore, even some of the core criminal law, on which there is strong consensus today, may have originally been devised to serve the interests of one segment of society. For instance, although we now categorize embezzlement as a crime, at one time it was not considered a crime at all. Taking possession of entrusted property or money was then perceived as a matter of personal injury to one person who foolishly trusted another with his or her money or goods. It was not deemed as criminal theft. Legally, theft had to involve actual trespass on someone's property to steal valuables. The landed aristocracy was served by the trespass law, whereas the interests of the merchant class were better served by adding laws that defined the conversion of entrusted property as a crime. At that time the power of the aristocracy was in decline, whereas the rising class of entrepreneurs was gaining power. Hence, the ultimate change in law reflected that shifting power balance in society (Hall, 1952).

Even when the law has been subjected to direct pressure by interest groups or modified to the benefit of powerful classes or segments of society, broad public opinion may still be a factor. A powerful group or coalition of groups frequently tries to shape public sentiments, so they at least take on the appearance of consensus. At the same time, a group that champions a cause that is consistent with existing common values and public opinion has a far better chance of success in winning over a conflict with other groups. The news media play a major role in this process (Hollinger and Lanza-Kaduce, 1988; Castellano and McGarrell, 1991; see also Barak, 1994). Politicians and the public alike may be alerted to a problem perceived to be in need of legislation through news stories and editorials. Public opinion both shapes and, in turn, is shaped by media coverage.

Conflict theory's focus on power and coercion also highlights the role that "social threat" plays in the formation of law and the operation of the criminal justice system. According to the conflict perspective, "the greater the number of acts and people threatening to the interests of the powerful, the greater the level of deviance and crime control" (Liska, 1992:18). Members of minority groups, the poor, and youth pose a real or symbolic threat to the interests of more powerful groups, generating a greater fear of crime and increased crime reporting, especially by non-minority citizens, more restrictive laws, and increases in law enforcement activity, court processing, and punishment. Conflict theorists also contend that the social threat presented by the underclasses affects the decision making of criminal justice officials, who use their discretionary power to impose more punitive responses on offenders belonging to threatening groups and more lenient responses on offenders belonging to more powerful groups.

This conflict approach to law and criminal justice was incorporated into labeling theory, which also was developed in the 1950s and 1960s (see chap. 7). Therefore, there is essentially no difference between conflict and labeling theory in explaining the formation and operation of social and legal norms. The two do offer different explanations of criminal and deviant behavior.

Empirical Validity of Consensus and Conflict Theories of Law and Criminal Justice

Research on Legislation and Public Opinion on Crime and Criminal Justice

There are four types of empirical studies that try to evaluate the validity of conflict and labeling theory as an explanation of criminal law and justice. The first type studies the influence of interest groups on legislation, administrative regulations, and court decisions. It may involve research on law making during early historical periods or on law and policy in more recent, contemporary times. These studies have investigated the background and nature of group conflict in the formation of laws on theft, vagrancy, prostitution, drugs, smoking, kidnapping, gun control, juvenile delinquency, computer crimes, and other areas of crime-control policy.[3]

These studies have identified specific groups involved in influencing the enactment of the law and the establishment of public policy. Some of these are well-organized pressure groups, whereas others are more diffuse regional, labor, business, farm, religious, professional, and other interests. Even law enforcement agencies and government bureaucracies have themselves acted as special-interest groups in the formation and enforcement of laws. The preponderance of evidence from these studies provides little support for either a pure consensus model or a model in which one elite group controls all legislation. The findings are most consistent with a pluralistic conflict model:

> What emerges [from the research] is a picture of crime-control legislation that is the product of conflict and competition among a number of interest groups that differ over time and issue. The consistent finding of conflict over values and interests, and the finding that most laws appear targeted at the urban poor, raise fundamental questions about the moral functionalist position. The lack of identifiable business or

capital involvement raises questions about the moral Marxist interpretation. (McGarrell and Castellano, 1991:176)

The second type of study relevant to evaluating conflict theory includes research on the consensus or dissensus in public opinion about what, and how strongly, acts are disapproved. If the laws resonate with agreed-on public morality and values, then there ought to be some consensus in public opinion and some congruence between the legal and social definitions of wrong-doing and consequent penalties. These studies show that there is a consensus that cuts across class, age, sex, educational, racial, and regional groups on the condemnation of criminal behavior found in the core criminal law. Those acts defined by criminal law as the most serious offenses that carry the most severe penalties (e.g., murder, assault, rape, robbery, and theft) are the same ones that citizens agree are the most heinous and threatening to society. Violent personal crimes are rated as the most serious, with drug trafficking offenses not far behind and property offenses ranking somewhat lower. Offenses to public morality and order (e.g., public drunkenness or disorderly conduct) and consensual acts committed in private (e.g., prostitution) rank the lowest, with considerably more disagreement on their disapproval (Rossi, Waite, Bose, and Berk, 1974; Wellford, 1975; Pease, Ireson, and Thorpe, 1975; Thomas, Cage, and Foster, 1976; Wolfgang, Figlio, Tracy, and Singer, 1985).

There is a sizable variation in the average opinion for some kinds of behavior (Miethe, 1982). Differing circumstances often mitigate the severity of sanctions advocated by certain people for different acts, even when there is a consensual agreement that they are wrong and should be defined as illegal (Lanza-Kaduce, Krohn, Akers, and Radosevich, 1979; Cullen et al., 2000). The consensus found in these studies is real and not simply an artifact of the research methods. However, the findings do not support a pure consensus model of the law. Rather, they are more in line with a pluralistic conflict explanation. The acts prohibited by criminal law are the ones over which there is the most consensus and greatest moral condemnation in society. But there are many areas of the law over which there is just as much conflict and disagreement.

Research on Social Threat and Extra-Legal Variables in Criminal Justice Decision Making

The third type of study examines the relationship between the presence of threatening social groups and its impact on crime control efforts within a geographic area. The primary approach in this research is a macro-level focus on the demographic composition of an area and various measures of punitiveness. The results of this research are mixed, largely due to methodological variations and shortcomings. Most studies attempting to test the threat hypothesis have found weak to moderate support for a positive correlation between the percentage of Black or poor and crime control efforts such as police size and funding, police use of excessive force, and arrest.[4]

Chamlin and Cochran (2000:84) argued, however, that most of these studies represent only indirect tests of the threat hypothesis, measuring "structural antecedents" of social threat in which the dominant group's perception of threat is assumed rather than measured. Eitle, D'Alessio, and Stolzenberg (2002) offered more specific measures of threat, including political threat (ratio of Black-to-White voters in a community), economic threat (ratio of White-to-Black employment), and the threat of Black crime (Black offender/White victim felony crime rate). Their research indicates that neither political nor economic threat increases the likelihood of arrest of Black offenders, and that Black-on-White crime rates, but not Black-on-Black crime rates, lead to more arrests of Black offenders. Although these results may point to an inherent bias in policing that favors White over Black victims,[5] the demonstrated effect of Black-on-White crime on Black arrests may also reflect a functionalist interpretation, in that rising crime rates trigger a police response of increased arrest (Chamlin and Cochran, 2000; Elaine B. Sharp, 2006).

The measure of social threat has also been expanded to accommodate a more global context. In their study of social threat and punishment in 140 nations around the world, Ruddell and Urbina (2004) took social threat beyond its customary racial dimensions to include religious, ethnic (tribal), and linguistic diversity within the population. They found that after controlling for economic stress, modernization, political stability, and violent crime, population diversity increases the rate of imprisonment and decreases the likelihood of abolishing the death penalty among the nations studied. However, the study cannot discern the effect of within-nation variability in diversity and the extent to which the residential segregation of large minorities can diminish the perceived need to respond to this growing threat with greater social control (Stolzenberg, D'Alessio, and Eitle, 2004; Kent and Jacobs, 2005).

The idea of social threat is also implicit in the fourth, and most frequently conducted, type of study relevant to conflict theory. This research examines the exercise of discretion in applying the law against accused or suspected juvenile or adult law violators. Conflict and labeling theorists contend that criminal justice decisions (to arrest, prosecute, convict, and punish) will be biased against the less powerful individuals in society. In their view, the criminal justice system upholds the values and interests of the middle and upper classes, protects property and business, and favors the protection of the more influential and powerful members of society. Therefore, members of less powerful groups are more likely to be arrested, prosecuted, convicted, and given more severe penalties for committing the same offenses than the members of favored groups. Specifically, the hypothesis proposes that when examining the characteristics of individual offenders, criminal justice decisions are based more on *extra-legal variables* such as race, class, age, and gender, than on relevant behavioral and *legal variables* such as the defendant's charged offenses, prior criminal record, and guilt or innocence.[6] Paternoster and Iovanni (1989) asserted that labeling and conflict theories make no strong claims in this regard. They argue that they only hypothesize that extra-legal variables play "some" role, however minor or insignificant, in formal labeling decisions. This would be a very minimal claim that, if it were the main prediction by the theory, would be very easy to support, because finding anything with more than a zero effect of extra-legal variables would count in its favor. However, labeling and conflict theories can just as easily be interpreted as making the more extreme prediction that *only* extra-legal variables determine who gets labeled as criminal. In this version, the offense behavior and other legally relevant variables play no part whatsoever in the actions by police, courts, and correctional officials. It would be very difficult to find evidence to verify this prediction, because a finding of anything more than a zero effect of the legal variables would falsify it. Neither of these extremes, however, represents the most common and reasonable interpretation of the conflict perspective on criminal justice. It is usually interpreted to predict that extra-legal variables have substantial effects on criminal justice decisions that are as strong as, or stronger than, the effects of legal variables.

This makes the theory much more testable. It is some version of this hypothesis that usually gets tested in empirical research. The preponderance of evidence from that research weighs against the hypothesis. Criminal justice decisions are more likely to be based on legally relevant, neutral, and non-biased legal factors than they are on extra-legal variables. There is little question that disproportionate numbers of some groups undergo arrest, conviction, and imprisonment. Adolescent and young adult, lower class, and minority males are very much over-represented in arrests, prosecutions, convictions, and imprisonments. But by itself, a finding of differences by race, class, sex, or age in the criminal justice system does not support conflict theory. One cannot simply assume that the observed differences have resulted primarily from decisions biased against the less powerful. Before such a conclusion can be accepted, other questions must be answered.

The first question is, do the differences correspond to the ones hypothesized in the theory? Some in fact do. For instance, Blacks and the poor are over-represented in the criminal justice system (Walker et al., 2007). But other differences contradict the hypothesis that the less powerful will be treated more harshly and be more stigmatized than the more powerful. For example, as a group, men have more power and status in society than women; yet, male offenders vastly outnumber female offenders in the criminal and juvenile justice systems. They are much more likely to be arrested, convicted, and given long prison sentences than women (see chap. 11).

Second, and more important, is the question of the extent to which the decisions are based on these social characteristics, rather than on the behavior of the offender and the legal aspects of the case. To support the conflict/labeling hypothesis, research must demonstrate that people are treated differently based on their social status, even for the same criminal behavior and legal circumstances; that is, to support the hypothesis, the observed differences should be based primarily on something other than law-violative behavior and legally relevant variations in offense seriousness and criminal background. Even if men were less powerful than women, the theory would not be confirmed—because men are much more likely than women to be the most serious and frequent criminal offenders. Men's predominance in arrested, convicted, and incarcerated populations, then, results from their predominance in the population of offenders rather than from their gender. Thus, one must control for legal variables to determine if the extra-legal variables have a substantial independent effect on criminal justice decisions.

It is on this point that research evidence is the most damaging to the hypothesis that decisions in the criminal justice process are predominantly based on extra-legal variables. When legal variables (e.g., seriousness of the offense, prior criminal record, and aggravating circumstances) are controlled, differences in arrests, court outcomes, and the severity of sentencing by race, class, sex, age, and ethnicity either disappear or are reduced to small, substantively insignificant levels.[7]

One theorist became so convinced by research on the primacy of legal over extra-legal variables in the criminal justice system that he called the common assumption of racism in the system a "myth" (Wilbanks, 1987). This overstates the case, however. It may be a myth that the system is grossly discriminatory, with legal niceties always laid aside in favor of race-based or other biased decisions. Overall, research has found a relatively even-handed law enforcement, judicial, and correctional system. It is not a myth, however, that race, class, and other extra-legal variables in some places do in fact influence some decisions about adults and juveniles in the justice system.[8] As Walker et al. (2007) noted, there is "contextual discrimination" in which race-based decisions occur in some parts, at some stages, and by some individuals but not by others in the criminal justice system.

For example, Bishop and Frazier (1996) found significant disparities by race that remain, even controlling for legal variables in juvenile cases. In Florida, Black youth were treated more harshly in the juvenile justice system for major offenses, whereas White youth were treated more harshly for minor status offenses. However, Bishop and Frazier (1996:412) found that these differences were not based on deliberate, "intentional race discrimination." Instead, they conclude that "institutional racism" was in evidence, where formally race-neutral policies, practices, and judicial philosophies that affect judges' decisions were in practice correlated with race, favorable to White youth in delinquency cases, and unfavorable to them in dependency and status offense cases.

In most research, the more serious the offense, the more likely it is that decisions will remain neutral on race, class, and other status characteristics of the offender. Discretionary decisions are more apt to produce such disparities in minor offenses. There appears to be some racism, sexism, and class bias in the system, but they have a relatively weak effect on actual arrest, conviction, and sanctioning outcomes. On the whole, whatever effect these factors may have operates in a subtle, complex fashion, rather than in a direct, unequivocally discriminatory manner.

An illustration of this complex intertwining of variables is found in research involving race effects on the imposition of the death penalty in homicide convictions. Despite a "history of capital punishment in the United States prior to the Furman decision [that] is marked by inequality and discrimination" (Radelet, 1981:918), research on the death penalty has not found significant disparities in capital sentencing based on the race of the offender. Indeed, when racial differences are found, convicted White murderers face double the risk of a death sentence than do Black murderers. However, there *is* a pattern of prosecution and sentencing disparities based on the race of the homicide *victim*. The greater probability of a death penalty for White murderers appears to result from the fact that their victims are also likely to be White. When murder victims are White, regardless of the race of the offender, the convicted murderer is more likely to be sentenced to death. This is primarily because the one who murders a White person is more likely to be indicted and prosecuted for first-degree homicide, the only conviction that carries the possibility of capital punishment. The most likely offender-victim combination to result in prosecution for first-degree murder and the death penalty is that of a Black murderer and a White victim, even when all measurable legal variables are controlled (Radelet, 1981; Radelet and Pierce, 1991). Neither race of offender nor offender/victim race category is related to rate of incarceration or length of sentence for violent crimes in general; rather, the strongest predictors of sentencing are legal variables, such as seriousness of the crime committed and the offender's prior criminal record. But the race of offender/race of victim is a significant variable in sentencing for murder and sex offenses (Spohn, 1994).

A similar pattern is observed in sentencing of female murderers in Alabama from 1929 to 1985. White female murderers were twice as likely to be given life sentences as Black female murderers. However, there is a noticeable difference in life sentencing among the small number (20) of cases of interracial homicides. In those cases, half of the Black offenders who had murdered White victims received life sentences, whereas no White offender who had murdered a Black victim received a life sentence. Moreover, this sentencing inequity was more prominent in the pre–civil rights era (1929–1964) than in the post–civil rights era (Hanke, 1995).

Darrell Steffensmeier and his colleagues have examined the effects of age, gender, race, and ethnicity on sentencing outcomes (Steffensmeier, Ulmer, and Kramer, 1998; Steffensmeier and Demuth, 2000; 2001; 2006). His research demonstrated that both the judicial decision to sentence to prison and the length of the sentence imposed are most strongly affected by the legally relevant and non-discriminatory variables of offense severity and the offender's prior criminal record. However, even when these legal variables are controlled, some small to moderate effects of these extra-legal variables remain. For example, given similar prior records and offense seriousness, Whites receive the most lenient sentences, whereas Hispanics receive harsher penalties than both Blacks and Whites (Steffensmeier and Demuth, 2000; 2001; 2006). However, even these conditional race and ethnicity effects are moderated by gender: Among males, both Blacks and Hispanics receive harsher treatment at sentencing; however, among females, the race and ethnicity effects on sentencing outcomes disappear. Steffensmeier hypothesized that these differences result primarily from judges' "focal concerns" of offender blameworthiness, dangerousness, and considerations about how some defendants would stand up to "hard time" in prison. Although in general, judges and other court actors may perceive Blacks and Hispanics to be "more dangerous, more likely to recidivate, and less likely to be deterred," it appears that "*all* female defendants [regardless of race or ethnicity] ... benefit from beliefs viewing them as less culpable, as less dangerous, as less likely to recidivate (partly because of stronger ties to kin/family including children), and as more essential for providing child care" (Steffensmeier and Demuth, 2006:246–247; emphasis in original).

Not all racial differences can be interpreted as racially motivated. Rather they may reflect what Petersilia and Turner (1987) called "disparities" rather than "discrimination" in the system:

> Racial *discrimination* occurs if the system officials make *ad hoc* decisions based on race rather than on clearly defined objective standards. ... However, racial *disparity* occurs when such standards are applied but

have different results for different racial groups. (Petersilia and Turner, 1987:153; emphasis in original)

The final question that remains is, how is it that a system found by careful research to be relatively even-handed in arrest, prosecution, conviction, and sentencing can produce a prison population that is so disproportionately Black, male, and poor? Research conducted at any stage of criminal justice processing reports little difference by race, class, or gender when the proper legalistic variables are controlled. Yet, as one moves from the beginning stage of arrest to the end stage of imprisonment or intermediate sanctioning, class, gender, and other disparities increase. One answer may be that relatively small differences at each decision point accumulate to the extent that larger differences seem to exist at the end of the process (Liska and Tausig, 1979; Bishop and Frazier, 1988; Horowitz and Pottieger, 1991).

Another answer may lie in the research on habitual and career criminals. These are the chronic offenders who commit multiple offenses, continue their criminal activity at a high level, fill the jails, and populate the prisons. For example, a study of an urban birth cohort found that, by 18 years of age, 50% of Black male youths and 28% of White male youths have had at least one encounter with police. Among these delinquent offenders was found a small group of chronic recidivists (6%) who accounted for more than one half (52%) of police arrests. Race and social class were among those variables most strongly related to the seriousness and repetitiveness of their delinquency (Wolfgang et al., 1972). Although most of those with juvenile arrest records did not continue into adulthood with a criminal record, almost 80% of the small group of chronic juvenile offenders pursued criminal careers as adults, again with Black and lower class men over-represented among them (Wolfgang et al., 1987; see also Shannon, 1982).

These "chronic persisters" (Blumstein, Farrington, and Moitra, 1985), whose behavior and lifestyle place them most at risk for official attention by the criminal justice system, are disproportionately Black and poor. This results in more frequent arrests, accumulating an official record on which later criminal justice sanctioning decisions are based. They may also be subjected to the policy of "selective incapacitation" (Blumstein et al., 1978; Bernard and Ritti, 1991) in which habitual offenders are singled out for longer prison terms to keep them off the streets for a longer time. The over-representation of certain groups in prison populations, then, may be the end product of a combination of their higher frequency and longer lasting criminal behavior and the greater attention they attract at an early stage from law enforcement.

The research on disparities in the criminal justice system almost exclusively examines formal decision points: arrest, indictment, conviction, and sentencing. It does not look closely at racial and neighborhood disparities in informal and unauthorized actions taken on the street. Daniel Georges-Abeyie (1990) drew the distinction between "grand apartheid" in which racism is embodied explicitly and overtly within a government's laws and procedures, and "petit apartheid" in which racism is embedded covertly and perhaps even unintentionally within mores and custom (see also Milovanovic and Russell, 2001). It may be that racial and class biases are found in the patterns of police patrols, citizen harassment, stop and search, stop and interrogate, use of excessive force, and other actions taken by the police in the community (Chambliss, 1994).

One notable example is the practice of racial profiling by police. Outlawed in several states and under increasing scrutiny by many of the nation's courts, racial profiling, or race-biased law enforcement, involves police action taken *solely* on the basis of race rather than the behavior of the individual. Anecdotal accounts of "driving while Black" (or even "running while Black" or "standing while Black") have led to a variety of more systematic analyses of data collected on traffic stops and field interrogations. Most of these studies have found disproportionate numbers of minorities stopped by the police.[9]

The research on racial profiling has been subjected to numerous methodological criticisms, especially the questionable use of census data on proportions of minorities in the residential population as the "benchmark" (Fridell, 2004) against which proportions of minorities in traffic stops or field interrogations are compared. Engel et al. (2002) also question the conceptual basis of the extant racial profiling research. Most of these studies are purely descriptive and offer no attempt to examine the intent of the racial basis for police action. Because racial profiling is defined as the use of race as the *sole* criterion for police action, the officer's (or police department's) intention or motivation becomes paramount. It is therefore necessary that studies examining racial profiling also take into account the numerous social psychological, organizational, and social structural variables proposed to explain the race-based actions of police officers and agencies.

Conflict Theory of Criminal Behavior

Conflict theory views the whole process of law-making, law-breaking, and law enforcement as implicated in the conflict and power differentials among social, economic, and political interest groups. Criminal behavior is a reflection of this ongoing collective conflict. This conflict explanation is best exemplified in Vold's (1958:203–219) group conflict theory. It also bears a relation to the cultural and normative conflict theories of crime by Thorsten Sellin (1938) and Edwin Sutherland (1947; 1973). Conflict theory explains crime and deviant behavior as the ordinary, learned, and normal behavior of individuals caught up in *cultural* and *group* conflict. Crime is an expression of that conflict and results when persons acting according to the norms and values of their own group violate those of another group that have been enacted into law (Sellin, 1938; Sutherland, 1947; Sutherland and Cressey, 1978).

For example, foreign immigrants may violate the laws of a new country simply by behaving according to the customs of the old country. Even rural migrants within the same country may carry a set of conduct norms and values with them into a city, which results in a conflict with urban laws. Religious, ethnic, and other cultural minority groups may adhere to a set of behavioral standards that conflict with those of dominant conventional society.

Other crimes may result from direct group conflict. Both major and minor crimes are committed by dissident groups protesting against or trying to induce change in the established political and social order. Civil rights protesters have engaged in civil disobedience and broken the law, not because they were personally motivated to commit crime, but because they espoused the interests of a group that defined the laws as instruments of an unjust system. On the other side of the coin, Blacks have been lynched, churches have been bombed, and other acts of violence have been inflicted on both Blacks and Whites by those (including some in law enforcement) who support a system they believed to be right and just.

Law violation growing out of group conflict may be a non-violent disruption or simply non-compliance with police orders to disperse, but often it goes beyond this to violence and property damage. For example, anti-abortion activists have damaged property and broken laws in their efforts to close down abortion clinics; on the other hand, pro-choice activists have assaulted anti-abortion protesters. A clinic abortionist has been murdered by an anti-abortion zealot. Both sides adamantly believe they are right, resulting in violence and an open defiance of the law.

If such protest reached the point of questioning the entire system, the outcome could be a violent revolution. During the Vietnam War era, for example, protests against the war and the draft often resulted in large-scale conflict with the law. Radical groups, determined to change the system, bombed buildings and committed violence in the name of their own brand of justice. In a revolution, all forms of terrorism are justified by ideology. As radical groups clash with the police, such criminal offenses as murder, sabotage, seizure of property, destruction, theft, and burglary may occur. To protect the established legal system, the police and other authorities may also violate the law (e.g., "police brutality") in the course of controlling the protests.

Such crimes are typically *political crimes* (Vold, 1958; Quinney, 1964). Political crimes are best defined as law violations motivated by the desire to influence existing public policy, the political system, or power relations (Minor, 1975). Political crime may be committed by those who oppose the existing system and want to change or destroy it. It may also be committed by officials in the government, law enforcement, or the criminal justice system to defend the status quo or change the system in the desired direction. The infamous crimes and obstruction of justice committed by President Richard Nixon and his White House staff in the 1970s, commonly known as Watergate, are a clear historical example of political crime. They used the power of government and law enforcement agencies against groups and individuals who were perceived as threats to the power and authority of the established regime.[10]

Who is deemed a criminal depends on which side prevails in the conflict. If a protest or revolution is successful, the former rulers become the criminals; if not, the rebels remain the criminals. White supremacists, who previously enforced the Jim Crow laws and branded Blacks who broke them as criminals, later became the ones who were more likely to be considered criminals for violating civil rights laws. The collapse of the Soviet Union and communist regimes in Eastern Europe is another example. Those who were dissidents violated communist law under the old regimes, but many of those former dissidents came to power in the new regimes. Former rulers were indicted and convicted of crimes or became fugitives sought by law enforcement under the control of the newly elected governments. In politically or ideologically motivated crimes, offenders perceive themselves as fighters for the cause of higher loyalties and values. They publicly announce their violations and disavow the law. Conflict theorists, however, often try to explain crime even when these elements are absent and the offenders acknowledge the legitimacy of the laws they are breaking. For instance, Vold viewed delinquent gangs as groups supporting values in conflict with the dominant majority. He also analyzed organized crime as a type of business system that is in conflict with the laws of legitimate society.

Empirical Validity of Conflict Theory of Criminal Behavior

Many other illustrations of crime related to group and culture conflict could be given here, but research that explicitly tests hypotheses from conflict theory of criminal behavior is quite rare. One study found no correlation between the number of political interest groups and the crime rate, but did find some relationship between crime and the *type* of interest groups (Brunk and Wilson, 1991). The dearth of such studies means that the validity and scope of conflict theory have not been adequately tested. Despite this fact, some observations can be made on the theory's empirical applicability to crime.

Conflict theory portrays modern society as so heterogeneous that there is little value consensus among the population at large. Crisscrossing and balancing cleavages and group compromises form the basis for the organization of society today. There is some validity to this conflict image, but it remains incomplete. There is more to society than the working arrangement of a congeries of conflicting groups and interests. Society is also held together by the larger or smaller number of widely supported values, common assumptions, and images of the world. This is a chief factor in providing some continuity and unity in a diversified society. We cannot explain the criminal behavior of those who violate these broad values and norms as simply acting on behalf of some group interest in conflict with the dominant view. Of course, groups and their values clash in the enactment of laws, but it does not necessarily follow that most crime is simply the result of a continuation of that conflict beyond legislative battles, nor is it true that those from groups who win a political battle will faithfully adhere to the law, whereas those on the losing side will typically violate the law.

Vold emphasized conflict among more or less organized interest groups. He excluded the "impulsive, irrational acts of a criminal nature that are quite unrelated to any battle between different interest groups in organized society" (Vold, 1958:219). He also warned that the "group conflict hypothesis should not be stretched too far" (Vold, 1958:219). Nevertheless, he stretched the theory to cover many types of crime, including organized crime and white-collar crime, and "a considerable amount of crime" in general (Vold, 1958:219).

However, the empirical scope of conflict theory is much less than this. Conflict theory applies accurately to a narrow range of crimes, of which only politically or ideologically motivated crimes will fit the model well. The vast majority of juvenile delinquency and adult crime cannot be explained as simply behavior incidental to group and cultural conflict. Most crime is intra-group, committed by members inside a group against one another, rather than inter-group.

Partly acknowledging the limited scope of conflict theory to explain criminal behavior, other conflict theorists have typically refrained from or disavowed efforts to explain criminal behavior as the result of group or cultural conflict. Rather, they have emphasized group power and conflict in the process of making and enforcing laws while turning to other explanations to answer the question of why people violate the law. Quinney (1970), for instance, used power and conflict to explain the formulation and application of criminal law. But when addressing the behavior of those who violate the law, he relied on differential association, learning, self-concept, and other variables outside of conflict theory. Bernard (Vold et al., 2002:240) proposed a "unified conflict theory of crime" to explain both criminal behavior and criminal law, which retains Vold's emphasis on "different and conflicting values and interests." In so doing, Bernard incorporated into the context of Vold's argument the principles of social learning theory,

Policy Implications of Conflict Theory

The conflict approach to law and criminal justice obviously implies support for fair representation of differing interests and values in the law and a policy of non-discrimination with regard to race, gender, and class in the criminal justice system. However, such a policy would be equally implied by the consensus approach to law and criminal justice because it would reflect common, widely held values of fairness, equal protection of the law, and non-discrimination in American society. Administering legally fair and equitable policies, procedures, and decisions in the criminal justice system is already the official policy. Findings from research on discrimination, legal versus extra-legal factors, and the other kinds of research discussed in this chapter are useful in judging how well the official policy is carried out in practice. But there is not much in the theory that would inform us on how to make practice come closer to the ideal. Also, it is difficult to discern the policy implications of the conflict explanation of criminal behavior.

Conflict theory would lead one to conclude that without fundamental structural changes in society, not much can be done about crime. One could argue that because the theory says that criminal behavior results from the clash of group interests, reduction of conflict should reduce crime. But because the theory also views conflict as a necessary, universal aspect of society, any effort to reduce group conflict would seem to be futile or inconsistent with the theory.

Turk (1995) challenged the view that conflict theory has little direct application to legal or criminal justice policy. He argued that the policy implications of conflict theory have been underappreciated because "non-partisan conflict" [non-radical, pluralistic conflict] theory is too often confused with "radical revolutionism," which

> ...assumes that the *only* policy worth considering is how to bring about the destruction of the current social order. Whether the essential character of that order is thought to be capitalism, racism, sexism, militarism, or some other basis of social inequality, the impossibility of improving or transforming it is taken for granted. (Turk, 1995:16)

However, beyond noting that non-partisan conflict theory rejects both piecemeal reformism and revolution, Turk does not spell out what specific policies would be recommended by conflict theory.

Summary

Law is the formal part of the overall social control system of society. It both reflects and has an impact on social, economic, political, and other institutions in society. Consensus theory explains the content and operation of the law by reference to a broad-based agreement in society on social and moral norms and the common interests of all elements of society. Conflict theory proposes that law and the criminal justice system primarily embody the interests and norms of the most powerful groups in society, rather than those of the society as a whole; and that the law will be enforced by the criminal justice system in a manner that unfairly labels and punishes the less powerful in society.

The empirical evidence on consensus and conflict theories stems from studies of the enactment of law, studies of public opinion on crime, and both macro- and micro-level studies of race, class, sex, and age disparities in arrests, convictions, and penalties. The research tends to favor a pluralistic conflict model in which there is consensus on core legal norms but conflict among competing interest groups in making and enforcing the law. Research evidence does not show that racism and sexism blatantly infest the criminal justice system. At the same time, it does not show that the system is free of bias. The preponderance of research findings, however, support the conclusion, contrary to extreme conflict theory but consistent with pluralistic conflict theory (Walker et al., 2007), that the criminal justice system makes decisions based more on legally relevant variables than on extra-legal variables.

Conflict theory explains crime as the behavior of individuals caught up in cultural and group conflict. There is very little research, however, to test this theory of criminal behavior. Politically or ideologically motivated crime would seem to fit the conflict model well. On the other hand, conflict theory does not fit juvenile delinquency or the vast majority of crime such as murder, theft, burglary, rape, arson, white-collar crime, and organized crime. Conflict theory has greater empirical support as an explanation of law formation than as an explanation of the operation of the criminal justice system or as an explanation of criminal behavior. Both conflict and consensus theories imply support for fair representation of differing interests and values and non-discrimination in the law and criminal justice system, but there seem to be few specific programmatic implications of the conflict theory of criminal behavior.

Notes

1. For early statements of the conflict theory of criminal law, see Chambliss (1964; 1969), Chambliss and Seidman (1971), Quinney (1969; 1970), Turk (1966; 1969a), and Hills (1971). For later statements, see Akers and Hawkins (1975), Akers (1985), Turk (1977; 1979), Alix (1978), Reasons and Rich (1978), and Chambliss (1974; 1988). For a more recent review and update of conflict theory, see Bridges and Myers (1994).

2. Ironically, some contemporary proponents of radical, critical, and Marxist theories have returned to pluralistic conflict models, acknowledging that capitalism alone cannot adequately account for criminality and designating "identity" (i.e., race, class, or gender) as a dominant concept in theories of law and criminal justice. See Messerschmidt (1997), Barak, Flavin, and Leighton (2001), and Lynch and Michalowski (2006) for discussions of these issues.

3. See Hall (1952), Becker (1963), Chambliss (1964), Dickson (1968), Roby (1969), Platt (1969), Alix (1978), Galliher and Walker (1977), Hagan and Leon (1977), Hagan (1980), Troyer and Markle (1983), Hollinger and Lanza-Kaduce (1988), and Castellano and McGarrell (1991).

4. For reviews of this literature, see Liska (1992) and Eitle et al. (2002).

5. Liska and Chamlin (1984) referred to this phenomenon as "benign neglect." See also LaFree (1980), Paternoster (1984), and Kleck (1981).

6. For tests of a different set of hypotheses regarding police–citizen contacts taken from Turk's conflict theory, see Lanza-Kaduce and Greenleaf (1994).

7. There is a very large body of literature on this point. For narrative reviews of this research, see Hagan (1974), Wilbanks (1987), Tittle and Curran (1988), and Free (2002). A recent meta-analysis of the race and sentencing research (Mitchell, 2005) also concluded that the race effect on sentencing is substantially reduced when more precise measures of prior record and offense severity are controlled. A related body of literature has to do with what effect the "demeanor" of the suspect toward the police has on the police decision to arrest. Research on this issue finds that controlling for demeanor reduces racial differences in arrests and that even when suspected criminal conduct is held constant, a hostile or disrespectful demeanor increases the chances that the suspect will be arrested (Klinger, 1996; Worden and Shepard, 1996; see also Dunham, Alpert, Stroshine, and Bennett, 2005, for an observational analysis of factors affecting the formation of police suspicion). This finding suggests that hostility is interpreted by the police as a challenge to authority. However, because demeanor may be seen as relevant to probable cause, it is unclear whether it is a legal or extra-legal variable.

8. See the findings in Petersilia (1983), Petersilia and Turner (1987), Kempf and Austin (1986), Bridges and Crutchfield (1988), Bishop and Frazier

(1988), Horowitz and Pottieger (1991), Smith and Akers (1993); and research reviewed by Spohn (2000), Zatz (2000), and Walker et al. (2007).

9. For a good review, see Withrow (2006).

10. Crimes by public officials for personal monetary or political gain, on the other hand, are instances of occupational or white-collar crime, rather than politically motivated crime.

Chapter 10

Marxist and Critical Theories

Marxist Theory

Conflict theory, along with labeling theory, gained prominence in American sociology and criminology in the 1960s. By the mid-1970s, Richard Quinney (1974a; 1974b), William Chambliss (1975; Chambliss and Seidman, 1982), Anthony Platt (1977; Platt and Takagi, 1981), Herman and Julia Schwendinger (1983; 1985), and others had shifted from their earlier adherence to conflict theory of law and criminal justice and toward embracing Marxist theory or "radical" and "critical" approaches that were viewed as synonymous with or closely related to Marxist theory.[1] This historical connection of Marxist theory with conflict theory presents an "interesting paradox of a Marxism reared in the womb of theoretical structures to which it was, and is, ostensibly largely opposed" (Beirne and Quinney, 1982:8).

Marxist theory has in common with conflict theory an interest in explaining both law and criminal justice but rejects the multi-group conflict image of society and endorses a power-elite model of society in which social, economic, and political power has been concentrated into the hands of a small ruling class in "late-stage capitalism." Late-stage or advanced capitalism is the label that Marxists have given to highly industrially developed democracies (Mankoff, 1970). In Marxist theory, capitalism is a two-class system comprised of the ruling class that owns the means of production (the capitalists or the bourgeoisie) versus the proletariat, the workers or masses who have only their labor to sell. The capitalists' monopoly on the means of production allows them also to control the political state. This political power is used to manipulate the legal and criminal justice system to promote the interests of the capitalist class and to perpetuate its position of power. Repressed by this system, the masses of workers have no power whatsoever to ameliorate or modify their oppression. This situation will remain until they become organized for revolution, take power into their hands, overthrow the government, and destroy the capitalist economy. After this revolutionary period, the proletariat will establish a socialist system that will ultimately evolve into a class-free communist system in which there will be economic and social equality, justice will prevail, the political state will wither away, and the law will be unnecessary.

A major example of Marxist theory in criminology is found in the work of Richard Quinney (1974a; 1974b; 1979; 1980). Quinney proposed that whatever conflicts exist amidst the diversity of interests in society are concentrated within the basic, underlying struggle between the proletariat and the bourgeoisie. What appears to be internal conflict within each of these two main classes is not real. In America and other late-stage capitalist societies, we are all either members of the ruling elite or members of the oppressed masses. If we are not owners of the means of production, we are workers subject to capitalist oppression, some of whom serve as lackeys to do the bidding (willingly or unwillingly) of the ruling elite. The objective interests of the masses lie with the proletariat. Any worker who does not recognize this objective interest and subjectively identifies with the bourgeois class possesses "false class-consciousness." Quinney (1979) claims that most intellectuals and academics in American society have false class-consciousness. This includes non-Marxist, "traditional" criminologists, who provide knowledge of criminals and criminal law for use by the ruling class to manipulate the crime problem in its own interests. Although criminologists may view themselves as objective social scientists, in reality they serve the interests of the capitalist class.

All real power and authority are exclusive to the ruling class, whose primary goals are to maintain power and continue the existing capitalist order. In pursuit of these goals, capitalists promote interests that are antithetical to those of the proletariat, trampling the rights and aspirations of the masses. This basic contradiction between the reality of oppression and the democratic ideals of freedom and equality forces the capitalist elite to face a constant "crisis of legitimacy." If the masses ever reach the point of fully recognizing their repression by the elite, they will organize, revolt, and overthrow the system. They cannot be kept forever in check by force alone. Therefore, the elite must wage a ceaseless battle to maintain a cultural and ideological "hegemony" (sovereign control) over the "ruling ideas" of society. The ruling class manipulates the mass media, the intellectual and academic community, and other sources of public opinion, so that the masses will continue to believe in the legitimacy of the system. Quinney recognized that there may be consensus on certain laws, but this does not necessarily show that these laws reflect the common experiences and support the interests of society as a whole. Existing consensus and order are imposed from above through force and the manipulation of public opinion.

Marxist Theory of Law and Criminal Justice

The law appears to operate in the interests of the whole society, whereas in reality it is structured to serve only the interests of the ruling elite. The criminal justice system is used against, rather than for, the people. Under capitalism, the system of law and punishment is inherently unjust, designed not to control crime for the good of society but to subjugate the population. For instance, imprisonment is imposed less as a direct punishment for convicted offenders than as a way to siphon off surplus labor from the population (Rusche, 1933/1978; Rusche and Kirchheimer, 2003). Because a "long cycle" of growth and depression is inherent in capitalism (Gordon et al., 1982), there will be times when there are too many workers that the economy cannot absorb. These surplus laborers are a potential threat to the capitalists because they could mobilize and organize themselves into a revolutionary movement. Therefore, the theory explains the imprisonment of criminal offenders as simply another way to regulate the availability and cost of labor. Imprisonment rates are expected to be high during times of recession and high unemployment, which is indicative of the capitalists' efforts to remove surplus workers from society until they are needed again for production.[2]

According to Quinney, the criminal justice system is designed not to protect society against crime but, along with other institutions of the capitalist state, to repress the people. Because this is inevitable in a capitalist system, there is no way to accomplish real reform to ameliorate the plight of the proletariat. The whole system must be, and inevitably will be, destroyed. The only real solution to the crime problem is to join the class struggle, overthrow the capitalist system, and establish a socialist state. Marxist ideology maintains that this can only be brought about by violent means. In this case, however, Quinney departed from the Marxist stance, arguing that the system can be overthrown nonviolently and replaced with some form of democratic socialism.

Instrumentalist and Structuralist Marxism

Quinney's and similar explanations of law and the criminal justice system (see Balkan, Berger, and Schmidt, 1980) are known as *instrumentalist* Marxism. This theory of the political state as only and always an instrument of the capitalist class underwent strong criticism by other criminologists. Some of the critics were themselves Marxist scholars who proposed an alternative *structuralist* model of Marxism

(Balbus, 1977; Chambliss and Seidman, 1982). Partially in response to these criticisms, Quinney and other instrumental Marxists modified their position to adhere more closely to this structuralist model (Beirne and Quinney, 1982).

The principal difference between the two is that the structuralists view the political state as having "relative autonomy." In other words, the state is not totally under the dominion of the ruling elite, and the law is not always just an instrument for the promotion of its interests. In the short run, then, the state may be autonomous. Much of the law and the criminal justice system does not automatically mirror the interests of the capitalists. Indeed, many laws may be passed that are directly counter to capitalist interests. Even individual members of the ruling class, if discovered breaking the law, may be apprehended and punished. Moreover, the structural model does not propose that this capitalist class is an entirely monolithic group. There may be internal factions within it that clash with each other. Particular laws and policies may promote the interests of some ruling-class members yet work against the interests of others (see Balbus, 1977; Beirne, 1979; Greenberg, 1981a; Beirne and Quinney, 1982; Chambliss and Seidman, 1982; Chambliss, 1988).

This distinction between instrumentalist and structuralist Marxism can be sustained only in the short run. In the long run there is no difference between instrumentalist and structuralist Marxism. Both agree that the long-term historical tendency of the legal system is to reflect and protect the interest of the capitalist class and oppress the masses (Lynch and Groves, 1986). The only difference is that structural Marxism contends that in the short run, there are conflicts beyond the clash between capitalists and the proletariat, and that other power centers exist in society with the ability to counterbalance the power elite. The greater the extent to which Marxist theory is modified to account for a multiplicity of conflicts, power groups, and contradictions in society (Chambliss, 1988), the closer it becomes a variation on pluralistic conflict theory. Therefore, the structuralist model represents something of a movement by some Marxist criminologists back toward conflict theory.

Empirical Adequacy of Marxist Theory of Law and Justice

Marxist theory has been criticized for stating tautological propositions and dogmatic ideology rather than stating a testable theory of law making and law enforcement. Akers (1979) argued that much of what passes for Marxist theory is really an ideological condemnation of Western democracies and a call for revolutionary action to overthrow them. But he distinguishes the political philosophy of Marxism from Marxian analysis that does offer a verifiable theory.

The Marxist contention that criminal justice responses to crime are affected by the political economy of a society has been subjected to empirical testing. One hypothesis that was explained earlier is that the elite will ensure that imprisonment rates are high in times of depression and low in times of economic prosperity to control the labor supply. This effect of unemployment on imprisonment should remain even when changes in the crime rate are taken into account. However, the historical evidence to support this hypothesis is contradictory. Imprisonment rates were high during the Great Depression of the 1930s; yet, during times of economic growth, relatively low unemployment, and little surplus labor over the past 2 decades, there has been the greatest increase in the prison population in American history. This hypothesis has also been tested both directly and indirectly with quantitative data, but the evidence is mixed. One review of the empirical literature concludes positive support for the unemployment–imprisonment relationship, but critics observe that only 60% of the correlations in the studies reviewed were statistically significant in the expected direction (Chiricos and DeLone, 1992; Jacobs and Helms, 1996). A later study shows that the strength of the unemployment-imprisonment correlation depends on the unique relationships among capital, labor, and the state during each period of economic decline (Michalowski and Carlson, 1999). Nevertheless, other research demonstrates that conditions of capital (e.g., business and bank failures, trade deficits) rather than conditions of labor influence the enactment of punitive legislation, and then only weakly (Barlow, Barlow, and Johnson, 1996; Lynch, Hogan, and Stretesky, 1999). Moreover, the apparent effects of unemployment on imprisonment seem to weaken or disappear when variables such as conservative party dominance and family disorganization are controlled (D'Alessio and Stolzenberg, 1995; Sutton, 2000; Jacobs and Helms, 1996; 2001; Jacobs and Carmichael, 2001).

As a whole, there is little in Marxist theory of law and criminal justice that is empirically testable in this way. Many Marxists will argue that such attempts to create testable hypotheses and judge them on the basis of quantitative data is "bourgeois positivism" and not the proper way to evaluate Marxist theory.[3] The only way to apply Marxist theory, they contend, is to examine history. Critics respond that, when Marxist theorists use historical analysis, they tend to focus only on the failings, fallacies, and injustices in Western democracies and pay scant attention to the historical elitism, repression, and injustices in systems founded on Marxist principles (Turk, 1979; Klockars, 1979; Akers, 1979).

This does not necessarily mean that the Marxist critiques of capitalist society have no validity. There is little doubt that the historical tendency in capitalist systems leans toward greater concentrations of wealth and power. We are currently in an era that seems to concern itself primarily with promoting and protecting a global system of trade and commerce that treats labor as a fungible commodity. In the process of downsizing, large corporations eliminate jobs in countries with relatively high income for the labor force, such as the United States, and move their industrial facilities to countries where workers are more impoverished and powerless. One does not need to read beyond newspaper headlines to know that the power of unions and the living standards of middle-class and working-class populations have been severely curtailed, whereas the living standards of the executives and owners of manufacturing and financial corporations are maintained or elevated. Domestic policies and the foreign policies of free trade serve more the interest of multinational corporations and international financial institutions than the interest of common workers. Marxist theory provides one way to explain how these high concentrations of economic power have an impact on law and justice in a capitalist society.

However, examining the structure and operation of capitalist systems alone is not adequate to evaluate Marxist theory. Akers (1979) argued that, to substantiate their theory, Marxist criminologists must make the proper kinds of comparisons between real socialist and real capitalist societies. As yet, Marxists have been very reluctant to make such comparisons. Instead, they compare an idealized, future socialist utopia with the realities of historical and present-day capitalist democracies. This is not a valid method for determining the validity of a theory.

Serious doubt has been raised about the historical accuracy of Marxist explanations for the formation and operation of law in society. Marxists make reference to the inherent contradictions and injustices of capitalism as an economic system, under which a repressive legal system is seen as inevitable. But, in fact, although some capitalistic societies have indeed been ruled by authoritarian political systems that use the police, courts, and prisons to repress the population, the most open, free, and democratic societies in history have had capitalist economies. On the other hand, Marxist theory denigrates civil liberties and individual rights as "bourgeois democracy" and favors instead a dictatorship of the proletariat in which there is no protection of human rights (Lipset, 1960).

Despite adopting such names as "people's democratic republic," Marxist regimes have invariably been totalitarian or authoritarian. They have not progressed to the point of instituting a classless society with a non-repressive system of law and criminal justice. Instead, they have produced a command economy in which a small group of rulers control the economy, the law, and the criminal justice system to repress political dissent and protect its own power.

If ever there was any further doubt about it, the collapse of the communist regimes around the world in the latter part of the 1980s finally unveiled the repressive police-state law enforcement systems that existed in Marxist governments. Even before the failure of Marxist political-economic systems, comparisons of real societies could not support Marxist assertions that the law is inevitably a repressive tool of the elite in a capitalist society while it is used to promote justice in a socialist society. The injustices attributed to Western capitalist democracies by Marxists better describe the now defunct systems in the former Soviet Union and Eastern Europe and the current regimes in Cuba, China, Vietnam, and North Korea. In these systems, the privileged elite has co-opted the state, law, and criminal justice to perpetuate its own interests. In addition, Marxist theory cannot account for the rise of the most extremely and comprehensively repressive systems, such as the former Taliban regime in Afghanistan, in societies that can be described as neither late-stage capitalism nor socialism.

Historical realities such these have often been ignored in Marxist analyses of law and criminal justice. However, structural Marxists are more likely than instrumental Marxists to acknowledge some of the realities of socialist systems. Many American Marxist scholars disavowed the Soviet Union and similar regimes as not truly socialist even before their dissolution. For example, there was some recognition of the political repression and power conflict in the Soviet system (Chambliss and Seidman, 1982; Greenberg, 1981a). Although earlier Marxist thought failed "to see that the political, conflict processes through which definitions of deviance (criminality) are created and enforced are not peculiar to 'capitalist' societies" (Turk, 1969b:14), some Marxist and radical scholars did see that:

> All societies represent a set of social relations characterized by attempts to resolve conflicts generated by contradictions inherent in the social structure.... Modern-day socialist societies share some of the contradictions and conflicts of capitalist societies and have their own unique ones as well.... Crime in both socialist and capitalist societies reflects the particular contradictions of those societies. (Chambliss, 1988:304, 325)

Others dismissed whatever problems there were in socialist systems as unfortunate aberrations unreflective of true socialism while viewing the problems in Western democracies as inherent and unavoidable in late-stage capitalism or simply denied that there were any problems of human rights and repression in communist societies (Chase-Dunn, 1980; Szymanski, 1981).

Marxist Theory of Crime

Karl Marx wrote virtually nothing about criminal behavior, and many Marxist criminologists have long recognized that there can be no purely Marxist theory of crime (Taylor et al., 1973; 1975). As do conflict theorists, Marxists concentrate on criminal law and the criminal justice system. They have less to say about the causes of criminal behavior.

Even when examining the causes of crime, Marxists tend to refer more to the control by the system than to the behavior of criminal offenders. For example, Steven Spitzer (1975) proposed a "Marxian theory of deviance," which is widely cited as an example of a Marxist explanation for crime. Spitzer's model, however, is largely devoted to how those who steal, participate in delinquent gangs, become involved in revolutionary activities, or become unemployed are defined and controlled by capitalists as "problem populations." Little attention is paid to the etiology of crime among these problem populations. Spitzer does no more than sketch out the general features of capitalism, such as its "contradictions," that may induce criminal behavior. Such general reference to capitalism as embodying the causes of crime is typical of Marxist explanations of crime.

Bonger: Early Marxist Theory of Crime

The first systematic application of Marxism to the etiology of crime was offered by the Dutch criminologist Willem Bonger (1876–1940), who hypothesized that crime is produced by the "capitalistic organization of society" (Bonger, 1916/1969; van Bemmelen, 1972). Private ownership of the means of production, as well as the profit motive found in capitalist society, induces "egoistic tendencies," encourages greed and selfishness, and fails to promote "social instincts" that would otherwise prevent "egoistic thoughts from leading to egoistic acts." Bonger further claimed, "We shall show that, as a consequence of the present [capitalist economic system], man has become very egoistic and hence more *capable of crime* than if the environment had developed the germs of altruism" (Bonger, 1916/1969:40–41; emphasis in original).

All classes are affected by the egoism and greed produced by capitalism; but because the law is controlled by the bourgeoisie, it is the egoistic actions of the proletariat that are defined as criminal. The cause of crime in all classes, therefore, is the capitalist mode of economic organization by which one's class position in society is defined by one's relationship to the means of production. Adult crime and juvenile delinquency, the criminality of women, prostitution, alcoholism, and other aspects of crime are to be expected because of economic conditions under capitalism.

Quinney: Class, State, and Crime

Bonger's theory received little acceptance when it first appeared. By the 1940s, its single-factor economic explanation of crime and naive faith in socialism had been essentially discounted in American criminology (Gillen, 1945:152–157). Non-Marxist class analysis predominated, and economic factors were seen as just one set among a large number of causes of crime. Mainstream sociological theory of class and crime (e.g., anomie theory) prevailed over Marxist class analysis. There was strong emphasis on social class and the "root" causes of crime, but this did not include the notion that the capitalist social structure itself was the root cause of all crime.

Marxist theory enjoyed an intellectual boom in the 1970s, as it came to occupy a position of influence and respect in Western social science. When these neo-Marxists turned their attention to the issue of crime causation, however, they offered essentially the same explanation of crime that Bonger had given several decades earlier: Capitalism is the central cause of crime.

Among them were the British scholars Ian Taylor, Paul Walton, and Jock Young (Taylor et al., 1973; 1975), who delivered a scathing critique of the ideological and theoretical shortcomings of such "traditional" sociological theories of crime as anomie, social disorganization, social control, labeling, and social learning. Yet, they offered little more than an outline of what a radical theory of crime should be and failed to provide a viable alternative to these other theories. According to Taylor et al. (1973), crime is one significant consequence of the exploitation and oppression of the working class under capitalism. Most proletarian lawbreakers are motivated to commit crimes of "accommodation" (e.g., professional crime, theft, prostitution, and organized crime). Their offenses have no relevance for the proletarian class struggle, because they are simply surviving the best they can in an unjust society without trying to change it. Other offenders, however, commit crimes of "rebellion," political crimes carried out as part of the revolutionary struggle against the capitalist system.

Richard Quinney (1980) upheld the same view of crime as an inevitable response to the material conditions of capitalism. Echoing Taylor et al. (1973), he proposed that the crimes of the working class are either "crimes of accommodation" or "crimes of resistance" to the capitalist system. Crimes of accommodation are predatory crimes, such as burglary and robbery, which simply "reproduce" the capitalist system of acquisition of property by expropriating the income and property of others. Violent crimes, such as murder, assault, and rape, are also crimes of accommodation committed by those who have been "brutalized" by the capitalist system. Similarly, Michalowski (1985) viewed both violent and property crimes as "crimes of the powerless." Crimes of resistance, according to Quinney, include both non-revolutionary, unconscious reactions against exploitation and crimes deliberately committed by the proletariat as acts of rebellion against capitalism.

Quinney's theory extends beyond the causes of crime among the proletariat; even the crimes committed by the ruling class are the result of the capitalist system. These are "crimes of domination and repression" committed by ruling capitalists to protect their interests. Corporate crimes (e.g., bid rigging, price fixing, security and exchange violations) are forms of "economic domination" by the ruling class. "Crimes of control" are committed by criminal justice personnel, and "crimes of government" are committed by both appointed and elected officials. Even organized crime, according to Quinney, is part of the capitalist class' effort to ensure its continued domination in society. He also defined acts of sexism and racism, whether or not they violate the law, as crimes of the ruling class intended to maintain control over the working class. (For similar conceptions of crime, see Michalowski, 1985; Lynch and Michalowski, 2006; Henry and Lanier, 1998.) Thus, Quinney and others have constructed a typology of crimes found in any modern industrial society, from ordinary street crimes to corporate crimes, then attribute the cause of each type to some feature of capitalism. But the addition of this typology does not advance their theory much beyond the basic Marxist assertion that crime is caused by capitalism.

Modifications of Marxist Theory

In response to critiques of Marxist theory as too simplistic, ideological, and utopian (Akers, 1979; Turk, 1979; Inciardi, 1980), Michael J. Lynch and W. Byron Groves (1986:45) and other radical criminologists moved toward explanations of crime that avoided any "oversimplified, 'unicausal' approach where the only source of crime is capitalism." These explanations stressed the effects of economic inequality on crime through alienation, family disorganization, parental socialization practices, and other variables from strain and control theories. Vold and Bernard agreed that by the 1980s the explanation of criminal behavior as simply a reaction to capitalist oppression had been "rejected by Marxists, who look for more complex explanations of crime within the context of the Marxist theory of history and of social change" (Vold and Bernard, 1986:305–306).

David Greenberg (1981a) also called for a modification of the Marxian explanation for crime:

> Marxists do not deny that social-psychological processes and face-to-face interactions may have some importance for understanding crime and criminal justice, but they try to see these as shaped by larger social structures. And in characterizing these structures, they give particular attention to the organization of economic activity, without neglecting the political and ideological dimensions of society. (Greenberg, 1981a:18)

Although he covered a number of different areas and questions that a multi-dimensional Marxist theory of crime should address, Greenberg (1981a) did not actually propose a Marxist theory of crime that could be distinguished from non-Marxist structural theories. But he came closer to presenting a specific theory of crime in his analysis of the age distribution of crime, arguing that the disproportionate number of juveniles involved in crime "is not readily explained by current sociological theories of delinquency, but it can be readily understood as a consequence of the historically changing position of juveniles in....the long-term tendencies of a capitalist economic system" (Greenberg, 1977:189).

The assumption in Greenberg's theory is that juveniles in *all* social classes in capitalist societies are relatively deprived of access to the labor market. Faced with peer influences to possess certain material goods but without any parental ability or willingness to purchase these desired goods, juveniles must turn to other means to gain them. Because their adolescent status prevents them from integrating into the legitimate labor market, they turn to delinquent means. They will only do so, however, if they believe that the costs of crime, which are principally age-dependent, will not be too great. The younger they are, the less likely their criminal behavior will carry serious negative legal and social consequences. Hence, both the rewards and costs of crime in capitalist society are related to age. Greenberg noted that delinquency was also found in socialist societies, but he believes that it was decreasing and not as much of a problem as in capitalist societies (Greenberg, 1981b).

Whatever the empirical merits of Greenberg's theory of the age distribution of crime, it is difficult to see how it qualifies as a Marxist theory. Except for the assertion that juvenile age status is more likely to produce crime in capitalist than in socialist society, the theory basically utilizes concepts and propositions from non-Marxist theories, such as differential opportunity, social control, and social learning theories to account for age variations in crime.

Another explanation of delinquency that is frequently cited as a good example of an "integrated structural-Marxist" theory was subsequently proposed by Mark Colvin and John Pauly (1983). They argued that the practices of parents in the socialization and discipline of their children reflect the kind of control that the parents are themselves subjected to in the workplace. White-collar workers experience control at work through the development of strong internal moral norms; in turn, they socialize their children in a positive way to develop strong moral bonds to the family. Other workers on the lower rungs of the economic structure are more subject to coercion and direct manipulation by employers and managers; thus, they carry over such workplace subjugations into their disciplinary control over their own children. Blue-collar workers are controlled on the job by material rewards, so they tend to raise their children in the same utilitarian way by direct reward and punishment. Parents who hold very low-level, economically marginal jobs have little consistency in the workplace and are coercively controlled by their bosses. Likewise, they are inconsistent, alternately permissive and punitive, in disciplining their children. Socialization patterns in the family produce delinquent or conforming behavior, and these same patterns reflect the parents' status in the workplace. Not only are lower class youth raised in a negative family environment, they are faced with negative school experiences and other social conditions related to delinquent behavior.

There is research showing some connection between school, family, and parental socialization practices and delinquency. But there is little that shows how parents' disciplinary practices are determined by the type of job they hold. To date, there has been little empirical testing of this theory and what has been done reports positive but fairly weak empirical validity of the theory (Messner and Krohn, 1990; Simpson and Elis, 1994). Simpson and Elis (1994) tested the Colvin and Pauly theory by examining the effect on delinquent behavior of the class position of the parents, as measured by type of work in which they were employed, and the other family, school, and peer variables specified in the theory. They found that all the relevant variables in the theory combined accounted for little of the variation in the frequency of either violent (3% of variance explained) or property juvenile offenses (1%). Moreover, they report that the relationships are sometimes not in the predicted direction and that the type of parental work, the main variable in the theory, had the weakest effects. Finally, the effects of class, family, and school variables differ somewhat by gender, a variable that is ignored in the Colvin and Pauly modification of Marxist theory.

Even if stronger research support for the Colvin and Pauly theory were to be found, it would still be difficult to distinguish this explanation from non-Marxist theory. Simply referring to the class position of parents and youth, especially when this is measured by occupational classifications similar to those used by non-Marxists, does not substantiate it as Marxist theory (see Akers, 1980). One could arrive at exactly the same propositions without any reference whatsoever to Marxist theory or to the class structure of capitalist society as defined by its relationship to the means of production. Those parts of the theory that give it some empirical credibility, such as its reference to family socialization and school experiences, are drawn from social bonding theory rather than from Marxist theory.

As these examples demonstrate, when Marxist theorists offer explanations of crime that go beyond simply attributing the causes of all crime to capitalism, they rely on concepts taken directly from the same "traditional" criminological theories of which they have been so critical and which they have declared to be inadequate. As Jensen (1980) pointed out long ago, the specific factors used in modified Marxist theories to explain crime, such as economic and racial inequality, urban density, industrialization, family, and peers, are exactly the same factors proposed in mainstream, non-Marxist sociological theories. The more Marxist theory in criminology is modified to incorporate age, gender, socialization, strain, differential opportunity, and social learning patterns, the less it differs from non-Marxist theories. Except for nuances of emphasis and terminology, it becomes virtually indistinguishable from the main sociological theories of crime that it was meant to replace.

Is Crime the Result of a Capitalist Economy?

If the Marxist view of capitalist society as criminogenic is valid, then crime should be very low, if not non-existent, in all socialist societies. Conversely, it should be very high in all capitalist systems. The theory explains differences in the crime rate across types of society, but it does not explain differences in individual or group behavior within the same society. Therefore, any analysis of variations in crime solely within the same society cannot test the theory. The inherent, crime-generating contradictions of capitalism can only be tested by cross-national comparisons of crime in capitalist systems with crime in pre-capitalist and socialist systems.[4]

Marxist criminologists have shown little interest in such comparisons of real societies, preferring to compare existing capitalist society with ideal, future socialist systems. Many Marxists have long argued that none of the currently defunct socialist states of the Soviet Union and Eastern Europe were truly socialist. These systems were state capitalism, collectivism, or at best imperfectly and improperly applied socialism (see Greenberg, 1981a). During the time that countries such as Sweden moved from more capitalistic economies and voted in social democratic governments with policies that are often described as socialist, both violent and property crime rates skyrocketed (Felson, 1994:12). But Marxists would not accept the political economy of these societies as truly socialist. This concept of socialist society as a future utopia that has yet to be established in reality renders Marxist theory untestable. If no such society based on Marxist principles exists or has ever existed, then there can be no empirical comparison of crime between capitalist and socialist systems; hence, it would be impossible to test the Marxist hypothesis that capitalism causes crime and socialism prevents crime. Such utopianism changes Marxism from a theoretical explanation of crime as it exists in reality into a moral philosophy about a crime-free ideal society.

Even when this utopian Marxism is rejected and real socialist systems are examined, effective comparisons are difficult, because the comparative data are usually not available. The former communist societies of the Soviet Union and Eastern Europe were all closed systems in which the party-controlled government withheld information. Independent social science research was practically unknown. Valid and reliable official or unofficial data on crime either did not exist or was not openly reported. This is still the case in China, Cuba, and North Korea.

Despite this, some relevant comparative observations can be made to allow at least a partial assessment of the validity of the Marxist theory of crime. One variable to consider is the differences in types of crime between the two political systems. Any type of political dissent, forming independent labor unions, complaining about the government, or simply not having a job are all illegal under communist law. A whole range of activities, which in Western democracies are defined as legitimate variations in lifestyles or are protected by constitutional rights, are defined as criminal acts in socialist systems (see Klockars, 1979; Nettler, 1984).

Therefore, the commission of these acts greatly increases the crime rate in communist societies, whereas the commission of the same acts would have no effect on the crime rate in Western democracies. In contrast, crimes by private corporations is a serious category of crime in capitalist society; but because there are no private corporations in communist societies, no such crime exists there. At the same time, black-market crimes in currency or ordinary merchandise run rampant in socialist economies but are relatively unknown or considered minor in capitalist systems. The range of acts outlawed in socialist societies is as great or greater than in capitalist systems, although many of the acts that are criminal in one system may not be criminal in the other.

The lack of data on crime in communist societies makes it extremely difficult to determine if there is more or less crime when comparing acts that are defined as criminal in *both* types of societies, such as the "ordinary" street crimes of violence, theft, fraud, and property damage. However, the little research that was done on the causes of crime in socialist states before the democratic changes of the 1980s and 1990s found that the same socioeconomic and social-psychological variables were related to crime there as they were to crime in the United States (see Chalidze, 1977; Shelley, 1980).

There have been reports of dramatic increases in crime in the major cities of Russia and other component republics of the former Soviet Union since the transition from communist control to more open-market, free-enterprise economies. Whether this is the result of the change from a socialist to a capitalist system is debatable, because it may be attributable to an economic and social breakdown and to the destruction of a once highly restrictive law-enforcement system. One finds few reports of similar crime increases in former East Germany, which because of its unification with West Germany may have been better able to maintain public order and avert the social disorganization that followed the dismantling of the Soviet Union.

The United States, Japan, Germany, Great Britain, and virtually all other industrialized nations, including the social welfare capitalism such as that found in the Scandinavian countries, as well as most of the developing nations, are more or less capitalist. Yet, they have widely varying crime rates, some of which are lower and others of which are higher than the crime rates that prevailed under communist rule. If there is something inherently criminogenic in a capitalist mode of production, then all capitalist societies should have similar crime rates and these rates should all be higher than those found in any socialist system. Historically, this has not been found to be true.

For most of the 20th century, both property and violent crime rates were considerably higher in the United States than in other Western democracies with capitalist economies. However, in the past 2 decades the crime problems in some of these other countries have come to equal or exceed that of the United States. For instance, both household victimization surveys and official police statistics show that while rates for some types of crimes were stable or falling in this country, they were rising in England (and Wales). Since the mid-1990s, the rates for several major crimes (motor vehicle theft, burglary, assault, and robbery) have been higher in England than in the United States, whereas rape and homicide rates remain higher in the United States (Langan and Farrington, 1998). As shown in chapter 8, the crime rates have increased in several countries and are now higher than the rate in the United States where both property and violent crime have generally been declining since the 1980s. As noted in that chapter, these changes and differences are inconsistent with anomie theory. It is important to note that they also clearly run counter to Marxist theory. There may be explanations for these cross-societal variations and changes in crime rates. These explanations, however, cannot reasonably include the one that the changes and differences are the result of the United States having become less capitalistic and more socialistic than England and other societies.

Policy Implications of Marxist Theory

Marxist criminologists have long emphasized the idea of *praxis*, the application of Marxist theory through deliberate actions to bring about social change (Lynch and Michalowski, 2006). Indeed, for some Marxist scholars the truth of any theory is not judged by empirical evidence, but by whether the theory contributes to the class struggle to overthrow the capitalist system and to replace it with a socialist (and, ultimately, a communist) system. According to Marxist theory, crime will always be high in capitalist society, and there can be no solution to crime under capitalism. If socialism, a system of "having the means of production held in common," were substituted for the present capitalist mode of property ownership, "material poverty would be no longer known" (Bonger, 1916/1969:198). The profit motive would be eliminated, concern for the general social welfare would dominate over selfish privilege and competitiveness, and crime would be reduced to negligible levels:

> Such a [socialist] society will not only remove the causes that now make men egoistic ... [but also] there can be no question of crime properly understood. ... There will be crimes committed by pathological individuals, but this will come rather within the sphere of the physician than that of the judge. (Bonger, 1916/1969:200)

The policy recommendations of Quinney and later Marxist theorists are the same as those of Bonger. Because both "crime control and criminality ... are understood in terms of the conditions resulting from the capitalist appropriation of labor" (Quinney, 1980:67), it follows that:

> The only lasting solution to the crisis of capitalism is socialism. Under late, advanced capitalism, socialism will be achieved in the struggle of all people who are oppressed by the capitalist mode of production. ... The *essential meaning* of crime in the development of capitalism is the need for a socialist society. (Quinney, 1980:67–68; emphasis added)

> The purely radical strain of critical criminology obviously views corporate violence as an absolutely inevitable feature of a modern capitalist society, which cannot be obliterated or even diminished significantly without a revolutionary structural transformation of the political economy. (Schwartz and Friedrichs, 1994:235)

If crime is the result of capitalism, and the criminal justice system is at bottom a tool of the capitalist class to maintain control of labor and problem populations, then nothing short of elimination of capitalism and adoption of the socialist system will eliminate capitalist injustices and solve the crime problem (Schwendinger and Schwendinger, 1976). Social actions and reforms in the existing criminal justice system are futile because they do nothing about the underlying pathology of capitalist society.

> These reforms never go beyond the interests of the capitalist system itself....Reform is the adaptive mechanism of advanced capitalism. ...Our praxis is one of critical thought and action. ...Our theory and our practice are formed in the struggle to make a socialist society. (Quinney, 1974a:168–169, 197–198)

This rejection of practical reforms and the reliance on a highly improbable revolutionary scenario to solve the crime problem are principal reasons that Marxist theory came to be "dismissed as a utopian realm of thought with no relevant policy implications except revolution" (Lynch and Groves, 1986:105). "[B]y the 1980s and into the 1990s it had become clear that ... the merit in these ideas [is] limited, especially in their romantic call for socialism as the solution to the crime problem. ..." (Henry and Einstadter, 1998:7). For this and other reasons, Marxist and radical criminologists muted their revolutionary language and called for non-revolutionary reforms such as "equal justice in the bail system, the abolition of mandatory sentences, prosecution of corporate crimes, increased employment opportunities, and promoting community alternatives to imprisonment" (Lynch and Groves, 1986:107). Whatever the merit of these policies, they appear to be essentially the same list of mainstream humanitarian and liberal reform proposals based on non-Marxist thought that Marxists previously had rejected as simply ameliorative and futile. What is it that now transforms them into practical applications of Marxist theory?

Critical Criminology

As we have seen, the Marxist label became highly visible in American criminology in the middle of the 1970s as an outgrowth of conflict theory. In the process, many criminologists used the terms "critical" and "radical" as synonyms for Marxist theory. These terms have continued to be used over the years to identify perspectives that resonate well with Marxist theory and share with it a "critical" stance toward capitalist society, toward law and justice in Western democracies, and toward "mainstream" criminology. These critiques are often coupled with what are defined as "radical" policy analyses and proposals. In the Marxist boom in academic circles of the 1970s and 1980s, these terms tended to be seen less often and the Marxist label became dominant. But the Marxist label in criminological articles and books has been seen less often since the 1980s; radical, critical, leftist, and other designations are more often found. However, critical and radical criminology has never been fully synonymous with Marxist criminology, and in the past decade the former labels have come in for renewed attention while broadening their identity beyond Marxist theory to feminist, left realist, and a variety of other viewpoints. Therefore, much of what comes under the heading of critical criminology is not Marxist. Assessing the content and validity of critical criminology, however, is made more difficult, because what does come under this heading is not clear, at least not to criminologists who are readers rather than authors of critical criminology. Don Gibbons (1994:60) stated:

> A sizable body of theorizing, in the broad sense, has accumulated in recent years and can be identified as critical criminology, but this work does not form a coherent whole, that is, a shared body of broad propositions or generalizations and supporting evidence. Indeed, critical criminology is an intellectual posture around which a variety of criminological endeavors have been pursued.

Critical/Constitutive Criminology: Postmodernism and Beyond

This lack of clarity as to what is critical criminology was shown in an overview of critical criminology by Stuart Henry and Dragan Milovanovic (1991; 1996). They suggested that, instead of critical criminology, the term "constitutive criminology" be used and that this umbrella label be used to encompass a variety of critical or "postmodern" perspectives. Milovanovic (2002) presented semiotics, edgework, chaos theory, and catastrophe theory as "emerging perspectives" within critical criminology. Arrigo (2000) added critical race theory, "queer" theory, anarchism, peacemaking, prophetic criticism, socialist feminism, and postmodern feminism to this list.[5] Schwartz and Friedrichs (1994:222) said that postmodernism "is linked most closely to critical criminology and should be viewed in that context."

Although recognizing that much of what goes by the name of postmodernism "is only a pretentious intellectual fad," Schwartz and Friedrichs (1994:222) argued that postmodernist theory can "uncover pretensions and contradictions of traditional scholarship," that it provides "a highlighting of the significance of language and signs in the realm of crime and criminal justice" and serves as "a source of metaphors and concepts (e.g., 'hyper-reality') that capture elements of an emerging reality." What does and does not qualify as postmodern criminology is especially murky, but a common theme is uncovering and overturning the hidden power of language and text to confer privilege and power on one view over another. In the process, postmodernists seem to be relentless relativists who do not want "to privilege" any mode of thought and language. At the same time, they seem to be particularly worried about the hegemony of modern scientific thought that attempts to find testable explanations and causes of crime. They want to dethrone it and replace it with linguistically based non-scientific views that recognize "a need to advance a progressive agenda favoring disprivileged people" (Schwartz and Friedrichs, 1994:22).

Constitutive criminology shares an obvious affinity to these themes, but Henry and Milovanovic (1996) believed that they have gone "beyond postmodernism." Although Henry and Milovanovic claimed that constitutive criminology is not "oppositional," they continued the tradition in critical criminology of not only opposing but rejecting what they view as mainstream criminology. Indeed, Gibbons (1994) argued that constitutive criminology appears to recommend abandoning criminology altogether. Henry and Milovanovic explicitly rejected the search for causes of crime, but they were silent regarding accepting or rejecting the search for causes of the law and criminal justice system. Instead, they assert that crime is a "discursive production" that somehow comes about when "agents act out criminal patterns, when others seek to control criminal behavior, and when yet others attempt to research, philosophize about, and explain crime" (Henry and Milovanovic, 1991:293).

At one level, this is an unexceptional, descriptive statement about crime, criminal justice, and criminology that is self-evident or true by definition. It simply says that some people commit crime (offenders who act out criminal patterns), others seek to control that crime (criminal justice agencies), and others (criminologists and other social scientists) seek to explain it. Both this description and the assertion by Henry and Milovanovic (1991:295) that crime is the outcome of human interaction are mundane statements that would be immediately accepted by virtually all criminologists. On another level, however, such statements seem to take an extreme position that denies that crime as such really exists. Crime exists only because it is a "discursive production"; that is, a product not only of the interaction of offenders, control agents, criminologists, or other people, but also simply by their talking about it. "Discursive practices" that refer to various kinds of "talk," such as control talk, organizational talk, and law talk, constitute the narrative medium through which "codetermination" of crime, victims, and control take place. This implies that there is no such thing as crime as an objective behavioral reality to be explained; crime, criminal justice, social structure, and institutions are merely the products of talk, text, and discursive practices (Henry and Milovanovic, 1991:299). Does this mean that criminal behavior would not exist if we did not talk about it?

It is not clear that Henry and Milovanovic meant an affirmative answer to this question, because their statements also imply that crime does exist as something that is "co-determined" in this process that includes the very acts of talking about it, trying to explain it, and attempting to control it. Thus, there may be some internal logical inconsistencies in constitutive criminology. If the search for causes must be abandoned, as clearly stated by Henry and Milovanovic, or if crime does not exist as an objective reality in the discursive process as they may imply, then how can crime be "enabled and constrained" (i.e., caused or prevented) and at the same time have reciprocal "shaping" effects on social structure? Victims and control agents are also real entities in the process. It would seem that constitutive criminology has not really abandoned the search for causes, because crime, victims, and control are "shaped" (i.e., caused) by both micro-level events, "individual choice or predisposition," and by macro-level structural arrangements. In turn, crime and control, or at least talk about them, "shape" both individual actions and social structure:

> Advocates decline the seduction that either human agents, through choice or predisposition, or structural arrangements at institutional and societal levels have priority in shaping crime, victims, and control. ...[T]hey see social structure and its constituent control institutions as the emerging outcome of human interaction that both constrains and enables criminal action and recognizes that those structures are simultaneously shaped by the crime and crime control talk that is part of its reproduction. Constitutive criminology is not an exercise in polemics, in which human agency is separated from the structures that it makes.

> Constitutive criminology, then, is concerned with identifying the ways in which the interrelationships among human agents constitute crime, victims, and control as realities. Simultaneously, it is concerned with how these emergent realities themselves constitute human agents. (Henry and Milovanovic, 1991:295)

The concept of "transpraxis" is introduced by Henry and Milovanovic to heighten awareness of unintended consequences in this process and to go beyond the Marxist concept of praxis. Building on labeling theory's notion of the unintended consequences of societal labeling and control in producing deviance, they argue that praxis often legitimizes the very capitalist control structures that it is meant to oppose. Thus, actions both by control agents and by those whom they attempt to control can produce unintended outcomes. Whatever the truth of these assertions, there is little in this application of the concept of unintended consequences that constitutes a special or new insight of constitutive criminology. This is an old concept that has been applied in sociology to the full range of human behavior and social structures.

Henry and Milovanovic also claimed that criminologists exclude the informal control system and do not understand mutual obligations, loyalties, gratitude, and other processes in the informal system that constitute "symbolic violence" undergirding "ideological domination." Criminologists overlook this, do not understand it, or consign it to the past as "custom" rather than "law." Again, one would have to object to this characterization of criminology. It is simply not true that the informal control system or informal mechanisms in the criminal justice system are excluded from the purview of traditional, mainstream criminology. In fact, with the possible exception of classical deterrence theory and old-style biological theory, processes of informal interaction and control are recognized in virtually every criminological theory.

Henry and Milovanovic (1991:307) concluded as follows:

> Our position calls for abandoning of the futile search for causes of crime because that simply elaborates the distinctions that maintain crime as a separate reality while failing to address how it is that crime is constituted as part of society. We are concerned, instead, with the ways in which human agents actively co-produce that which they take to be crime.

To be "concerned" about how people co-produce what they construe to be crime only states the question; it does not offer an answer. It does not offer an explanation of crime. Although these authors discuss "talking about" crime and criminal justice and how they are "co-determined" both by human agents and social structure, constitutive criminology has not yet offered a testable explanation of either crime or criminal justice. Indeed, it rejects the very effort to explain or do anything about crime because these actions themselves constitute part of the process by which crime is produced. This presents a problem for the theory. If crime or criminal justice is not what constitutive criminology intends to explain, then what *is* it intended to explain? Constitutive criminology, as well as other varieties of critical and postmodern criminology, focuses more on a critique of the shortcomings of other criminologists than on offering an alternative explanation of crime. According to this critique, criminologists who are uninformed about constitutive criminology do not realize that they are actually participating in the production of crime by talking about it, studying it, and recommending policies to control it.

This stance produces another apparent internal inconsistency in constitutive theory because talking, studying, and proposing policies about crime are precisely what Henry and Milovanovic (1996) continued to do, not only in explicating their theory but also in outlining its implications for "justice practice." Their policy recommendations are primarily meant to replace current "technologies of discipline" with new "languages of possibility." The goal of this "replacement discourse" is to work toward "harm reduction" (Henry and Milovanovic, 1996:214), achieved through four main strategies:

1. Criminologists should practice "newsmaking criminology" (Barak, 1988) by intervening in the news media to produce "an alternative, discursive, resource base for reflexive, celebrative, and expansive transpraxis" (Henry and Milovanovic, 1996:214).

2. Various ways of exercising "social judo" should be implemented "where people act together to defensively employ the strength and power of oppressors toward their self-limitation" (Henry and Milovanovic 1996:221). An example would be "narrative therapy" in which a therapist helps the client to redirect "the constitutive energy of the excessive investor and an affirmative medium for her/his authorship (a de-reification), particularly in interpersonal relations" (Henry and Milovanovic, 1996:225).

3. Victims of crime should be restored through support groups and mutual aid.

4. There must be a "critical transformation" of the political economy by replacing the current "state and institutional systems that are discursively entrenched" with a "superliberal, empowered democracy." This would promote, among other things, shifting "role making" whereby judges, probation officers, police, and counselors periodically exchange positions to prevent them from getting entrenched in "narrowly drawn discursive subject positions" (Henry and Milovanovic, 1996:238).

The jargonistic and insider language in which this kind of discourse is couched interferes with a clear appraisal of policy recommendations coming from constitutive criminology. Moreover, how policies such as these can be expected to reduce the harm from crime, control or prevent criminal behavior, rehabilitate offenders, or avoid the problem of thereby participating in the production of crime is left vague; and empirical evidence on their effectiveness is absent. Constitutive criminology, therefore, can be criticized for not offering viable theoretical alternatives and for being unrealistic about the crime problem. In fact, these criticisms have been leveled against some versions of critical criminology by another group of critical and radical criminologists who call themselves "left realists."

Left Realism

Left realism refers primarily to the writings of a group of British criminologists, some of whom, such as Jock Young, were in the forefront of radical criminology in the 1970s in Great Britain. Left realism was developed by Young (1987) and others largely in reaction to what they call "left idealism," extreme positions that radical/critical criminology had come to take regarding crime and criminal justice. They were also responding to the rising tide of criminal victimization in British society, to the political changes that had taken place in the rise to power of political conservatism, and to the development of "right realism" (Matthews and Young, 1992).

By "left idealism," these authors mean the tendency in many radical and Marxist critiques of capitalist society and its oppressive criminal justice system to overlook the reality of pain and suffering generated by criminal offenders who victimize their fellow human beings, usually the poor and powerless. Left idealists view street crime

> either as a diversion from class struggle, or as a vehicle for marketing news, and treat crime as an epiphenomenon, with the criminal conceived of as a sort of socialist homunculus or proto-revolutionary being viewed as determined and blameless, punishment as unwarranted or amplificatory. (Lowman, 1992:141)

Left realists point out that neither the street-level criminal offender nor the White-collar offender is a revolutionary soldier in the class struggle.

The growing crime problem in society and the ascendancy of conservative government in Great Britain and the United States with very strong public support for get-tough, punitive criminal justice policies to control crime produced what the left realists thought was a "crisis" in criminology. This crisis called for a reappraisal of the radical, as well as the traditional liberal, approaches to crime. They were concerned that "conservative" criminology or "realism of the right," represented by biological and rational choice perspectives, would overwhelm radical views that had become sterile critiques of existing society with little direct relevance for alleviating the genuine problems of crime for ordinary members of society.

Left realists criticize left idealists and orthodox Marxists for believing that crime is nothing but a fiction created by the ruling class to maintain its hegemony, that the criminal justice system does nothing but repress the population without providing any real control of crime, and that the only proper fate for the criminal justice system is to be totally dismantled. On the other hand, they propose that the inequities of the criminal justice system be rectified and that the system be made more effective, efficient, and just. Political repression can be reduced while improving governmental services to the poor and the working class. Matthews and Young

(1992) rejected the view that crime is an arbitrary social category that can be modified at will through verbal construction and narrative discourse. Left realists assert that street crime is real, relevant, important, and serious; moreover, there is a real consensus in society on the core of criminal law, and criminal justice reform and crime prevention are the most important immediate goals toward which criminologists and policy makers should strive (Lowman, 1992). In promoting this reform, left realists have toned down critiques of police and have provided vocal support for such policies as crime prevention, victim services, restitution, community service, community policing, and minimal use of prison sentences (Gibbons, 1994; Curran and Renzetti, 2001; Einstadter and Henry, 1995).

Left realists differentiate themselves from other critical criminologists by going beyond criticizing the punitive, conservative approaches of right realists to criticizing the unrealistic approaches of the left idealists. But there is little in the positions taken by left realists to differentiate them from advocates of mainstream liberal crime-control policies. Left realism

> argues that only socialist intervention will fundamentally reduce the causes of crime rooted as they are in social inequality, that only the universality of crime prevention will guard the poor against crime, that only a genuinely democratic control of the police force will ensure that community safety is achieved. (Matthews and Young, 1992:6)

It is difficult to tell what "socialist intervention" means here. Nevertheless, exhortations to deal with the root causes of crime, promote crime prevention, institute victim restitution, reform punitive crime control and sentencing policies, and control police excesses to make criminal justice both more effective and more just are found in the mainstream policy and reform proposals over the past 50 years.

In short, left realists are former radical or critical criminologists who have recognized the reality of crime, have softened their critique of capitalist society and the criminal justice system, and are now advocating less radical and more ameliorative reform. The empirical validity of left realism, however, has not been established. The question is what theory of crime or criminal justice is proposed by left realists that can be tested? Reactions to the idealism of the left and proposals for more realistic reform of the system are not theoretical explanations; they are philosophical and political statements about what society should be and how the system ought to operate. Do left realists go beyond these statements to offer a new testable explanation of crime or of criminal justice as an alternative to existing theory? Despite calls by left realists themselves to "engage in detailed empirical investigation ... rather than dogmatically reiterate abstract beliefs" (Matthews, 1987:377), the answer is, not yet.

The left realist movement in criminology is a reappraisal of critical criminology and a movement back toward the middle ground of intellectual discourse in the field. It has inspired victimization surveys and other kinds of research in Great Britain, promoted reform in the police, and exposed deficiencies in critical perspectives in criminology. However, just as was true for the earlier radical "new" criminology of Taylor et al. (1973) in England many years ago, Young's left realism of today stops with an outline of categories of variables and sketches out what a sound theory should do. It does not actually offer a new theory of either criminal justice or crime. Left realism is really defined by its reaction to left idealism, its stance on the issues of social change, the significance of crime in society, and its attitude toward criminal justice policy. Its implications for these seem clear, but it is not at this time a testable theory that can be empirically validated.

Peacemaking Criminology

The left realists' concern for the real suffering created by crime is also reflected in what is known as "peacemaking" criminology, chief proponents of which are Harold E. Pepinsky and Richard Quinney (1991; see also Fuller and Wozniak, 2006). They likened crime and its control to war and declare that it is time to try peace between offenders and victims, police, and the community. Peacemaking criminology advocates mediation, conflict resolution, reconciliation, and reintegration of the offender into the community in an effort to "alleviate suffering and thereby reduce crime" (Pepinsky and Quinney, 1991:ix). Peacemaking criminology is described as emerging out of religious, humanist, feminist, and critical/Marxist traditions (Pepinsky, 1991; Fuller and Wozniak, 2006).

As we have seen, Quinney's previous theoretical views were first conflict and, later, Marxist. But his peacemaking criminology is religious (primarily Christian but with elements of Buddhism). It is a spiritual, transcendental, and visionary preaching of non-violence and a plea to end suffering. Because Quinney defined crime itself as a form of suffering, his central contention is tautological: If suffering can be ended, crime will be ended. In his view, the criminal justice system as currently organized is based on the principle of violence. This must be done away with and replaced with the principles of love and non-violence as the only solution to crime. "When our hearts are filled with love and our minds with willingness to serve, we will know what has to be done and how it is to be done. Such is the basis of a non-violent criminology" (Quinney, 1991:12).

Others take more secular approaches to peacemaking criminology. For instance, Anderson (1991) argued that both Gandhian and Marxist humanism offer guidelines for peaceful resolution of the problems of crime. Harris (1991:88) claimed that feminist theory values harmony and "felicity" above all else and that "feminists stress the themes of caring, sharing, nurturing, and loving." This is contrasted with the "power/control," "rights/justice" male perspective that dominates criminological thinking and government actions in the war on crime. Thus, the incorporation of this feminist perspective will lead to a resolution of conflict and peace in the criminal justice system.

Although it is claimed that "peacemaking criminology does not directly address the issues of crime and criminality in quite the same manner as traditional criminological theories" (Fuller and Wozniak, 2006:256), it is not stated how peacemaking criminologists actually address these issues. In fact, peacemaking criminology does not offer a theory of crime or of the criminal justice system that can be evaluated empirically in comparison with "traditional" theories, as even peacemaking criminologists admit:

> [T]he peacemaking perspective has not been a recognized theory in academic criminology for very long. In fact, it is still so new [that] the necessary groundwork has yet to be done in forming testable propositions and gathering empirical evidence. There are no programs that label themselves peacemaking that can be examined. In short, unlike other criminological theories, *there is little more than direct anecdotal evidence from which to evaluate peacemaking criminology*. (Fuller and Wozniak, 2006:264; emphasis added)

Explanations of crime and the criminal justice system might or might not be consistent with the religious and other precepts espoused by peacemaking criminologists, but these precepts do not themselves constitute a testable theory. It may be possible to construct a testable, parsimonious, and valid theory from peacemaking criminology, but at this point it remains a philosophy rather than a theory. It has a utopian vision of society that calls for reforming and restructuring to get away from war, crime, and violence and to institute a society with a justice system characterized by non-violence, the peaceful resolution of conflict, and the restoration of offenders to the community. This is a highly laudable philosophy of criminal justice, but it does not offer an explanation of why the system operates as it does or why offenders commit crime. It can be evaluated on other grounds but not on empirical validity.

Although not all religious beliefs and practices are non-violent and religion is not the only basis for non-violence, the notion that the religious values of some of the criminologists underpin their peacemaking perspective is quite understandable. Christianity honors the commandment to love your neighbor as yourself and to love those who spitefully use you. It preaches non-violence, forgiveness, reconciliation, and redemption. Although wrongdoing is not to be condoned, one does not cast stones at the wrongdoers. Rather, one restores them and admonishes them to sin no more. In Christianity, righteousness is based on serving others, not gaining power or control over them. Long before the peacemaking criminology label was adopted by Pepinsky, Quinney, and others, the in-prison religious programs and the many prison ministries run by churches and lay groups were practicing peacemaking; they have long applied the tenets of love and peaceful reformation of offenders, by persuading them toward a religious commitment and lifestyle incompatible with committing crime and causing suffering. The kind of coalition of churches and synagogues to provide aid, comfort, and shelter to transients and the homeless described by Barak (1991) for one city has long been duplicated in thousands of other communities around the country. (See the discussion of faith-based programs in chap. 7.) Buddhist and other religious traditions also preach non-violence and reconciliation. Gandhian and other philosophies, religious and secular, also preach non-violent social change.

Nevertheless, on other counts, peacemaking criminology has some internal inconsistencies and contradictions that are difficult to reconcile. For instance, it seems to be contradictory to claim Marxist/critical criminology as one of the main foundations for peacemaking criminology. It is true, as Anderson (1991) shows, that there are humanistic elements in Marx's own writing. But are they enough to overcome the major thrust of Marxist theory that capitalist society is based on irreconcilable class conflict and Marx's own endorsement of violent revolution? Whether from the original Marx or some variety of neo-Marxism, the major policy recommendation of this theoretical tradition has long been to meet power with power, violence with violence to overthrow capitalist society. Further, how does one reconcile the peacemaking image with the characteristics of governments based on Marxist principles: the violent repression of citizens, intolerance of dissent, punitive control of deviance, and rule by terror? Certainly there is nothing particularly violent about non-Marxist varieties of critical criminology, but at the same time there is very little about them that is conciliatory and peacemaking. By its very name, it is critical and oppositional; it is not known for advocating peacemaking with those who are the subjects of its criticisms.

There also seems to be some logical inconsistency in claiming feminist theory as a foundation for peacemaking criminology. The distinction that Harris (1991) made between the peacemaking orientation of women and the control orientation of men may be valid. She cited research that shows that women do tend to support nurturing and caring values more than men, who tend to endorse power relationships. But this celebration of the nurturing, caring, loving, and peaceful orientation of women is not a significant part of the feminist tradition (see chap. 11). Indeed, it is more identified with the traditional "hegemonic definitions" of the "feminine" role and of "acting like a woman." Feminists have long rejected this role as itself a reflection of the patriarchal system of oppression of women. How, then, does its incorporation into peacemaking criminology or into criminal justice practice represent feminist theory?

The assertion by peacemaking criminologists that no "traditional" criminologist or no one in the criminal justice system recognizes the real suffering created by crime, or that none has advocated peaceful, non-violent ways of dealing with crime, is simply inaccurate. None of the policy implications of peacemaking criminology is unique to those who self-consciously identify themselves with this perspective. As we saw in chapter 7, all these policies, such as non-punitive treatment of offenders, mediation, restitution, offender reintegration, rehabilitation, and so on, have long been mainstays of the policy recommendations coming from "traditional" criminology. More to the point, they are already common practices in the criminal justice system.

Fuller and Wozniak (2006) characterized peacemaking criminologists as opposing capital punishment, advocating gun control, opposing terrorism, war, and the war on drugs, and advocating human rights. But none of this is any way different from the political positions taken by most academic criminologists.

As Don Gibbons (1994) pointed out, peacemaking criminologists have not shown how to get beyond those policies already in place to the large-scale structural changes in society that they claim are needed to perpetuate non-violent and peaceful crime control.

Summary

Marxist theory explains the law and criminal justice system as being controlled by and serving the interests of the ruling capitalist elite. Instrumental Marxists view all aspects of the political state, including its law and justice system, as inevitably and always an instrument of the ruling class. Structural Marxists modify this somewhat by arguing that, in the short term, the political state is relatively independent of the ruling class and may reflect the interests of the proletariat.

In Marxist theory, capitalism itself is the major cause of crime. Ownership of the means of production by the capitalist ruling class produces a society that is inherently criminogenic. Some Marxists propose that all forms of crime simply reflect the crime-producing system of capitalism. The crimes of the working class are either "crimes of accommodation" or "crimes of resistance" to the capitalist system. Crimes committed by the ruling class are "crimes of domination and repression" that are committed to protect and promote the interests of the ruling class. Other Marxist theorists have departed from this oversimplified approach. However, the more complex models that they offer essentially rely on concepts and explanations from non-Marxist theories.

Because Marxist theory focuses on the inherent contradictions of capitalist society as a source of law and criminal justice, as well as crime, it cannot be tested by examining only capitalist systems. Whether the more simplified or complex Marxist theories are valid can be adequately judged only on the basis of direct comparisons of real capitalist with real socialist societies. When such comparisons are made, Marxist theory does not fare well as an explanation of the law and operation of the criminal justice system, and such comparisons do not offer much empirical validation of the primary Marxist argument that crime is a problem in capitalism but not a problem in socialism. The only unique policy flowing from Marxist theory is advocating the overthrow of capitalism (while dismissing any effort to reform the system) and replacing it with socialism. Other policies now supported by radical and Marxist theorists are more likely to include reform policies of the type that mirror what had previously been dismissed as ineffective amelioration.

Constitutive criminology, postmodern, left realism, and peacemaking criminology have all been identified as varieties of critical criminology. All offer a critique of criminology as practiced by others and a critique of society and the criminal justice system. Constitutive criminology rejects the search for causes of crime as an objective reality and views it as the product of "discursive practices" among offenders, controllers, and victims. Proponents recommend various policies and practices such as newsmaking criminology, social judo, and narrative therapy. Left realism rejects this kind of reasoning and policy as unrealistic and proposes reform in the criminal justice system to deal with the real pain and suffering of crime in society. Peacemaking criminology draws on religious, humanist, feminist, and Marxist traditions to advocate a non-violent, restitutive, and reconciling approach to the crime problem. None of these varieties of critical criminology offers a testable theory of crime or the criminal justice system.

Notes

1. For additional references, reviews, critiques, and differentiations made among radical, critical, and Marxist models, see Meier (1977), Inciardi (1980), and Bohm (1982).

2. For additional discussions of the Rusche and Kirchheimer hypothesis, see Sutton (2000), Weiss (2001), and Melossi (2003).

3. Lynch, Schwendinger, and Schwendinger (2006) took exception to this characterization of Marxist and radical theory, although they attributed some of the blame to postmodernists who at one time affiliated themselves with Marxist thought. In addition to the research on the political economy and punishment, they also cited numerous quantitative empirical studies on environmental harms and justice that link class oppression with crime.

4. As we have seen in chapter 8 on social disorganization and anomie theories, the question of the unequal class distribution of crime has not yet been empirically resolved. But even if research finds a concentration of crime in an "under-class" or among the "truly disadvantaged" (Wilson, 1987), it is unclear how this would support Marxist theory. The research and theory on the class distribution of crime has developed out of a non-Marxist sociology.

5. Although characterized by some critical criminologists as at the "cutting edge" of criminology, many of the ideas embodied in this approach are hardly new. Semiotics, the study of the impact of language and rhetoric on speaker, listener, and subject of discourse, can be found in mainstream criminological concepts such as Cressey's (1953) "vocabulary of motives" and Sykes and Matza's (1957) "techniques of neutralization." Edgework, which examines the nonmaterial, emotional rewards of crime and deviance, cannot be distinguished from the impulsiveness dimension of self-control theory (chap. 6) or from the principle of differential reinforcement in social learning theory (chap. 5). Critical race and "queer" theories are variants of conflict theory. Chaos and catastrophe theory are not explanations at all but are merely frameworks upon which highly complex, nonlinear theoretical models of crime and justice can be constructed; ironically, these models can be subjected to the very empirical testing that postmodernists so ardently oppose.

Chapter 11

Feminist Theories

Introduction

The primary aim of feminist theory, according to Kathleen Daly and Meda Chesney-Lind (1988:490), is to draw on women's "ways of knowing" in contrast to criminological theory, "rooted in men's experience." Its objective is to eliminate "androcentric science" and produce a distinctly feminist approach to crime and criminal justice. Knowledge is assumed to be determined by experiences conditioned by one's gender (as well as one's race, class, and ethnicity).[1] Because criminology has been dominated by males, existing criminological theory is seriously flawed by the "masculinist" perspective. Both the questions asked and the answers given in criminology are the "product of white, economically privileged men's experiences" (Daly and Chesney-Lind, 1988:506). Feminist theory is designed to counter this bias and to produce a new, deeper understanding of gender relations in society and how they affect both crime and criminal justice.

There is no single feminist theory. Rather, there are liberal, radical, Marxist, socialist, postmodern, and other varieties of feminist thought.[2] Moreover, there is some disagreement in the feminist literature on how various gender-related theories and empirical studies are classified according to these categories, or even whether or not they can lay claim to being feminist at all. Although all are critical of traditional criminology, many of these feminist perspectives were also created to critique other forms of feminist scholarship on crime and criminal justice. Yet, all these variations share a feminist perspective on gender issues that is not captured by mainstream criminological theories (Daly and Chesney-Lind, 1988; Burgess-Proctor, 2006).

Feminist Theories of Criminal Justice

Feminist theories identify the major blind spot in traditional "male-stream" criminological theory as the failure to understand the profound significance of gender and sex roles in society (Gelsthorpe and Morris, 1990). For some, this significance is reflected in the ongoing differential in sex roles and gender inequality. For others, the inequalities run deeper: "Patriarchy" is a fundamental principle of societal organization. A patriarchal society in which the rights and privileges of males are superior and those of females are subordinated characterizes the vast majority of societies throughout history and the world. Although patriarchy is not universal and varies in intensity, it reigns in capitalist and socialist systems and in industrialized and non-industrialized societies. Conflict and labeling theories of criminal justice recognize male-female differences in power; however, feminist theories propose that the power differential between men and women is at least as important as, if not more important than, the power differentials by race, class, and age. Marxists view class as the fundamental, bifurcating force in capitalist society. Feminist theories posit that patriarchy is equally as important as class and may even override class in the division of society into the dominant and the subordinate. Feminist theories explain criminal justice decisions as reflecting this male dominance and functioning to support patriarchy by discriminating against women and reinforcing traditional female sex and family roles.[3]

Empirical Validity of Feminist Theories of Criminal Justice

At one level, to examine the empirical validity of feminist theories of criminal justice entails the same kind of historical cross-societal comparisons of patriarchal and non-patriarchal societies as in the evaluation of Marxist theory by comparison of socialist and capitalist societies. However, its empirical validity can also be judged by research on the male-female disparities in criminal justice decisions in American society.

The first issue that feminist theories of criminal justice must address, however, is the nature of those gender disparities in the criminal justice system. Given a patriarchal society in which masculinity is favored over femininity and males possess more power than females, a feminist theory of criminal justice, like labeling and conflict theories, would predict that adolescent girls and adult women should receive harsher treatment in the system for the same offense than boys and men. Research evidence on sentencing outcomes does not confirm this hypothesis; it shows instead that, when legally relevant variables are taken into account, there is little disparity by sex, age, race, or class in the criminal and juvenile justice systems. (See Bridges and Myers, 1994, and the research reviewed in chap. 9.) Indeed, when sex differences in sentencing are found, the system is almost always harder on men and more lenient with women (Daly, 1994b):

> What is intriguing about the statistical sentencing literature is that gender differences, favoring women, are more often found than race differences, favoring whites. (Daly, 1989:137)

> The criminal justice system is filled with males (it is hard to ignore this), and when gender is studied, at every legal decision point its effect tends to be small and it frequently favors females. (Liska and Messner, 1999:207)

This tendency to treat female offenders more leniently than male offenders has been subjected to a number of interpretations (Crew, 1991; Farnworth and Teske, 1995). The most common and longstanding has been the "chivalry" hypothesis (Pollak, 1950). This hypothesis proposes that predominantly male police, prosecutors, and judges have a traditional, chivalrous attitude toward women and extend this attitude even to women offenders; therefore, they treat them with more leniency than men. The chivalry hypothesis has been dismissed by most feminists, and leniency toward female offenders has been reinterpreted as a product of "paternalism." Rather than viewing women as objects of admiration and respect and gallantly refusing to subject female offenders to the harsh realities of the criminal justice system, decision makers take a paternalistic stance toward women, viewing them as too weak and passive to withstand or even learn from punishment by the criminal justice system (Chesney-Lind, 1988; 1989; Horowitz and Pottieger, 1991). Paternalism is viewed as having twin effects in that leniency in the name of protection of essentially powerless women can easily transform into harsher treatment of these same women in the name of control. Margaret Farnworth and Raymond Teske (1995) asserted, however, that both the chivalry and paternalism hypotheses oversimplify the treatment that female offenders receive in the criminal justice system. They argued that chivalry is extended only to certain types of women: women who are middle class and White ("selectivity hypothesis") and women who are charged with crimes consistent with traditional feminine stereotypes ("typicality hypothesis"). By contrast, poor and minority women and offenders who have committed crimes that violate normative expectations of femininity (e.g., aggravated assault, armed robbery) are likely to be treated more harshly.

The research evidence is mixed in its support of these various hypotheses explaining gender disparity in criminal justice processing. As discussed earlier, the sentencing research indicates that leniency toward adult female defendants remains, even when legal variables such as offense seriousness and prior record are accounted for (Steffensmeier, Kramer, and Streifel, 1993). However, Chesney-Lind (1988; 1989; Chesney-Lind and Shelden, 2004) claimed that the juvenile justice system has been especially punitive toward girls. A higher proportion of girls than of boys are brought into juvenile court for status offenses, such as running away from home, truancy, and incorrigibility. Moreover, girls are more likely than boys to be incarcerated for status offenses, although less likely for serious offenses. Chesney-Lind (1988; 1989; Chesney-Lind and Shelden, 2004) contended that girls are treated more harshly for minor offenses than boys because the system "sexualizes" their offenses as a threat to traditional sex-role expectations. This is one example of how male-dominated society maintains control over women. Other research also finds that young adult women tend more often to be imprisoned for less serious offenses than men (Horowitz and Pottieger, 1991). However, these findings do not necessarily support the paternalism hypothesis because the difference may simply result from factors other than sex bias. For instance, prostitution may result in more frequent convictions and incarcerations simply because it is easier to charge and prove in court and less likely than other charges to be dismissed. Also, women are very unlikely to be charged with major felonies, but more likely than men to be charged with petty theft. Yet, these male-female differences may reflect something other than gender bias in arrest and adjudication, such as the lower "visibility" of females involved in such "male" offenses as major felonies (Horowitz and Pottieger, 1991).

Research testing the selectivity hypothesis has also been mixed. In early studies of the interactive effects of race and sex on sentencing, Black female offenders are sentenced less harshly than Black male offenders (Spohn et al., 1985) and only slightly more harshly than White female offenders (Steffensmeier et al., 1998). Farnworth and Teske (1995) found only partial support for the hypothesis, in that Black females are more likely than Black males to receive a reduction in charges, but their likelihood of a charge reduction is no different from that of White females; moreover, even these weak results disappear when examining severity of sentence. In a more recent study directly addressing the selectivity hypothesis, Darrell Steffensmeier and Stephen Demuth (2006) demonstrated that although female offenders receive more lenient sentences than male offenders regardless of race or ethnicity after controlling for legal variables, there are no significant differences among White, Black, and Hispanic female defendants in their sentence severity. The sentencing practices examined in this study do not reflect a "selective chivalry" that benefits White female offenders and disadvantages minority female offenders.

Daly (1989) claimed that neither the chivalry nor paternalism hypotheses properly account for the findings on gender variations in court decisions. She hypothesized that judicial discretion in pre-trial releases and sentencing are very much influenced by the family status and relations of the defendants. Her research found that these family variables affect judges' decisions for both male and female defendants as well as for different racial and ethnic groups. Judges tended to be more lenient with defendants, men and women, who had stronger family ties and obligations to children. Women with familial ties were treated more leniently than men with such ties. Because such ties characterize more female than male defendants, the judges gave more frequent pre-trial releases and lenient sentences to women. Daly's findings from two court systems showed that such legal variables as the offense charged and prior record were the key ingredients in judicial decisions. But her findings also supported the hypotheses that these legal variables interact with the family situation, so that "familied" defendants were given more lenient treatment. Therefore, the "initially significant sex effects can be explained by differences in treatment of some familied women and familied men" (Daly, 1989:152).

If judges' considerations of such factors as family status is an example of applying double-standard, sex-role expectations, then the findings are consistent with feminist theory. However, the fact that the same family factors were considered for both male and female defendants undercuts this feminist interpretation. The finding that judges based their decisions on offenses, prior records, and family variables equally for men and women runs counter to the theory.

Daly (1994a; 1992) also reported the findings from a unique study of felony court cases. She conducted a statistical analysis of a "wide sample" of 300 felony court cases. Then she combined that with a qualitative analysis of pre-sentence reports and court transcripts for a "deep sample" of 40 female defendants matched by crime, prior record, age, and race with 40 male defendants. Although men were much more likely to receive prison sentences than women for convictions within the same offense category, on closer examination of the matched pairs of defendants, she found that the men, ostensibly with the same criminal charge, actually had committed a more serious offense:

> I set out to determine whether men and women accused and convicted of statutorily similar crimes committed offenses of the same seriousness. Of the forty deep-sample pairs, I judged 48 percent to be comparably serious, but for 40 percent the men's offenses were more serious, and for 12 percent, the women's were. (Daly 1994a:110)

Thus, what appeared to be harsher penalties for men for the same crime could be justified by the characteristics of individual cases. Therefore, there are few cases in which the outcome was based mainly on gender. Although the felony court judges viewed women as more reformable than men, the justifications for sentencing used by the judges were the same for men and women.

Feminist theories expect criminal justice decisions to be based solely or primarily on considerations of gender or sex roles, yet this has not gained much support from the research literature. The fact that delinquent girls run a higher risk of confinement for status offenses, and that a higher proportion of women convicts serve time for lesser offenses, may reflect society's preference that women live up to certain sexual and family roles. But it is not solid evidence for the hypothesis that it is a patriarchally dominated system in which decisions are exercised to the detriment of women, because the same system severely punishes a higher proportion of men over women for serious offenses. It is difficult to sustain the argument that minor offenses by women violate social rules of femininity but that serious felonies do not. In addition, the high proportion of women serving time for lesser offenses may simply indicate a low proportion of female offenders committing serious offenses. The probability of serving time is about equal for men and women convicted of the same offense and with the same prior record.

Research thus far shows that the independent effects of gender on criminal justice actions are weak or absent. The overall conclusion from research on gender disparities in juvenile and adult justice decisions is similar to the conclusion in chapter 9 about the effect of other extra-legal variables in the criminal justice system. The strongest effect on criminal justice decisions comes from legally relevant, non-discriminatory factors, such as the seriousness of the charged offenses and the criminal characteristics of the offenders. Gender disparities favoring women exist, but they have less effect than legally relevant variables. When these variables are controlled, the remaining gender disparities are inconsequential.

Feminist Theories of Crime

Just as gender is the central issue in feminist explanations of criminal justice, it is at the center of feminist explanations of crime. Daly and Chesney-Lind (1988) identified two main gender-related issues that have engaged the attention of feminist theories of crime (see also Miller and Mullins, 2006). These are not the only concerns or the exclusive domain of feminist theory, but they are critical to understanding the feminist perspective on crime. The first issue is the "generalizability problem" that asks, "Do the theories of men's crime apply to women?" (Daly and Chesney-Lind, 1988:514). Were existing theories of crime and delinquency developed only with male offenders in mind, and do they hold up only when tested with male populations? One answer offered is that, although some theories do have relevance for both men and women, as a whole the traditional body of criminological theory inadequately accounts for female crime. The second issue is the "gender ratio problem" that poses the question, "Can extant theory explain the well-known gender difference in crime?" Why do women commit so much less crime than males? Again, different answers are provided, but feminist theorists tend to criticize those offered by mainstream theory and hypothesize that gender-specific variables explain and predict inter-gender differences in crime.[4]

This dissatisfaction with "traditional" theories of crime and delinquency as too male-centered is a distinguishing feature of proponents of feminist theories. The common theme is that all current etiological theories, such as biological, psychological, anomie, control, differential association, conflict, labeling, social disorganization, and social learning theories, were designed to explain only male criminality and have been tested only with male populations (Einstadter and Henry, 1995). There may be certain parts of these theories that are useful, but neither one single theory nor all the theories combined are capable of explaining female criminality or the male/female differences in crime (Leonard, 1982; Chesney-Lind and Pasko, 2004).[5]

Some feminist theorists, however, disagree with this general critical assessment of all traditional criminological theories. For instance, Allison Morris (1987) contended that, although biological, psychiatric, and women's liberation theories are mistaken, traditional sociological explanations of crime have the potential of explaining female crime and why it occurs less frequently than male crime:

> Special theories for women's crimes have not been particularly successful.... One implication of this ... is that we need to reconsider the relevance to women of general criminological theories. [T]here is no reason to suppose that explanations for women's crime should be fundamentally different from explanations for men's crime, though gender must play a part in any such explanation.... There are a number of criminological theories, however, which, though not originally developed for women, do contribute to our understanding of women's crime.... (Morris, 1987:75)

She found special relevance in anomie, differential association, and social bonding theories and concludes, "Differential opportunity structure, associations, socialization, and social bonding can aid our understanding of crimes committed both by men and women and can take account of differences in the nature and extent of their crimes" (Morris, 1987:76).

There is not yet a well-developed, uniquely feminist explanation of crime and delinquency that can answer the generalizability or gender ratio questions. However, feminist theorists have approached the task of constructing such a theory by paying close attention to the dimensions of gender and sex roles that they believe other theories have ignored or misunderstood. This includes not only different sex-role expectations, but the significance of the underlying patriarchal structure that permeates all aspects of society:

> It is increasingly clear that gender stratification in patriarchal society is as powerful a system as is class. A feminist approach to delinquency means construction of explanations of female behavior that are sensitive to its patriarchal context. Feminist analysis of delinquency would also examine ways in which agencies of social control ... act in ways to reinforce women's place in male society. (Chesney-Lind, 1989:19)

Women's Liberation and Female Crime

The earliest self-described feminist theories of crime focus on presumed changes in the gender difference in crime in the United States in the 1970s, concomitant with social changes generated from the women's liberation movement. During this time, the media began to report instances of women committing crimes that ran counter to traditional stereotypes of feminine roles. In 1975, two books were published that attempted to account for the behavior of these female offenders, each with somewhat different interpretations.

Masculinity Hypothesis. In her book, *Sisters in Crime,* Freda Adler (1975) used some statistical but mostly anecdotal evidence to support her claim that the nature and extent of female crime is on a trajectory to converge with those of male crime. Adler began by showing a faster rate of increase in female arrests than in male arrests, concluding that the differences in male and female criminality are decreasing rapidly. Her theoretical explanation for this was that the women's movement had brought about changes in traditional sex roles, greater equality for women, and an increase in the female labor force. An unintended consequence of this availability to women of a wider range of social roles previously reserved only for men is their greater involvement in another arena traditionally dominated by men—crime:

> In the same way that women are demanding equal opportunity in fields of legitimate endeavor, a similar number of determined women are forcing their way into the world of major crimes ... formerly committed by males only.... Like her sisters in legitimate fields, the female criminal is fighting for her niche in the hierarchy [of crime].... (Adler, 1975:13–14)

Adler's explanation has been called the "masculinity thesis" (Simon and Ahn-Redding, 2005) because it predicts that as women gain equality with men they will increasingly assume masculine characteristics, some of which result in negative outcomes such as a greater tendency to commit crime:

> It would, therefore, seem justified to predict that if present social trends continue women will be sharing with men not only ulcers, coronaries, hypertension, and lung cancer (until recently considered almost exclusively masculine diseases) but will also compete increasingly in such traditionally male activities as crimes against the person, more aggressive property offenses, and especially white collar crime. As women invade the business world, there is no reason to expect them to be any more honest than men.... (Adler, 1975:251–252)

Opportunity Hypothesis. In a second book published in 1975, Rita Simon offered a somewhat narrower interpretation of the apparent confluence of rising crime patterns among women and the women's liberation movement. She showed that female property offenses increased, for which more women were being arrested and incarcerated, but contrary to Adler's assertion, violent offenses by women did not increase. Her focus was almost exclusively on property crime, and her prediction was that white-collar, occupationally related crimes by women will increase even more as women take on more positions in the work force, allowing them greater opportunities to commit such crimes. Violent crimes by women, however, are not likely to rise because increasingly educated and independent women will no longer accept victimization and will thus extricate themselves from violence-prone relationships and situations.

Neither the masculinity nor the opportunity hypothesis has received much empirical support (Mann, 1984; Chesney-Lind and Pasko, 2004). It has not been demonstrated that female equality increased dramatically during the time of changing female crime rates, or that the two are somehow connected. Steffensmeier (1980) and others showed that the increases in female crime predated the women's liberation movement. Furthermore, male-to-female ratios of crime have decreased somewhat, but the changes have not narrowed the gap all that much. Crime is still overwhelmingly a male phenomenon, and recent trends do not show much change in the female rate of crime or in the ratio of male to female offenders (Steffensmeier and Streifel, 1992). Patterns of female delinquency and its relationship to male delinquency have remained little changed for a long time, and there is no relationship between feminist attitudes or ideology and female delinquency (Chesney-Lind and Shelden, 2004). Contrary to Simon's thesis, increases in female crime have been reported in non–white collar types of offenses, such as shoplifting (Datesman and Scarpitti, 1980). Chesney-Lind and Pasko (2004) challenged notions about the "liberated female crook," who is male-like in her violent behavior, as a sign that females are at last free to be what they want to be in society. One version of this is the media-reported explosion of female involvement in violent gangs. They showed that girls always have been and continue to be only marginally involved in the delinquent activity of gangs. Even those who do become involved in gangs have not closed much of the criminality gap between themselves and gang boys.

Economic Marginalization Hypothesis. The linking of the women's liberation movement with rising female crime rates has been subjected to a third interpretation. The economic marginalization hypothesis was originally advanced as a rival hypothesis to those proposing that women's advances in employment and education would result in an increase in their criminal involvement. Critics of the masculinity and opportunity theses have argued that female offenders are largely poor, under- or unemployed, and lacking alternatives to criminal means of providing for themselves and their dependents (Crites, 1976; Chapman, 1980; Box and Hale, 1984), hardly the image of the increasingly powerful emancipated woman. A wide variety of research lends support to the claims of the marginalization hypothesis (Box and Hale, 1984; Miller, 1986; Steffensmeier, Allan, and Streifel, 1989):

> [F]eminization of poverty, not women's liberation, is the social trend most relevant to female criminality.... [T]he economic pressures on women caused by unemployment, poorly paid employment, and/or inadequate welfare payments, combined with the increasing numbers of female-headed households supporting dependent children, lead more and more women to seek the benefits of criminal activity as supplements or alternatives to employment. In other words, economic necessity is forcing the emancipation of women from more law-abiding standards of conduct. (Simon and Ahn-Redding, 2005:16)

Although economic marginalization has been posed as a rival to earlier liberation hypotheses, the assertions of the marginalization hypothesis are not necessarily contradictory to those of its predecessors. Hunnicutt and Broidy (2004:135) argued that these competing models may in fact offer complementary explanations. They proposed that there exists a

> disjunction between ideology and material reality ... where women may be expected to be liberated and independent, but are still dependent on men for economic support.... [For example,] higher divorce rates are in part a consequence of liberation, yet women are more economically vulnerable after divorce....

In their cross-national study of male and female conviction rates, Hunnicutt and Broidy (2004) found that measures of both economic marginality and liberation are associated with higher female conviction rates. Female conviction rates are also associated with male economic marginalization, indicating that women's economic fortunes are still intertwined with those of men. The results of this study suggest that the equality of opportunity afforded by the women's liberation movement has not resulted in equality of outcome. Instead, the movement has had the consequence of releasing men from a cultural imperative to financially support and protect women, leaving women in an economically marginalized position due to structural limitations that remain on employment and income. This increasing feminization of poverty is an unintended consequence of women's liberation and is thought to be at the root of female crime. There is the question of what uniquely feminist theory is reflected in this explanation that crime among women is an adaptation to economic deprivation, marginalization, and lack of legitimate opportunities. It is the central argument of anomie theory and corresponds to one source of strain in general strain theory (see chap. 8), traditional theories that many feminist theorists reject as applicable only to men.

Power-Control Theory. At the heart of women's liberation theories of female crime is the effect of women's increased labor force participation on the gender gap in crime rates. John Hagan's (1989a; Hagan, Gillis, and Simpson, 1985; Hagan, Simpson, and Gillis, 1987) "power-control theory" examined this effect within a complex structural and relational context. The theory set out explicitly to account for gender differences in delinquent involvement and how those gender differences expand or contract, depending on the type of family structure and the degree of parental controls over boys relative to girls. Central to Hagan's theory is the notion that class relations within the capitalist economic system "reproduce" themselves in gender relations within the family. Earlier statements (Hagan et al., 1985; Hagan et al., 1987) of power-control theory emphasize gender power—wife's occupational authority relative to husband's occupational authority—as the determinant of relatively patriarchal or egalitarian family structures. Patriarchal families are those wherein the father's occupation places him in a "command" position, giving orders to others, and the mother either does not work outside the home or works in a job where she occupies an "obey" position, taking orders from supervisors. In egalitarian families, both mother and father work in "command" positions, both work in "obey" positions, or the father is absent (Hagan et al., 1987).[6] In both patriarchal and egalitarian families, mothers are more likely than fathers to exert both "instrumental control" (supervision) and "relational control" (emotional bonds that indirectly constrain deviant behavior) over sons and daughters, but in patriarchal families mothers exert greater controls over daughters than sons. Mothers in egalitarian families may exert either less control over daughters or more control over sons than mothers in patriarchal families. Although gender differences in maternal controls still remain in egalitarian families, these differences are not pronounced. Variations in maternal control practices across family types differentially influence sons' and daughters' orientations toward risks. In patriarchal families, given greater freedom from control, sons are more likely than daughters to prefer risky activities (including delinquent activities) and to pursue them without fear of consequences. Gender differences in risk preference and perceptions are likely to be reduced in egalitarian families. This earlier version of power-control theory predicts that boys will commit more delinquency than girls in patriarchal families. In such families, sons are subject to fewer controls, view risk-taking as more pleasurable, and perceive fewer negative consequences of risky behavior than daughters. In egalitarian families, boys are still more likely than girls to engage in delinquent activities, but the gender difference will be smaller.

Hagan's own Canadian data tend to support this version of power-control theory,[7] but findings from other research have been mixed.[8] Some studies have found that the effect of gender on delinquency or deviance is significantly reduced, as the theory would predict, when parental controls, risk preferences, and perceived sanction threats are added to the model, but others have found only weak effects for these mediating variables. The research also offers little support for Hagan's contention that mothers play a more important role than fathers in the control of children; instead, daughters tend to be the objects of maternal control and sons the objects of paternal controls (Hill and Atkinson, 1988; Morash and Chesney-Lind, 1991; Lieber and Wacker, 1997). Most damaging to the theory's empirical adequacy is the lack of support for the effect of family structure on gender differences in control, risk, and delinquency. One reason for the failure to replicate Hagan's findings on this relationship stems from variation in measurement of patriarchal and egalitarian family structures. Some studies use only gradational measures of social class or indirect measures of occupational types rather than explicit measures of occupational authority of husbands relative to wives (Jensen and Thompson, 1990; Morash and Chesney-Lind, 1991; Avakame, 1997). Nevertheless, even studies using measures similar to Hagan's have failed to demonstrate substantive or statistically significant variations in the gender gap in delinquency or deviance across family type (Blackwell, 2000; Blackwell, Sellers, and Schlaupitz, 2002).

The dubious empirical adequacy of power-control theory has also been attributed to testing with inappropriate samples. Most power-control studies have examined gender differences in delinquency among unrelated individuals, notwithstanding that the theory actually predicts differences in delinquency between opposite-sex siblings within the same family. Hagan's recent research using opposite-sex siblings (Hagan, Boehnke, and Merkens, 2004; Hadjar, Baier, Boehnke, and Hagan, 2007) offered support for the theory, and Blackwell and Reed (2003) demonstrated that the theory's ability to predict variation in the gender gap in delinquency across family type increases somewhat when examining within-household rather than between-household gender differences in delinquency.

Hagan recognized the problematic nature of the occupational patriarchy concept and has recently revised power-control theory (McCarthy, Hagan, and Woodward, 1999; Hagan et al., 2004; Hadjar et al., 2007). He observed that over the past 2 decades, less patriarchal families have become more common than more patriarchal families in Western societies. Nevertheless, gender differences in parental controls have not changed much. Hagan and colleagues (2004) theorized that as women's authority in the workplace has increased, mothers have "decoupled" patriarchal gender-role beliefs, or "gendered schemas" from parental control practices. In patriarchal families, mothers give sons more freedoms, consistent with gendered schemas supportive of male domination and female subordination. In more occupationally balanced families, mothers do not simply supply these same freedoms to their daughters, as the earlier power-control theory predicted; instead these empowered mothers use their control to "advance the opportunities of daughters along the paths of more conventional achievement that have become more available to women" (Hagan et al., 2004:662). Hagan et al.'s (2004) data from two-parent families containing opposite-sex siblings in Toronto and Berlin demonstrated that mothers lacking occupational power still control daughters more than sons, but mothers who possess high levels of occupational power actually control sons more than daughters, and among middle-status mothers, relative occupational authority is unrelated to gendered parental controls.

Patriarchal Society and Crime

Although counted by some as "liberal feminism," women's liberation theories are often not considered to be feminist theories. Chesney-Lind (1989:19) referred to them rather as examples of "flawed theory building" that have been "more or less discredited." These authors also do not consider power-control theory, at least its initial statement, to be feminist theory either, but simply a variation on the liberation hypothesis, because it is "arguing that mothers' work force participation ... leads to daughters' delinquency." In effect, then, "mother's liberation causes daughter's crime" (Chesney-Lind, 1989:20). If liberation and power-control theories are not feminist explanations of male and female crime, then what is?

> It is not easy to know when a work or action is feminist....Neither a scholar's gender nor the focus of scholarship ... can be used to distinguish feminist, non-feminist, or even anti-feminist works. Research on women or on gender differences, whether conducted by a male or female criminologist, does not in itself qualify it as feminist....[F]eminist inquiry is not limited to topics about women, it focuses on men as well. (Daly and Chesney-Lind, 1988:503)

Despite this uncertainty about the distinguishing features of feminist theory, its theoretical development has apparently moved away from themes of female liberation and sex-role differentiation in family socialization. The themes emphasized in later feminist theories of crime are the pervasiveness of male dominance in patriarchal society and its impact on crimes committed both by and against women. This emphasis on patriarchy would seem to distinguish feminist from non-feminist theories of criminal behavior more clearly than the emphasis on women's liberation or family structure to account for gender differences in crime. It does not, however, represent a total departure from mainstream criminological theory. For instance, the primary dimension of power relations in feminist theory is no different than the power dimension in traditional, male-formulated conflict and Marxist theories. The difference lies in what type of power is placed at the center. In conflict theory, the dominant theme is the conflict between various powerful and powerless groups; whereas in Marxism, ruling class power dominates the proletariat. In feminist theory, male power over women is the dominant theme.

James Messerschmidt (1986), for example, modified the Marxist position that capitalism is criminogenic because it exploits the working class to incorporate the feminist focus on patriarchy. His theory was that crime is caused by the combination of a male-dominated, patriarchal social structure and a capitalist economic system. To Messerschmidt, the criminality of women and the violent crime of lower class men both result from their powerlessness, whereas corporate crimes and sexual crimes against women, especially rape, are the result of male power.

This patriarchal dominance is not only useful in understanding the gender differential in the rates of crime, according to feminist theories, it can also lead to a better understanding of such gender-specific offenses as prostitution by women and the commission of rape by men against women. Nowhere is the gender ratio more skewed toward male offenders than in the universality of males as perpetrators and the rarity of males as victims of rape. Closely related to this is the great disparity of males as offenders and females as victims of sexual and domestic abuse. Explaining rape and abuse is hardly unique to feminist theory, and differing feminist views have not yet coalesced into a coherent theory of rape and violence against women. Nevertheless, feminist research, theoretical, and policy agendas have brought attention to the issue of the extremely disadvantaged role of women as victims of rape and abuse. This issue has been defined not only in terms of female victimization and survivorship, but also in terms of the treatment of rape victims in the criminal justice system (Daly and Chesney-Lind, 1988).

Chesney-Lind (1989) spelled out one possible process by which the patriarchal system, the family, physical and sexual abuse, "survival strategies" (e.g., running away from home), and other gender-relevant factors may cause female delinquency. Status offenses and minor delinquencies by girls are ways of responding to conflict in the family. The enforcement of a double standard of conduct for sons and daughters, even in non-traditional families, is one common source of this conflict. Sexual and physical abuse by stepfathers and others in the home is another. Girls who run away to the streets and engage in prostitution, theft, and other crimes are more likely than boys who run away to have been victims of abuse. Thus, serious juvenile delinquency and, by extension, adult criminal careers are linked to the survival response of leaving home. These processes are similar for abused boys, but, "unlike boys, girls' victimization and their response to that victimization are specifically shaped by their status as young women" (Chesney-Lind, 1989:23). She argued that there are dramatic differences in childhood and adolescence for boys and girls. They live in very different worlds with very different choices. Even when boys and girls share similar circumstances, these are filtered by gender. Therefore, family abuse, although also affecting boys, is especially important in the etiology of female delinquency and crime (Chesney-Lind and Shelden, 2004).

Masculinities and Structured Action

Many feminist scholars look to the concept of patriarchy as a means of shifting the emphasis in mainstream criminology from the individual characteristics that distinguish male offenders and non-offenders toward a focus on the structural power and domination of women shared by all men. More recently, however, some feminist theorists, including James Messerschmidt (1993:59), have rejected patriarchy as a concept that has "lost its strength and usefulness as an analytical tool." Messerschmidt (1993:57) acknowledged criticisms that his patriarchal theory "merely tacked on an analysis of gender relations to an unaltered androcentric Marxism" and "failed to account for the intentions of actors and for how action, including crime, is a meaningful construct in itself."

According to Messerschmidt (1993:58), the primary shortcoming of patriarchy theory is that it "explains away any real variation in the construction of masculinity within a particular society and, consequently, encourages the theorization of [only] one type of masculinity—the 'typical' (patriarchal) male." He argued instead that crime should be conceptualized as "structured action," where gendered social structural features (specifically, a division of labor along gender lines, gender differences in power, and heterosexuality) are created by and at the same time produce gendered social action. "Social structures are constituted by social action and, in turn, provide resources and power from which individuals construct 'strategies of action'" (Messerschmidt, 1993:77). Closely tied to this conceptualization of crime is the notion of gender as a "situated accomplishment" (West and Zimmerman, 1987; West and Fenstermaker, 1993). In social interaction, individuals' *sex* may be judged by others as male or female on the basis of distinctive biological features or, absent such knowledge, social signs such as hair, clothing, or speech; *gender*, however, constitutes social action that verifies that categorization:

> We configure our behaviors so we are seen unquestionably by others in particular social situations as expressing our "essential natures"—*we do masculinity or femininity.* ... In this view, then, masculinity is accomplished, it is not something done to men or something settled beforehand. And masculinity is never static, never a finished product. Rather men construct masculinities in specific social situations ... in so doing, men reproduce (and sometimes change) social structures. (Messerschmidt, 1993:80; emphasis added)

Because masculinity is accomplished in a variety of specific social situations, we are encouraged to conceptualize multiple masculinities. For example, the construction of masculinities depends on men's position in society as determined by class, race, or sexual orientation. Masculinities may therefore be "hegemonic" (adhering to a culturally idealized form of masculinity) or "subordinated" (anything other than the ideal; Connell, 1987).

Messerschmidt (1993:85) tied these concepts of crime as structured action and masculinities as situated accomplishments into an explanation of the gender difference in crime. Essentially, "crime by men is a form of social practice invoked as a resource, when other resources are unavailable, for accomplishing masculinity." Especially in situations where a man's masculinity may be doubted or called into question, some men who have no other means at hand for "doing masculinity" may resort to crime as an expression of masculinity. Messerschmidt applied masculinities theory to a variety of crimes committed by males of varying ages, races, and classes in different social settings. He illustrated that the ways of "doing masculinity" for White, middle class boys may produce entirely different forms of crime committed in different settings than for White working-class boys and racial-minority, lower working-class boys. Likewise, crimes committed on the street differ from those committed in the workplace and in the family, depending on the man's position of authority, which in turn determines the form of expressed masculinity.

Patriarchy theory shifted attention away from notions of individual differences between criminal and non-criminal men and toward notions of structural universalities shared by men. Masculinities theory in its turn shifted the focus away from this universalism to recognize that masculinities, and therefore types of criminal actions, vary depending on such factors as class and race. Nevertheless, the theory has been criticized on a number of grounds, primarily by other feminists. Although acknowledging multiple masculinities based on class, race, or other identities, the theory still cannot answer why all men do not use crime (of whatever type) as a resource for "doing masculinity" (Jefferson, 1996). Masculinities theory has also been criticized for presenting a tautological explanation of crime (Walklate, 1995; Hood-Williams, 2001). The theory states that men commit crime because crime affirms their masculinity. But what makes crimes masculine? Undoubtedly, it is because men commit them. Feminists have also been wary of a theory that seems to refocus theoretical attention on men and, like traditional criminological theories, runs the risk of holding up men as the norm against which women are compared as the "other" (Daly, 1997; Cain, 1990). If men who commit crime are "doing masculinity," are the women who do not commit crime "doing femininity"? What about women who do commit crime? Do their crimes serve to accomplish some sort of subordinated rather than hegemonic femininity? Or does the social structure that subordinates them (through economic or social marginalization) simply close off opportunities to achieve hegemonic femininity? If the latter, then the theory promotes the image of woman as passive (see Naffine, 1987). On the other hand, if women are actively seeking expression of subordinated rather than hegemonic femininity through the commission of crime, why would they be motivated to do so? Daly (1997) cautioned, however, that femininity and masculinity need not be viewed as polar opposites. "Researchers must be mindful that categories taken from theorizing masculinity may be inappropriately applied to femininity. Gender categories are not neutral, and the terms used to describe men and women 'doing gender' are not likely to be interchangeable" (Daly, 1997:37).

Gendered Pathways and Gendered Contexts

Recent work in criminological theory has seen a shift toward greater acceptance of feminist perspectives on crime and delinquency. Increasingly, mainstream criminologists are actively considering gender, including its structural, cultural, social, and psychological implications.[9] Also increasingly, feminist criminologists are acknowledging the utility of retaining many components of general criminological theories (Steffensmeier and Allan, 1996; Bottcher, 2001; Belknap and Holsinger, 2006; Heimer, De Coster, and Unal, 2006):

> The best feminist work—and the most promising direction for the future of feminist criminology—is that which remains critically engaged with the gendered life situations of women and men while drawing from, and enriching its analysis from, the insights of broader criminological thought. (Miller and Mullins, 2006:217)

The incorporation of mainstream criminological theory into feminist theories of gender and crime is most evident in two areas of inquiry: gendered pathways to crime and gendered contexts of crime. The "gendered pathways" (Daly, 1998) approach has much in common with the life-course perspective (see chap. 12); work in this area focuses on the life experiences and developmental trajectories of girls and women who become involved in crime. Feminist researchers typically engage in ethnographic field observations and interviews with female offenders, allowing these women a "voice" in describing the events in their own lives that may be linked to their criminal involvement. One of the most common themes to emerge in gendered pathways research is the experience of physical and sexual victimization in the lives of female offenders. However, identifying the "blurred boundaries" (Daly and Maher, 1998) between victimization and offending does little to explain offending; instead, this phenomenon *requires* explanation. In mainstream criminological theory, for example, Agnew (1992; Broidy and Agnew, 1997) incorporated victimization into general strain theory (see chap. 8), arguing that victimization represents a strain that produces a negative emotion (anger, depression, anxiety) that may ultimately lead to delinquency as a means of escaping the victimization. By itself, then, the gendered pathways approach is more descriptive than explanatory.

Offering more promise as a testable explanation of the gendered nature of crime is the gendered context approach. The gendered context approach examines the degree to which males and females encounter different normative expectations and opportunities for offending, as well as the degree to which males and females attribute different meanings, and thus respond differently, to similar events and situations. The gendered context approach can and often does draw from traditional criminological theory. Darrell Steffensmeier and Emilie Allan (1996), for example, conceded that theoretical variables such as those derived from social learning, social bonding, and anomie theories, might serve to account for gender differences in minor delinquency; however, a gendered approach is necessary to account for differences in serious criminal involvement:

> Even when men and women commit the same statutory offense, the "gestalt" of their offending is frequently quite different. Because the gender differences in context are small for trivial or mild forms of law-breaking, but large for violent and other serious forms of crime, contextual analysis can shed light on the gender differences for serious offenses....(Steffensmeier and Allan, 1996:474)

Steffensmeier and Allan argued that the "organization of gender," that is, the structural arrangements that determine gender differences in norms, morals and values, and ultimately social controls placed on the behaviors of males and females, produce gender differences in opportunities, motivations, and contexts for crime. Women more than men are expected to be nurturing, to emphasize relational concerns (an "ethic of care") over instrumental concerns, and are often subjected to more informal social controls to maintain the organization of gender. These structural gender differences influence, among other things, the kinds of associates one encounters, perceptions of risks and rewards, and levels of self-control differentially among males and females. Likewise, males and females carry out their crimes within different contexts. For example, in spousal homicide, men rarely kill their wives out of fear of violent victimization from them, but a sizeable number of women who kill their husbands have used murder in response to longstanding patterns of abuse in the relationship (Steffensmeier and Allan, 1996).

Karen Heimer et al. (2006) used similar reasoning in their analysis of "hegemonic gender definitions" and their subsequent influence on social psychological correlates of delinquency. These gender definitions "are built into major institutions, permeate most social interactions, are extolled at the symbolic level, and are influential in the judgments of most types of behavior by both females and males" (Heimer et al., 2006:112). Hegemonic gender definitions produce differences in males' and females' exposure to associations, definitions, and reinforcement contingencies and elicit through socialization different levels and forms of morality, empathy, and shame. These gender definitions also create differences in the impact that other social psychological factors have on the individual. For example, because of hegemonic gender definitions, the meaning and importance of emotional bonds may be different for males and females; angry males may act on that emotion differently than angry females; and women who enjoy taking risks may choose very different activities from men who enjoy taking risks. These gender differences in social psychological characteristics are likely to produce differentially gendered outcomes in delinquent and conventional behavior.

Empirical Validity of Feminist Theories of Criminal Behavior

As shown earlier, theories drawing on women's liberation and increased labor force participation, including power-control theory, have been tested directly, but they have encountered non-supportive and contrary evidence. These theories, however, are often defined as non-feminist theories by feminist criminologists.

Hypotheses generally acknowledged as feminist have rarely been directly tested. A generalized reliance on patriarchal social structure, such as Messerschmidt's (1986), as an explanation of all types of crime has the same problem as the Marxist explanation that "capitalism causes crime." Unless there is some way to measure degrees of patriarchy in different parts of society, any research within that same society will not allow for any variation in the independent variable. To test this theory, one would have to conduct cross-cultural comparisons of societies with greater or lesser patriarchy and examine the differences in male and female crime patterns. Some cross-national research has been done in which the degree of gender inequality is measured in different societies. For example, Steffensmeier et al. (1989) compared the female percentage of arrests for homicide, major property crimes, and minor property crimes across a wide range of societies. They found that the ratio of female-to-male arrestees in different societies was related neither to their measure of "gender inequality" nor to "female economic marginality," but rather to the formalization of social control and greater access by women to consumer goods. Findings such as these do not lend much support to the theory that the gender ratio in crime reflects patriarchal inequalities. It will take considerably more research than this study to measure more directly the concept of patriarchy to provide better tests of the theory.

Masculinities theory has not been subjected to a great deal of empirical evaluation, and what has been done has been indirect. Simpson and Elis (1995), for example, examined the effects of hegemonic femininity and masculinity on crime in a national probability sample of youth aged 14 to 21. Hegemonic femininity was measured among women by disapproval of a career orientation for women and a projection of being married and raising a family rather than working by age 35. They found that career-oriented women were more likely to engage in violent and property offenses than women adhering to more traditional feminine

ideals, but this was true only for White women. The impact of hegemonic masculinity on male crime was even less clear. The only measure of hegemonic masculinity used in the study was men's projections
of being married and having a family as opposed to working by age 35.
Yet, it can be argued that for men, both options represent some form of
masculinity. By using this measure, the theory would be impossible to
refute because any result could be interpreted as supportive. The measure of hegemonic masculinity had no impact on men's violent offenses
but reduced White men's and increased Black men's property offenses.
These results seem to support the existence of multiple masculinities
based on race but call into question whether gender power supercedes
race or class power.

Feminist research on gendered pathways to crime has relied on both
quantitative[10] and qualitative[11] data to support the claim that physical
and sexual abuse in childhood, adolescence, and even adulthood can
account for involvement in delinquency and crime among girls and
women. National victimization surveys, such as the National Crime
Victimization and the American Correctional Association surveys,
estimate that approximately half of all female offenders in prison have
been subjected to some form of physical or sexual abuse in their lifetime. Qualitative studies involving intensive interviews with women
in prison also find consistent evidence of victimization among female
offenders, but sample sizes are generally small (but see Owen, 1998, for
an exception). However, for the most part, feminist research on gendered pathways has neglected to conduct analyses that compare the
victimization histories of female offenders with that of male offenders.
Research generally shows that victims of child and adolescent maltreatment are more likely than non-victims to become offenders (Brezina,
1998; Widom and Maxfield, 2001), but the research is less clear whether
female victims are at any greater risk of offending than male victims.
Cathy Spatz Widom found in her prospective study of 667 matched
pairs of abused and non-abused children no differences between
male and female victims in their likelihood of becoming offenders,
having increased numbers of offenses, being arrested at earlier ages,
and being chronic offenders (Widom, 1989); however, she did find that
female victims, but not male victims, demonstrate a greater prevalence
of violent offending and are more likely to be arrested for an alcohol-
related offense than non-victims (Widom and Maxfield, 2001; Ireland
and Widom, 1994). Thus, there is little support for the contention that
the "pathway" to crime is "gendered" with respect to victimization.

No direct tests of the gendered context of crime exist, and indirect
tests demonstrate little support for the hypothesis of major differences
in the etiology of male and female crime. The same variables that are
related to male offending are also related to female offending; gender

moderates, but does not dramatically alter, the effects of these variables (Simpson and Elis, 1995). Other research supports these conclusions. There is little empirically to sustain the feminist criticism that extant theories are falsified or inadequate when applied to the criminal behavior of women, or to uphold the conclusion that gender-specific theories are needed to account for the gender-ratios in crime and deviance. Variables from social learning, social bonding, self-control, and other theories account for differences between male and female rates and for individual variations in criminal and deviant behavior among both men and women. Differences in exposure to these same variables largely, and in some research almost completely, explain the greater tendency of males to commit offenses (Esbensen and Deschenes, 1998; Mears et al., 1998; Liu and Kaplan, 1999; Moffitt et al., 2001; Hartjen and Priyadarsini, 2003; Chapple, McQuillan, and Berdahl, 2005; Piquero, Gover, MacDonald, and Piquero, 2005; Meadows, 2007). Mears et al. (1998:263) concluded that it is "fruitless to construct utterly different theories to explain the delinquency of males and females. As we have seen, both males and females are affected—although to different degrees—by a common factor: association with delinquent friends." For some offenses (such as rape), the gender ratio is so great that something beyond gender variations in common causes of sexual aggression will probably be needed to explain it. But to the extent that feminist theories of criminal behavior reject "traditional" explanations as applicable to female offenders (see Chesney-Lind and Pasko, 2004) and rely on gender-specific explanations of crime, they do not conform to the research evidence.

Policy Implications of Feminist Theories

Feminist theories would clearly imply that patriarchy must be ended or at least fundamental changes must be made in gendered institutions and social relations in society. The goal would be to reduce gender-based disparities and inequalities in society in general and in the law and criminal justice system in particular. Sentencing guidelines that limit judges' discretion in sentencing is one way that the criminal justice system has attempted to eliminate gender and other disparities in the treatment of offenders. Koons-Witt (2002) examined the extent to which sentencing guidelines accomplished this mission. Comparing sentencing decisions prior to, immediately after, and long after sentencing guidelines were implemented in Minnesota, she found that, although some gender disparities disappeared immediately after the implementation of the guidelines, they reappeared several years later as courts discovered how to circumvent the guidelines. In a similar study undertaken in Ohio, Griffin and Wooldredge (2006) found that gender disparities remained even immediately after sentencing guidelines were implemented.

There are other implications of feminist theory for crime control, prevention, or treatment. For instance, Chesney-Lind and Pasko (2004) suggested that prevention and treatment are to be preferred over punitive policies for female offenders. Although they have much in common, there are some special, perhaps unique, life circumstances faced by girls and women. These include special vulnerability to sexual assault and intimate violence, unplanned pregnancy, and adolescent motherhood. These and other gendered events and contingencies must be taken into account when designing treatment and prevention programs. As it stands now, only a very small portion of such programs serve females, and many of those do not provide for the specialized counseling needs of girls (e.g., special risks and consequences of sexual abuse). This research confirms that women are less violent and more amenable to treatment and prevention than men in both residential and non-residential community programs, and they respond better than men to such programs rather than those carried out in prisons or detention facilities.

Chesney-Lind and Pasko (2004) did not say specifically how such community-based prevention and treatment techniques, procedures, or strategies for females would differ from those for males, and they do not report research showing the differential effectiveness of gender-specific programs. Nevertheless, the general point of treating women differently from men is well made, cogent, and sound. Without great care, however, programs geared to the special needs of women could turn out to be of the type that would be inconsistent with the feminist perspective of Chesney-Lind and others. Depending on how it is implemented, the policy of treating female offenders differently in rehabilitation and prevention programs could perpetuate rather than counter sexist stereotypes and gender disparities in treatment and rehabilitation.

Summary

Feminist theory focuses on the patriarchal system as the root division in society between the dominant and subordinate groups. Privileged males rule, make the rules, and enforce the rules. In this system, women are more disadvantaged, restricted, and controlled. Male dominance is maintained, and women are kept in their place in part by sex-role expectations that are enforced by both the informal and formal control systems. Gender disparities in the criminal justice system reflect male dominance and restrictive female sex roles. Women may be treated paternalistically by more lenient judgment in the system or punished more harshly for certain offenses that go strongly against traditional female sex-role expectations. Research on male-female differences in criminal justice decisions for offenders provides some data consistent with feminist theory, but for the most part, the gender of the offender has little or no direct effect on the criminal justice outcomes.

Feminist theories of criminal behavior have addressed two basic issues: whether explanations of law violations committed by males also apply to those committed by females, and what accounts for the high ratio of male-to-female crime rates. Earlier feminist theories postulated that committing crime and delinquency is a consequence of learning the male role; therefore, as women's liberation has increased the equality between men and women, female crime has risen to greater equality with male crime. Power-control theory proposed that the patriarchal family system creates more delinquent boys and fewer delinquent girls. These liberation theories have had trouble in the face of empirical evidence and have been repudiated by many feminist theorists, who explain crime by reference to the basic patriarchal structure of society. No distinctive feminist theory on the etiology of crime has yet been formulated, but feminist theorists have utilized patriarchy to analyze rape and other sexual and physical violence by men against women and offenses by females. Masculinities theory seeks to explain men's greater involvement in crime as a means to accomplish masculinity, but it has been criticized as tautological, and there is little empirical evidence to support its claims. More recently, some feminist criminologists have hypothesized that causes derived from mainstream criminological theory may affect males and females differently, and that the context within which crime is committed is distinctively different for males and females. Feminist theory is still in formation, and the paucity of direct tests of its hypotheses and implementation of its policy implications has not yet provided a clear evaluation of its empirical validity or policy usefulness.

Notes

1. A recent emphasis in feminist criminology is "intersectionality" (Susan F. Sharp, 2006; Burgess-Proctor, 2006). This approach to the study of crime acknowledges that women cannot be assumed to share identical experiences simply by virtue of their shared gender. Instead, the experiences of individuals in the criminal justice system are structurally shaped by their multiple and simultaneous social locations: gender *and* race *and* class *and*

other identities including age, sexual orientation, and physical abilities. Thus, the experiences of poor women of color are not identical to the experiences of either White, middle class women or young Black men.

2. Although detailed descriptions of these types of feminism can be found in the literature (Tong, 1989; Walklate, 1995; Belknap, 2007; Chesney-Lind and Faith, 2001), many feminist writers refer instead to "phases" of feminist inquiry into which these five types of feminism may or may not be loosely fitted. These phases include the progression from "feminist empiricism" to "standpoint feminism" and then to postmodern feminism (Harding, 1987; but see also Naffine, 1995; Smart, 1995; Daly, 1997; and Daly and Maher, 1998, for other ways of describing the progression of feminist thought). Rather than "privilege" a single classification scheme, we simply acknowledge, present, and evaluate multiple feminist perspectives on law, criminal justice, and crime.

3. See Bowker with Chesney-Lind and Pollock (1978), Mann (1984), Messerschmidt (1986), Morris (1987), Daly and Chesney-Lind (1988), Simpson (1989; 1991), Daly (1989), Chesney-Lind (1988; 1989), Gelsthorpe and Morris (1990), Chesney-Lind and Shelden (2004), and Daly (1992; 1994a; 1994b).

4. Virtually all criminologists recognize that in the past, the subject of female crime has been less studied than male crime. A theory that limits its scope only to male crime is certain to be viewed as non-feminist, but even those theories that have traditionally been proposed as general explanations of all crime, both male and female, are defined as non-feminist theory. Further, simply concentrating on female crime or explaining female versus male crime rates is insufficient to define feminist theory. Almost all of the research and theory on female crime and delinquency from the time of Lombroso to the 1970s has been defined as non-feminist theory (see, for instance, Chesney-Lind and Shelden, 2004). A theory that offers a specific explanation for female crime by modifying and extending extant theory (e.g., Ogle, Katkin, and Bernard, 1995) will not be interpreted as a feminist theory. If a "traditional" theory is used to explain the gender ratio in crime, especially if the theory leans on biological differences between male and female, it is very unlikely to be defined as a feminist theory.

5. Leonard (1982) contended that all "traditional" theories are incapable of explaining female crime, but her critique mainly repeated the same empirical and logical flaws in the traditional theories that have long been identified by non-feminist critics. Contrary to her original assumption about the inadequacies of traditional theories, Leonard's analysis showed that some non-feminist theories, especially differential association and social learning, are quite capable of providing some explanation for both male and female crime. In fact, her suggestions for moving "toward a feminist theory of crime" were primarily selections of certain concepts and variables from the same traditional theories she had been criticizing for their insensitivity to feminist issues.

Similarly, Chesney-Lind and Pasko referred to the "androcentric bias in the *major theories of delinquent behavior, old and new*" (2004:15; emphasis added). They attempted to show that female offenders have always been "invisible" in the major criminological theories because they were developed only to explain male crime and delinquency. However, their review of criminological theories to support this contention focused almost exclusively on the older subcultural theories of Cohen, Cloward and Ohlin, and Miller, which were meant explicitly to explain only male gang delinquency. They cannot be expected to offer a general, non-gender specific theory of crime. Their characterization of criminological theory would be different if they had gone beyond this narrow range of theories to consider the major criminological theories such as those discussed in this book. Many of these theories were not designed exclusively to explain male crime. They have been tested with male, female, and combined samples; and those that successfully explain the behavior of males also successfully explain the behavior of females.

6. Hagan has never been consistent in his descriptions or measurement of patriarchal and egalitarian family structures. For example, the measure of patriarchal family type (also termed "more patriarchal") has sometimes been restricted only to situations where the husband has authority and the wife is unemployed. Measures of egalitarian (or "less patriarchal") family type are even more variable, sometimes excluding families where both husband and wife are employed without authority and sometimes broadening the measure to include all situations in which husband and wife hold similar positions. Hagan also recognizes a "matriarchal" family structure where the wife is employed with authority and the husband is employed without authority. Power-control theory has been relatively silent about the relationship between gender and delinquency in this type of family and tends to dismiss it as an outlier. Patriarchal, egalitarian, and matriarchal families all require two-parent households. However, single-parent households, especially female-headed families, are also quite common in contemporary society. Power-control theory has also been inconsistent in its predictions about the gender–delinquency relationship in female-headed families. At times, Hagan and others (Lieber and Wacker, 1997; see also Bates, Bader, and Mencken, 2003; Mack and Lieber, 2005) characterized these families as less patriarchal, although they have also been likened to matriarchal families (McCarthy et al., 1999). In all probability, female-headed families constitute a singular family structure that cannot be blended easily into any category that characterizes two-parent families (see Blackwell, 2000). Both matriarchal and female-headed families are theoretically underdeveloped in power-control theory, leaving the theory at present relatively narrow in its explanatory scope.

7. See the following studies by Hagan and associates that test various models of power-control theory: Hagan et al. (1985; 1990; 1993), Hagan et al. (1987; 1988), Hagan (1990), Hagan and Kay (1990), McCarthy and Hagan (1987), Boritch and Hagan (1990), McCarthy et al. (1999), Hagan et al. (2004), Hadjar et al. (2007).

8. See the following studies, which have attempted to replicate Hagan's findings or otherwise test Hagan's earlier version of power-control theory: Hill and Atkinson (1988); Singer and Levine (1988); Jensen and Thompson (1990); Morash and Chesney-Lind (1991); Grasmick, Hagan, Blackwell, and Arneklev (1996); Avakame (1997); Lieber and Wacker (1997); Uggen (2000a); Blackwell (2000); Blackwell et al. (2002); Blackwell and Reed (2003).

9. For example, Akers (1998) incorporated gender in his social structure-social learning model, acknowledging that one's gender will determine the extent to which one is exposed to associations, reinforcements, definitions, and models conducive to crime. Broidy and Agnew (1997) theorized gender differences in sources of strain and the negative affect which such strains produce, as well as differences in coping strategies that differentially affect delinquent outcomes.

10. Quantitative studies of pathways to crime among girls and women include the American Correctional Association (1990); Snell and Morton (1994); Browne, Miller, and Maguin (1999); Bloom, Owen, and Rosenbaum (2003); Fagan (2005); Lansford et al. (2007).

11. Qualitative studies of pathways to crime among girls and women include Chesney-Lind and Rodriguez (1983), Arnold (1990), Gilfus (1992), Richie (1996), Moore (1999), Owen (1998).

Chapter 12

Integrating Criminological Theories

Theory Competition Versus Theory Integration

There are three principal ways by which theories can be evaluated and developed. The first is to consider each theory on its own. To the extent that the theory's predictions are confirmed by the data, it can be accepted; to the extent that they are disconfirmed by the evidence, it can be modified or discarded. The second way is to subject two or more theories to "theory competition" (Liska, Krohn, and Messner, 1989). Theory competition is the logical, conceptual, or empirical comparison of two or more theories to determine which offers the better or best explanation of crime. In the previous chapters, the focus was on single-theory explication and assessment, during which some attention was given to the comparison of theories.

Evaluation of the evidence on a single theory seldom leads to a complete rejection of that theory. A modicum of truth can usually be found in each theory. At the other extreme, no theory has been able to explain all variations in crime. The evidence in support of, or counter to, most theories lies in between these two extremes. Theories differ in implications for policy; there are some applied implications with each theory, but no theory can form the basis for all policy or programs. The question remains, how well does each theory do in comparison with other theories? Criticism of one theory from the perspective of another is common, and direct competitive testing of two or more rival theories is often reported in the literature. Table 12.1 provides a summary overview of the major proponents, concepts, propositions, empirical validity, and policy implications of each of the principal theories discussed in the preceding chapters and three theories selected from this chapter (as indicated in the table) that should be useful in reviewing and comparing the theories.

Table 12.1: Overview of Theories of Criminal and Deviant Behavior

Theory/Chapter	Main Concept(s)	Main Proposition(s)	Empirical Validity	Main Policy Implications
Classical/Deterrence Chap. 2 Beccaria, Bentham	certainty, celerity, severity of legal punishment	punishment of crimes produces specific and general deterrence	weak large body of research	tough criminal justice policies and programs
Rational Choice Chap. 2 Cornish Clarke	rewards/costs expected utility of crime rational choice	decision to violate the law made after rational consideration of rewards/costs	none for pure rational choice, weak to moderate for modified models, sizeable body of research	similar to deterrence and routine activities theories; situation specific prevention
Routine Activities Chap. 2 Felson Cohen	motivated offender vulnerable targets or victims capable guardians	crime occurs when routine activities produce lack of guardianship of targets in the presence of motivated offenders	weak little direct testing	routine precautions and prevention, target hardening, change in routine activities
Early Biological Chap. 3 Lombroso Hooton	born criminal atavism biological inferiority	criminals are born; criminals are inherently defective	essentially none small body of research	eugenics permanent segregation from society
Modern Biosocial Chap. 3 Mednick Ellis Rowe	genetic heritability, slow neurological arousal, low IQ, biochemical imbalances, other biological susceptibility	crime results from genetically or biologically caused criminal susceptibility in interaction with social factors	weak modest but growing body of research	prenatal care, genetic counseling, community programs to counter genetic susceptibility

Theory	Central Concepts	Explanation of Criminal/Deviant Behavior	Empirical Validity	Policy Implications
Psychoanalytic Chap. 4 Friedlander	abnormalities of id, ego, superego, psychiatric disorder	crime is symptom of irrational, unconscious motives and psychiatric disturbance	very weak small body of direct research	in-depth, individualized psychotherapy
Personality Traits Chap. 4 Hathaway	antisocial or maladjusted personality traits	crime results from the individual's personality traits	weak to moderate large body of research	individual/group psychological counseling
Psychopathic Personality Chap. 4 Hare	psychopathy; sociopathy; personality syndrome of shallowness, selfishness, no conscience	psychopaths have very high probability of committing serious and persistent crime	weak sizeable body of research	little chance of changing psychopaths with treatment or early intervention
Social Learning Chap. 5 Sutherland Akers	differential association definitions differential reinforcement imitation	Deviant/criminal and conforming behavior results from the same SL process depending on the balance and direction of the SL variables	moderate to strong large body of research	cognitive/behavioral treatment/prevention and intervention programs with individuals, families, peers, other groups
Social Bonding Chap. 6 Hirschi	attachment, commitment, involvement, belief	Conformity results from stronger; deviance/crime from weaker, bonds to others/society	weak to moderate large body of research	treatment/prevention programs with individuals and families to strengthen bonds

Table 12.1: *Continued*

Theory/Chapter	Main Concept(s)	Main Proposition(s)	Empirical Validity	Main Policy Implications
Self-Control Chap. 6 Gottfredson Hirschi	self-control	Conformity results from high, and deviance from low, self-control	moderate large body of research	early childhood intervention with families; no treatment or rehabilitation
Labeling Chap. 7 Lemert Becker Schur	societal reaction stigmatized labeling	stigmatizing labels cause secondary deviance	very weak large body of research	juvenile diversion
Reintegrative Shaming Chap. 7 Braithwaite	stigmatizing and reintegrative shaming	reintegrative shaming prevents secondary deviance	not determinable very little direct research	restorative justice
Social Disorganization Chap. 8 Shaw/McKay Sampson Bursik	social disorganization, weak informal social control, in neighborhood or community; low collective efficacy	social disorganization results in higher rates of crime/deviance	moderate to strong substantial body of indirect research, little direct research	neighborhood, community projects, gang intervention
Anomie/Strain Chap. 8 Merton Cloward and Ohlin Messner/Rosenfeld	anomie; inequality of opportunity/access to means; overemphasis on monetary/success goals; expectations/aspirations discrepancy	anomie, blocked opportunities, inequality result in deviant adaptations, higher rates of crime/deviance, and delinquent subcultures	weak at individual level, sizeable body of research; weak to moderate at structural level, little direct research	structural change, neighborhood, community projects, gang intervention, job skill training

Theory	Key Concepts	Causes of Crime	Research Support	Policy Implications
General Strain Chap. 8 Agnew	strain; failure to achieve goals; loss of positive stimuli; confrontation with negative stimuli, negative effect	criminal/deviant behavior is an individual adaptation to strain/stress operating through learning, control, personality variables	weak to moderate growing body of research	family and individual counseling/therapy; indirectly, restorative justice
Conflict Chap. 9 Vold Sellin Sutherland	group and cultural conflict power	criminal behavior is an expression of group and cultural conflict	not determinable very little research	uncertain; implies structural change to equalize group power
Marxist Chap. 10 Bonger Quinney	class conflict capitalism power	crime caused by capitalism and class conflict	weak small body of historical, comparative research	overthrow capitalism and replace with socialism/communism
Feminist Chap. 11 Adler/Simon Chesney-Lind Messerschmidt Steffensmeier	inequality in gender and sex role expectations patriarchy	female crime and gender ratio in crime is a reflection of gender inequality and patriarchal society	weak small body of direct research	uncertain; implies structural change toward gender equality and reduction of patriarchy
Social Networks Chap. 12 Krohn Haynie	social networks; density, multiplexity, peer networks	delinquency related to lower network density and multiplex networks with proportionately more delinquent friends	weak for density; strong for delinquent networks; small body of research	intervention with gangs and other deviant networks

Table 12.1: *Continued*

Theory/Chapter	Main Concept(s)	Main Proposition(s)	Empirical Validity	Main Policy Implications
Control Balance Chap. 12 Tittle	balance, surplus, and deficit in control exercised over or by the individual	crime committed in effort to balance control surpluses or deficits	weak to moderate small body of research	uncertain; implies that application would vary by individual's deficit or surplus of control
Age-graded Informal Social Control Chap. 12 Laub Sampson	informal social control social bonds	age variations in onset, persistence, and desistance reflect informal control and social bonds through the life course	moderate small body of research	uncertain; similar to implications of social bonding theory adjusted for age

Note: This table includes only the major theories of criminal and deviant behavior found in chapters 2 through 11 and selected theories in chapter 12. Perspectives such as left realism, postmodernism, and peacemaking criminology, that either offer no theory of criminal behavior, or reject efforts to explain such behavior, are not listed. Theories of law and criminal justice, even when stated from the same general perspective as the theories listed in this table (such as labeling, conflict, Marxist, and feminist theories) are not listed. The entries in the columns are intended only to be summary and illustrative, not exhaustive or mutually exclusive, of the theorists, central concepts, propositions, empirical research, and policy implications of the different theories listed. The table is based on the content of the relevant chapters with regard to the concepts and propositions of the theories, research testing the theories, and the explicit or implicit policy and program practices or implications of the theories. It does not reflect other sources or assessments of the theories which, it is recognized, may differ.

The third way to assess and construct theory is by theoretical integration. Having made brief reference to theoretical integration in previous chapters, we now return to it in some detail in this concluding chapter. The goal of theory integration is to identify commonalities in two or more theories to produce a synthesis that is superior to any one theory individually.

Theoretical integration often involves deliberate attempts to fuse together two closely related theories, but it may also stem from theory competition. On closer examination, two opposing theories may not be as incompatible as thought. All of the theories reviewed in previous chapters have been subjected, to some degree, both to competition and to integration with other theories. When each theory was first formulated, it more or less leaned on prior theories and drew from a number of different sources. Moreover, all these theories have been revised in some fashion after their original statements. These revisions almost always borrow from the insights and explanations found in other theories, or are response to critiques from proponents of other theories, and constitute at least a partial integration of theories. (For example, see the revisions suggested for deterrence theory in chap. 2, for strain theory in chap. 8, and for labeling theory in chap. 7.) At the same time, the proponents of each theory implicitly or explicitly compare its explanatory power with alternative explanations. Both theory competition and integration have been vigorously defended (see the various contributors to Messner, Krohn, and Liska, 1989). Hirschi and Gottfredson (Hirschi, 1979; 1989; Gottfredson and Hirschi, 1990) are strong proponents of the oppositional strategy of pitting theories against one another, whereas Elliott advocates theoretical integration (Elliott, 1985; Elliott et al., 1985). Hirschi argued that what passes for theoretical integration in criminology usually involves ignoring crucial differences between the theories undergoing integration. He pointed out that some "integrated theories are merely oppositional theories in disguise, theories that pretend to open-mindedness while in fact taking sides in theoretical disputes" (Hirschi, 1989:41–42):

> I do not favor efforts to link theories together unless it can be shown that they are for all intents and purposes the same theory....
>
> The first purpose of oppositional theory construction is to make the world safe for a theory contrary to currently accepted views.... Therefore, oppositional theorists should not make life easy for those interested in preserving the status quo. They should instead remain at all times blind to the weaknesses of their own position and stubborn in its defense. Finally, they should never smile. (Hirschi, 1989:44–45)

Akers (1989) agreed with Hirschi that the integration of theories, if done without regard to incompatibilities, can result in useless "theoretical mush." On the other hand, a strictly oppositional strategy often overlooks important compatibilities between theories:

> [T]he insistence on keeping theories separate and competing carries ... the risk of ignoring similarities and overlap between two theories even when they are different....

> If concepts and propositions from two or more theories are essentially the same, why pretend they are different and ignore the similarity merely for the sake of retaining separate theories? Such an attitude results in theories that are different in name only. (Akers, 1989:24–25)

Bernard and Snipes (1995) argued that Hirschi's opposition to integration is based on his characterization of theories as falling into three main categories: "control, strain, and cultural deviance." Hirschi believed that these are inherently incompatible theories resting on irreconcilable assumptions. Bernard and Snipes (1995) maintained that Hirschi reached this conclusion because he misinterpreted and distorted both strain and cultural deviance theory. A clear example of this is the way in which Gottfredson and Hirschi (1990; see also Hirschi, 2004) mistakenly described social learning theory as cultural deviance theory and a pure "positivist" theory that led them to ignore the many similarities between control and learning theories (see Akers, 1991; 1996).

Varieties of Theoretical Integration in Criminology

Liska et al. (1989) identified different types of theoretical integration. One type is conceptual integration, by which concepts from one theory are shown to overlap in meaning with concepts from another theory. *Propositional integration* relates propositions from different theories. This can be accomplished by showing how two or more theories make the same predictions about crime, although each begins with different concepts and assumptions (e.g., anomie, social disorganization, and conflict theories would each predict higher crime rates in the lower class). Propositional integration can also be done by placing the explanatory variables from different theories into some kind of causal or explanatory sequence. The sequence starts with the variables from one theory (e.g., social disorganization) to explain the variations in variables from another theory (e.g., attachment to family), which in turn can be used to explain delinquency. Theoretical integration can also be *within-level* (only micro-level or only macro-level) or *cross-level* (structural–processual).[1] To explicate all the instances of theoretical integration would take us beyond the purposes of this book. Instead, a few are presented here to illustrate integration of criminological theories.[2]

Conceptual Integration

Akers: Integration by Conceptual Absorption

Akers (1973; 1977) long ago showed the ways in which social learning theory concepts and propositions overlap with and complement social bonding, labeling, conflict, anomie, and deterrence theories.[3] Later, he proposed that integration could be achieved by "conceptual absorption." Conceptual absorption means subsuming concepts from one theory as special cases of the phenomena defined by the concepts of another (Akers and Cochran, 1985; Akers, 1989).

For instance, in social bonding theory, the concept of "belief" refers to general moral beliefs that, if strongly adhered to, constrain delinquency. The belief concept can be absorbed into the more general social learning concept of "definitions" favorable or unfavorable to crime and delinquency. This broader concept incorporates both general and specific beliefs and attitudes that constrain criminal and delinquent behavior, and those that approve of or justify the behavior under certain circumstances. Strong adherence to conventional beliefs, therefore, is only one type of definition unfavorable to deviance, just as weak adherence to conventional moral beliefs is only one type of definition favorable to deviance. There is nothing in "beliefs" that is not included in "definitions," but definitions includes phenomena left out of the belief concept.

The social bonding concept of "attachment" refers to the closeness of relationships and affectional ties with parents, peers, and others. According to Akers, this can be subsumed under the concept of the modalities of differential association as one measure of "intensity" of association specified in social learning theory. Attachment also means identification with others as role models, obviously subsumable under the general concept of imitation in social learning theory.

Akers notes that these areas of conceptual commonalities do not necessarily lead to the same propositions about delinquency. Conceptual integration does not by itself produce propositional integration. For example, whereas social bonding theory predicts that strong attachment to others will inhibit delinquency, even if that attachment is to delinquent friends, social learning theory predicts the opposite outcome: that delinquency will be facilitated by intense association or attachment with or to delinquent friends.

Thornberry (1989) contended that this subsuming of concepts from theories under social learning concepts, although interesting, stops well short of a fully integrated model. Charles Tittle said that Akers is taking a "pac man" approach to theory integration that simply gobbles up other theories and does not really integrate them. If absorption means only that concepts from other theories are subsumed under existing social learning concepts without producing anything more than what is already there, then social learning has not integrated other theories. It has simply executed a hostile takeover.

Cullen and Colvin: Social Support and Coercion

Francis Cullen (1994; Cullen and Wright, 1997) proposed that "social support" (social integration in a group relationship in which emotional, material, and social assistance is provided to one another) can be used as the central organizing concept around which all of criminology can be unified. According to Cullen, social support prevents crime and therefore, the greater the social support the lower crime and victimization. Mark Colvin (2000), on the other hand, said that "coercion" (defined as whatever forces one to act through fear, anxiety, or intimidation) may be the unifying concept in criminology because crime is a reaction or response to coercion. These two positions are reminiscent of the contention by some theories (e.g., anomie/strain) that people are motivated to commit crime as a response to strain or pressure (see chap. 8) compared to the contention by other theories (e.g. social bonding) that crime is prevented by strong bonds to society (see chap. 6). But Colvin and Cullen teamed up to argue that there is an "emerging theoretical and public policy consensus" that "coercion causes crime" and "social support prevents crime" and that concepts (and variables) from a "wide variety of theories" can be subsumed under these two general concepts (Colvin, Cullen, and Vander Ven, 2002:19). They contended that coercion and support are not polar opposites but rather two different general conceptual categories under which a range of crime preventative and crime causative factors may be classified. Although a propositional model is presented, the focus on these two constructs subsuming concepts from several theories make these efforts more akin to conceptual than to propositional integration.

Contained within the concept of coercion are coercive family discipline that weakens social bonds (coercive family model), sources of strain (general strain theory), economic inequality (anomie theory), and repression (control balance theory). Coercion comes from both interpersonal (individuals and small groups) and impersonal sources (economy, government, and criminal justice) and varies in strength and consistency. According to Colvin et al. (2002:24), the general concept of coercion comes more from strain theory, whereas "social support is rooted in the idea, first promoted by the Chicago School, that organized networks of human relations can assist people in meeting both expressive and instrumental needs, which prevents crime."

Expressive or emotional support affirms the individual's value and worth as a person. Instrumental support provides assistance with physical or monetary needs as well as guidance, aid, and help in getting along in society. Informal social support is found in primary groups (family, peers, neighborhoods) and formal social support is provided by schools, workplaces, criminal justice, government, and public organizations. Just as with coercion, there is variation in the strength and consistency of social support. Consistent social support induces stronger self-control and social bonds to conventional society while counteracting the effects of strain. Drawing on social learning concepts (see chap. 5), Colvin et al. (2002) recognized that social support may not always undergird conformity and prevent crime. Rather, if the social support comes disproportionately from illegitimate or deviant sources (differential association), criminal, not conventional, behavior is more likely. Similarly, the authors drew a parallel to the concept of differential opportunity (see chap. 8) and pointed out that experiencing limited access to legitimate networks, connections, and role models may lead to seeking out social support from illegitimate sources.

Colvin et al. (2002:33) did not present any research testing the predicted effects of coercion and support, but they do offer policy implications. In general, they would support social or criminal justice policies that would "enhance the legitimate sources of social support and reduce the forces of coercion" (Colvin et al., 2002:33). Many of the programs and policies of restorative justice in the criminal and juvenile justice system (see chap. 7), social policies in support of families and parental skill training, family leave, Head Start school programs, early intervention, positive peer and mentoring programs, positive reinforcement of prosocial behavior, rehabilitative and reintegrative correctional programs, and similar policies combined with appropriate and consistent punishment would all fit with the concepts and tenets of the theory.

Propositional Integration

Elliott's Integrative Model of Strain, Bonding, and Learning

Delbert S. Elliott and his associates proposed the best-known theoretical integration of strain, control, and social learning theories. As shown in Figure 12.1, their integrated model proposed that (1) strain (in the family and school) weakens (2) social bonds to conventional society, which in turn promotes (3) strong bonds to delinquent peers (delinquent definitions, reinforcement, modeling, and association from

Figure 12.1

Elliott's Integrated Theory of Delinquent Behavior			
(1)	**(2)**	**(3)**	**(4)**
Strain →	**Weak Conventional Bonding** →	**Strong Bonding to Delinquent Peers** →	**Delinquent Behavior**
Discrepancy in aspirations/achievements and other strain in the family and school	Family and school involvement, commitment, and attachment	Exposure to deviant peers compared to non-deviant peers; social reinforcement for delinquent behavior; peers' and one's own attitudes favorable to delinquency	Self-reported

(Adapted from Elliott et al., 1985:94 and 146)

social learning theory). It is these strong bonds to delinquent peers, therefore, that are principal factors in (4) the commission of delinquent behavior.

Elliott et al. (1985) argued that strain, control, and learning theories share some basic assumptions, propositions, and implications for social policy. However, they recognized some differences in assumptions that must be reconciled before propositional integration can be done. For instance, control theory starts with the assumption of a disposition by everyone to deviate from the law, so that the only source of variation in criminal or delinquent behavior is how strongly or weakly social control prevents deviant behavior. Strain theory, on the other hand, makes no assumptions about the inherent motives shared by all of us to commit crime. It makes no reference to the strength of social controls and hypothesizes that persons exposed to strain are more highly motivated to commit deviant acts than those who are not. Social learning theory proposes variation in motivation both to commit and refrain from offenses.

In social bonding theory, the content and direction of socialization are always conventional; deviance results only from weaknesses or failures of socialization. In social learning theory, the direction in which the individual is socialized may be conforming or deviant. Delinquency is learned in the same way that conforming behavior is learned, and socialization may be more or less successful or unsuccessful in either direction.

Elliott et al. (1985) reconciled these positions by essentially taking the side of strain and learning theory. They do away with the assumption of a natural or uniform motivation to crime, allowing for bonding to produce either conventional or deviant outcomes, depending on the involvement with conforming or deviant peers. Not surprisingly, Hirschi (1989) objected to this method of reconciling the differences among the theories. He contended that it is not integration at all, but simply a rejection of the assumptions of social bonding theory in favor of those of the two other theories.

Elliott et al. (1985) provided a rationale for building the assumptions of strain and learning theory into their integrated model, while retaining social bonding terminology and propositions. They pointed out that Hirschi and other control theorists have themselves previously recognized that the assumption of no variation in the positive motivation to commit crime is not tenable. They saw no logical or empirical necessity for the assumption of uniform criminal motivation. (See the discussion of this issue in chap. 6.) Therefore, their integrated model begins with the assumption that there is variation in motivations both to deviate and to conform.

Because family and school are the major conventionally socializing agencies in society, the model hypothesizes that any strong attachment to them promotes the learning of non-delinquent behavior. The attitudes, models, and rewards in these groups are more conducive to conforming than to delinquent behavior. By the same process, strong bonds to delinquent peers promote the learning of delinquent behavior more so than conventional behavior. Conventional socialization begins in the home, but it may be inadequate; therefore, weakened bonds to the family will enhance bonding to peers. The weaker the bond to conventional peers and the stronger the bond to delinquent peers, the greater the probability of delinquent behavior.

Elliott et al. (1985) tested this model with longitudinal data from their National Youth Survey and found that the integrated model was strongly supported by the findings. The original model proposed that the main direct effect on delinquent behavior would come from bonding to delinquent/non-delinquent peers. Most of the effect of strain and conventional bonding on delinquent behavior should come about indirectly through the effect that strain and bonding have on peer bonding. However, the hypothesis in the integrated theory, that bonding and strain variables have direct effects on delinquent behavior separate from their relationship with peer bonding, was not supported by the data. Strain and conventional bonding had no direct effect on delinquent behavior. Only bonding to delinquent peers had a strong, direct effect. This was the most predictive variable in the model. All the other variables had only indirect effects by their relationship with delinquent peer bonds. The rest of the variables added very little to the explanation of delinquency beyond that given by the direct effect of delinquent peer variables.

Elliott et al. recognized that the final integrated model that best fits the data could be stated as a social learning theory, but they chose instead to use the language of social bonding theory in the integrative model. They did this because:

> It is not clear that a social learning model would have predicted a conditional relationship between conventional bonding (restraints) and deviant bonding (rewards)....The predictive efficiency resulting from adding the interaction effects to the linear regression model was relatively small (a 4 percent relative increase ...) but statistically significant and substantively important. (Elliott et al., 1985:137)

In our opinion, even with the addition of the interactive effects of conventional bonding, the final model reported by Elliott et al. (1985) is more a variation on social learning theory (with bonding modifications) than it is a variation on social bonding theory (with learning modifications). The concepts and measures of differential attachment and involvement with family and school (under (2) in Figure 12.1) and differential involvement with non-delinquent or delinquent peers (under (3) in Figure 12.1) correspond much more closely with concepts in social learning theory, and the way in which these concepts have been measured in previous research, than with social bonding concepts. Indeed, the measures of deviant peer bonds used by Elliott et al. are essentially measures of the main variables in social learning theory of differential associations, reinforcement, modeling, and definitions.

Most important, the findings on the relationship of peer bonding to delinquency in the model agree with predictions from social learning, rather than predictions from social bonding. Agnew's (1993) re-analysis of the data from the National Youth Survey confirms this conclusion. It is precisely on this issue that social learning and social bonding make opposing predictions. Social learning theory predicts that delinquent behavior is related to involvement with deviant peers, and conforming behavior is related to involvement with conventional peers. The social bonding proposition that strong attachment to others prevents delinquent behavior, even when that attachment is to unconventional peers, is not supported. It cannot be sustained either in a pure social bonding theory or a theory integrating bonding and learning. Thus, in any empirically valid integration of bonding and learning theory, only the learning theory proposition can survive. Any resulting integration would not be acceptable to social bonding theorists.

Krohn's Network Analysis

Marvin D. Krohn (1986) proposed an explanation of delinquency that draws on both social learning and social bonding theory. His network theory is also a cross-level integration that connects the structural characteristics of social networks and interactional processes. His theory does not represent a full integration of the two theories, but rather represents what Krohn referred to as a "bridging" of theoretical propositions regarding the delinquency-enhancing effects of differential association and the delinquency-constraining effects of social bonds.

A social network is a set of actors, individuals, or groups linked by friendship or some other relationship. A personal network refers to an individual's set of linkages to others (e.g., family, friends, church, and school). Consistent with social control theory, Krohn hypothesized that "a social network constrains individual behavior ... and the probability of behavior consistent with the continuance of their network relationships will increase" (Krohn, 1986:S82–S83). He made the same decision as Elliott et al. (1985), rejecting the social bonding hypothesis that this constraint will lead only to conformity to conventional norms. Instead, consistent with social learning theory, his network analysis hypothesizes that "the network could be formed around participation in deviant activities and, as a consequence, the constraining effect of the network would be toward deviant behavior" (Krohn, 1986:S83).

Krohn identified two major structural characteristics of social networks—multiplexity and density. Multiplexity is the *number* of different relationships or contexts that two or more persons have in common. For instance, two boys may be friends, live in the same neighborhood, go to the same church, belong to the same scout troop, attend the same school in the same grade, and so on. The greater the network multiplexity, the greater the constraint on the individual's behavior. The direction of this constraint is usually to lower delinquent behavior, but this is only because the multiplexity is most likely to be within family, school, and other conventionally oriented contexts, rather than within delinquent contexts. This recognizes both "what individuals' associates do (differential association) and the kind of activities in which they are mutually involved (commitment and/or involvement)" (Krohn, 1986:S84).

Network density refers to the *ratio* of existing social relationships to the maximum total number of possible relationships in a network. A small community in which everyone knows and interacts with everyone else would have a high network density. The higher the network density, the lower the delinquency rate. Network density is inversely related to population density (the number of persons within a given geographical area). The higher the population density, the lower the network density; therefore, the higher the delinquency rate.

Haynie (2002) reported research in which friendship networks among adolescents are measured by asking respondents to identify up to five of their closest female and five of their closest male friends in the same school (as well as ties to friends outside of the school). She found that it is the "relative nature" of friendship networks—that is, the *proportion* or ratio of delinquent and non-delinquent friends (the standard measure of differential peer association found in the literature)—that is most strongly related to subsequent delinquency. This proportion of delinquent friends had a stronger effect than did the absolute level of delinquency among the friends, average delinquency, or total number of friends. Proportion of delinquent friends remained a strong predictor, even taking into account prior delinquency and other dimensions of the friendship network (e.g., involvement, attachment, density, average age). Although Haynie would likely agree with Krohn's leaning on both social bonding and social learning in social network theory, her empirical findings clearly favor the latter:

> [C]ontrary to the common-sense idea that adolescents become involved in crime/delinquency because of a lack of social and/or human capital (e.g., social control and social disorganization theory) or due to an impulsive personality trait (e.g., self-control theory), adolescents become delinquent if they are located in friendship networks that support and facilitate delinquency. (Haynie, 2002:104)

> The relevance of delinquent peers for youth's later involvement in delinquency is consistent with differential association and social learning explanations for behavior that suggests adolescents follow the behavioral examples of significant others. (Haynie, 2002:124)

Also, McGloin (2005) and others showed that network analysis is of value in the study of delinquent gangs with implications for policies of direct gang intervention (see chap. 5).

Thornberry's Interactional Theory

Terence P. Thornberry (1987; Thornberry et al., 1991) integrated elements of social structure, social bonding, and social learning theory into an "interactional theory" of delinquency. Social class, race, community, and neighborhood characteristics affect both the elements of the social bond and social learning variables. The underlying cause of delinquency is the weakening of the bonds to society. But this weakening simply renders a youngster a more likely candidate for delinquency. Delinquent acts will not occur until they have been learned through association, reinforcement, and definitions. To the extent that this continues over time, delinquency will become a stable part of a person's behavioral patterns.

These influences are not static but vary by age and at different stages of onset, continuation, or cessation of delinquency. Moreover, the relationships among bonding, learning, and delinquency do not all run in one direction. For instance, a lower attachment to parents can lead to a lowered commitment to school, which in turn can reduce the attachment to parents. Similarly, lowered commitment and attachment lead to delinquent behavior; this involvement in delinquency, in turn, will tend to interfere with the attachment to parents and the commitment to school.

Thornberry et al. (1991) found no support for the hypotheses about the reciprocal effects of parental attachment and school commitment. They did find reciprocal effects by which the effects of delinquency on attachment and commitment were greater than the effects of attachment and commitment on delinquency. However, all the relationships were weak. Later, Thornberry (Thornberry et al., 1994; Thornberry, 1996) reported reciprocal effects of social learning and bonding variables and delinquency. This and other research has found that the social learning variable of differential association has significant influence in all phases of delinquency (Smith, Visher, and Jarjoura, 1991).

Kaplan's Self-Derogation Theory

Howard B. Kaplan (1975) proposed a self-esteem/derogation theory of adolescent deviance that brings together deviant peer influences (social learning theory), family and school factors (control theory), dealing with failure to live up to conventional expectations (strain theory), and self-concept (symbolic interactionism and labeling theory). In this theory, delinquency and drug use are viewed as the response of certain adolescents to feelings of low self-esteem or self-derogation. According to Kaplan, each person has a "self-esteem motive" to take actions that minimize negative self-attitudes and maximize positive perceptions of self. For most people, experiences in conventional groups and conformity to their expectations produce positive self-concepts. But those adolescents for whom this is not true will turn to deviant groups and activities in an effort to get rid of self-derogatory attitudes and develop self-esteem.

If the inability to conform to conventional standards and interaction with others in the family, school, and peer groups is self-devaluing, then the social control exercised in these conventional groups becomes less effective. An individual's motivation to conform is lessened, and the motivation to deviate is increased. Conventionality becomes associated with self-derogation. As the adolescent becomes aware of delinquent alternatives, he or she will gravitate to those deviant groups that are perceived as offering an enhancement of self-esteem and as countering self-derogatory attitudes. Persistence and escalation of delinquency and drug use and greater involvement in deviant groups will occur to the extent that such actions continue to satisfy the need for positive self-evaluation. Positively conforming to the standards of a new reference group by committing deviant acts, as well as the reactions of deviant peers, allows a person to develop a positive, albeit deviant, identity. At the same time, the deviant affiliations enable that person to escape from the stress of self-derogation brought on by the failure to live up to the conventional expectations of family and school.

Kaplan and his associates have conducted a series of research projects to test out this general model, primarily involving adolescent substance abuse, and find some support for it. The overall model accounts for moderate amounts of variation in delinquent behavior. However, the strongest effects in the model come from peer associations, whereas the self-attitude measures are not as strongly related to delinquent outcomes (Kaplan, Martin, and Robbins, 1982; Kaplan, Martin, Johnson, and Robbins, 1986). Research has generally supported the hypothesis in self-derogation theory that deviance is one way of adapting to self-identity problems, again with the strongest effects on that adaptation coming from peer associations (Kaplan, 1995; 1996; Vega et al., 1998).

Tittle's Control Balance Theory

Charles Tittle proposed a "synthetic integration" in which "control balance" is the unifying causal process in criminal and deviant behavior. Control balance is defined as the ratio of how much the individual is liable to control to how much he or she is able to control. This control balance is implicated in both motivation and inhibition of deviant behavior:

> The central premise of the theory is that the amount of control to which people are subject relative to the amount of control they can exercise affects their general probability that they will commit specific types of deviance. Deviant behavior is interpreted as a device, or maneuver, that helps people escape deficits and extend surpluses of control.
>
> An unbalanced control ratio, in combination with a desire for autonomy and fundamental bodily and psychic needs, predisposes an individual to act deviantly. (Tittle, 1995:142, 147–148)

Control balance operates in the context of four main variables: *predisposition* (deviant motivation), *provocation* (positive and negative situational stimulation), *opportunity* (to commit specific types of deviance), and *constraint* (actual or perceived likelihood that one will be subject to restraining reactions by others). These incorporate concepts from social learning, anomie, deterrence/rational choice, and social bonding theory. The probability of deviance occurring is higher when the control ratio is imbalanced, either negatively or positively, and is lower when control is balanced. Those individuals experiencing "control deficits" will be predisposed toward predatory, defiant, or submissive deviance, whereas those with "control surpluses" will be predisposed toward "exploitative" or "decadent" deviance. "The theory contends that deviant behavior is undertaken mainly to alter the deviant's control ratio, even if temporarily" (Tittle, 1995:192). The predisposed individual must perceive that a deviant act will alter the balance of control, be in a situation that affords the opportunity to commit the act, and expect that the chance of counter control is not enough to overwhelm the balancing expected to be produced by the deviant act. The major sources of motivation and constraints on behavior, as well as opportunity and situational variables, are incorporated in a sequence of events leading to the commission of crime and deviance in which control balance is the central process.

Tittle reviewed the known relationships of crime and delinquency to a series of sociodemographic variables (age, gender, race, marital and parental status, urban living, and class) and offered an explanation of each by reference to control balance or imbalance. But he recognized that this does not provide a direct test of the theory. "Firmer judgment about the empirical credibility of the theory must wait for tests with more precise and directly applicable data, which existing data sets do not permit" (Tittle, 1995:261). A body of research of the kind Tittle called for to test the theory, although still relatively small, is developing. Piquero and Hickman (1999; see also Hickman and Piquero, 2001), studying self-reported likelihood of committing deviant acts in a sample of college students, reported findings that favor the hypothesis that control deficits are related to predatory offenses (assault) and defiant behavior (deviant sexual practices). However, contrary to the theory, both of these offenses were also related to control surpluses. Piquero and Piquero (2006), using a similar methodology in a college sample, found that control surpluses account for "corporate exploitative crime" and review other studies that, although producing somewhat mixed findings, are still generally supportive of control balance theory (see also Tittle, 2004). Baron and Forde (2007) reported that both control surpluses and deficits were related to the self-reported likelihood of assault and serious (but not minor) theft in a sample of homeless youth.

Tittle continued to develop the theory to take into account research findings and to

> address a logical flaw, mistaken categorization, and inconsistencies and conceptual ambiguity in the original formulation. . . . The reformulated theory [does away with distinctions among types of deviance and] addresses

three forms of behavior—conformity, deviance, and submission–and introduces the concept of "control balance desirability" to help resolve some issues in the original formulation. (Tittle, 2004:395)

The reformulated theory proposes the same causative process as the original (i.e., the cognitive balancing of the gain in control expected from committing a particular deviant act against the counter control it is likely to encounter), but refers only to a single continuum of deviance. The *control balance desirability* of different deviant or criminal acts does not refer to the extent to which the potential acts personally appeal to an individual. Rather, the deviant acts are more desirable the more likely they are to change a control imbalance in the long term and the less they necessitate confronting a victim in-person. The hypothesis is that the higher the control balance desirability of a deviant act the more likely it is to be committed, but which act the individual chooses to commit from among a set of alternatives having about the same level of control balance desirability depends on the effects of other variables identified in the theory—control ratio, opportunity, constraint, and self-control.

Life-Course Criminology

The goal of life-course criminology is to understand better the stability and changes in criminal and deviant behavior through time and at different life stages. Among the many scholars developing "life-course" and "developmental" criminology are John Laub and Robert Sampson (Sampson and Laub,1993; 1997; 2005; Laub and Sampson, 1993; 2003; Laub et al., 2006), David P. Farrington (2005; 2006), Terrie E. Moffitt (1993; 2006), Rolf Loeber (Loeber and LeBlanc, 1990; Loeber, 1996; Loeber et al., 1998), J. David Hawkins and Richard Catalano (Hawkins and Weis, 1985; Catalano and Hawkins, 1996; Catalano et al., 2005), Ronald Simons and Rand Conger (Conger and Simons, 1995; Simons, Johnson, Conger, and Elder, 1998; Simons et al., 2004), Alex Piquero (Piquero and Mazerolle, 2001; Piquero and Moffitt, 2005), Daniel Nagin and Richard Tremblay (Nagin and Tremblay, 2005; Blokland, Nagin, and Nieuwbeerta, 2005) and Michael Benson (2002). By focusing on age variations, careers, and "trajectories" in criminal and deviant behavior over time, life-course criminologists view age or life stage as the central focus of criminology in much the same way that Marxist and conflict theorists focus on class and race and feminist theorists focus on gender. "What I have argued here is that criminology should adopt life-course criminology as its paradigm for the causes and dynamics of crime" and that this paradigm should be the "soul" and "core" of criminology around which all of the facts, research agendas, and theories of the entire field can be organized (Laub, 2006:250).

Laub and Sampson located the cohort of boys (later in life) who were the participants in the famous Gluecks's study of the 1950s (Glueck and Glueck, 1959). They first collected and analyzed data on these participants up to middle age (Sampson and Laub, 1993), and later reported on subsequent events in these men's lives (some of whom were 70 years of age by the time of the second study; Laub and Sampson, 2003; see also Sampson and Laub, 2003; 2005; Laub et al., 2006). This remarkable study obtaining data on the same participants over such a long period of life is rare in all of social science and nearly unique in criminology. (For a Dutch cohort study following participants from ages 15 to 72, see Blokland et al, 2005.) In their earlier analysis, Sampson and Laub (1993) invoked control theory concepts but also, although they did not directly acknowledge doing so, depended on social learning processes in the family (see Patterson, 1982). They proposed that abrupt "turning points" and gradual changes that come with growing older, such as getting married and finding stable employment, increase social bonds to society. This explains why most who were delinquent at a younger age discontinue law violations later in life, whereas others continue offending. Those who do not experience these changes or have disruptive family or employment experiences are more likely to persist in offending. The stability of causative factors in the social environment as one ages produces stability of behavior; changes in those same factors produce changes in behavior through the life course primarily through their effects on informal social control.

Sampson and Laub find support for this explanation in their research. Similarly, Piquero, Brame, Mazerolle, and Haapanen (2002) found that marriage and full-time employment lowered official recidivism among parolees in "emerging adulthood" (18–25). Uggen (2000b) also found that employment lowered recidivism (self-reported), but contrary to the Piquero et al. (2002) study, he found that work has this effect among offenders 27 and older, not in the younger age group.

Warr (1998) agreed with Sampson and Laub that life-course transitions in family and work account for persistence and change in deviant behavior. Warr (1998:183) differed with them, however, in finding that "marriage is followed by a dramatic decline in time spent with friends as well as reduced exposure to delinquent peers, and that these factors [rather than formation of preventive social bonds] largely explain the association between marital status and delinquent behavior." Earlier he found that the dramatic increases in delinquent behavior from the early to the later teenage years were explained by dramatic increases in exposure to delinquent peers (Warr, 1993b). Simons et al. (1998) maintained that both bonding and learning processes are involved because the relationship between early antisocial behavior and later adolescent delinquency disappears when parenting effects, school, and peer variables are taken into account (Simons et al., 1998; 2004). Akers and Lee (1999) found that both sets of variables had an effect on development of adolescent substance use, but the social learning variables of peer association, definitions, and differential reinforcement had a stronger effect than the social bonding variables of attachment, commitment, and beliefs.

Laub and Sampson's later analysis of data on the men into old age confirmed and extended their earlier work. This time they included detailed life-history information and interviews so that in addition to analysis of "trajectory groups" exhibiting various patterns of onset, persistence, and desistance, they reported individual variations within groups. The findings raise serious questions about identifying and defining criminal typologies and developmental models such as Moffitt's (1993; 2006; Piquero and Moffitt, 2005) that project qualitatively different life-course trajectories for different types of offenders (limited, less serious versus persistent, most serious). They objected to making predictions, based on these typologies, about individuals' criminal behavior later in life and to support for policies that are based primarily on the assumption that effective prevention requires intervention early in life. All of the men in the Laub and Sampson study would qualify in adolescence as "life course persistent" but virtually all desisted at some point. The differences in persistence and timing of desistance among these men revolved around employment, military service, incarceration/criminal justice experience, and especially marriage. Laub and Sampson continued to rely on their theory of "age-graded" or age-related informal social control (Laub and Sampson, 2003; Sampson and Laub, 2005). However, they have now added various "nuances" to the model by explicitly referring to, and drawing on concepts and variables from, other general criminological theories, not only bonding, but also learning, strain, and routine activities theories (Laub and Sampson, 2003; Sampson and Laub, 2003; Laub et a., 2006) and other "concepts equally relevant for understanding persistent offending and desistance from crime over the life course ... personal agency and situated choice ... macro-level historical events, and local culture and community context" (Laub and Sampson, 2003:293).

Moffitt's theory (Moffitt; 1993; Bartusch et al., 1997) drew from concepts in neuropsychology and developmental psychology. She argued that those who have behavioral problems as children and begin delinquent involvement at an early age (life-course persistent delinquents) differ qualitatively from those who begin in the teenage years. The former will continue in the adolescent and later years with a high probability of violating the social and legal norms, whereas the latter are much less likely to continue on as adults (adolescence-limited delinquents). The causes of childhood antisocial behavior and persistence into adulthood are low verbal ability, hyperactivity, and impulsive personality. Peer influence for the life-course persistent offenders is slight. On the other hand, the adolescence-limited offender, who is unlikely to continue offending into adulthood, is more strongly influenced by peer associations. This agrees, in part, with the models previously developed by Patterson (1982; Patterson et al., 1989) that peer influence is apt to be more important for late starters, but the two differ in that Patterson allowed for significant peer influence also for the early starting offenders. Further, Patterson's social learning "coercion model," proposes that for both early and late onset offenders the "persistence and desistance of offending in adulthood cannot be explained fully by individual characteristics and environmental influences in early childhood or adolescence. Age-graded changes in adulthood have to be considered as well" (Weisner et al., 2003:327). Paternoster and Brame (1997) found exposure to delinquent peers and parental variables had similar effects on both early and late onset delinquency. Loeber (1996; Kelley, Loeber, Keenan, and DeLamatre, 1998) proposed that even the early onset persisters do not develop along a single pathway, but rather differ by whether they evince behavior in conflict with authority, violent patterns, or property offending.

As the foregoing shows, there is some overlap in how variables from personality, learning, bonding, and other theories are utilized in life-course models, but there are also considerable differences among them. There is no single agreed-on model. The most important common denominator among them is the effort to explain similarities, differences, and changes in criminal and deviant behavior at different ages, stages of development, or periods of the life course:

> Thus criminologists who employ a life-course perspective are concerned with identifying the processes whereby childhood disruptive behavior escalates to delinquency and crime, and with discovering the factors that enable some anti-social children to assume a more conventional lifestyle during adolescence. (Simons et al., 1998:221)

These criminologists are responding not only to the issue of whether there are different types of offenders who begin committing law violations at different times in life (earlier or later) and follow different behavioral trajectories (frequency, persistence, and seriousness) as they age. Most of them are also responding to the theoretical challenges made by Gottfredson and Hirschi (1990) regarding the age–crime relationship. Many other criminologists have also reacted to the challenge to explain the age–crime relationship (see the review of this literature in Akers, 1998). Since the early 1980s, Hirschi and Gottfredson (1983) contended that there is an inverted-J curve relationship between crime and age. That is, age-specific rates for offenses increase rapidly during adolescence, peak in the late teenage and early adult years, and then decline thereafter. In their view, the shape of this curve is invariant across time, cross-culturally, across groups within the same society, and across all types of criminal behavior. There is strong disagreement on just how invariant this curve is (see Benson, 2002), but the shape of the curve is generally accepted as accurate for most offenses. What is not generally accepted is Hirschi and Gottfredson's related argument that age is a direct, unmediated, cause of crime. To them, the age–crime relationship not only needs no further explanation, in fact, no known criminological theory or set of known causal variables is capable of explaining this curvilinear relationship of crime and age. They argue further that once formed in childhood, differences in self-control or propensity to commit law violations persist throughout life with essentially no change; therefore, the cause of crime and deviance is the same at all ages.

Those who reject this argument point out that there is both persistence and change in deviant, delinquent, and criminal behavior and theorize that age-related variables can explain both. They attempt to explain what it is that produces the age–crime relationship. Some posit different causes of crime and deviance depending on age (e.g., the Moffitt model). Others agree with Gottfredson and Hirschi that the causes are the same for all age groups; they disagree with them by hypothesizing that it is age-related variations in the magnitude or value of those causes (social bonds, rewards and costs, peer influences, etc.) that account for age-related variations in offending. The empirical evidence thus far favors this hypothesis (see Akers, 1998).

Michael Benson (2002) reiterated that both continuity and change in criminal behavior are central to the life course perspective. Continuity is based on both *cumulative continuity* in which behavior and events at one time have an effect on later opportunities and behavior, and *self-selection* of similar behavior at both earlier and later stages in life consistent with persistent individual traits present at both times. Change is based on both developmental changes and changes in circumstances. He argued that biological and early childhood effects on criminal behavior later in life are relatively weak. "Predicting the life course of an individual based only on factors present at an early age ignores all of the causal factors that come into play later" (Benson, 2002:14). According to Benson, there are different trajectories of offending careers (short-term, long-term, high-rate, low-rate) and each stage in the life course (childhood, adolescence, adulthood) presents factors that are conducive to or inhibit antisocial or criminal behavior. Cumulative economic and social disadvantage makes for persistence in offending from adolescence into adulthood, whereas marriage, family, children, and employment make for desistance; and of course, antisocial behavior, in turn, can have a negative effect on employment and marriage. He pointed to "theoretical diversity" in the field and how difficult it is to apply any life course perspective to both street crime and white-collar crime.

A key question is whether life course criminology has produced new general theories or rather represents ways of pulling in concepts and propositions from existing theories at different ages or stages of life. In our view, it is hard to identify any new explanatory variable introduced by the life course perspective. Instead, life course criminologists lean heavily on concepts and propositions from biological, developmental, social bonding, social learning, and other extant theories. The assertion by some that there are different explanations of offending at different life stages has primarily led to their taking those different explanations from elements of extant theory. On the other hand, others have argued that the explanatory variables are the same at any age but have different values at different ages. This is a sound argument, but again has not resulted in new explanatory variables. The empirical findings are that the strong explanatory variables from existing theories, such as peer associations, attitudes, and social bonds (which, in turn, are affected by employment, marriage, and family that vary by age), account for delinquent and criminal behavior both during the adolescent years and in later years, with some variation in strength of effects. Moreover, these same variables at one stage of life are predictive of outcomes in later stages of life. The common disagreement with Gottfredson and Hirschi's claim that no theory is capable of explaining age variations in crime is not unique to life course criminology and is not itself a theoretical explanation of those age variations. The focus on both behavioral stability and change across the life course, as a counter to self-control theory's almost exclusive emphasis on behavioral stability, may sensitize criminology more to age variations and trajectories of behavior through time, but that is not the same as offering a new explanation of why behavior is stable or changes. Theoretical models in life-course criminology are mainly elaborations or modifications of existing general criminological theories (e.g., learning, strain, control, rational choice) sometimes producing very complex models (see especially Farrington, 2005; 2006). Laub and Sampson (2003:587) recognized that their age-graded informal social control theory as an explanation of stability and change in crime over the life course is

in some respects more compatible with general theories like Gottfredson and Hirschi than with developmental theories [such as Moffitt's], although the latter are often viewed as synonymous with life-course perspectives.... This claim may also be true for social learning theory, general strain theory, and control balance theory.

Of course, as we have seen in this chapter, attempts at theoretical integration always draw on existing theories and concepts. However, life-course criminologists often write about integrated life-course/ developmental theory *of* crime as if it is to be considered a distinct alternative to genetic, personality, social bonding, self-control, social learning, anomie, strain, and the other theories of criminal behavior that have been reviewed in previous chapters. We may more accurately speak of *theoretical explanations of the relationship between age and crime or variations in offending over the life course* drawing on the explanatory concepts and variables from current general theories rather than *life-course theories of all variations in criminal offending* as alternatives to those theories.

How Successful Has Theoretical Integration Been in Criminology?

Notwithstanding the value of theoretical integration as an ideal, in practice integrated models in criminology have met with mixed success and acceptance. Some have received empirical support, whereas others have received little or no testing. Many have been ignored. Only a small percentage of criminologists seem to prefer "integrated theory" over one or the other of the "separate" theories of crime (Ellis and Walsh, 1999). There remains an overall favorable climate of opinion in criminology toward theoretical integration, but there continues to be a considerable indifference and a healthy skepticism toward integration as a theory-building strategy.

Akers's own work on social learning theory underscores the value of both oppositional and integrative strategies. He used the competitive approach in pitting social learning against alternative explanations of criminal and deviant behavior (Akers and Cochran, 1985; Krohn et al., 1984; Akers and Lee, 1999), while at the same time pursuing efforts at conceptual integration discussed in this chapter and cross-level integration discussed in chapter 5. Indeed, it must be remembered that social learning theory is itself an integration of principles of differential association and reinforcement. However, social learning theory and many other more recent theoretical integrations are not usually treated as integrative theory in the literature. Although they may be recognized for a while as integrative, they tend over time to be cited and tested as separate theories either in competition with or subject to integration with other theories, sometimes with the very theories they were intended to integrate.[4] The issue of theory competition versus theory integration has not yet been, and perhaps should not necessarily be, fully resolved.

Summary

Theoretical development takes place through explicating, testing, and modifying a single theory, through competition of rival theories, and through theoretical integration. Theoretical integration can be conceptual and/or propositional. It entails either theories at the same level of explanation or theories from different explanatory levels. Social learning theory, in one way or another, is a main component of integrative models in criminology, along with social bonding and strain theories.

Akers proposed the absorption of concepts from other theories by social learning concepts. Cullen and Colvin saw social support and coercion as the overarching unifying concepts in criminology. Elliott proposed a theory of delinquency that integrates propositions of strain, control, and social learning theories. Krohn drew on bonding and social learning theory in social network theory. Thornberry integrated structural, bonding, learning, and other variables in an interactive theory. Kaplan used self-esteem as the central variable that ties learning, bonding, and labeling effects together. Tittle offered a general integrative theory that relied on the concept of control balance. Life-course theories integrate explanatory variables primarily from psychological, social learning, and social bonding theories to account for stability and change in criminal behavior at different stages of the life course. Although there has been much integrative activity and a positive orientation toward theoretical integration in criminology, there remains controversy and skepticism about the value of building theory by melding together different explanations of crime and delinquency.

Notes

1. The literature contains many examples of conceptual and propositional integration, within-level integration, and cross-level integration: *biological and psychosocial theories* (Jeffery, 1977; Gove and Hughes, 1989; Wellford, 1989); *anomie, labeling, and control theories* (Aultman and Wellford, 1979); *deterrence and social bonding theories* (Minor, 1977; Hawkins and Williams, 1989; Williams and Hawkins, 1989); *conflict and control theories* (Hagan, 1989a; 1989b); *Marxist and control/learning theories* (Colvin and Pauly, 1983); *Marxist and feminist theory* (Messerschmidt, 1986); *labeling, anomie, and social learning theories* (Braithwaite, 1989); and other theories (Farrell, 1989). For reviews and discussions of issues in theoretical integration, see Bernard and Snipes (1995), Tittle (1995), and Agnew (2001a).

2. The theoretical integrations reviewed in this chapter involve social learning theory in one way or another, and most of them also encompass social

bonding theory. Concepts and hypotheses from these two theories are those most frequently used in the theoretical integrations found in the literature. There are many other examples of partial or full integration with social learning besides those given here, several of which have been discussed or alluded to in previous chapters.

3. Pearson and Weiner (1985) also showed how the principal concepts of all major theories, including social bonding, deterrence, rational choice, and strain as well as macro-level theories, can be seen as variations on, or subtypes of, eight general concepts derived from social learning theory. The scope of Pearson and Weiner's integration of these concepts into a consistent, coherent framework is impressive. To our knowledge, however, this framework has not received much attention in criminological discourse (but see Bernard and Snipes, 1995).

4. For example, one still sees references in the literature to differential association theory without any mention whatsoever of its integration with behavioral principles into social learning theory, as well as separate references to differential association and social learning, as if they were unrelated or even rival theories. Another example is control balance theory. The research literature testing the theory makes no mention of the fact that it is supposed to be a "synthetic synthesis." In fact, it is treated in the literature as separate from, and often as competitive with, the very theories that Tittle intended to integrate through the control balance concept.

References

Abrams, Laura S., Kyoungho Kim, and Ben Anderson-Nathe
2005 "Paradoxes of treatment in juvenile corrections," Child and Youth Care Forum 34:7–25.

Adams, Stuart
1970 "The PICO Project," pp. 548–561 in Norman Johnston, Leonard Savitz, and Marvin E. Wolfgang (eds.), The Sociology of Punishment and Correction. Second Edition. New York: Wiley.

Adler, Freda
1975 Sisters in Crime: The Rise of the New Female Criminal. New York: McGraw-Hill.

Adler, Patricia and Peter Adler
1978 "Tinydopers: A case study of deviant socialization," Symbolic Interaction 1:90–105.

Agnew, Robert
1985a "Social control theory and delinquency: A longitudinal test," Criminology 23:47–62.
1985b "A revised strain theory of delinquency," Social Forces 64:151–167.
1991a "The interactive effect of peer variables on delinquency," Criminology 29:47–72.
1991b "A longitudinal test of social control theory and delinquency," Journal of Research of Crime and Delinquency 28:126–156.
1992 "Foundation for a general strain theory of crime and delinquency," Criminology 30:47–88.
1993 "Why do they do it? An examination of the intervening mechanisms between 'social control' variables and delinquency," Journal of Research in Crime and Delinquency 30:245–266.
1995a "Determinism, indeterminism, and crime: An empirical exploration," Criminology 33:83–110.
1995b "Testing the leading crime theories: An alternative strategy focusing on motivational processes," Journal of Research in Crime and Delinquency 32:363–398.
1995c "Controlling delinquency: Recommendations from general strain theory," pp. 43–70 in Hugh Barlow (ed.), Crime and Public Policy: Putting Theory to Work. Boulder, CO: Westview.
2001a Juvenile Delinquency: Causes and Control. Los Angeles: Roxbury.
2001b "Building on the foundation of general strain theory: Specifying the types of strain most likely to lead to crime and delinquency," Journal of Research in Crime and Delinquency 38:319–361.
2006a Pressured Into Crime: An Overview of General Strain Theory. Los Angeles: Roxbury.
2006b "General strain theory: current status and directions for further research," pp. 101–123 in Francis T. Cullen, John Paul Wright, and Kristie R. Blevins (eds.), Taking Stock: The Status of Criminological Theory. Advances in Criminological Theory. Volume 15. New Brunswick, NJ: Transaction.

Agnew, Robert F., special ed.
1999 Symposium on Ronald L. Akers, Social Learning and Social Structure: A General Theory of Crime and Deviance, Theoretical Criminology 3:437–494.

Agnew, Robert, Timothy Brezina, John Paul Wright, and Francis T. Cullen
2002 "Strain, personality traits, and delinquency: Extending general strain theory," Criminology 40:43–72.

Agnew, Robert, Francis Cullen, Velmer Burton, T. David Evans,
and R. Gregory Dunaway

1996 "A new test of classic strain theory," Justice Quarterly 13:681–704.

Agnew, Robert and Helene Raskin White

1992 "An empirical test of general strain theory," Criminology 30:475–500.

Aichhorn, August

1963 Wayward Youth. New York: Viking.

Akers, Ronald L.

1964 "Socioeconomic status and delinquent behavior: A retest," Journal of Research in Crime and Delinquency 1:38–46.

1965 "Toward a comparative definition of law," Journal of Criminal Law, Criminology, and Police Science 56:301–306.

1968 "Problems in the sociology of deviance: Social definitions and behavior," Social Forces 46:455–465.

1973 Deviant Behavior: A Social Learning Approach. Belmont, CA: Wadsworth.

1977 Deviant Behavior: A Social Learning Approach. Second Edition. Belmont, CA: Wadsworth.

1979 "Theory and ideology in Marxist criminology," Criminology 16:527–544.

1980 "Further critical thoughts on Marxist criminology: Comment on Turk, Toby, and Klockars," pp. 133–138 in James A. Inciardi (ed.), Radical Criminology: The Coming Crises. Beverly Hills, CA: Sage.

1985 Deviant Behavior: A Social Learning Approach. Third Edition. Belmont, CA: Wadsworth. Reprinted 1992. Fairfax, VA: Techbooks.

1989 "A social behaviorist's perspective on integration of theories of crime and deviance," pp. 23–36 in Steven Messner, Marvin D. Krohn, and Allen Liska (eds.), Theoretical Integration in the Study of Crime and Deviance: Problems and Prospects. Albany: State University of New York Press.

1990 "Rational choice, deterrence, and social learning theory: The path not taken," Journal of Criminal Law and Criminology 81:653–676.

1991 "Self control as a general theory of crime," Journal of Quantitative Criminology 7:201–211.

1992a "Linking sociology and its specialties: The case of criminology," Social Forces 71:1–16.

1992b Drugs, Alcohol, and Society: Social Structure, Process and Policy. Belmont, CA: Wadsworth.

1996 "Is differential association/social learning cultural deviance theory?" Criminology 34:229–248.1998 Social Learning and Social Structure: A General Theory of Crime and Deviance. Boston: Northeastern University Press.

1999 "Social learning and social structure: Reply to Sampson, Morash, and Krohn," Theoretical Criminology 3:477–493.

2005 "Sociological theory and practice: The case of criminology," Journal of Applied Sociology/Sociological Practice: A Journal of Applied and Clinical Sociology 22/7: 24–41.

Akers, Ronald L. and John K. Cochran

1985 "Adolescent marijuana use: A test of three theories of deviant behavior," Deviant Behavior 6:323–346.

Akers, Ronald L. and Richard Hawkins

1975 Law and Control in Society. Englewood Cliffs, NJ: Prentice Hall.

Akers, Ronald L. and Gary F. Jensen, eds.

2003 Social Learning Theory and the Explanation of Crime: A Guide for the New Century. Advances in Criminological Theory. Volume 11. New Brunswick, NJ: Transaction.

Akers, Ronald L. and Gary F. Jensen

2006 "The empirical status of social learning theory of crime and deviance: The past, present, and future," pp. 37–76 in Francis T. Cullen, John Paul Wright, and Kristie R. Blevins (eds.), Taking Stock: The Status of Criminology Theory. Advances in Criminological Theory. Volume 15. New Brunswick, NJ: Transaction.

Akers, Ronald L., Marvin D. Krohn, Lonn Lanza-Kaduce, and Marcia Radosevich

1979 "Social learning and deviant behavior: A specific test of a general theory," American Sociological Review 44:635–655.

Akers, Ronald L. and Anthony J. La Greca

1991 "Alcohol use among the elderly: Social learning, community context, and life events," pp. 242–262 in David J. Pittman and Helene Raskin White (eds.), Society, Culture, and Drinking Patterns Re-examined. New Brunswick, NJ: Rutgers Center of Alcohol Studies.

Akers, Ronald L., Anthony J. La Greca, John K. Cochran, and Christine S. Sellers

1989 "Social learning theory and alcohol behavior among the elderly," Sociological Quarterly 30:625–638.

Akers, Ronald L. and Gang Lee

1996 "A longitudinal test of social learning theory: Adolescent smoking," Journal of Drug Issues 26:317–343.

1999 "Age, social learning, and social bonding in adolescent substance use," Deviant Behavior 19:1–25.

Akers, Ronald L., Lonn Lanza-Kaduce, Paul Cromwell, and Roger Dunham

1994 "Hurricane Andrew: Exploring its impact on law and social control." Paper presented at the annual meetings of the American Society of Criminology, Miami, November.

Akers, Ronald L. and Ross Matsueda

1989 "Donald Cressey: An intellectual portrait of a criminologist," Sociological Inquiry 29:423–438.

Akers, Ronald L. and Adam Silverman

2004 "Toward a social learning model of violence and terrorism," pp. 19–35 in Margaret A. Zahn, Henry H. Brownstein, and Shelly L. Jackson (eds.), Violence: From Theory to Research. Cincinnati, OH: Lexis Nexis–Anderson.

Alexander, Jeffrey C., Bernhard Giesen, Richard Munch, and Neil J. Smelser, eds.

1987 The Micro Macro Link. Berkeley: University of California Press.

Alix, Ernest K.

1978 Ransom Kidnapping in America, 1874–1974: The Creation of a Capital Crime. Carbondale: Southern Illinois Press.

American Correctional Association

1990 The Female Offender: What Does the Future Hold? Washington, DC: St. Mary's Press.

Andenaes, Johannes

1971 "The moral or educative influence of criminal law," Journal of Social Issues 24:17–31.

Anderson, Elijah

1999 Code of the Street: Decency, Violence, and the Moral Life of the Inner City. New York: Norton.

Anderson, Kevin

1991 "Radical criminology and the overcoming of alienation: Perspectives from Marxian and Gandhian humanism," pp. 14–30 in Harold E. Pepinsky and Richard Quinney (eds.), Criminology as Peacemaking. Bloomington: Indiana University Press.

Anderson, Linda S., Theodore G. Chiricos, and Gordon P. Waldo

1977 "Formal and informal sanctions: A comparison of deterrent effects," Social Problems 25:103–112.

Andrews, D. A.

1980 "Some experimental investigations of the principles of differential association through deliberate manipulations of the structure of service systems," American Sociological Review 45:448–462.

Andrews, D. A. and James Bonta

1998 Psychology of Criminal Conduct. Second Edition. OH: Anderson.
2003 The Psychology of Criminal Conduct. Third Edition. Cincinnati, OH: Anderson.

Andrews, Kenneth H. and Denise B. Kandel

1979 "Attitude and behavior: A specification of the contingent consistency hypothesis," American Sociological Review 44:298–310.

Ardelt, Monika and Laurie Day

2002 "Parents, siblings, and peers: Close social relationships and adolescent deviance," Journal of Early Adolescence 22:310–349.

Arneklev, Bruce J., Harold G. Grasmick, and Robert Bursik, Jr.

1999 "Evaluating the dimensionality and invariance of 'low self-control'," Journal of Quantitative Criminology 15:307–331.

Arnold, Regina A.

1990 "Women of color: Processes of victimization and criminalization of Black women," Social Justice 17:153–166.

Arnold, Robert

1970 "Mobilization for youth: Patchwork or solution?" pp. 448–453 in Harwin L. Voss (ed.), Society, Delinquency, and Delinquent Behavior. Boston: Little, Brown.

Arrigo, Bruce A.

2000 "Social justice and critical criminology: On integrating knowledge," Contemporary Justice Review 3:7–37.

Aultman, Madeline and Charles F. Wellford

1979 "Towards an integrated model of delinquency causation: An empirical analysis," Sociology and Social Research 63:316–327.

Avakame, Edem F.

1997 "Modeling the patriarchal factor in juvenile delinquency: Is there room for peers, church, and television?" Criminal Justice and Behavior 24:477–494.

Baier, Colin and Bradley R. E. Wright

2001 "'If you love me, keep my commandments': A meta-analysis of the effect of religion on crime," Journal of Research in Crime and Delinquency 38:3–21.

Balbus, Isaac D.

1977 "Commodity form and legal form: An essay on the 'relative autonomy' of the state," Law and Society Review 11:571–588.

Balkan, Sheila, Ronald J. Berger, and Janet Schmidt

1980 Crime and Deviance in America: A Critical Approach. Belmont, CA: Wadsworth.

Ball, John C.

1955 "The deterrent concept in criminology and the law," Journal of Criminal Law, Criminology, and Police Science 46:349–354.

Ball, Harry V. and George O. Simpson

1962 "Law and social change: Sumner reconsidered," American Journal of Sociology 67:532–540.

Ball, Richard A.

1968 "An empirical exploration of neutralization theory," pp. 255–265 in Mark Lefton, James K. Skipper, and Charles H. McCaghy (eds.), Approaches to Deviance. New York: Appleton-Century-Crofts.

Bandura, Albert

1969 Principles of Behavior Modification. New York: Holt, Rinehart & Winston.

1973 Aggression: A Social Learning Analysis. Englewood Cliffs, NJ: Prentice Hall.

1977a Social Learning Theory. Englewood Cliffs, NJ: Prentice Hall.

1977b "Self-efficacy: Toward a unifying theory of behavioral change," Psychological Review 84:191–215.

1986 Social Foundations of Thought and Action: A Social Cognitive Theory. Englewood Cliffs, NJ: Prentice Hall.

1990 "Selective activation and disengagement of moral control," Journal of Social Issues 46:27–46.

Bandura, Albert and Richard H. Walters

1963 Social Learning and Personality Development. New York: Holt, Rinehart & Winston.

Barak, Gregg

1988 "Newsmaking criminology: Reflections on the media, intellectuals, and crime," Justice Quarterly 5:565–587.

1991 "Homelessness and the case for community based initiatives: The emergence of a model shelter as a short-term response to the deepening crisis in housing," pp. 47–68 in Harold E. Pepinsky and Richard Quinney (eds.), Criminology as Peacemaking. Bloomington: Indiana University Press.

Barak, Gregg, ed.

1994 Media, Process, and the Social Construction of Crime. New York: Garland.

Barak, Gregg, Jeanne M. Flavin, and Paul S. Leighton

2001 Class, Race, Gender, and Crime. Los Angeles: Roxbury.

Barlow, David, Melissa Hickman Barlow, and Wesley Johnson

1996 "The political economy of criminal justice policy: A time-series analysis of economic conditions, crime, and federal criminal justice legislation, 1948–1987," Justice Quarterly 13:223–242.

Barlow, Hugh

1995 "Introduction: Public policy and the explanation of crime," pp. 1–14 in Hugh Barlow (ed.), Crime and Public Policy: Putting Theory to Work. Boulder, CO: Westview.

Barlow, Hugh D. and Theodore N. Ferdinand

1992 Understanding Delinquency. New York: HarperCollins.

Baron, Reuben M. and David A. Kenny

1986 "The moderator-mediator distinction in social psychological research: Conceptual, strategic, and statistical Considerations," Journal of Personality and Social Psychology 51:1173–1182.

Baron, Stephen W. and David R. Forde

2007 "Street youth crime: A test of control balance theory," Justice Quarterly 24:335–355.

Bartusch, Dawn Jeglum, Donald R. Lynam, Terrie A. Moffitt, and Phil A. Silva

1997 "Is age important? Testing a general versus a developmental theory of antisocial behavior," Criminology 35:375–406.

Bates, Kristin A., Christopher D. Bader, and F. C. Mencken

2003 "Family structure, power-control theory, and deviance: Extending power-control theory to include alternative family forms," Western Criminology Review 4:170–190.

Battin, Sara R., Karl G. Hill, Robert D. Abbott, Richard F. Catalano, and J. David Hawkins

1998 "The contribution of gang membership to delinquency: Beyond delinquent friends," Criminology 36:93–115.

Batton, Candice and Gary Jensen

2002 "Decommodification and homicide rates in the 20th century United States," Homicide Studies 6:6–38.

Batton, Candice and Robbin S. Ogle

2003 "'Who's it gonna be—You or me?' The potential of social learning for integrated homicide-suicide theory," pp. 85–108 in Ronald L. Akers and Gary F. Jensen (eds.), Social Learning Theory and the Explanation of Crime: A Guide for the New Century. Advances in Criminological Theory. Volume 11. New Brunswick, NJ: Transaction.

Bazemore, Gordon and Susan E. Day

1996 "Restoring the balance: Juvenile and community justice," Juvenile Justice 3:3–14.

Bazemore, Gordon and Mara Schiff, eds.

2001 Restorative Community Justice: Repairing Harm and Transforming Communities. Cincinnati, OH: Anderson.

Bazemore, Gordon and Mark Umbreit

1998 Guide for Implementing the Balanced and Restorative Justice Model. Washington, DC: U.S. Department of Justice, Office of Juvenile Justice and Delinquency Prevention.

Beccaria, Cesare

1963 On Crimes and Punishments. Translated with an introduction by Henry Paolucci. New York: Macmillan.

1972 "On crimes and punishment," pp. 11–24 in Sawyer F. Sylvester (ed.), The Heritage of Modern Criminology. Cambridge, MA: Schenkman.

Becker, Gary S.

1968 "Crime and punishment: An economic approach," Journal of Political Economy 76:169–217.

Becker, Howard S.

1963 Outsiders: Studies in the Sociology of Deviance. New York: Free Press.

1973 Outsiders: Studies in the Sociology of Deviance. Revised Edition. New York: Free Press.

Bedau, Hugo, ed.

1964 The Death Penalty in America. New York: Anchor.

Beirne, Piers

1979 "Empiricism and the critique of Marxism on law and crime," Social Problems 26:373–385.

1991 "Inventing criminology: The 'science of man' in Cesare Beccaria's *dei delitte e delle pene* (1764)," Criminology 29:777–820.

Beirne, Piers and Richard Quinney, eds.

1982 Marxism and Law. New York: Wiley.

Belknap, Joanne

2007 The Invisible Woman: Gender, Crime and Justice. Belmont, CA: Wadsworth.

Belknap, Joanne and Kristi Holsinger

2006 "The gendered nature of risk factors for delinquency," Feminist Criminology 1:48–71.

Bellair, Paul, Vincent J. Roscigno, and Maria B. Velez

2003 "Occupational structure, social learning, and adolescent violence," pp. 197–226 in Ronald L. Akers and Gary F. Jensen (eds.), Social Learning Theory and the Explanation of Crime: A Guide for the New Century. Advances in Criminological Theory. Volume 11. New Brunswick, NJ: Transaction.

Benda, Brent B.

1994 "Testing competing theoretical concepts: Adolescent alcohol consumption," Deviant Behavior 15:375–396.

Benoit, Ellen, Doris Randolph, Eloise Dunalp, and Bruce Johnson

2003 "Code switching and inverse imitation among marijuana-using crack sellers," British Journal of Criminology 43:506–525.

Benson, Michael L.

2002 Crime and the Life Course: An Introduction. Los Angeles: Roxbury.

Benson, Michael L. and Elizabeth Moore

1992 "Are white collar and common offenders the same? An empirical and theoretical critique of a recently proposed general theory of crime," Journal of Research in Crime and Delinquency 29:251–272.

Bentham, Jeremy

1948 An Introduction to the Principles of Morals and Legislation. Edited with an introduction by Laurence J. Lafleur. New York: Hafner.

Ben-Yehuda, Nachman, Richard A. Brymer, Steven C. Dubin, Douglass Harper, Rosanna Hertz, and William Shaffer

1989 "Howard S. Becker: A portrait of an intellectual's sociological imagination," Sociological Inquiry 59:467–489.

Bernard, Thomas J.

1983 The Consensus Conflict Debate: Form and Content in Social Theories. New York: Columbia University Press.

1987 "Testing structural strain theories," Journal of Research in Crime and Delinquency 24:262–290.

1990 "Angry aggression among the 'truly disadvantaged,'" Criminology 28:73–96.

Bernard, Thomas J. and Robin Shepard Engel

2001 "Conceptualizing criminal justice theory," Justice Quarterly 18:1–30.

Bernard, Thomas J. and R. Richard Ritti

1991 "The Philadelphia birth cohort and selective incapacitation," Journal of Research in Crime and Delinquency 28:33–54.

Bernard, Thomas J. and Jeffrey B. Snipes

1995 "Theoretical integration in criminology," pp. 1–48 in Michael Tonry (ed.), Crime and Justice. Chicago: University of Chicago Press.

Bernburg, Jon Gunnar and Thorolfur Thorlindsson

2001 "Routine activities in social context: A closer look at the role of opportunity in deviant behavior," Justice Quarterly 18:543–568.

Bishop, Donna M. and Charles E. Frazier

1988 "The influence of race in juvenile justice processing," Journal of Research in Crime and Delinquency 25:244–263.

1996 "Race effects in juvenile justice decision making: Findings of a statewide analysis," Journal of Criminal Law and Criminology 86:392–414.

Black, Donald J.

1976 The Behavior of Law. New York: Academic.

Blackwell, Brenda Sims

2000 "Perceived sanction threats, gender, and crime: A test and elaboration of power-control theory," Criminology 38:439–488.

Blackwell, Brenda S. and Mark D. Reed

2003 "Power-control as a between- and within-family model: Reconsidering the unit of analysis," Journal of Youth and Adolescence 32:385–400.

Blackwell, Brenda Sims, Christine S. Sellers, and Sheila M. Schlaupitz

2002 "A power-control theory of vulnerability to crime and adolescent role exits revisited," Canadian Review of Sociology and Anthropology 39:199–218.

Blokland, Arjan A. J., Daniel S. Nagin, and Paul Nieuwbeerta

2005 "Life span offending trajectories of a Dutch conviction cohort," Criminology 43:955–988.

Bloom, Barbara, Barbara Owen, and Jill Rosenbaum

2003 "Focusing on girls and young women: A gendered perspective on female delinquency," Women & Criminal Justice 14:117–136.

Blumer, Herbert

1969 Symbolic Interactionism: Perspective and Method. Englewood Cliffs, NJ: Prentice Hall.

Blumstein, Alfred, Jacqueline Cohen, and Daniel Nagin

1978 Deterrence and Incapacitation: Estimating the Effects of Sanctions on the Crime Rate. Washington, DC: National Academy Press.

Blumstein, Alfred, David P. Farrington, and S. Moitra

1985 "Delinquency careers: Innocents, desisters, and persisters," pp. 137–168 in Michael Tonry and Norval Morris (eds.), Crime and Justice. Volume 6. Chicago: University of Chicago Press.

Boeringer, Scot, Constance L. Shehan, and Ronald L. Akers

1991 "Social contexts and social learning in sexual coercion and aggression: Assessing the contribution of fraternity membership," Family Relations 40:558–564.

Bohm, Robert M.

1982 "Radical criminology: An explication," Criminology 19:565–589.

Bonger, Willem

1916/1969 Criminality and Economic Conditions. Abridged with an introduction by Austin T. Turk. Bloomington: Indiana University Press.

Booth, Alan and D. Wayne Osgood

1993 "The influence of testosterone on deviance in adulthood: Assessing and explaining the relationship," Criminology 31:93–117.

Bordua, David J.

1967 "Recent trends: Deviant behavior and social control," Annals 369:149–163.

Boritch, Helen and John Hagan

1990 "A century of crime in Toronto: Gender, class, and patterns of social control, 1859 to 1955," Criminology 28:567–600.

Bottcher, Jean

2001 "Social practices of gender: How gender relates to delinquency in the everyday lives of high-risk youths," Criminology 39:893–932.

Botvin, Gilbert J., Eli Baker, Linda Dusenbury, Elizabeth M. Botvin, and Tracy Diaz

1995 "Long term follow up results of a randomized drug abuse prevention trial in a White middle class population," Journal of the American Medical Association. 273:1106–1118.

Bourque, Blair B., Mei Han, and Sarah M. Hill

1996 A National Survey of Aftercare Provisions for Boot Camp Graduates. National Institute of Justice Research in Brief. Washington, DC: U.S. Department of Justice, National Institute of Justice.

Bowker, Lee H. with contributions by Meda Chesney-Lind and Joy Pollock

1978 Women, Crime, and the Criminal Justice System. Lexington, MA: Lexington.

Box, Steven and Chris Hale

1984 "Liberation/emancipation, economic marginalization, or less chivalry," Criminology 22:473–498.

Braithwaite, John

1989 Crime, Shame, and Reintegration. Cambridge, England: Cambridge University Press.

1995 "Reintegrative shaming, republicanism, and policy," pp. 191–204 in Hugh Barlow (ed.), Crime and Public Policy: Putting Theory to Work. Boulder, CO: Westview.

1997 "Charles Tittle's control balance and criminological theory," Theoretical Criminology 1:77–97.

2002 Restorative Justice and Responsive Regulation. New York: Oxford University Press.

Braithwaite, John, Eliza Ahmed, and Valerie Braithwaite

2006 "Shame, restorative justice, and crime," pp. 397–412 in Francis T. Cullen, John Paul Wright, and Kristie R. Blevins (eds), Taking Stock: The Status of Criminological Theory. Advances in Criminological Theory. Volume 15. New Brunswick, NJ: Transaction.

Braithwaite, John and Peter Drahos

2002 "Zero tolerance, naming and shaming: Is there a case for it with crimes of the powerful?" Australian and New Zealand Journal of Criminology 35:269–88.

Braukmann, Curtis J. and Montrose M. Wolf

1987 "Behaviorally based group homes for juveniles offenders," pp. 135–159 in Edward K. Morris and Curtis J. Braukmann (eds.), Behavioral Approaches to Crime and Delinquency: A Handbook of Application, Research, and Concepts. New York: Plenum.

Brennan, Patricia A., Sarnoff Mednick, and Jan Volavka

1995 "Biomedical factors in crime," pp. 65–90 in James Q. Wilson and Joan Petersilia (eds.), Crime. San Francisco: ICS Press.

Brezina, Timothy

1996 "Adapting to strain: An examination of delinquent coping responses," Criminology 34:39–60.

1998 "Adolescent maltreatment and delinquency: The question of intervening processes," Journal of Research in Crime and Delinquency 35:71–99.

Brezina, Timothy and Alex R. Piquero

2003 "Exploring the relationship between social and non-social reinforcement in the context of social learning theory," pp. 265–288 in Ronald L. Akers and Gary F. Jensen (eds.), Social Learning Theory and the Explanation of Crime: A Guide for the New Century. Advances in Criminological Theory. Volume 11. New Brunswick, NJ: Transaction.

Briar, Scott and Irving Piliavin

1965 "Delinquency, situational inducements, and commitment to conformity," Social Problems 13:35–45.

Bridges, George and Robert Crutchfield

1988 "Law, social standing, and racial disparities in imprisonment," Social Forces 66:699–724.

Bridges, George S. and Martha A. Myers, eds.

1994 Inequality, Crime, and Social Control. Boulder, CO: Westview.

Broadhurst, Roderic

2006 "Crime and security in Asia: Diversity and development," Asian Journal of Criminology 1:1–7.

Broidy, Lisa M.

2001 "A test of general strain theory," Criminology 39:9–36.

Broidy, Lisa and Robert Agnew

1997 "Gender and crime: A general strain theory perspective," Journal of Research in Crime and Delinquency 34:275–305.

Brown, Eric C., Richard F. Catalano, Charles B. Fleming, Kevin P. Haggerty, and Robert D. Abbott

2005 "Adolescent substance use outcomes in the Raising Healthy Children Project: A two-part latent growth curve analysis," Journal of Consulting and Clinical Psychology 73:699–710.

Browne Angela, Brenda Miller, and Eugene Maguin

1999 "Prevalence and severity of lifetime physical and sexual victimization among incarcerated women," International Journal of Law and Psychiatry 22:301–322.

Bruinsma, Gerben J. N.

1992 "Differential association theory reconsidered: An extension and its empirical test," Journal of Quantitative Criminology 8:29–49.

Brunk, Gregory G. and Laura Ann Wilson

1991 "Interest groups and criminal behavior," Journal of Research in Crime and Delinquency 28:157–173.

Budziszewski, J.

1997 Written on the Heart: The Case for Natural Law. Downers Grove, IL: Intervarsity Press.

Burgess, Robert L. and Ronald L. Akers

1966a "Are operant principles tautological?" Psychological Record 16:305–312.
1966b "A differential association reinforcement theory of criminal behavior," Social Problems 14:128–47.

Burgess-Proctor, Amanda

2006 "Intersections of race, class, gender, and crime: Future directions for feminist criminology," Feminist Criminology 1:27–47.

Burkett, Steven and Bruce O. Warren

1987 "Religiosity, peer associations, and adolescent marijuana use: A panel study of underlying causal structures," Criminology 25:109–132.

Bursik, Robert J.

1988 "Social disorganization and theories of crime and delinquency: Problems and prospects," Criminology 26:519–551.

Bursik, Robert J. and Harold G. Grasmick

1993 Neighborhoods and Crime: The Dimensions of Effective Community Control. New York: Lexington.

1995 "Neighborhood based networks and the control of crime and delinquency," pp. 107–130 in Hugh Barlow (ed.), Crime and Public Policy: Putting Theory to Work. Boulder, CO: Westview.

Burt, Callie Harbin, Ronald L. Simons, and Leslie G. Simons

2006 "A longitudinal test of the effects of parenting and the stability of self-control: Negative evidence for the general theory of crime," Criminology 44:353–396

Burton, Velmer S. and Francis T. Cullen

1992 "The empirical status of strain theory," Journal of Crime and Justice 15:1–30.

Burton, Velmer, Frances Cullen, David Evans, and R. Gregory Dunaway

1994 "Reconsidering strain theory: Operationalization, rival theories, and adult criminality," Journal of Quantitative Criminology 10:213–239.

Bynum, Jack E. and William E. Thompson

1992 Juvenile Delinquency: A Sociological Approach. Boston: Allyn & Bacon.

Cain, Maureen

1990 "Realist philosophy and the standpoint epistemologies or feminist criminology as successor science," pp. 124–140 in Loraine Gelsthorpe and Allison Morris (eds.), Feminist Perspectives in Criminology. Philadelphia: Open Press.

Cantor, David and Kenneth C. Land

1985 "Unemployment and crime rates in the post World War II United States: A theoretical and empirical analysis," American Sociological Review 50:317–332.

Capaldi, D. M., P. Chamberlain, and G. R. Patterson

1997 "Ineffective discipline and conduct problems in males: Association, late adolescent outcomes, and prevention," Aggression and Violent Behavior 2:343–353.

Carey, Gregory

1992 "Twin imitation for antisocial behavior: Implications for genetic and family environment research," Journal of Abnormal Psychology 101:18–22.

Carmines, Edward G. and Richard A. Zeller

1979 Reliability and Validity Assessment. Beverly Hills, CA: Sage.

Caspi, Avshalom, Terrie E. Moffitt, Phil A. Silva, Magda Stouthamer Loeber, Robert F. Krueger, and Pamela S. Schmutte

1994 "Are some people crime prone? Replications of the personality crime relationship across countries, genders, races, and methods," Criminology 32:163–196.

Castellano, Thomas C. and Edmund F. McGarrell

1991 "The politics of law and order: Case study evidence for the conflict model of the criminal law formation process," Journal of Research in Crime and Delinquency 28:304–329.

Catalano, Richard and J. David Hawkins

1996 "The social development model: A theory of antisocial behavior," pp. 149–197 in J. David Hawkins (ed.), Delinquency and Crime: Current Theories. New York: Cambridge University Press.

Catalano, Richard F., Rick Kosterman, J. David Hawkins, Robert D. Abbott, and Michael D. Newcomb

1996 "Modeling the etiology of adolescent substance use: A test of the social development model," Journal of Drug Issues 26: 429–456.

Catalano, Richard F., Jisuk Park, Tracy W. Harachi, Kevin P. Haggerty, Robert D. Abbott, and J. David Hawkins

2005 "Mediating the effects of poverty, gender, individual characteristics, and external constraints on antisocial behavior: A test of the Social Development Model and implications for developmental life-course theory," pp. 93–124 in David Farrington (ed.), Integrated Developmental & Life Course Theories of Offending. Advances in Criminological Theory. Volume 14. New Brunswick, NJ: Transaction.

Cernkovich, Stephen and Peggy Giordano

1992 "School bonding, race, and delinquency," Criminology 30:261–291.

Chadwick-Jones, J. K.

1976 Social Exchange Theory: Its Structure and Influence in Social Psychology. London: Academic.

Chalidze, Valery

1977 Criminal Russia: Crime in the Soviet Union. New York: Random House.

Chamberlain, Patricia, Philip A. Fisher, and Kevin Moore

2002 "Multidimensional treatment foster care: Applications of the OSLC intervention model to high risk youth and their families," pp. 203–218 in John B. Reid, Gerald R. Patterson, and James Snyder (eds.), Antisocial Behavior in Children and Adolescents: A Developmental Analysis and Model for Intervention. Washington, DC: American Psychological Association.

Chambliss, William J.

1964 "A sociological analysis of the law of vagrancy," Social Problems 12:67–77.
1974 "The state, the law, and the definition of behavior as criminal or delinquent," pp 7–43 in Daniel Glaser (ed.), Handbook of Criminology. Chicago: Rand McNally.
1988 Exploring Criminology. New York: Macmillan.
1994 "Policing the ghetto underclass: The politics of law and law enforcement," Social Problems 41:177–194.

Chambliss, William J., ed.

1969 Crime and the Legal Process. New York: McGraw-Hill.
1975 Criminal Law in Action. Santa Barbara, CA: Hamilton.

Chambliss, William J. and Robert B. Seidman

1971 Law, Order, and Power. Reading, MA: Addison-Wesley.
1982 Law, Order, and Power. Second Edition. Reading, MA: Addison-Wesley.

Chamlin, Mitchell and John K. Cochran

1995 "Assessing Messner and Rosenfeld's institutional-anomie theory: A partial test," Criminology 33:411.
2000 "Race riots and robbery arrests: Toward a direct test of the threat hypothesis," Social Pathology 6:83–101.

Chapman, Jane R.

1980 Economic Realities and the Female Offender. Lexington, MA: Lexington.

Chappell, Allison T. and Alex R. Piquero

2004 "Applying social learning theory to police misconduct," Deviant Behavior 25:89–108.

Chapple, Constance L., Julia A. McQuillan, and Terceira A. Berdahl

2005 "Gender, social bonds, and delinquency: a comparison of boys' and girls' models," Social Science Research 34:357–383.

Chase-Dunn, Christopher K.

1980 "Socialist states in the capitalist world economy," Social Problems 27:505–525.

Chesney-Lind, Meda

1988 "Girls in jail," Crime and Delinquency 34:150–168.

1989 "Girls' crime and woman's place: Toward a feminist model of female delinquency," Crime and Delinquency 35:5–29.

Chesney-Lind, Meda and Karlene Faith

2001 "What about feminism? Engendering theory-making in criminology," pp. 287–302 in Raymond Paternoster and Ronet Bachman (eds.), Explaining Criminals and Crime. Los Angeles: Roxbury.

Chesney-Lind, Meda and Lisa Pasko

2004 The Female Offender: Girls, Women, and Crime. Second Edition. Thousand Oaks, CA: Sage.

Chesney-Lind, Meda and Noelie Rodriguez

1983 "Women under lock and key: A view from the inside," The Prison Journal 63:47–65.

Chesney-Lind, Meda and Randall G. Shelden

2004 Girls, Delinquency, and Juvenile Justice. Third Edition. Belmont, CA: Wadsworth/Thomson Learning.

Chiricos, Theodore

1991 "Unemployment and punishment: An empirical assessment," Criminology 29:701–724.

Chiricos, Theodore G. and Miriam A. DeLone

1992 "Labor surplus and punishment: A review and assessment of theory and evidence," Social Problems 39:421–446.

Chiricos, Theodore G. and Gordon P. Waldo

1970 "Punishment and crime: An examination of some empirical evidence," Social Problems 18:200–217.

Clark, Robert

1972 Reference Group Theory and Delinquency. New York: Behavioral Publications.

Cloward, Richard

1959 "Illegitimate means, anomie, and deviant behavior," American Sociological Review 24:164–77.

Cloward, Richard and Lloyd Ohlin

1960 Delinquency and Opportunity. Glencoe, IL: Free Press.

Cochran, John K. and Ronald L. Akers

1989 "Beyond hellfire: An exploration of the variable effects of religiosity on adolescent marijuana and alcohol use," Journal of Research in Crime and Delinquency 26:198–225.

Cochran, John K. and Mitchell B. Chamlin

2000 "Deterrence and brutalization: The dual effects of executions," Justice Quarterly 17:685–706.

Cochran, John, Jennifer Wareham, Peter Wood, and Bruce Arneklev

2002 "Is the school attachment/commitment-delinquency relationship spurious? An exploratory test of arousal theory," Journal of Crime and Justice 25:49–70.

Cochran, John K., Peter B. Wood, and Bruce J. Arneklev

1994 "Is the religiosity delinquency relationship spurious? A test of arousal and social control theories," Journal of Research in Crime and Delinquency 31:92–123.

Cochran, John K., Peter B. Wood, Christine S. Sellers, Wendy Wilerson, and Mitchell B. Chamlin

1998 "Academic dishonesty and low self control: An empirical test of a general theory of crime," Deviant Behavior 19:227–255.

Cohen, Albert K.

1955 Delinquent Boys. Glencoe, IL: Free Press.

Cohen, Albert K., Alfred R. Lindesmith, and Karl F. Schuessler, eds.

1956 The Sutherland Papers. Bloomington: Indiana University Press.

Cohen, Lawrence E. and Marcus Felson

1979 "Social change and crime rate trends: A routine activities approach," American Sociological Review 44:588–608.

Cohen, Lawrence E., James Kluegel, and Kenneth Land

1981 "Social inequality and predatory criminal victimization: An exposition and test of a formal theory," American Sociological Review 46:505–524.

Cole, Simon A.

2001 Suspect Identities: A History of Fingerprinting and Criminal Identifications. Cambridge, MA: Harvard University Press.

Colvin, Mark

2000 Crime and Coercion: An Integrated Theory of Chronic Criminality. New York: St. Martin's Press.

Colvin, Mark, Francis T. Cullen, and Thomas Vander Ven

2002 "Coercion, social support, and crime: An emerging theoretical consensus," Criminology 40:19–42.

Colvin, Mark and John Pauly

1983 "A critique of criminology: Toward an integrated structural Marxist theory of delinquency production," American Journal of Sociology 89:513–551.

Conger, Rand

1976 "Social control and social learning models of delinquency: A synthesis," Criminology 14:17–40.

Conger, Rand D. and Ronald L. Simons

1995 "Life course contingencies in the development of adolescent antisocial behavior: A matching law approach," in Terrance P. Thornberry (ed.), Developmental Theories of Crime and Delinquency. New Brunswick, NJ: Transaction.

Connell, Robert W.

1987 Gender and Power. Stanford, CA: Stanford University Press.

Cooley, Charles Horton

1902 Human Nature and the Social Order. New York: Scribner.

Cornish, Derek B. and Ronald V. Clarke, eds.

1986 The Reasoning Criminal: Rational Choice Perspectives on Offending. New York: Springer.

Costello, Barbara J.

2000 "Techniques of neutralization and self-esteem: A critical test of social control and neutralization theory," Deviant Behavior 21:307–330.

Costello, Barbara J. and Paul R. Vowell

1999 "Testing control theory and differential association: A reanalysis of the Richmond Youth Project data," Criminology 37:815–842.

Creechan, James H.

1994 "A test of the general theory of crime: Delinquency and school dropouts," pp. 233–256 in James H. Creechan and Robert A. Silverman (eds.), Canadian Juvenile Delinquency. Canada: Prentice Hall.

Cressey, Donald R.

1953 Other People's Money. Glencoe, IL: Free Press.

1955 "Changing criminals: The application of the theory of differential association," American Journal of Sociology 61:116–120.

1960 "Epidemiology and individual conduct: A case from criminology," Pacific Sociological Review 3:47–58.

Crew, B. Keith

1991 "Sex differences in criminal sentencing: Chivalry or patriarchy?" Justice Quarterly 8:59–84.

Crites, Laura, ed.

1976 The Female Offender. Lexington, MA: Lexington.

Cromwell, Paul F., Roger Dunham, Ronald Akers, and Lonn Lanza-Kaduce

1995 "Routine activities and social control in the aftermath of a natural catastrophe," European Journal of Criminal Policy and Research 3:56–69.

Cromwell, Paul F., James N. Olson, and D'Aunn Wester Avary

1991 Breaking and Entering: An Ethnographic Analysis of Burglary. Newbury Park, CA: Sage.

Crouch, Robert L.

1979 Human Behavior: An Economic Approach. North Scituate, MA: Duxbury.

Cullen, Francis T.

1983 Rethinking Crime and Deviance Theory: The Emergence of a Structuring Tradition. Totowa, NJ: Rowman and Allanheld.

1994 "Social support as an organizing concept for criminology: Presidential address to the Academy of Criminal Justice Sciences," Justice Quarterly 11:528–559.

Cullen, Francis T., Bonnie S. Fisher, and Brandon K. Applegate

2000 "Public opinion about punishment and corrections," Crime and Justice: A Review of Research 27:1–79.

Cullen, Francis T., Paul Gendreau, G. Roger Jarjoura, and John Paul Wright

1997 "Crime and the bell curve: Lessons from intelligent criminology," Crime and Delinquency 43:387–411.

Cullen, Francis T., Jody L. Sundt, and John F. Wozniak

2001 "The virtuous prison: Toward a restorative rehabilitation," pp. 265–286 in Henry N. Pontell and David Shichor (eds.), Contemporary Issues in Crime and Criminal Justice: Essays in Honor of Gilbert Geis. Upper Saddle River, NJ: Prentice Hall.

Cullen, Francis T. and John Paul Wright

1997 "Liberating the anomie strain paradigm: Implications from social support theory," pp. 187–206 in Nikos Passas and Robert Agnew (eds.), The Future of Anomie Theory. Boston: Northeastern University Press.

Cullen, Francis T., John Paul Wright, and Kristie R. Blevins, eds.

2006 Taking Stock: The Status of Criminology Theory. Advances in Criminological Theory. Volume 15. New Brunswick, NJ: Transaction.

Cullen, Francis T., John Paul Wright, Paul Gendreau, and D. A. Andrews

2003 "What correctional treatment can tell us about criminological theory: Implications for social learning theory," pp. 339–362 in Ronald L. Akers and Gary F. Jensen (eds.), Social Learning Theory and the Explanation of Crime: A Guide for the New Century. Advances in Criminological Theory. Volume 11. New Brunswick, NJ: Transaction.

Curran, Daniel J. and Claire M. Renzetti

2001 Theories of Crime. Second Edition. Boston: Allyn & Bacon.

Curry, G. David, Scott H. Decker, and Arlen Egley, Jr.

2002 "Gang involvement and delinquency in a middle school population," Justice Quarterly 19:275–292.

D'Alessio, Stewart and Lisa Stolzenberg

1995 "Unemployment and incarceration of pretrial defendants," American Sociological Review 60:350–359.

1998 "Crime, arrests, and pretrial jail incarceration: An examination of the deterrence thesis," Criminology 36:735–762.

Daly, Kathleen

1989 "Neither conflict nor labeling nor paternalism will suffice: Intersections of race, ethnicity, gender, and family in criminal court decisions," Crime and Delinquency 35:136–168.

1992 "Women's pathways to felony court: Feminist theories of lawbreaking and problems of representation," Review of Law and Women's Studies 2:11–52.

1994a Gender, Crime, and Punishment. New Haven, CT: Yale University Press.

1994b "Gender and punishment disparity," pp. 117–133 in George S. Bridges and Martha A. Myers (eds.), Inequality, Crime, and Social Control. Boulder, CO: Westview.

1997 "Different ways of conceptualizing sex/gender in feminist theory and their implications for criminology," Theoretical Criminology 1:25–51.

1998 "Gender, crime, and criminology," pp. 85–108 in Michael Tonry (ed.), The Handbook of Crime and Justice. Oxford, England: Oxford University Press.

Daly, Kathleen and Meda Chesney-Lind

1988 "Feminism and criminology," Justice Quarterly 5:497–538.

Daly, Kathleen and Lisa Maher

1998 Criminology at the Crossroads. New York: Oxford University Press.

Datesman, Susan K. and Frank R. Scarpitti, eds.

1980 Women, Crime, and Justice. New York: Oxford University Press.

Davis, F. James

1962 "Law as a type of social control," pp. 39–61 in F. James Davis, Henry H. Foster, C. Ray Jeffery, and E. Eugene Davis (eds.), Society and the Law: New Meanings for an Old Profession. New York: Free Press.

Davis, Kingsley

1966 "Sexual behavior," pp. 322–408 in Robert K. Merton and Robert A. Nisbet (eds.), Contemporary Social Problems. Second Edition. New York: Harcourt Brace Jovanovich.

De Haan, Willem and Jaco Vos

2003 "A crying shame: The over-rationalized conception of man in the rational choice perspective," Theoretical Criminology 7:29–54.

Dickson, Donald T.

1968 "Bureaucracy and morality: An organizational perspective on a moral crusade," Social Problems 16:43–56.

Dishion, Thomas J., Gerald R. Patterson, and Kathryn A. Kavanagh

1992 "An experimental test of the coercion model: Linking theory, measurement, and intervention," pp. 253–282 in Joan McCord and Richard E. Tremblay (eds.), Preventing Antisocial Behavior: Interventions From Birth Through Adolescence. New York: Guilford.

Dishion, Thomas J., Joan McCord, and Francia Poulin

1999 "When interventions harm: Peer groups and problem behavior," American Psychologist 54:755–764.

Donnerstein, Edward and Daniel Linz

1995 "The media," pp. 237–266 in James Q. Wilson and Joan Petersilia (eds.), Crime. San Francisco: ICS Press.

Driver, Edwin D.

1972 "Charles Buckman Goring, 1870–1919," in Hermann Mannheim (ed.), Pioneers in Criminology. Second Edition Enlarged. Montclair, NJ: Patterson Smith.

Dugan, Laura, Gary LaFree, and Alex R. Piquero

2005 "Testing a rational choice model of airline hijackings," Criminology 43: 1031–1066

Dunaway, Gregory R., Francis T. Cullen, Velmer S. Burton, Jr., and T. David Evans

2000 "The myth of social class and crime revisited: An examination of class and adult criminality," Criminology 38:589–632.

Dunham, Roger G., Geoffrey P. Alpert, Meghan S. Stroshine, and Katherine Bennett

2005 "Transforming citizens into suspects: Factors that influence the formation of police suspicion," Police Quarterly 8:366–393.

Durkheim, Emile

1893/1964 The Division of Labor in Society. New York: Free Press of Glencoe.
1897/1951 Suicide. Translated by John A. Spaulding and George Simpson. New York: Free Press.

Durkin, Keith F., Timothy W. Wolfe, and Gregory A. Clark

2005 "College students and binge drinking: An evaluation of social learning theory," Sociological Spectrum 25:255–272.

Eddy, J. Mark and Patricia Chamberlain

2000 "Family management and deviant peer association as mediators of the impact of treatment condition on youth antisocial behavior," Journal of Consulting and Clinical Psychology 68:857–863.

Eddy, J. M., J. B. Reid, and R. A. Fetrow

2000 "An elementary-school based prevention program targeting modifiable antecedents of youth delinquency and violence: Linking the Interests of Families and Teachers (LIFT)," Journal of Emotional and Behavioral Disorders 8:165–176.

Edens, John F., David K. Marcus, Scott O. Lilienfeld, and Norman G. Poythress Jr.

2006 "Psychopathic, Not Psychopath: Taxometric Evidence for the Dimensional Structure of Psychopath," Journal of Abnormal Psychology 115:131–144

Einstadter, Werner and Stuart Henry

1995 Criminological Theory: An Analysis of Its Underlying Assumptions. Ft. Worth, TX: Harcourt Brace.

Eisenberg, Michael and Brittani Trusty

2002 Overview of the InnerChange Freedom Initiative: The Faith-Based Prison Program within the Texas Department of Criminal Justice. Austin: Criminal Justice Policy Council. [Online]. Available at http://www.cjpc.state.tx.us/reports/alphalist/IFI.pdf

Eitle, David, Stewart J. D'Alessio, and Lisa Stolzenberg

2002 "Racial threat and social control: A test of the political, economic, and threat of Black crime hypotheses," Social Forces 81:557–576.

Elliott, Delbert S.

1985 "The assumption that theories can be combined with increased explanatory power," pp. 123–149 in Robert F. Meier (ed.), Theoretical Methods in Criminology. Beverly Hills, CA: Sage.

1994 "Serious violent offenders: Onset, developmental course, and termination," Criminology 32:1–22.

Elliott, Delbert S. and Susan S. Ageton

1980 "Reconciling race and class differences in self reported and official estimates of delinquency," American Sociological Review 45:95–110.

Elliott, Delbert S., David Huizinga, and Suzanne S. Ageton

1985 Explaining Delinquency and Drug Use. Beverly Hills: Sage.

Elliott, Delbert S. and Scott Menard

1996 "Delinquent friends and delinquent behavior: Temporal and developmental patterns," pp. 28–67 in J. David Hawkins (ed.), Delinquency and Crime: Current Theories. New York: Cambridge University Press.

Elliott, Delbert S. and Harwin L. Voss

1974 Delinquency and Dropout. Lexington, MA: Lexington.

Ellis, Lee

1987a "Criminal behavior and r/K selection: An extension of gene based evolutionary theory," Deviant Behavior 8:148–176.

1987b "Neurohormonal bases of varying tendencies to learn delinquent and criminal behavior," pp. 499–518 in Morris, Edward K. and Curtis J. Braukmann (eds.), Behavioral Approaches to Crime and Delinquency: A Handbook of Application, Research, and Concepts. New York: Plenum.

1987c "Religiosity and criminality from the perspective of arousal theory," Journal of Research in Crime and Delinquency 24:215–232.

Ellis, Lee and Anthony Walsh

1997 "Gene based evolutionary theories in criminology," Criminology 35:229–275.

1999 "Criminologists' opinions about causes and theories of crime and delinquency," The Criminologist 24(4):1, 4–6.

Ellis, Rodney and Karen Sowers

2001 Juvenile Justice Practice: A Cross-Disciplinary Approach to Intervention. Belmont, CA: Wadsworth/Brooks Cole.

Empey, LaMar T.

1967 "Delinquency theory and recent research," Journal of Research in Crime and Delinquency 4:28–42.

Empey, LaMar T. and Maynard L. Erickson

1972 The Provo Experiment: Evaluating Community Control of Delinquency. Lexington, MA: Lexington.

Engel, Robin Shepard, Jennifer M. Calnon, and Thomas J. Bernard
2002 "Theory and racial profiling: Shortcomings and future directions in research," Justice Quarterly 19:249–273.

Erikson, Kai T.
1964 "Notes on the sociology of deviance," pp. 9–23 in Howard S. Becker (ed.), The Other Side. New York: Free Press.

Erlanger, Howard S.
1974 "The empirical status of the subculture of violence thesis," Social Problems 22:280–291.
1976 "Is there a 'subculture of violence' in the South?" Journal of Criminal Law and Criminology 66:483–490.

Esbensen, Finn Aage, and Elizabeth Piper Deschenes
1998 "A multisite examination of youth gang membership: Does gender matter?" Criminology 36:799–827.

Esbensen, Finn-Aage, D. Wayne Osgood, Terrance J. Taylor, Dana Peterson, and Adrience Freng
2001 "How great is G.R.E.A.T.? Results from a longitudinal quasi-experimental design," Criminology and Public Policy 1:87–118.

Evans, T. David, Francis T. Cullen, R. Gregory Dunaway, and Velmer S. Burton, Jr.
1995 "Religion and crime re examined: The impact of religion, secular controls, and social ecology on adult criminality," Criminology 33:195–224.

Eysenck, Hans J. and Gisli H. Gudjonsson
1989 The Causes and Cures of Criminality. New York: Plenum.

Fagan, Abigail A.
2005 "The relationship between adolescent physical abuse and criminal offending: Support for an enduring and generalized cycle of violence," Journal of Family Violence 20:279–290.

Farnworth, Margaret and Michael J. Leiber
1989 "Strain theory revisited: Economic goals, educational means, and delinquency," American Sociological Review 54:263–274.

Farnworth, Margaret and Raymond Teske
1995 "Gender differences in felony court processing: Three hypotheses of disparity," Women and Criminal Justice 6:23–44.

Farrell, Ronald A.
1989 "Cognitive consistency in deviance causation: A psychological elaboration of an integrated systems model," pp. 77–92 in Steven F. Messner, Marvin D. Krohn, and Allen E. Liska (eds.), Theoretical Integration in the Study of Deviance and Crime. Albany: State University of New York Press.

Farrington, David P.
1977 "The effects of public labeling," British Journal of Criminology 17:112–125.
2006 "Building developmental and life-course theories of offending," pp. 335–364 in Francis T. Cullen, John Paul Wright, and Kristie R. Blevins (eds.), Taking Stock: The Status of Criminological Theory. Advances in Criminological Theory. Volume 15. New Brunswick, NJ: Transaction.

Farrington, David P., ed.
2005 Integrated Developmental & Life Course Theories of Offending. Volume 14. Advances in Criminological Theory. Volume 14. New Brunswick, NJ: Transaction.

Felson, Marcus

1994 Crime and Everyday Life. Thousand Oaks, CA: Pine Forge Press.
1998 Crime and Everyday Life. Second Edition. Thousand Oaks, CA: Pine Forge Press.
2002 Crime and Everyday Life. Third Edition. Thousand Oaks, CA: Sage.
2006 Crime and Nature. Thousand Oaks, CA: Sage.

Felson, Marcus and Ronald V. Clarke

1995 "Routine precautions, criminology, and crime prevention," pp. 179–190 in Hugh Barlow (ed.), Crime and Public Policy: Putting Theory to Work. Boulder, CO: Westview.

Finckenauer, James O.

1982 Scared Straight and the Panacea Phenomenon. Englewood Cliffs, NJ: Prentice Hall.

Finestone, Harold

1976 Victims of Change. Westport, CT: Greenwood.

Fishbein, Diana H.

1990 "Biological perspectives in criminology," Criminology 28:27–72.
2001 Biobehavioral Perspectives on Criminology. Belmont, CA: Wadsworth.
2006 "Integrating findings from neurobiology into criminological thought," pp. 43–68 in Stuart Henry and Mark M. Lanier (eds.), The Essential Criminology Reader. Boulder, CO: Westview.

Forthun, Larry F., Nancy J. Bell, Charles W. Peek, and Sheh Wei Sun

1999 "Religiosity, sensation seeking, and alcohol/drug use in denominational and gender contexts," Journal of Drug Issues 29:75–90.

Free, Marvin D.

2002 "Race and presentencing decisions in the United States: A summary and critique of the research," Criminal Justice Review 27:203–232.

Fridell, Lorie

2004 By the Numbers: A Guide for Analyzing Race Data from Vehicle Stops. Washington, DC: Police Executive Research Forum.

Friedlander, Kate

1947 The Psychoanalytic Approach to Juvenile Delinquency. London: Kegan Paul.

Friedman, Lawrence

1975 The Legal System. New York: Russell Sage Foundation.

Fuller, John Randolph and John F. Wozniak

2006 "Peacemaking criminology: Past, present, and future," pp. 251–273 in Francis T. Cullen, John Paul Wright, and Kristie R. Blevins (eds.), Taking Stock: The Status of Criminological Theory. Advances in Criminological Theory. Volume 15. New Brunswick, NJ: Transaction.

Galliher, John F. and A. Walker

1977 "The puzzle of the origin of the Marijuana Tax Act of 1937," Social Problems 24:367–376.

Gaylord, Mark S. and John F. Galliher

1988 The Criminology of Edwin Sutherland. New Brunswick: Transaction.

Geis, Gilbert

1972 "Jeremy Bentham 1748–1832," pp. 51–68 in Hermann Mannheim (ed.), Pioneers in Criminology. Second Edition Enlarged. Montclair, NJ: Patterson Smith.

Gelsthorpe, Loraine and Allison Morris, eds.

1990 Feminist Perspectives in Criminology. Philadelphia: Open University Press.

Gendreau, Paul, Paula Smith, and Sheila K. A. French

2006 "The theory of effective correctional intervention: empirical status and future directions, pp. 419–446 in Francis T. Cullen, John Paul Wright, and Kristie R. Blevins (eds.), Taking Stock: The Status of Criminological Theory. Advances in Criminological Theory. Volume 15. New Brunswick, NJ: Transaction.

Georges-Abeyie, Daniel E.

1990 "The myth of a racist criminal justice system?" pp. 11–14 in Brian MacLean and Dragan Milovanovic (eds.), Racism, Empiricism, and Criminal Justice. Vancouver, Canada: Collective Press.

Gibbons, Don C.

1994 Talking About Crime and Criminals: Problems and Issues in Theory Development in Criminology. Englewood Cliffs, NJ: Prentice Hall.

Gibbons, Don C. and Marvin D. Krohn

1986 Delinquent Behavior. Fourth Edition. Englewood Cliffs, NJ: Prentice Hall.

Gibbs, Jack P.

1966 "Conceptions of deviant behavior: The old and the new," Pacific Sociological Review 9:9–14.

1968 "Crime, punishment, and deterrence," Southwestern Social Science Quarterly 48:515–530.

1975 Crime, Punishment, and Deterrence. New York: Elsevier.

1986 "Punishment and deterrence: Theory, research, and penal policy," pp. 319–368 in Leon Lipson and Stanton Wheeler (eds.), Law and the Social Sciences. New York: Russell Sage Foundation.

1990 "The notion of a theory in sociology," National Journal of Sociology 4:129–158.

1995 "The notion of control and criminology's policy implications," pp. 71–89 in Hugh Barlow (ed.), Crime and Public Policy: Putting Theory to Work. Boulder, CO: Westview.

Gilfus, Mary E.

1992 "From victims to survivors to offenders: Women's routes of entry and immersion into street crime," Women and Criminal Justice 4:63-90.

Gillen, John L.

1945 Criminology and Penology. New York: Appleton-Century-Crofts.

Glaser, Daniel

1956 "Criminality theories and behavioral images," American Journal of Sociology 61:433–444.

Glueck, Sheldon and Eleanor Glueck

1959 Predicting Delinquency and Crime. Cambridge, MA: Harvard University Press.

Goffman, Erving

1963 Stigma: Notes on the Management of Spoiled Identity. Englewood Cliffs, NJ: Prentice Hall.

Goode, Erich

1975 "On behalf of labeling theory," Social Problems 22:570–583.

Gordon, David, Richard Edwards, and Michael Reich

1982 Segmented Work, Divided Workers: The Historical Transformation of Labor in the United States. New York: Cambridge University Press.

Gordon, Rachel A., Benjamin B. Lahey, Eriko Kawai, Rolf Loeber, Magda Stouthamer-Loeber, and David P. Farrington

2004 "Anti-social behavior and youth gang membership: Selection and socialization," Criminology 42:55–87.

Gordon, Robert A.

1980 "Research on IQ, race, and delinquency: Taboo or not taboo?" pp. 37–66 in Edward Sagarin (ed.), Taboos in Criminology. Beverly Hills, CA: Sage.

1987 "SES versus IQ in the race IQ delinquency model," International Journal of Sociology and Social Policy 7:29–96.

Goring, Charles

1913 The English Convict: A Statistical Study. Patterson Smith Reprint, 1972. Montclair, NJ: Patterson Smith.

Gottfredson, Denise C., Richard J. McNeil, III, and Gary Gottfredson

1991 "Social area influences on delinquency: A multilevel analysis," Journal of Research in Crime and Delinquency 28:197–226.

Gottfredson, Michael and Travis Hirschi

1990 A General Theory of Crime. Palo Alto, CA: Stanford University Press.

Gove, Walter R.

1982 "Labeling theory's explanation of mental illness: An update of recent evidence," Deviant Behavior 3:307–327.

Gove, Walter R., ed.

1980 The Labeling of Deviance. Second Edition. Beverly Hills, CA: Sage.

Gove, Walter R. and Michael Hughes

1989 "A theory of mental illness: An attempted integration of biological, psychological, and social variables," pp. 61–76 in Steven F. Messner, Marvin D. Krohn, and Allen E. Liska (eds.), Theoretical Integration in the Study of Deviance and Crime. Albany: State University of New York Press.

Grasmick, Harold G. and Robert J. Bursik

1990 "Conscience, significant others, and rational choice: Extending the deterrence model," Law and Society Review 24:837–862.

Grasmick, Harold G. and Donald E. Green

1980 "Legal punishment, social disapproval, and internalization as inhibitors of illegal behavior," Journal of Criminal Law and Criminology 71:325–335.

Grasmick, Harold, John Hagan, Brenda Sims Blackwell, and Bruce Arneklev

1996 "Risk preferences and patriarchy: Extending power-control theory," Social Forces 75:177–199.

Green, Donald E.

1989 "Measures of illegal behavior in individual level research," Journal of Research in Crime and Delinquency 26:253–275.

Greenberg, David F.

1977 "Delinquency and the age structure of society," Contemporary Crises: Crime, Law, and Social Policy 1:189–223.

1981b "Delinquency and the age structure of society," pp. 118–139 in David F. Greenberg (ed.), Crime and Capitalism. Palo Alto, CA: Mayfield.

Greenberg, David F., ed.

1981a Crime and Capitalism: Readings in Marxist Criminology. Palo Alto, CA: Mayfield.

Greenwood, Peter W.

1998 Investing in Our Children: What We Know and Don't Know About the Costs and Benefits of Early Childhood Interventions. Santa Monica, CA: Rand Corporation.

Griffin, Robin and Scott Akins

2000 "Multiple birth rates and racial type: A research note regarding r/K theory," Deviant Behavior 21:15–22.

Griffin, Timothy and John Wooldredge

2006 "Sex-based disparities in felony dispositions before versus after sentencing reform in Ohio," Criminology 44:893–923.

Grimes, Ruth Ellen M. and Austin T. Turk

1978 "Labeling in context: Conflict, power, and self definition," pp. 39–58 in Marvin D. Krohn and Ronald L. Akers (eds.), Crime, Law, and Sanctions: Theoretical Perspectives. Berkeley, CA: Sage.

Hackler, James C.

1966 "Boys, blisters, and behavior: The impact of a work program in an urban central area," Journal of Research in Crime and Delinquency 3:155–164.

Hadjar, Andreas, Dirk Baier, Klaus Boehnke, and John Hagan

2007 "Juvenile delinquency and gender revisited: The family and power-control theory reconceived," European Journal of Criminology 4:33–58.

Hagan, John

1973 "Labeling and deviance: A case study in the 'sociology of the interesting'," Social Problems 20:447–458.

1974 "Extra legal attributes in criminal sentencing: An assessment of a sociological viewpoint," Law and Society Review 8:357–383.

1980 "The legislation of crime and delinquency: A review of theory, method, and research," Law and Society Review 14:603–628.

1989a Structural Criminology. New Brunswick, NJ: Rutgers University Press.

1989b "Micro and macro structures of delinquency causation and a power control theory of gender and delinquency," pp. 213–228 in Steven F. Messner, Marvin D. Krohn, and Allen E. Liska (eds.), Theoretical Integration in the Study of Deviance and Crime. Albany: State University of New York Press.

1989c "Why is there so little criminal justice theory? Neglected macro and micro level links between organizations and power," Journal of Research in Crime and Delinquency 26:116–135.

1990 "The structuration of gender and deviance: A power-control theory of vulnerability to crime and the search for deviant role exits," Canadian Review of Sociology and Anthropology 27:137–156.

Hagan, John, Klaus Boehnke, and Hans Merkens

2004 "Gender differences in capitalization processes and the delinquency of siblings in Toronto and Berlin," British Journal of Criminology 44:659–676.

Hagan, John, A. R. Gillis, and John Simpson

1985 "The class structure of gender and delinquency: Toward a power-control theory of common delinquent behavior," American Journal of Sociology 90:1151–1178.

1990 "Clarifying and extending power-control theory," American Journal of Sociology 95:1024–1037.

1993 "The power of control in sociological theories," pp. 381–398 in Freda Adler and William S. Laufer (eds.), New Directions in Criminological Theory. Advances in Criminological Theory. Volume 4. New Brunswick, NJ: Transaction.

Hagan, John and Fiona Kay

1990 "Gender and delinquency in white-collar families: A power-control perspective," Crime and Delinquency 36:391–407.

Hagan, John and Jeffrey Leon

1977 "Rediscovering delinquency: Social history, political ideology, and the sociology of law," American Sociological Review 42:587–598.

Hagan, John and Alberto Palloni

1990 "The social reproduction of a criminal class in working class London, circa 1950–1980," American Journal of Sociology 96:265–299.

Hagan, John, John H. Simpson, and A. R. Gillis

1987 "Class in the household: A power control theory of gender and delinquency," American Journal of Sociology 92:788–816.

1988 "Feminist scholarship, relational and instrumental control, and a power-control theory of gender and delinquency," British Journal of Sociology 39:301–336.

Hall, Jerome

1952 Theft, Law, and Society. Revised Edition. Indianapolis: Bobbs-Merrill.

Hall, S. T.

2003 "Faith-based cognitive programs in corrections," Corrections Today 65(7):108–137.

Halleck, Seymour L.

1967 Psychiatry and the Dilemmas of Crime. New York: Harper & Row.

Hamblin, Robert L.

1979 "Behavioral choice and social reinforcement: Step function versus matching," Social Forces 57:1141–1156.

Haney, Craig and Philip Zimbardo

1998 "The past and future of U.S. prison policy: Twenty-five years after the Stanford prison experiment," American Psychologist 53:709–727.

Hanke, Penelope J.

1995 "Sentencing disparities by race of offender and victim: Women homicide offenders in Alabama 1929–1985," Sociological Spectrum 15:277–298.

Harding, Sandra, ed.

1987 Feminism and Methodology. Philadelphia: Open University Press.

Hare, Robert D.

1965 "A conflict and learning theory analysis of psychopathic behavior," Journal of Research in Crime and Delinquency 2:12–19.

1999 Without Conscience: The Disturbing World of the Psychopaths Among Us. New York: Guilford.

2003 The Psychopathy Checklist Revised Manual. Second Edition. Toronto, Ontario, Canada: Multi-Health Systems.

Harris, Judith Rich

1998 The Nurture Assumption. New York: Free Press

Harris, M. Kay

1991 "Moving into the new millennium: Toward a feminist vision of justice," pp. 83–97 in Harold E. Pepinsky and Richard Quinney (eds.), Criminology as Peacemaking. Bloomington: Indiana University Press.

Hartjen, Clayton A. and S. Priyadarsini

2003 "Gender, peers and delinquency: A study of boys and girls in rural France," Youth & Society 34:387–414.

Hathaway, Starke

1939 "The personality inventory as an aid in the diagnosis of psychopathic inferiors," Journal of Consulting Psychology 3:112–117.

Hathaway, Starke and Paul E. Meehl

1951 An Atlas for the Clinical Use of the MMPI. Minneapolis: University of Minnesota Press.

Hathaway, Starke and Elio Monachesi

1953 Analyzing and Predicting Juvenile Delinquency with the MMPI. Minneapolis: University of Minnesota Press.

Hathaway, Starke R. and Elio D. Monachesi

1963 Adolescent Personality and Behavior. Minneapolis, MN: University of Minnesota Press.

Hawkins, J. David, Richard F. Catalano, Rick Kosterman, Robert Abbott, and Karl G. Hill

1999 "Preventing adolescent health–risk behaviors by strengthening protection during childhood," Archives of Pediatric and Adolescent Medicine 153:226–234.

Hawkins, J. David, Richard F. Catalano, Daine M. Morrison, Julie O'Donnell, Robert D. Abbott, and L. Edward Day

1992 "The Seattle Social Development Project: Effects of the first four years on protective factors and problem behaviors," pp. 139–161 in Joan McCord and Richard E. Tremblay (eds.), Preventing Antisocial Behavior: Interventions From Birth Through Adolescence. New York: Guilford.

Hawkins, J. David, Elizabeth Von Cleve, and Richard F. Catalano, Jr.

1991 "Reducing early childhood aggression: Results of a primary prevention program," Journal of the Academy of Child and Adolescent Psychiatry 30:208–217.

Hawkins, J. David and Joseph G. Weis

1985 "The social development model: An integrated approach to delinquency prevention," Journal of Primary Prevention 6:73–97.

Hawkins, Richard and Gary Tiedeman

1975 The Creation of Deviance: Interpersonal and Organizational Determinants. Columbus, OH: Merrill.

Hawkins, Richard and Kirk B. Williams

1989 "Acts, arrests, and the deterrence process: The case of wife assault." Paper presented to the Society for the Study of Social Problems, Berkeley, CA.

Hay, Carter

2001a "Parenting, self-control, and delinquency: A test of self-control theory," Criminology 39:707–736.
2001b "An exploratory test of Braithwaite's reintegrative shaming theory," Journal of Research and Crime and Delinquency 38:132–153.

Hay, Carter and Walter Forrest

2006 "The development of self-control: examining self-control theory's stability thesis," Criminology 44:739–774.

Haynie, Dana L.

2002 "Friendship networks and delinquency: The relative nature of peer delinquency," Journal of Quantitative Criminology 18:99–134.

Haynie, Dana L. and Scott J. South

2005 "Residential mobility and adolescent violence," Social Forces 84:361–374

Heimer, Karen, Stacy De Coster, and Halime Unal

2006 "Opening the black box: The social psychology of gender and delinquency," Sociology of Crime, Law, and Deviance 7:109–135.

Heineke, J. M., ed.

1978 Economic Models of Criminal Behavior. Amsterdam: North-Holland.

Henry, Stuart and Dragan Milovanovic

1991 "Constitutive criminology: The maturation of critical theory," Criminology 29:293–315.

1996 Constitutive Criminology: Beyond Postmodernism. London: Sage.

Henry, Stuart and Werner Einstadter, eds.

1998 The Criminology Theory Reader. New York: New York University Press.

Henry, Stuart and Mark M. Lanier

1998 "The prism of crime: Arguments for an integrated definition of crime," Justice Quarterly 15:609–627.

Herrnstein, Richard J.

1961 "Relative and absolute strength of response as a function of frequency of reinforcement," Journal of the Experimental Analysis of Behavior 4:267–272.

Herrnstein, Richard J. and Charles Murray

1994 The Bell Curve: Intelligence and Class Structure in American Life. New York: Free Press.

Hersen, Michel and Johan Rosqviist, eds.

2005 Encyclopedia of Behavior Modification and Cognitive Behavior Therapy. Volume 1 Adult Clinical Applications. Volume 2 Child Clinical Applications. Thousands Oaks, CA: Sage.

Hewitt, John P. and Randall Stokes

1975 "Disclaimers," American Sociological Review 40:1–11.

Hickman, Matthew and Alex Piquero

2001 "Exploring the relationships between gender, control balance, and deviance," Deviant Behavior 22:323–352.

Hill, Gary D. and Maxine P. Atkinson

1988 "Gender, familial control, and delinquency," Criminology 26:127–149.

Hill, Karl G., James C. Howell, J. David Hawkins, and Sara R. Battin-Pearson

1999 "Childhood risk factors for adolescent gang membership: Results from the Seattle Social Development Project," Journal of Research in Crime and Delinquency 36:300–322.

Hills, Stuart L.

1971 Crime, Power, and Morality: The Criminal Law Process in the United States. Scranton, PA: Chandler Publishing.

Hindelang, Michael J.

1970 "The commitment of delinquents to their misdeeds: Do delinquents drift?" Social Problems 17:502–509.

1973 "Causes of delinquency: A partial replication and extension," Social Problems 20:471–487.

Hindelang, Michael J., Travis Hirschi, and Joseph C. Weis

1979 "Correlates of delinquency: The illusion of discrepancy between self report and official measures," American Sociological Review 44:995–1014.

1980 Measuring Delinquency. Beverly Hills, CA: Sage.

Hirschi, Travis

1969 Causes of Delinquency. Berkeley, CA: University of California Press.

1973 "Procedural rules and the study of deviant behavior," Social Problems 21:159–173.

1979 "Separate and unequal is better," Journal of Research in Crime and Delinquency 16:34–38.

1989 "Exploring alternatives to integrated theory," pp. 37–49 in Steven F. Messner, Marvin D. Krohn, and Allen E. Liska (eds.), Theoretical Integration in the Study of Deviance and Crime. Albany: State University of New York Press.

2004 "Self-control and Crime," pp. 537–552 in Roy F. Baumeister and Kathleen D. Vohs (eds.), Handbook of Self-Regulation: Research, Theory, and Applications. New York: Guilford.

Hirschi, Travis and Michael Gottfredson

1983 "Age and the explanation of crime," American Journal of Sociology 89:552–584.

1993 "Commentary: Testing the general theory of crime," Journal of Research in Crime and Delinquency 30:47–54.

2006 "Social control and self-control theory," pp. 111–128 in Stuart Henry and Mark M. Lanier (eds.), The Essential Criminology Reader. Boulder, CO: Westview.

Hirschi, Travis and Michael Gottfredson, eds.

1994 The Generality of Deviance. New Brunswick, NJ: Transaction.

Hirschi, Travis and Michael J. Hindelang

1977 "Intelligence and delinquency: A revisionist review," American Sociological Review 42:571–587.

Hirschi, Travis and Rodney Stark

1969 "Hellfire and delinquency," Social Problems 17:202–213.

Hoffman, John P. and Felicia Gray Cerbone

1999 "Stressful life events and delinquency escalation in early adolescence," Criminology 37:343–374.

Hoffman, John P. and Alan S. Miller

1998 "A latent variable analysis of general strain theory," Journal of Quantitative Criminology 14:83–110.

Hoffman, John P. and S. Susan Su

1997 "The conditional effects of stress on delinquency and drug use: A strain theory assessment of sex differences," Journal of Research in Crime and Delinquency 34:46–78.

Hoffman, Kristi L., K. Jill Kiecolt, and John N. Edwards

2005 "Physical violence between siblings," Journal of Family Issues 26:1103–1130.

Holden, Gwen and Robert A. Kapler

1995 "Deinstitutionalizing status offenders: A record of progress," Juvenile Justice 2:3–10.

Holland-Davis, Lisa

2006 Putting Behavior in Context: A Test of the Social Structure Social Learning Model. Ph. D. Dissertation. Gainesville, FL: University of Florida.

Hollinger, Richard C.

1991 "Neutralizing in the workplace: An empirical analysis of property theft and production deviance," Deviant Behavior 12:169–202.

Hollinger, Richard and Lonn Lanza-Kaduce

1988 "The process of criminalization: The case of computer crime law," Criminology 26:101–126.

Holzman, Harold R.

1979 "Learning disabilities and juvenile delinquency: Biological and sociological theories," pp. 77–86 in C. R. Jeffery (ed.), Biology and Crime. Beverly Hills, CA: Sage.

Hood-Williams, John

2001 "Gender, masculinities, and crime: From structures to psyches," Theoretical Criminology 5:37–60.

Hooton, Earnest A.

1939 Crime and the Man. Cambridge, MA: Harvard University Press.

Horney, Julie

2006 "An alternative psychology of criminal behavior: The American Society of Criminology presidential address," Criminology 44: 1–16

Horowitz, Ruth and Anne E. Pottieger

1991 "Gender bias in juvenile justice handling of seriously crime involved youths," Journal of Research in Crime and Delinquency 28:75–100.

Huang, Bu, Rick Kosterman, Richard F. Catalano, J. David Hawkins, and Robert D. Abbott

2001 "Modeling mediation in the etiology of violent behavior in adolescence: A test of the social development model," Criminology 39:75–108.

Huff, C. Ronald, ed.

1990 Gangs in America. Newbury Park, CA: Sage.

Hunnicutt, Gwen and Lisa M. Broidy

2004 "Liberation and economic marginalization: A reformulation and test of (formerly?) competing models," Journal of Research in Crime and Delinquency 41:130–155.

Hutchings, Barry and Sarnoff A. Mednick

1977a "A review of studies of criminality among twins," pp. 45–88 in Sarnoff A. Mednick and Karl O. Christensen (eds.), Biosocial Bases of Criminal Behavior. New York: Gardner.

1977b "A preliminary study of criminality among twins," pp. 89–108 in Sarnoff A. Mednick and Karl O. Christensen (eds.), Biosocial Bases of Criminal Behavior. New York: Gardner.

1977c "Criminality in adoptees and their adoptive and biological parents: A pilot study," pp. 127–142 in Sarnoff A. Mednick and Karl O. Christensen (eds.), Biosocial Bases of Criminal Behavior. New York: Gardner.

Hwang, Sunghyun and Ronald L. Akers

2003 "Substance use by Korean adolescents: A cross-cultural test of social learning, social bonding, and self-control theories," pp. 39–64 in Ronald L. Akers and Gary F. Jensen (eds.), Social Learning Theory and the Explanation of Crime: A Guide for the New Century. Advances in Criminological Theory. Volume 11. New Brunswick, NJ: Transaction.

2006 "Parental and peer influences on adolescent drug use in Korea," Asian Journal of Criminology 1:59–69.

Iervolino, Alessandra, Alison Pike, Beth Manke, David Reiss, E. Mavis Hetherington, and Robert Plomin

2002 "Genetic and environmental influences in adolescent peer socialization: Evidence from two genetically sensitive designs," Child Development 73:162–174.

Inciardi, James, ed.

1980 Radical Criminology: The Coming Crises. Beverly Hills: Sage.

Inciardi, James A., Ruth Horowitz, and Anne E. Pottiger

1993 Street Kids, Street Drugs, Street Crime: An Examination of Drug Use and Serious Delinquency in Miami. Belmont, CA: Wadsworth.

InnerChange Freedom Initiative 2003 [Online]. Available at http://www.ifiprison.org/

Ireland, Timothy and Cathy Spatz Widom

1994 "Childhood victimization and risk for alcohol and drug arrests," International Journal of the Addictions 29:235–274.

Jacobs, David and Jason T. Carmichael

2001 "The politics of punishment across time and space: A pooled time-series analysis of imprisonment rates," Social Forces 80:61–89.

Jacobs, David and Ronald E. Helms

1996 "Toward a political model of incarceration: A time-series examination of multiple explanations for prison admission rates," American Journal of Sociology 102:323–357.

2001 "Toward a political sociology of punishment: Politics and changes in the incarcerated population," Social Science Research 30:171–194.

Jang, Sung Joon

2002 "The effects of family, school, peers, and attitudes on adolescents' drug use: Do they vary with age," Justice Quarterly 19:97–126.

Jang, Sung Joon and Byron R. Johnson

2001 "Neighborhood disorder, individual religiosity, and adolescent use of illicit drugs: A test of multilevel hypotheses," Criminology 39:109–144.

Jarjoura, G. Roger and Josine Junger-Tas

1993 "Does dropping out of school enhance delinquent involvement? Results from a large scale national probability sample," Criminology 2:149–171.

Jefferson, Tony

1996 "Introduction to Masculinities, Social Relations, and Crime," Special issue of the British Journal of Criminology 36:337–347.

Jeffery, C. Ray

1965 "Criminal behavior and learning theory," Journal of Criminal Law, Criminology, and Police Science 56:294–300.

1977 Crime Prevention Through Environmental Design. Second Edition. Beverly Hills, CA: Sage.

1980 "Sociobiology and criminology: The long lean years of the unthinkable and the unmentionable," pp. 115-124 in Edward Sagarin (ed.), Taboos in Criminology. Beverly Hills, CA: Sage.

Jeffery, C. Ray, ed.

1979 Biology and Crime. Beverly Hills, CA: Sage.

Jensen, Gary F.

1969 "'Crime doesn't pay': Correlates of a shared misunderstanding," Social Problems 17:189–201.

2003 "Gender variation in delinquency: Self-images, beliefs, and peers as mediating mechanisms," pp. 15–178 in Ronald L. Akers and Gary F. Jensen (eds.), Social Learning Theory and the Explanation of Crime: A Guide for the New Century. Advances in Criminological Theory. Volume 11. New Brunswick, NJ: Transaction.

Jensen, Gary F., ed.

1980 Sociology of Delinquency: Current Issues. Beverly Hills, CA: Sage.

Jensen, Gary F. and Ronald L. Akers

2003 "Taking social learning global: Micro-macro transitions in criminological theory," pp. 9–38 in Ronald L. Akers and Gary F. Jensen (eds.), Social Learning Theory and the Explanation of Crime: A Guide for the New Century. Advances in Criminological Theory. Volume 11. New Brunswick, NJ: Transaction.

Jensen, Gary F. and David Brownfield

1983 "Parents and drugs," Criminology 21:543–554.

1986 "Gender, lifestyle, and victimization: Beyond routine activity," Violence and Victims 2:85–99.

Jensen, Gary F., Maynard L. Erickson, and Jack P. Gibbs

1978 "Perceived risk of punishment and self reported delinquency," Social Forces 57:57–78.

Jensen, Gary F. and Dean G. Rojek

1998 Delinquency and Youth Crime. Third Edition. Prospect Heights, IL: Waveland.

Jensen, Gary F. and Ken Thompson

1990 "What's class go to do with it? A further examination of power control theory," American Journal of Sociology 95:1009–1023.

Jessor, Richard

1996 "Risk behavior in adolesence: A psychosocial framework for understanding and action," pp. 138–143 in Joseph G. Weis, Robert D. Crutchfield, and George S. Bridges (eds.), Juvenile Delinquency. Volume 2. Crime and Society. Thousand Oaks, CA: Pine Forge Press.

Johnson, Byron R.

2004 "Religious programs and recidivism among former inmates in prison fellowship programs: A long-term follow-up study," Justice Quarterly 21: 329–354.

Johnson, Byron R., David B. Larson, and Timothy C. Pitts

1997 "Religious programs, institutional adjustment, and recidivism among former inmates in prison fellowship programs," Justice Quarterly 14:145–166.

Johnson, Byron R., De Li Spencer, David B. Larson, and Michael McCullough

2000 "A systematic review of the religiosity and delinquency literature," Journal of Contemporary Criminal Justice 16:32–52.

Jones, Marshall and Donald R. Jones

2000 "The contagious nature of antisocial behavior," Criminology 38:25–46.

Jones, Shayne and Neil Quisenberry

2004 "The general theory of crime: How general is it?" Deviant Behavior 25:401–426.

Junger-Tas, Josine

1992 "An empirical test of social control theory," Journal of Quantitative Criminology 8:9–28.

Kandel, Denise B.

1978 "Homophily, selection, and socialization in adolescent friendships," American Journal of Sociology 84:427–436.

1996 "The parental and peer contexts of adolescent deviance: An algebra of interpersonal influences," Journal of Drug Issues 26:289–316.

Kandel, Denise and Israel Adler

1982 "Socialization into marijuana use among French adolescents: A cross cultural comparison with the United States," Journal of Health and Social Behavior 23:295–309.

Kandel, Denise and Mark Davies

1991 "Friendship networks, intimacy, and illicit drug use in young adulthood: A comparison of two competing theories," Criminology 29:441–469.

Kaplan, Howard B.

1975 Self Attitudes and Deviant Behavior. Pacific Palisades, CA: Goodyear.

1995 "Drugs, crime, and other deviant adaptations," pp. 3–46 in Howard B. Kaplan (ed.), Drugs, Crime, and Other Deviant Adaptations. New York: Plenum.

1996 "Empirical validation of the applicability of an integrative theory of deviant behavior to the study of drug use," Journal of Drug Issues 26:345–377.

Kaplan, Howard B., Richard J. Johnson, and C. A. Barley

1987 "Deviant peers and deviant behavior: Further elaboration of a model," Social Psychology Quarterly 50:277–284.

Kaplan, Howard B., Steven S. Martin, Robert J. Johnson, and Cynthia A. Robbins

1986 "Escalation of marijuana use: Application of a general theory of deviant behavior," Journal of Health and Social Behavior 27:44–61.

Kaplan, Howard B., Steven S. Martin, and Cynthia A. Robbins

1982 "Application of a general theory of deviant behavior: Self derogation and adolescent drug use," Journal of Health and Social Behavior 23:274–294.

Karp, David R. and Lynne Walther

2001 "Community reparative boards in Vermont: Theory and practice," pp. 199–217 in Gordon Bazemore and Mara Schiff (eds.), Restorative Community Justice: Repairing Harm and Transforming Communities. Cincinnati, OH: Anderson.

Keane, Carl, Paul S. Maxim, and James T. Teevan

1993 "Drinking and driving, self control, and gender: Testing a general theory of crime," Journal of Research in Crime and Delinquency 30:30–46.

Kelley, Barbara Tatem, Rolf Loeber, Kate Keenan, and Mary DeLamatre

1998 "Developmental pathways in boys' disruptive and delinquent behavior," Juvenile Justice Bulletin, Washington, DC: Office of Juvenile Justice and Delinquency Prevention.

Kempf, Kimberly and Roy L. Austin

1986 "Older and more recent evidence on racial discrimination in sentencing," Journal of Quantitative Criminology 2:29–48.

Kennedy, David

1998 "Pulling levers: Getting deterrence right," National Institute of Justice Journal (July):2–8.

Kennedy, Leslie W. and David R. Forde

1990 "Routine activities and crime: An analysis of victimization in Canada," Criminology 28:137–152.

Kent, Stephanie L. and David Jacobs

2005 "Minority threat and police strength from 1980 to 2000: A fixed-effects analysis of nonlinear and interactive effects in large U.S. cities," Criminology 43:731–760.

Kitsuse, John I.

1964 "Societal reaction to deviant behavior: Problems of theory and method," pp. 87–102 in Howard S. Becker (ed.), The Other Side. New York: Free Press.

Kleck, Gary

1981 "Racial discrimination in criminal sentencing: A critical evaluation of the evidence with additional evidence on the death penalty," American Sociological Review Washington DC 46:783–805.

Kleck, Gary and Ted Chiricos

2002 "Unemployment and property crime: A target-specific assessment of opportunity and motivation as mediating factors," Criminology 40:649–680.

Klepper, Steven and Daniel Nagin

1989 "The deterrent effect of perceived certainty and severity of punishment revisited," Criminology 27:721–746.

Klinger, David A.

1996 "More on demeanor and arrest in Dade County," Criminology 34:61–82.

Klockars, Carl

1979 "The contemporary crisis of Marxist criminology," Criminology 16:477–515.

Kobrin, Solomon

1959 "The Chicago Area Project—25 year assessment," Annals of the American Academy of Political and Social Science 322:19–29.

Koons-Witt, Barbara A.

2002 "The effect of gender on the decision to incarcerate before and after the introduction of sentencing guidelines," Criminology 40:297–328.

Kornhauser, Ruth Rosner

1978 Social Sources of Delinquency. Chicago: University of Chicago Press.

Krohn, Marvin D.

1986 "The web of conformity: A network approach to the explanation of delinquent behavior," Social Problems 33:S81–S93.

1999 "Social learning theory," Theoretical Criminology 3:462–476.

Krohn, Marvin D., Ronald L. Akers, Marcia J. Radosevich, and Lonn Lanza-Kaduce

1982 "Norm qualities and adolescent drinking and drug behavior," Journal of Drug Issues 12:343–359.

Krohn, Marvin D., Alan J. Lizotte, Terence P. Thornberry, Carolyn Smith, and David McDowall

1996 "Reciprocal causal relationships among drug use, peers, and beliefs: A five wave panel model," Journal of Drug Issues 26:405–428.

Krohn, Marvin D., Lonn Lanza-Kaduce, and Ronald L. Akers

1984 "Community context and theories of deviant behavior: An examination of social learning and social bonding theories," Sociological Quarterly 25:353–371.

Krohn, Marvin D. and James L. Massey

1980 "Social control and delinquent behavior: An examination of the elements of the social bond," Sociological Quarterly 21:529–543.

Krohn, Marvin D., William F. Skinner, James L. Massey, and Ronald L. Akers

1985 "Social learning theory and adolescent cigarette smoking: A longitudinal study," Social Problem 32:455–473.

Lab, Steven P.

1997 "Reconciling Hirschi's 1969 control theory with the general theory of crime," pp. 31–40 in Steven Lab (ed.), Crime Prevention at a Crossroads. Cincinnati, OH: Anderson.

LaFree, Gary D.

1980 "The effect of sexual stratification by race on official reactions to rape," American Sociological Review 45:842–854.

LaFree, Gary, Kriss A. Drass, and Patrick O'Day

1992 "Race and crime in post war America: Determinants of African American and White rates, 1957–1988," Criminology 30:157–188.

LaGrange, Teresa C. and Robert A. Silverman

1999 "Low self control and opportunity: Testing the general theory of crime as an explanation for gender differences in delinquency," Criminology 37:41–72.

Land, Kenneth C., Patricia L. McCall, and Lawrence E. Cohen
1990 "Structural covariates of homicide rates: Are there any invariances across time and social space?" American Journal of Sociology 95:922–963.

Lander, Bernard
1954 Towards an Understanding of Juvenile Delinquency. New York: Columbia University Press.

Langan, Patrick A. and David P. Farrington
1998 Crime and Justice in the United States and in England and Wales, 1981–1996: Executive Summary. Washington, DC: Bureau of Justice Statistics, U.S. Department of Justice.

Lanier, Mark H. and Stuart Henry
1998 Essential Criminology. Boulder, CO: Westwood Press.

Lansford, Jennifer E., Shari Miller-Johnson, Lisa J. Berlin, Kenneth A. Dodge, John E. Bates, and Gregory S. Pettit
2007 "Early physical abuse and later violent delinquency: A prospective longitudinal study," Child Maltreatment 12:233–245.

Lanza-Kaduce, Lonn
1988 "Perceptual deterrence and drinking and driving among college students," Criminology 26:321–341.

Lanza-Kaduce, Lonn, Ronald L. Akers, Marvin D. Krohn, and Marcia Radosevich
1984 "Cessation of alcohol and drug use among adolescents: A social learning model," Deviant Behavior 5:79–96.

Lanza-Kaduce, Lonn and Michael Capece
2003 "A specific test of an integrated general theory," pp. 179–196 in Ronald L. Akers and Gary F. Jensen (eds.), Social Learning Theory and the Explanation of Crime: A Guide for the New Century. Advances in Criminological Theory. Volume 11. New Brunswick, NJ: Transaction.

Lanza-Kaduce, Lonn and Richard Greenleaf
1994 "Police citizen encounters: Turk on norm resistance," Justice Quarterly 11: 605–623.

Lanza-Kaduce, Lonn, Marvin D. Krohn, Ronald L. Akers, and Marcia Radosevich
1979 "Law and Durkheimian order," pp. 41–61 in Paul J. Brantingham and Jack M. Kress (eds.), Structure, Law, and Power: Essays in the Sociology of Law. Beverly Hills, CA: Sage.

Lasley, James R.
1988 "Toward a control theory of white collar offending," Journal of Quantitative Criminology 4:347–359.

Laub, John H.
2006 "Edwin H. Sutherland and the Michael-Adler Report: Searching for the soul of criminology seventy years later," Criminology 44:235-258.

Laub, John H. and Robert J. Sampson
1993 "Turning points in the life course: Why change matters to the study of crime," Criminology 31:301–326.
2003 Shared Beginnings, Divergent Lives: Delinquent Boys to Age 70. Cambridge, MA: Harvard University Press.

Laub, John H., Robert J. Sampson, and Gary A. Sweeten

2006 "Assessing Sampson and Laub's life-course theory of crime," pp. 313–333 in Francis T. Cullen, John Paul Wright, and Kristie R. Blevins (eds.), Taking Stock: The Status of Criminology Theory. Advances in Criminological Theory. Volume 15. New Brunswick, NJ: Transaction.

Lauer, Ronald M., Ronald L. Akers, James Massey, and William Clarke

1982 "The evaluation of cigarette smoking among adolescents: The Muscatine study," Preventive Medicine 11:417–428.

Lauritsen, Janet L.

1993 "Sibling resemblance in juvenile delinquency: Findings from the national youth survey," Criminology 31:387–410.

Lee, Gang, Ronald L. Akers, and Marian Borg

2004 "Social learning and structural factors in adolescent substance use," Western Criminology Review 5:17–34 [Online]. Available at http://wcr.sonoma.edu/v5n/lee.htm

Lemert, Edwin M.

1951 Social Pathology. New York: McGraw-Hill.
1967 Human Deviance, Social Problems, and Social Control. Englewood Cliffs, NJ: Prentice Hall.
1974 "Beyond Mead: The societal reaction to deviance," Social Problems 21:457–468.
1981 "Diversion in juvenile justice," Journal of Research in Crime and Delinquency 18:34–46.

Leonard, Eileen B.

1982 Women, Crime, and Society: A Critique of Theoretical Criminology. New York: Longman.

Levin, Steven

2006 "The case of the critics who missed the point: A reply to Webster et al.," Criminology and Public Policy 5:449–460.

Levrant, Sharon, Francis T. Cullen, Betsy Fulton, and John F. Wozniak

1999 "Reconsidering restorative justice: The corruption of benevolence revisited?" Crime and Delinquency 45:3–27.

Lieber, Michael J. and Mary Ellen Ellyson Wacker

1997 "A theoretical and empirical assessment of power-control theory and single-mother families," Youth and Society 28:317–350.

Lilly, J. Robert, Francis T. Cullen, and Richard A. Ball

2007 Criminological Theory: Context and Consequences. Fourth Edition. Thousand Oaks, CA: Sage.

Linden, Eric and James Hackler

1973 "Affective ties and delinquency," Pacific Sociological Review 16:27–46.

Lindner, Robert

1944 Rebel Without a Cause. New York: Grove.

Link, Bruce, G., Francis T. Cullen, Elmer Struening, Patrick E. Shrout, and Bruce P. Dohrenwend

1989 "A modified labeling theory approach to mental disorders: An empirical assessment," American Sociological Review 54:400–423.

Lipsey, M. W., and N. A. Landenberger

2005 "Cognitive-behavioral interventions," pp. 57–71 in B.C. Welsh and D. P. Farrington (eds.), Preventing Crime: What works for Children, Offenders, Victims, and Places. Dordrecht, The Netherlands: Springer.

Lipset, Seymour M.

1960 Political Man: The Social Bases of Politics. Garden City, NY: Doubleday.

Liska, Allen E.

1969 "Uses and misuses of tautologies in social psychology," Sociometry 33:444–457.

1971 "Aspirations, expectations, and delinquency: Stress and additive models," Sociological Quarterly 12:99–107.

1987 Perspectives on Deviance. Englewood Cliffs, NJ: Prentice Hall.

Liska, Allen E., ed.

1992 Social Threat and Social Control. Albany: State University of New York Press.

Liska, Allen E. and Mitchell Chamlin

1984 "Social structure and crime control among macro-social units," American Journal of Sociology 90:383–395.

Liska, Allen E., Marvin D. Krohn, and Steven F. Messner

1989 "Strategies and requisites for theoretical integration in the study of crime and deviance," pp. 1–20 in Steven F. Messner, Marvin D. Krohn, and Allen E. Liska (eds.), Theoretical Integration in the Study of Deviance and Crime. Albany: State University of New York Press.

Liska, Allen E. and Steven F. Messner

1999 Perspectives on Crime and Deviance. Third Edition. Upper Saddle River, NJ: Prentice Hall.

Liska, Allen E. and Mark Tausig

1979 "Theoretical interpretation of social class and racial differentials in legal decision making for juveniles," Sociological Quarterly 20:197–207.

Liu, Ruth Xiaoru

2003 "The moderating effects of internal and perceived external sanction threats on the relationship between deviant peer associations and criminal offending," Western Criminology Review 4:191–202

Liu, Xiaoru and Howard B. Kaplan

1999 "Explaining the gender difference in adolescent delinquent behavior: A longitudinal test of mediating mechanisms," Criminology 37:195–215.

Loeber, Rolf

1996 "Developmental continuity, change, and pathways in male juvenile problem behaviors and delinquency," pp. 1–27 in J. David Hawkins (ed.), Delinquency and Crime: Current Theories. New York: Cambridge University Press.

Loeber, Rolf and Thomas J. Dishion

1987 "Antisocial and delinquent youths: Methods for their early identification," pp. 75–89 in J. D. Burchard and Sara Burchard (eds.), Prevention of Delinquent Behavior. Newbury Park, CA: Sage.

Loeber, Rolf, David P. Farrington, M. Stouthamer Loeber, Terri Moffitt, and A. Caspi

1998 "The development of male offending: Key findings from the first decade of the Pittsburgh Youth Study," Studies in Crime and Crime Prevention 7:141–172.

Loeber, Rolf and M. LeBlanc

1990 "Toward a developmental criminology," pp. 375–475 in Michael Tonry and Norvel Morris (eds.), Crime and Justice: A Review of Research. Volume 12. Chicago: University of Chicago Press.

Loeber, Rolf and Magda Stouthamer-Loeber

1986 "Family factors as correlates and predictors of juvenile conduct problems and delinquency," pp. 29–149 in Michael Tonry and Norval Morris (eds.), Crime and Justice. Volume 7. Chicago: University of Chicago Press.

Loeber, Rolf, Magda Stouthamer-Loeber, Welmoet Van Kammen, and David P. Farrington

1991 "Initiation, escalation, and desistance in juvenile offending and their correlates," Journal of Criminal Law and Criminology 82:36–82.

Longshore, Douglas

1998 "Self control and criminal opportunity: A prospective test of the general theory of crime," Social Problems 45:102–113.

Longshore, Douglas, Susan Turner, and Judith A. Stein

1996 "Self control in a criminal sample: An examination of construct validity," Criminology 34:209–228.

Lombroso, Cesare

1876 The Criminal Man (L'uomo Delinquente). First Edition. Milan: Hoepli. Second Edition (1878) through Fifth Edition (1896). Turin: Bocca.

Lombroso, Cesare and William Ferrero

1897/1958 The Female Offender. New York: Philosophical Library.
1912 Crime: Its Causes and Remedies. Patterson Smith Reprint, 1968. Montclair, NJ: Patterson Smith.

Longshore, D. E., E. Chung, S. C. Hsieh, and N. Messi

2004 "Self-control and social bonds: A combined control perspective on deviance," Crime and Delinquency 50:542–564.

Lopez, Jose Manuel Otero, Lourdes Miron Redondo, and Angeles Luengo Martin

1989 "Influence of family and peer group on the use of drugs by adolescents," The International Journal of the Addictions 24:1065–1082.

Losel, Friedrich

2007 "It's never too early and never too late: Toward an integrated science of developmental intervention in criminology," The Criminologists 32 (5): 3–8.

Lowman, John

1992 "Rediscovering crime," pp. 141–160 in Jock Young and Roger Matthews (eds.), Rethinking Criminology: The Realist Debate. London: Sage.

Lundman, Richard J.

1993 Prevention and Control of Juvenile Delinquency. Second Edition. New York: Oxford University Press.

Lyman, Stanford M. and Marvin B. Scott

1970 A Sociology of the Absurd. New York: Appleton-Century-Crofts.

Lynch, James P. and William J. Sabol

1997 Did Getting Tough on Crime Pay? Washington, DC: The Urban Institute.

Lynch, Michael J. and W. Byron Groves

1986 A Primer in Radical Criminology. New York: Harrow and Heston.

Lynch, Michael J., Michael Hogan, and Paul Stretesky

1999 "A further look at long cycles and criminal justice legislation," Justice Quarterly 16:431–450.

Lynch, Michael J. and Raymond J. Michalowski

2006 The New Primer in Radical Criminology: Critical Perspectives on Crime, Power, and Identity. Fourth edition. Monsey, NY: Criminal Justice Press.

Lynch, Michael J., Herman Schwendinger, and Julia Schwendinger

2006 "The status of empirical research in radical criminology," pp. 191–215 in Francis T. Cullen, John Paul Wright, and Kristie R. Blevins (eds.), Taking Stock: The Status of Criminological Theory. Advances in Criminological Theory. Volume 15. New Brunswick, NJ: Transaction.

MacArthur Foundation

2006 "Assessing juvenile psychopathy: Development and legal implications," Issue Brief 4 of the Philadelphia: Temple University, MacArthur Foundation Research Network on Adolescent Development and Juvenile Justice.

MacKenzie, Doris Layton and Alex Piquero

1994 "The impact of shock incarceration programs on prison crowding," Crime and Delinquency 40:222–249.

MacKenzie, Doris L. and Claire Souryal

1994 Multisite Evaluation of Shock Incarceration. Washington, DC: U.S. Department of Justice, National Institute of Justice.

McCarthy, Bill and John Hagan

1987 "Gender, delinquency, and the Great Depression: A test of power-control theory," Canadian Review of Sociology and Anthropology 24:153–177.

McCarthy, Bill, John Hagan, and Todd Woodward

1999 "In the company of women: Structure and agency in a revised power-control theory of gender and delinquency," Criminology 37:761–788.

McCord, Joan

1978 "A thirty year follow up of treatment effects," American Psychologist 33:284–289.

1991a "Family relationships, juvenile delinquency, and adult criminality," Criminology 29:397–418.

1991b "The cycle of crime and socialization practices," Journal of Criminal Law and Criminology 82:211–228.

2003 "Cures that harm: Unanticipated outcomes of crime prevention programs," Annals of the American Academy of Political and Social Science, 587:16–30.

McCord, William and Joan McCord

1956 The Psychopath: An Essay on the Criminal Mind. Princeton, NJ: Van Nostrand.

1959 Origins of Crime: A New Evaluation of the Cambridge Sommerville Youth Study. New York: Columbia University.

McGarrell, Edmund F.

1993 "Institutional theory and the stability of a conflict model of the incarceration rate," Justice Quarterly 10:7–28.

McGarrell, Edmund F. and Thomas C. Castellano

1991 "An integrative conflict model of the criminal law formation process," Journal of Research in Crime and Delinquency 28:174–196.

McGee, Zina T.

1992 "Social class differences in parental and peer influence on adolescent drug use," Deviant Behavior 13:349–372.

McIntosh, W. Alex, Starla D. Fitch, J. Branton Wilson, and Kenneth L. Nyberg

1981 "The effect of mainstream religious social controls an adolescent drug use in rural areas," Review of Religious Research 23:54–75.

McGloin, Jean Marie

2005 "Policy and intervention considerations of a network analysis of street gangs," Criminology and Public Policy 4:607–636.

McGloin, Jean Marie, Travis C. Pratt, and Jeff Maahs

2004 "Rethinking the IQ-Delinquency Relationship: A Longitudinal Analysis of Multiple Theoretical Models," Justice Quarterly 21:603–631.

Mack, KristenY. and Michael J. Leiber

2005 "Race, gender, single-mother households, and delinquency: A further test of power-control theory," Youth & Society 37:115–144.

Mahoney, Ann Rankin

1974 "The effect of labeling upon youths in the juvenile justice system: A review of the evidence," Law and Society Review 8:583–614.

Makkai, Toni and John Braithwaite

1994 "Reintegrative shaming and compliance with regulatory standards," Criminology 32:361–386.

Mann, Coramae Richey

1984 Female Crime and Delinquency. Tuscaloosa: University of Alabama Press.

Marcos, Anastasios, C., Stephen J. Bahr, and Richard E. Johnson

1986 "Testing of a bonding/association theory of adolescent drug use," Social Forces 65:135–161.

Marcus, Bernd

2003 "An Empirical Examination of the Construct Validity of Two Alternative Self-Control Measures," Educational and Psychological Measurement 63:674–706.

Maruna, Shadd and Heith Copes

2005 "What have we learned from five decades of neutralization research?" pp. 221–320 in Michael Tonry (ed.), Crime and Justice: A Review of Research. Volume 32. Chicago: University of Chicago Press.

Massey, James, Marvin Krohn and Lisa Bonati

1989 "Property crime and the routine activities of individuals," Journal of Research in Crime and Delinquency 26:378–400.

Matsueda, Ross L.

1992 "Reflected appraisals, parental labeling, and delinquency: Specifying a symbolic interactionist theory," American Journal of Sociology 97:1577–1611.

Matsueda, Ross L. and Kathleen Anderson

1998 "The dynamics of delinquent peers and delinquent behavior," Criminology 36:269–308.

Matsueda, Ross L. and Karen Heimer

1987 "Race, family structure, and delinquency: A test of differential association and social control theories," American Sociological Review 52:826–840.

Matsueda, Ross L., Derek A. Kreager, and David Huizinga

2006 "Deterring delinquents: a rational choice model of theft and violence," American Sociological Review 71:95–122.

Matthews, Roger

1987 "Taking realist criminology seriously," Contemporary Crises 11:371–401.

Matthews, Roger and Jock Young

1992 "Reflections on realism," pp. 1–24 in Jock Young and Roger Matthews (eds.), Rethinking Criminology: The Realist Debate. London: Sage.

Matza, David

1964 Delinquency and Drift. New York: Wiley.

Matza, David and Gresham M. Sykes

1961 "Juvenile delinquency and subterranean values," American Sociological Review 26:712–719.

Mazerolle, Paul

1998 "Gender, general strain, and delinquency: An empirical examination," Justice Quarterly 15: 65–91.

Mazerolle, Paul, Velmer Burton, Francis Cullen, T. David Evans, and Gary Payne

2000 "Strain, anger, and delinquent adaptations: Specifying general strain theory," Journal of Criminal Justice 28:89–101.

Mazerolle, Paul and Jeff Maahs

2000 "General strain and delinquency: An alternative examination of conditioning influences," Justice Quarterly 2000 17:753–778.

Mazerolle, Paul and Alex Piquero

1998 "Linking exposure to strain with anger: An investigation of deviant adaptations," Journal of Criminal Justice 26:195–211.

Mead, George Herbert

1934 Mind, Self, and Society. Chicago: University of Chicago Press.

Meadows, Sarah O.

2007 "Evidence of parallel pathways: Gender similarity in the impact of social support on adolescent depression and delinquency," Social Forces 85:1143–1168.

Mears, Daniel P., Matthew Ploeger, and Mark Warr

1998 "Explaining the gender gap in delinquency: Peer influence and moral evaluations of behavior," Journal of Research in Crime and Delinquency 35:251–266.

Mednick, Sarnoff A.

1977 "A biosocial theory of the learning of law abiding behavior," pp. 1–8 in Sarnoff A. Mednick and Karl O. Christensen (eds.), Biosocial Bases of Criminal Behavior. New York: Gardner.

1987 "Biological factors in crime causation: The reactions of social scientists," pp. 1–6 in Sarnoff Mednick, Terrie E. Moffitt, and Susan A. Stack (eds.), The Causes of Crime: New Biological Approaches. Cambridge, England: Cambridge University Press.

Mednick, Sarnoff and Karl O. Christiansen, eds.

1977 Biosocial Bases of Criminal Behavior. New York: Gardner.

Mednick, Sarnoff, William Gabrielli and Barry Hutchings

1984 "Genetic influences in criminal convictions: Evidence from an adoption cohort," Science 224:891–894.

Mednick, Sarnoff A., Terrie E. Moffitt, and Susan A. Stack, eds.

1987 The Causes of Crime: New Biological Approaches. Cambridge, England: Cambridge University Press.

Mednick, Sarnoff and Giora Shoham, eds.

1979 New Paths in Criminology. Lexington, MA: Lexington.

Mednick, Sarnoff, Jan Volavka, William F. Gabrielli, and Turan M. Itil

1981 "EEG as a predictor of antisocial behavior," Criminology 19:219–229.

Meier, Robert F.

1977 "The new criminology: Continuity in criminological theory," Journal of Criminal Law and Criminology 67:461–469.

Meier, Robert F. and Weldon T. Johnson

1977 "Deterrence as social control: The legal and extralegal production of conformity," American Sociological Review 42:292–304.

Melossi, Dario

2003 "A new edition of Punishment and Social Structure thirty-five years later: A timely event," Social Justice 30:248–263.

Menard, Scott and Delbert S. Elliott

1990 "Longitudinal and cross sectional data collection and analysis in the study of crime and delinquency," Justice Quarterly 7:11–55.

1994 "Delinquent bonding, moral beliefs, and illegal behavior: A three wave panel model," Justice Quarterly 11:173–188.

Merton, Robert K.

1938 "Social structure and anomie," American Sociological Review 3:672–682.

1957 Social Theory and Social Structure. Glencoe, IL: Free Press.

Messerschmidt, James W.

1986 Capitalism, Patriarchy, and Crime: Toward a Socialist Feminist Criminology. Totowa, NJ: Rowman & Littlefield.

1993 Masculinities and Crime: Critique and Reconceptualization of Theory. Lanham, MD: Rowman & Littlefield.

1997 Crime as Structured Action: Gender, Race, Class, and Crime in the Making. Thousand Oaks, CA: Sage.

Messner, Steven F.

1988 "Merton's 'Social structure and anomie': The road not taken," Deviant Behavior 9:33–53.

Messner, Steven and Marvin Krohn

1990 "Class compliance structures and delinquency: Assessing integrated structural Marxist theory," American Journal of Sociology 96:300–328.

Messner, Steven F., Marvin D. Krohn, and Allen E. Liska, eds.

1989 Theoretical Integration in the Study of Deviance and Crime. Albany: State University of New York Press.

Messner, Steven F. and Richard Rosenfeld

1994 Crime and the American Dream. Belmont, CA: Wadsworth.

1997 "Political restraint of the market and levels of criminal homicide: A cross-national application of institutional-anomie theory," Social Forces 75:1393–1416.

2001a Crime and the American Dream. Third Edition. Belmont, CA: Wadsworth.

2001b "An institutional-anomie theory of crime," pp. 151–160 in Raymond Paternoster and Ronet Bachman (eds.), Explaining Criminals and Crime. Los Angeles: Roxbury.

2006 "The present and future of institutional-anomie theory," pp. 127–148 in Francis T. Cullen, John Paul Wright, and Kristie R. Blevins (eds.), Taking Stock: The Status of Criminological Theory. Advances in Criminological Theory. Volume 15. New Brunswick, NJ: Transaction.

2007 Crime and the American Dream. Fourth Edition. Belmont, CA: Thomson Wadsworth.

Messner, Steven F. and Kenneth Tardiff

1985 "The social ecology of urban homicide: An application of the 'routine activities' approach," Criminology 23:241–268.

Michalowski, Raymond J.

1985 Order, Law, and Crime. New York: Random House.

Michalowski, Raymond J. and Susan M. Carlson

1999 "Unemployment, imprisonment, and social structures of accumulation: Historical contingency in the Rusche-Kirchheimer hypothesis," Criminology 37:217–250.

Miethe, Terance D.

1982 "Public consensus on crime seriousness: Normative structure or methodological artifact?" Criminology 20:515–526.

Miethe, Terance D., Mark C. Stafford and J. Scott Long

1987 "Social differentiation in criminal victimization: A test of routine activities life-style theories," American Sociological Review 52:184–194.

Mihalic, Sharon Wofford and Delbert Elliott

1997 "A social learning theory model of marital violence," Journal of Family Violence 12:21–36.

Miller, Eleanor M.

1986 Street Woman. Philadelphia: Temple University Press.

Miller, Jody and Christopher W. Mullins

2006 "The status of feminist theories in criminology," pp. 217–249 in Francis T. Cullen, John Paul Wright, and Kristie R. Blevins (eds.), Taking Stock: The Status of Criminological Theory. Advances in Criminological Theory. Volume 15. New Brunswick, NJ: Transaction.

Miller, Neal E. and John Dollard

1941 Social Learning and Imitation. New Haven, CT: Yale University Press.

Miller, Susan L. and Lee Ann Iovanni

1994 "Determinants of perceived risk of formal sanction for courtship violence," Justice Quarterly 11:281–312.

Miller, Walter B.

1958a "Lower class culture as a generating milieu of gang delinquency," Journal of Social Issues 14:5–19.

1958b "Inter institutional conflict as a major impediment to delinquency prevention," Human Organization 17:20–23.

1962 "The impact of a 'total community' delinquency control project," Social Problems 10:168–191.

Milovanovic, Dragan

2002 Critical Criminology at the Edge. Westport, CT: Praeger.

Milovanovic, Dragan and Katheryn K. Russell

2001 Petit Apartheid in the U.S. Criminal Justice System. Durham, NC: Carolina Academic.

Minor, W. William

1975 "Political crime, political justice, and political prisoners," Criminology 12:385–398.

1977 "A deterrence control theory of crime," pp. 117–137 in Robert F. Meier (ed.), Theory in Criminology. Beverly Hills, CA: Sage.

1981 "Techniques of neutralization: A reconceptualization and empirical examination," Journal of Research in Crime and Delinquency 18:295–318.

Mitchell, Ojmarrh

2005 "A meta-analysis of race and sentencing research: Explaining the inconsistencies," Journal of Quantitative Criminology 21:439–466.

Moffitt, Terrie E.

1993 "Adolescence limited and life course persistent antisocial behavioral: A developmental taxonomy," Psychological Review 100:674–701.

2006 "A review of research on the taxonomy of life-course persistent versus adolescence-limited antisocial behavior," pp. 277–312 in Francis T. Cullen, John Paul Wright, and Kristie R. Blevins (eds.), Taking Stock: The Status of Criminological Theory. Advances in Criminological Theory. Volume 15. New Brunswick, NJ: Transaction.

Moffitt, Terrie E., Avshalom Caspi, Michael Rutter, and Phil A. Silva

2001 Sex Differences in Antisocial Behaviour: Conduct Disorder, Delinquency, and Violence in the Dunedin Longitudinal Study. Cambridge, England: Cambridge University Press.

Moffitt, Terrie E., Donald R. Lyman, and Phil A. Silva

1994 "Neuropsychological tests predicting persistent male delinquency," Criminology 32:277–300.

Monachesi, Elio

1972 "Cesare Beccaria, 1738–1794," pp. 36–50 in Hermann Mannheim (ed.), Pioneers in Criminology. Second Edition Enlarged. Montclair, NJ: Patterson Smith.

Moore, Joan W.

1999 "Gang members' families," pp. 159–176 in Meda Chesney-Lind and John M. Hagedorn (eds.), Female Gangs in America: Essays on Girls, Gangs, and Gender. Chicago: Lakeview.

Morash, Merry

1999 "A consideration of gender in relation to social learning and social structure: A general theory of crime and deviance," Theoretical Criminology 3:451–461.

Morash, Merry and Meda Chesney-Lind

1991 "A reformulation and partial test of the power-control theory of delinquency," Justice Quarterly 8:347–378.

Morris, Allison

1987 Women, Crime, and Criminal Justice. New York: Basil Blackwell.

Morris, Edward K. and Curtis J. Braukmann, eds.

1987 Behavioral Approaches to Crime and Delinquency: A Handbook of Application, Research, and Concepts. New York: Plenum.

Morselli, Carlo, Pierre Tremblay, and Bill McCarthy

2006 "Mentors and criminal achievement," Criminology 44:17–43.

Moyer, Kenneth

1979 "What is the potential for biological violence control?" pp. 19–46 in C. R. Jeffrey (ed.), Biology and Crime. Newbury Park, CA: Sage.

Murray, Charles A.

1976 The Link Between Learning Disabilities and Juvenile Delinquency. Washington, DC: U.S. Government Printing Office.

Mustaine, Elizabeth Ehrhardt and Richard Tewksbury

1998 "Predicting risks of larceny theft victimization: A routine activity analysis using refined lifestyle measures," Criminology 36:829–858.

Nadelman, Ethan A.

1989 "Drug prohibition in the United States: Costs, consequences, and alternatives," Science 245:921, 939–947.

Naffine, Ngaire

1987 Female Crime: The Construction of Women in Criminology. Boston: Allen & Unwin.
1995 Gender, Crime and Feminism. Aldershot, England: Dartmouth.

Nagin, Daniel S. and David P. Farrington

1992a "The stability of criminal potential from childhood to adulthood," Criminology 30:235–260.
1992b "The onset and persistence of offending," Criminology 30:501–523.

Nagin, Daniel S. and Raymond Paternoster

1991a "On the relationship of past to future participation in delinquency," Criminology 29:163–189.
1991b "Preventive effects of the perceived risk of arrest: Testing an expanded conception of deterrence," Criminology 29:561–585.
1993 "Enduring individual differences and rational choice theories of crime," Law and Society Review 27:201–230.
1994 "Personal capital and social control: The deterrence implications of a theory of individual differences in criminal offending," Criminology 32:581–606.

Nagin, Daniel S. and Greg Pogarsky

2001 "Integrating celerity, impulsivity, and extralegal sanction threats into a model of general deterrence: Theory and evidence," Criminology 39:865–892.

Nagin, Daniel S. and Richard E. Tremblay

2005 "Developmental trajectory groups: Fact or a useful statistical fiction?" Criminology 43:873–904.

Neff, Joan L. and Dennis E. Waite

2007 "Male versus female substance abuse patterns among incarcerated juvenile offenders: Comparing strain and social learning variables," Justice Quarterly 24:106–132.

Nettler, Gwyn

1984 Explaining Crime. Third Edition. New York: McGraw-Hill.

Newman, Graeme, Ronald V. Clarke, and S. Giora Shoham, eds.

1997 Rational Choice and Situational Crime Prevention: Theoretical Foundations. Aldershot, England: Ashgate Dartmouth.

Newman, Oscar

1972 Defensible Space: Crime Prevention Through Urban Design. New York: Macmillan.

Nye, F. Ivan

1958 Family Relationships and Delinquent Behavior. New York: Wiley.

Ogle, Robbin S., Daniel Maier Kaktin, and Thomas J. Bernard

1995 "A theory of homicidal behavior among women," Criminology 33:173–194.

Opp, Karl Dieter

1997 "'Limited rationality' and crime," pp. 47–63 in Graeme Newman, Ronald V. Clarke, and S. Giora Shoham (eds.), Rational Choice and Situational Crime Prevention: Theoretical Foundations. Aldershot, England: Ashgate Dartmouth.

Osgood, Wayne D. and Amy L. Anderson

2004 "Unstructured socializing and rates of delinquency," Criminology 42:519–549.

Owen, Barbara

1998 In the Mix: Struggle and Survival in a Women's Prison. Albany: State University of New York Press.

Pagani, Linda, Richard E. Tremblay, Frank Vitaro, and Sophie Parent

1998 "Does preschool help prevent delinquency in boys with a history of perinatal complications?" Criminology 36:245–267.

Pallone, Nathaniel J. and James J. Hennessy

1992 Criminal Behavior: A Process Psychology Analysis. New Brunswick, NJ: Transaction.

Palmer, Ted B.

1971 "California's community treatment program for delinquent adolescents," Journal of Research in Crime and Delinquency 8:74–92.

Park, Robert E.K., Ernest W. Burgess, and Roderick D. McKenzie

1928 The City. Chicago: University of Chicago Press.

Paternoster, Raymond

1984 "Prosecutorial discretion in requesting the death penalty: A case of victim-based racial discrimination," Law and Society Review 18:437–478.

1985 "Assessments of risk and behavioral experience: An explanatory study of change," Criminology 23:417–436.

1989a "Decisions to participate in and desist from four types of common delinquency: Deterrence and the rational choice perspective," Law and Society Review 23:7–40.

1989b "Absolute and restrictive deterrence in a panel of youth: Explaining the onset, persistence/desistance, and frequency of delinquent offending," Social Problems 36:289–309.

Paternoster, Raymond and Robert Brame

1997 "Multiple routes to delinquency? A test of developmental and general theories of crime," Criminology 35:49–84.

1998 "The structural similarity of processes of a generation of criminal and analogous behaviors," Criminology 36:633–669.

Paternoster, Raymond and Lee Ann Iovanni

1989 "The labeling perspective and delinquency: An elaboration of the theory and an assessment of the evidence," Justice Quarterly 6:379–394.

Paternoster, Raymond and Paul Mazerolle

1994 "General strain theory and delinquency: A replication and extension," Journal of Research in Crime and Delinquency 31:235–263.

Paternoster, Raymond, Linda E. Saltzman, Gordon P. Waldo, and Theodore G. Chiricos

1983 "Perceived risk and social control: Do sanctions really deter?" Law and Society Review 17:457–480.

Patterson, Gerald R.

1975 Families: Applications of Social Learning to Family Life. Champaign, IL: Research Press.

1982 A Social Learning Approach. Volume 3. Eugene, OR: Castalia.

1995 "Coercion as a basis for early age of onset for arrest," pp. 81–105 in Joan McCord (ed.), Coercion and Punishment in Long term Perspectives. Cambridge, England: Cambridge University Press.

2002 "A brief history of the Oregon Model," pp. 3–24 in John B. Reid, Gerald R. Patterson, and James Snyder (eds.), Antisocial Behavior in Children and Adolescents: A Developmental Analysis and Model for Intervention. Washington, DC: American Psychological Association.

Patterson, Gerald R., D. Capaldi, and L. Bank

1991 "The development and treatment of childhood aggression," pp. 139–168 in D. Pepler and R. K. Rubin (eds.), The Development and Treatment of Childhood Aggression. Hillsdale, IL: Lawrence Erlbaum Associates, Inc.

Patterson, Gerald R. and Patricia Chamberlain

1994 "A functional analysis of resistance during parent training therapy," Clinical Psychology: Science and Practice 1:53–70.

Patterson, Gerald R., B. D. Debaryshe, and E. Ramsey

1989 "A developmental perspective on antisocial behavior," American Psychologist 44:329–335.

Patterson, Gerald R., John B. Reid, and Thomas J. Dishion

1992 Antisocial Boys. Eugene, OR: Castalia.

Patterson, Gerald R., J. B. Reid, R. Q. Jones, and R. E. Conger

1975 A Social Learning Approach to Family Intervention. Volume 1. Eugene, OR: Castalia.

Pearson, Frank S., Douglas S. Lipton, Charles M. Cleland, and Dorline S. Yee

2002 "The effects of behavioral/cognitive-behavioral programs on recidivism," Crime and Delinquency 48:476–496.

Pearson, Frank S. and Neil Alan Weiner

1985 "Toward an integration of criminological theories," Journal of Criminal Law and Criminology 76:116–150.

Pease, Kenneth, Judith Ireson, and Jennifer Thorpe

1975 "Modified crime indices for eight countries," Journal of Criminal Law and Criminology 66:209–214.

Pepinsky, Harold E.

1991 "Peacemaking criminology and criminal justice," pp. 299–327 in Harold E. Pepinsky and Richard Quinney (eds.), Criminology as Peacemaking. Bloomington: Indiana University Press.

Pepinsky, Harold E. and Richard Quinney, eds.

1991 Criminology as Peacemaking. Bloomington: Indiana University Press.

Peters, Michael, David Thomas and Christopher Zamberian

1997 Boot Camps for Juvenile Offenders: Program Summary. Washington, DC: U.S. Department of Justice, Office of Juvenile Justice and Delinquency Prevention.

Petersilia, Joan

1983 Racial Disparities in the Criminal Justice System. Santa Monica, CA: Rand Corporation.

Petersilia, Joan and Susan Turner

1987 "Guideline based justice: The implications for racial minorities," pp. 151–182 in Don Gottfredson and Michael Tonry (eds.), Prediction and Classification in Criminal Justice Decision Making. Chicago: University of Chicago Press.

Petrosino, Anthony, Caroly-Turpin Petrosino, and John Buehler

2006 "Scared straight and other juvenile awareness programs," pp. 87–101 in Brandon C. Welsh and David P. Farrington, eds., Preventing Crime: What Works for Children, Offenders, Victims, and Places. Dordrecht, The Netherlands: Springer.

Piliavin, Irving, Graig Thornton, Rosemary Gartner, and Ross L. Matsueda

1986 "Crime, deterrence, and rational choice," American Sociological Review 51:101–119.

Piquero, Alex R. and Jeff A. Bouffard

2007 "Something old, something new: A preliminary investigation of Hirschi's redefined self-control," Justice Quarterly 24:1–27.

Piquero, Alex R., Robert Brame, Paul Mazerolle, and Rudy Haapanen

2002 "Crime in emerging adulthood," Criminology 40:137–170.

Piquero, Alex and Matthew Hickman.

1999 "An empirical test of Tittle's control balance theory," Criminology 37:319–342.

Piquero, Alex and Paul Mazerolle

2001 Life-Course Criminology: Contemporary and Classic Readings. Belmont, CA: Wadsworth/Thomson Learning.

Piquero, Alex R. and Terrie E. Moffitt

2005 "Explaining the facts of crime: How the developmental taxonomy replies to Farrington's invitation," pp. 51–72 in David P. Farrington (ed.), Integrated Developmental & Life Course Theories of Offending. Advances in Criminological Theory. Volume 14. New Brunswick, NJ: Transaction.

Piquero, Alex, Raymond Paternoster, Paul Mazerolle, Robert Brame, and Charles W. Dean

1999 "Onset and offense specialization," Journal of Research in Crime and Deliquency, 36:275–299.

Piquero, Nicole Leeper and Alex R. Piquero

2006 "Control balance and exploitative corporate crime," Criminology 44:397–430.

Piquero, Alex R. and Greg Pogarsky

2002 "Beyond Stafford and Warr's reconceptualization of deterrence: Personal and vicarious experiences, impulsivity, and offending behavior," Journal of Research in Crime and Delinquency 39:153–186.

Piquero, Alex and George F. Rengert

1999 "Studying deterrence with active residential burglars," Justice Quarterly 16:451–471.

Piquero, Nicole Leeper, Angela R. Gover, John M. MacDonald, and Alex R. Piquero

2005 "The influence of delinquent peers on delinquency: Does gender matter?" Youth & Society 36:251–275.

Piquero, Nicole Leeper and Miriam D. Sealock

2000 "Generalizing general strain theory: An examination of an offending population," Justice Quarterly 17: 449–484.

Platt, Anthony M.

1969 The Child Savers: The Invention of Delinquency. Chicago: University of Chicago Press.

1977 The Child Savers. Second Edition Enlarged. Chicago: University of Chicago Press.

Platt, Anthony and Paul Takagi, eds.

1981 Crime and Social Justice. Totowa, NJ: Barnes and Noble.

Polakowski, Michael

1994 "Linking self and social control with deviance: Illuminating the structure underlying a general theory of crime and its relations to deviant activity," Journal of Quantitative Criminology 10:41–78.

Pollak, Otto

1950 The Criminality of Women. Philadelphia: University of Pennsylvania Press.

Powers, Edwin and Helen Witmer

1951 An Experiment in the Prevention of Juvenile Delinquency: The Cambridge Somerville Youth Study. New York: Columbia University Press.

Pratt, Tavis C. and Francis T. Cullen

2000 "The empirical status of Gottfredson and Hirschi's General Theory of Crime: A meta-analysis," Criminology 38:931–964.

Pratt, Travis C., Francis T. Cullen, Kristie R. Blevins, Leah E. Daigle, and Tamara D. Madensen

2006 "The empirical status of deterrence theory: A meta-analysis," pp. 367–396 in Francis T. Cullen, John Paul Wright, and Kristie R. Blevins, eds. Taking Stock: The Status of Criminological Theory. Advances in Criminological Theory. Volume 15. New Brunswick, NJ: Transaction Publishers.

Preston, Pamela

2006 "Marijuana use as a coping response to psychological strain: racial, ethnic, and gender differences among young adults," Deviant Behavior 27:397–422.

Quinney, Richard

1964 "Crime in political perspective," American Behavioral Scientist 8:19–22.
1970 The Social Reality of Crime. Boston: Little, Brown.
1974a Critique of the Legal Order. Boston: Little, Brown.
1979 "The production of criminology," Criminology 16:445–458.
1980 Class, State, and Crime. Second Edition. New York: Longman.
1991 "The way of peace: On crime, suffering, and service," pp. 3–13 in Harold E. Pepinsky and Richard Quinney (eds.), Criminology as Peacemaking. Bloomington: Indiana University Press.

Quinney, Richard, ed.

1969 Crime and Justice in Society. Boston: Little, Brown.
1974b Criminal Justice in America: A Critical Understanding. Boston: Little, Brown.

Radelet, Michael L.

1981 "Racial characteristics and the imposition of the death penalty," American Sociological Review 46:918–927.

Radelet, Michael and Ronald L. Akers

1996 "Deterrence and the death penalty: The views of the experts," Journal of Criminal Law and Criminology 87:1–16.

Radelet, Michael L. and Glenn L. Pierce

1991 "Choosing those who will die: Race and the death penalty in Florida," Florida Law Review 43:1–43.

Rafter, Nicole Hahn

1992 "Criminal anthropology in the United States," Criminology 30:525–545.
2004 "Earnest A. Hooton and the biological tradition in American criminology," Criminololgy 42:735–771.
2006 "Cesare Lombroso and the Origins of Criminology," pp. 33–42 in Stuart Henry and Mark M. Lanier (eds.), The Essential Criminology Reader. Boulder, CO: Westview.

Rankin, Joseph H. and Roger Kern

1994 "Parental attachments and delinquency," Criminology 32:495–516.

Reasons, Charles E. and Robert M. Rich

1978 The Sociology of Law: A Conflict Perspective. Toronto, Canada: Butterworth.

Rebellon, Cesar J.

2002 "Reconsidering the broken homes/delinquency relationship and exploring its mediating mechanism(s)," Criminology 40:103–136.

Reckless, Walter

1961 "A new theory of delinquency and crime," Federal Probation 25:42–46.
1967 The Crime Problem. New York: Appleton-Century-Crofts.

Reckless, Walter, Simon Dinitz, and Ellen Murray

1956 "Self concept as an insulator against delinquency," American Sociological Review 21:744–756.

Reid, John B. and J. Mark Eddy

2002 "Preventive efforts during the elementary school years: The Linking of the Interests of Families and Teachers (LIFT) project," pp. 219–233 in John B. Reid, Gerald R. Patterson, and James Snyder (eds.), Antisocial Behavior in Children and Adolescents: A Developmental Analysis and Model for Intervention. Washington, DC: American Psychological Association.

Reid, John B., Gerald R. Patterson, and James Snyder, eds.

2002 Antisocial Behavior in Children and Adolescents: A Developmental Analysis and Model for Intervention. Washington, DC: American Psychological Association.

Reiss, Albert J.

1951 "Delinquency as the failure of personal and social controls," American Sociological Review 16:196–207.

Reynolds, Morgan O.

1998 Does Punishment Deter? Policy Backgrounder No. 148. Washington, DC: National Center for Policy Analysis.

Richie, Beth E.

1996 Compelled to Crime: The Gender Entrapment of Battered Black Women. New York: Routledge.

Ritzer, George

1992 Sociological Theory. Third Edition. New York: McGraw-Hill.

Roby, Pamela A.

1969 "Politics and criminal law: Revision of the New York State penal law on prostitution," Social Problems 17:83–109.

Rodriguez, Nancy

2005 "Restorative justice, communities and delinquency: Whom do we reintegrate," Criminology and Public Policy 4:103–130

Rogers, Joseph W. and M. D. Buffalo

1974 "Fighting back: Nine modes of adaptation to a deviant label," Social Problems 22:101–118.

Rojek, Dean G.

1982 "Juvenile diversion: A study of community cooptation," pp. 316–322 in Dean G. Rojek and Gary F. Jensen (eds.), Readings in Juvenile Delinquency. Lexington, MA: D.C. Heath.
1967 The Power Structure. New York: Oxford University Press.

Rose, Dina R. and Todd R. Clear

1998 "Incarceration, social capital, and crime: Implications for social disorganization theory," Criminology 36:441–479.

Ross, Edward Alsworth

1901 Social Control. New York: Macmillan.

Ross, Lawrence H.

1982 Deterring the Drinking Driver: Legal Policy and Social Control. Lexington, MA: Lexington Books.

Rossi, Peter H., Emily Waite, Christine E. Bose, and Richard Berk

1974 "The seriousness of crime: Normative structure and individual differences," American Sociological Review 39:224–237.

Rotter, Julian

1954 Social Learning and Clinical Psychology. Englewood Cliffs, NJ: Prenctice Hall.

Rowe, David C.

1985 "Sibling interaction and self reported delinquent behavior: A study of 265 twin pairs," Criminology 23:223–240.

1986 "Genetic and environmental components of antisocial behavior: A study of 265 twin pairs," Criminology 24:513–532.

2002 Biology and Crime. Los Angeles: Roxbury.

Rowe, David and David P. Farrington

1997 "The familial transmission of criminal convictions," Criminology 35:177–201.

Rowe, David C. and Bill L. Gulley

1992 "Sibling effects on substance use and delinquency," Criminology 30:217–234.

Rowe, David C. and D. Wayne Osgood

1984 "Heredity and sociological theories of delinquency: A reconsideration," American Sociological Review 49:526–540.

Ruddell, Rick and Martin G. Urbina

2004 "Minority threat and punishment: A cross-national analysis," Justice Quarterly 21:903–931.

Rusche, Georg

1933/1978 "Labor market and penal sanction: Thoughts on the sociology of criminal justice." Translated by G. Dinwiddie. Crime and Social Justice 10:2–8.

Rusche, Georg and Otto Kirchheimer

2003 Punishment and Social Structure. Piscataway, NJ: Transaction.

Rushton, J. P.

1996 "Self-report delinquency and violence in adult twins," Psychiatric Genetics 87–89

Sampson, Robert J.

1995 "The community," pp. 193–216 in James Q. Wilson and Joan Petersilia (eds.), Crime. San Francisco: ICS Press.

1999 "Techniques of research neutralization," Theoretical Criminology 3:438–450.

2006 "Collective efficacy theory: Lessons learned and directions for future inquiry," pp. 149–167 in Francis T. Cullen, John Paul Wright, and Kristie R. Blevins (eds.), Taking Stock: The Status of Criminological Theory. Advances in Criminological Theory. Volume 15. New Brunswick, NJ: Transaction.

Sampson, Robert J. and W. Byron Groves

1989 "Community structure and crime: Testing social disorganization theory," American Journal of Sociology 94:774–802.

Sampson, Robert J. and John H. Laub

1993 Crime in the Making: Pathways and Turning Points Through Life. Cambridge, MA: Harvard University Press.

1997 "A life course theory of cumulative disadvantage and the stability of delinquency," pp. 133–161 in Terence P. Thornberry (ed.), Advances in Criminological Theory. Volume 7: Developmental Theories of Crime and Delinquency. New Brunswick, NJ: Transaction.

2003 "Life-course desisters? Trajectories of crime among delinquent boys followed to age 70," Criminology 41:555–592.

2005 "A general age-graded theory of crime: Lessons learned and the future of life-course criminology," pp. 165–182 in David P. Farrington (ed.), Integrated Developmental & Life Course Theories of Offending. Advances in Criminological Theory. Volume 14. New Brunswick, NJ: Transaction

Sandstrom, Kent L., Daniel D. Martin, and Gary Alan Fine

2003 Symbols, Selves, and Social Reality: A Symbolic Interactionist Approach to Social Psychology and Sociology. Los Angeles: Roxbury.

Savolainen, Jukka

2000 "Inequality, welfare state, and homicide: Further support for the institutional anomie theory," Criminology 38:983–1020.

Scarpitti, Frank, Ellen Murray, Simon Dinitz, and Walter Reckless

1960 "The good boy in a high delinquency area: Four years later," American Sociological Review 23:555–558.

Scheider, Matthew C

2001 "Deterrence and the base rate fallacy: An application of expectancy theory," Justice Quarterly 18:63–86.

Schiff, Mara F

1998 "Restorative justice interventions for juvenile offenders: A research agenda for the next decade," Western Criminological Review 1(1). [Online]. Available at http://scr.sonoma.edu./v1n1/schiff.html

Schlossman, Steven and Michael Sedlak

1983 "The Chicago Area Project revisited," Crime and Delinquency 29:398–462.

Schlossman, Steven and Richard Shavelson with Michael Sedlak and Jane Cobb

1984 Delinquency Prevention in South Chicago: A Fifty Year Assessment of the Chicago Area. Santa Monica, CA: Rand Corporation.

Schrag, Clarence

1962 "Delinquency and opportunity: Analysis of a theory," Sociology and Social Research 46:168–175.

Schreiber, Flora Rheta

1984 The Shoemaker: The Anatomy of a Psychotic. New York: New American Library.

Schuessler, Karl and Donald R. Cressey

1950 "Personality characteristics of criminals," American Journal of Sociology 55:476–484.

Schur, Edwin M.

1965 Crimes Without Victims. Englewood Cliffs, NJ: Prentice Hall.

1971 Labeling Deviant Behavior. New York: Harper & Row.

1973 Radical Non Intervention: Rethinking the Delinquency Problem. Englewood Cliffs, NJ: Prentice Hall.

1979 Interpreting Deviance. New York: Harper & Row.

1984 Labeling Women Deviant: Gender, Stigma, and Social Control. New York: Random House.

Schwartz, Martin D. and David O. Friedrichs

1994 "Postmodern thought and criminological discontent: New metaphors for understanding violence," Criminology 32:221–246.

Schwartz, Richard D.

1986 "Law and normative order," pp. 63–108 in Leon Lipson and Stanton Wheeler (eds.), Law and the Social Sciences. New York: Russell Sage Foundation.

Schwendinger, Julia R. and Herman Schwendinger

1976 "Marginal youth and social policy," Social Problems 24:84–91.
1983 Rape and Inequality. Beverly Hills, CA: Sage.
1985 Adolescent Subcultures and Delinquency. New York: Praeger.

Sellers, Christine S.

1999 "Self control and intimate violence: An examination of the scope and specification of the general theory of crime," Criminology 37:375–404.

Sellers, Christine S. and Ronald L. Akers

2006 "Social learning theory: Correcting misconceptions," pp. 89–99 in Stuart Henry and Mark M. Lanier (eds.), The Essential Criminology Reader. Boulder, CO: Westview.

Sellers, Christine S. and Thomas L. Winfree

1990 "Differential associations and definitions: A panel study of youthful drinking behavior," International Journal of the Addictions 25:755–771.

Sellers, Christine S., John K. Cochran, and L. Thomas Winfree, Jr.

2003 "Social learning theory and courtship violence: An empirical test," pp. 109–129 in Ronald L. Akers and Gary F. Jensen (eds.), Social Learning Theory and the Explanation of Crime: A Guide for the New Century. Advances in Criminological Theory. Volume 11. New Brunswick, NJ: Transaction.

Sellin, Thorsten

1938 Culture Conflict and Crime. New York: Social Science Research Council.
1959 The Death Penalty. Philadelphia: American Law Institute.

Shah, Saleem A. and Loren H. Roth

1974 "Biological and psychophysiological factors in criminality," pp. 101–174 in Daniel Glaser (ed.), Handbook of Criminology. Chicago: Rand McNally.

Shannon, Lyle

1982 Assessing the Relationship of Adult Criminal Careers to Juvenile Careers. National Institute of Juvenile Justice and Delinquency Prevention. Washington, DC: U.S. Government Printing Office.

Sharp, Elaine B.

2006 "Policing urban america: A new look at the politics of agency size," Social Science Quarterly 87:291–307.

Sharp, Susan F.

2006 "It's not just men anymore: The criminal justice system and women in the 21st century," The Criminologist 31 (March/April):1–5.

Shaw, Clifford and Henry D. McKay

1942 Juvenile Delinquency and Urban Areas. Chicago: University of Chicago Press.
1969 Juvenile Delinquency and Urban Areas. Revised Edition. Chicago: University of Chicago Press.

Shelley, Louise

1980 "The geography of Soviet criminality," American Sociological Review 45:111–122.

Sherman, Lawrence W., Patrick R. Gartin, and Michael D. Buerger

1989 "Hot spots of predatory crime: Routine activities and the criminology of place," Criminology 27:27–56.

Sherman, Lawrence W., Denise C. Gottfredson, Doris L. MacKenzie, John Eck, Peter Retuer, and Shawn D. Bushway

1998 Preventing Crime: What Works, What Doesn't, What's Promising. Research in Brief. Washington, DC: National Institute of Justice.

Shoemaker, Donald J.

2004 Theories of Delinquency: An Examination of Explanations of Delinquent Behavior. Fifth Edition. New York: Oxford University Press.

Shoham, S. Giora and Mark Seis

1993 A Primer in the Psychology of Crime. New York: Harrow and Heston.

Short, James F.

1975 "The natural history of an applied theory: Differential opportunity and mobilization for youth," pp. 193–210 in Nicholas J. Demerath, Otto Larsen, and Karl Schuessler (eds.), Social Policy and Sociology. New York: Academic.

Short, James F. and Fred L. Strodtbeck

1965 Group Process and Gang Delinquency. Chicago: University of Chicago Press.

Shover, Neal and Andy Hochstetler

2005. Choosing White Collar Crime: Doing Deals and Making Mistakes. New York: Cambridge University Press.Silver, Eric.

2000 "Extending social disorganization theory: A multilevel approach to the study of violence among persons with mental illness," Criminology 38:1021–1042.

Simcha-Fagan, Ora and Joseph E. Schwartz

1986 "Neighborhood and delinquency: An assessment of contextual effects," Criminology 24:667–704.

Simmel, Georg

1950 The Sociology of Georg Simmel. Translation and Introduction by Kurt H. Wolff. Glencoe, IL: Free Press.

Simon, Rita

1975 Women and Crime. Lexington, MA: Lexington.

Simon, Rita J. and Heather Ahn-Redding

2005 The Crimes Women Commit. Third Edition. Lanham, MD: Lexington.

Simons, Ronald L., Christine Johnson, Rand D. Conger, and Glen Elder, Jr.

1998 "A test of latent trait versus life course perspectives on the stability of adolescent anti social behavior," Criminology 36:217–243.

Simons, Ronald L., C. Wu, Rand D. Conger, and F. O. Lorenz

1994 "Two routes to delinquency: Differences between early and late starters in the impact of parenting and deviant peers," Criminology 32:247–276.

Simons, Ronald L., Leslie Gordon Simons, and Lora Ebert Wallace

2004 Families, Delinquency, and Crime: Linking Society's Most Basic Institution to Antisocial Behavior. Los Angeles: Roxbury.

Simpson, Sally S.

1989 "Feminist theory, crime, and justice," Criminology 27:605–627.

1991 "Caste, class, and violent crime: Explaining differences in female offending," Criminology 29:115–135.

Simpson, Sally S. and Lori Elis

1994 "Is gender subordinate to class? An empirical assessment of Colvin and Pauly's structural Marxist theory of delinquency," Journal of Criminal Law and Criminology 85:453–480.

1995 "Doing gender: Sorting out the caste and crime conundrum," Criminology 33:47–82.

Singer, Simon I. and Murray Levine

1988 "Power control theory, gender, and delinquency: A partial replication with additional evidence on the effects of peers," Criminology 26:627–648.

Skinner, B. F.

1953 Science and Human Behavior. New York: Macmillan.

1959 Cumulative Record. New York: Appleton-Century-Crofts.

Skinner, William F. and A. M. Fream

1997 "A social learning theory analysis of computer crime among college students," Journal of Research in Crime and Delinquency 34:495–518.

Smart, Carol

1995 Law, Crime and Sexuality: Essays in Feminism. Thousand Oaks, CA: Sage.

Smith, Douglas A. and Raymond Paternoster

1990 "Formal processing and future delinquency: Deviance amplification as selection artifact," Law and Society Review 24:1109–1131.

Smith, Douglas A., Christy A. Visher, and G. Roger Jarjoura

1991 "Dimensions of delinquency: Exploring the correlates of participation, frequency, and persistence of delinquent behavior," Journal of Research in Crime and Delinquency 28:6–32.

Smith, Linda G. and Ronald L. Akers

1993 "A research note on racial disparity in sentencing to prison or community control." Unpublished paper, Department of Criminology, University of South Florida.

Smith, William R., Sharon Glave Frazee, and Elizabeth L. Davison

2000 "Furthering the integration of routine activity and social disorganization theories: Small units of analysis and the study of street robbery as a diffusion process," Criminology 38:489–524.

Snell, T. L. and D. C. Morton

1994 Women in Prison: Survey of State Prison Inmates, 1991. Washington, DC: U.S. Department of Justice.

Snyder, James

2002 "Reinforcement and Coercion Mechanisms in the Development of Antisocial Behavior: Peer Relationships," pp. 101–122 in John B. Reid, Gerald R. Patterson, and James Snyder (eds.), Antisocial Behavior in Children and Adolescents: A Developmental Analysis and Model for Intervention. Washington, DC: American Psychological Association.

Snyder, James J. and Gerald R. Patterson

1995 "Individual differences in social aggression: A test of a reinforcement model of socialization in the natural environment," Behavior Therapy 26:371–391.

Spear, Sherilyn and Ronald L. Akers

1988 "Social learning variables and the risk of habitual smoking among adolescents: The Muscatine Study," American Journal of Preventive Medicine 4:336–348.

Spergel, Irving

1964 Racketville, Slumtown, and Haulburg. Chicago: University of Chicago Press.

Spielberger, Charles, G. Jacobs, S. Russell, and R. S. Crane

1983 "Assessment of anger: The state-trait anger scale," pp. 161–189 in James Butcher and Charles Spielberger (eds.), Advances in Personality Assessment. Volume 2. Hillsdale, NJ: Lawrence Erlbaum Associates, Inc.

Spitzer, Steven

1975 "Toward a Marxian theory of deviance," Social Problems 22:638–651.

Spohn, Cassia

1994 "Crime and the social control of Blacks: Offender/victim race and the sentencing of violent offenders," pp. 249–268 in George S. Bridges and Martha A. Myers (eds.), Inequality, Crime, and Social Control. Boulder, CO: Westview.

2000 "Thirty years of sentencing reform: The quest for a racially neutral sentencing process," pp. 427–501 in Julie Horney (ed.), Policies, Processes, and Decisions of the Criminal Justice System: Criminal Justice 2000. Volume 3. Washington, DC: National Institute of Justice.

Spohn, Cassia, Susan Welch, and John Gruhl

1985 "Women defendants in court: The interaction between sex and race in convicting and sentencing," Social Science Quarterly 66:178–185.

Stafford, Mark and Mark Warr

1993 "A reconceptualization of general and specific deterrence," Journal of Research in Crime and Delinquency 30:123–135.

Stahura, John M. and John J. Sloan

1988 "Urban stratification of places, routine activities, and suburban crime rates," Social Forces 66:1102–1118.

Steffensmeier, Darrell J.

1980 "Sex differences in patterns of adult crime, 1965–77," Social Forces 58:1080–1109.

Steffensmeier, Darrell and Emilie Allan

1996 "Gender and crime: Toward a gendered theory of female offending," Annual Review of Sociology 22:459–487.

Steffensmeier, Darrell, Emilie Allan, and Cathy Streifel

1989 "Development and female crime: A cross national test of alternative explanations," Social Forces 68:262–283.

Steffensmeier, Darrell and Stephen Demuth

2000 "Ethnicity and sentencing outcomes in U.S. Federal Courts: Who is punished more harshly?" American Sociological Review 65:705–739.

2001 "Ethnicity and judges' sentencing decisions: Hispanic–Black–White comparisons," Criminology 39:145–178.

2006 "Does gender modify the effects of race-ethnicity on criminal sanctioning? Sentences for male and female, White, Black and Hispanic defendants," Journal of Quantitative Criminology 22:241–261.

Steffensmeier, Darrell, John Kramer, and Cathy Streifel

1993 "Gender and imprisonment decisions," Criminology 31:411–446.

Steffensmeier, Darrell and Cathy Streifel

1992 "Trends in female crime: 1960–1990," in Concetta Culliver (ed.), Female Criminality: The State of the Art. New York: Garland.

Steffensmeier, Darrell and Jeffery T. Ulmer

2005 Confessions of a Dying Thief: Understanding Criminal Careers and Criminal Enterprise. New Brunswick, NJ: Transaction Aldine.

Steffensmeier, Darrell, Jeffery Ulmer, and John Kramer

1998 "The interaction of race, gender, and age in criminal sentencing: The punishment cost of being young, Black, and male," Criminology 36:763–798.

Stewart, Eric A.

2003 "School, social bonds, school climate, and school misbehavior: A multilevel analysis," Justice Quarterly 20:575–604.

Stinchcombe, Arthur L.

1968 Constructing Social Theories. New York: Harcourt Brace and World.

Stitt, B. Grant and David J. Giacopassi

1992 "Trends in the connectivity of theory and research in criminology," The Criminologist 17:1, 3–6.

Stolzenberg, Lisa, Stewart J. D'Alessio, and David Eitle

2004 "A multilevel test of racial threat theory," Criminology 42:673–698.

Strodtbeck, Fred L. and James F. Short

1964 "Aleatory risks versus short run hedonism in explanation of gang action," Social Problems 12:127–140.

Stumphauzer, Jerome S.

1986 Helping Delinquents Change: A Treatment Manual of Social Learning Approaches. New York: Hayworth.

Stylianou, Stelios

2002 "The relationship between elements and manifestations of low self-control in a general theory of crime: two comments and a test," Deviant Behavior 23:531–557.

Sullivan, Christopher J., Jean Marie McGloin, Travis C. Pratt, and Alex R. Piquero

2006 "Rethinking the 'norm' of offender generality: Investigating specialization in the short-term," Criminology 44:199–233.

Sumner, William Graham

1906 Folkways. Boston: Ginn.

Sutherland, Edwin H.

1937 The Professional Thief. Chicago: University of Chicago Press.
1940 "White collar criminality," American Sociological Review 5:1–12.
1947 Principles of Criminology. Fourth Edition. Philadelphia: Lippincott.
1949 White Collar Crime. New York: Holt, Rinehart & Winston.
1973 On Analyzing Crime. Edited with an Introduction by Karl Schuessler. Chicago: University of Chicago Press.

Sutherland, Edwin H. and Donald R. Cressey

1960 Principles of Criminology. Sixth Edition. Chicago: Lippincott.
1978 Criminology. Tenth Edition. Philadelphia: Lippincott.

Sutherland, Edwin H., Donald R. Cressey, and David F. Luckenbill

1992 Principles of Criminology. Eleventh Edition. Dix Hills, NY: General Hall.

Sutton, John R.

2000 "Imprisonment and social classification in five common-law democracies, 1955–1985," American Journal of Sociology 106:350–386.

2004 "The political economy of imprisonment in affluent Western democracies, 1960–1990," American Sociological Review 69:170–189.

Sykes, Gresham and David Matza

1957 "Techniques of neutralization: A theory of delinquency," American Journal of Sociology 22:664–670.

Szymanski, Albert

1981 "Socialist societies and the capitalist system," Social Problems 28:521–526.

Tannenbaum, Frank

1938 Crime and the Community. Boston: Ginn.

Tarde, Gabriel

1912 Penal Philosophy. Translated by R. Howell. Boston: Little, Brown.

Taylor, Ian, Paul Walton, and Jock Young

1973 The New Criminology. New York: Harper & Row.

1975 "Marx and Engels on law, crime, and morality," pp. 203–230 in Paul Q. Hirst (ed.), Critical Criminology. London: Routledge & Kegan Paul.

Taylor, Lawrence

1984 Born to Crime: The Genetic Causes of Criminal Behavior. Westport, CT: Greenwood.

Taylor, Ralph B. and Adele V. Harrell

1996 Physical Environment and Crime. Washington, DC: U.S. Department of Justice, National Institute of Justice.

Thomas, Charles W. and Donna M. Bishop

1984 "The effects of formal and informal sanctions on delinquency: A longitudinal comparison of labeling and deterrence theories," Journal of Criminal Law and Criminology 75:1222–1245.

Thomas, Charles W., Robin J. Cage, and Samuel C. Foster

1976 "Public opinion on criminal law and legal sanctions: An examination of two conceptual models," Journal of Criminal Law and Criminology 67:110–116.

Thornberry, Terence P.

1987 "Towards an interactional theory of delinquency," Criminology 25:863–891.

1989 "Reflections on the advantages and disadvantages of theoretical integration," pp. 51–60 in Steven F. Messner, Marvin D. Krohn, and Allen E. Liska (eds.), Theoretical Integration in the Study of Deviance and Crime. Albany: State University of New York Press.

1996 "Empirical support for interactional theory: A review of the literature," pp. 198–235 in J. David Hawkins (ed.), Delinquency and Crime: Current Theories. New York: Cambridge University Press.

Thornberry, Terence P. and R. L. Christenson

1984 "Unemployment and criminal involvement," American Sociological Review 49:398–411.

Thornberry, Terence P. and Margaret Farnworth

1982 "Social correlates of criminal involvement," American Sociological Review 47:505–517.

Thornberry, Terence P., Melanie Moore, and R. L. Christenson

1985 "The effect of dropping out of high school on subsequent criminal behavior," Criminology 23:3–18. Thornberry, Terence P., Alan J. Lizotte, Marvin D. Krohn, Margaret Farnworth, and Sung Joon Jang

1991 "Testing interactional theory: An examination of reciprocal causal relationships among family, school, and delinquency," Journal of Criminal Law and Criminology 82:3–33.

1994 "Delinquent peers, beliefs, and delinquent behavior: A longitudinal test of interactional theory," Criminology 32:47–84.

Tibbetts, Stephen G. and Alex R. Piquero

1999 "The influence of gender, low birth weight, and disadvantaged environment in predicting early onset of offending: A test of Moffitt's interactional hypothesis," Criminology 37:843–878.

Tittle, Charles R.

1969 "Crime rates and legal sanctions," Social Problems 16:409–422.

1975 "Deterrents or labeling?" Social Forces 53:399–410.

1980 Sanctions and Social Deviance. New York: Praeger.

1995 Control Balance: Toward a General Theory of Deviance. Boulder, CO: Westview.

2004 "Refining control balance theory," Theoretical Criminology 8:395–428.

Tittle, Charles R. and Ekaterina V. Botchkovar

2005 "Self-control, criminal motivation and deterrence: An investigation using Russian respondents," Criminology 43:307–353.

Tittle, Charles R. and Debra Curran

1988 "Contingencies for dispositional disparities in juvenile justice," Social Forces 67:23–58.

Tittle, Charles R. and Robert F. Meier

1990 "Specifying the SES/delinquency relationship," Criminology 28:271–299.

Tittle, Charles R. and Raymond Paternoster

2000 Social Deviance and Crime: An Organizational and Theoretical Approach. Los Angeles: Roxbury.

Tittle, Charles R., David A. Ward, and Harold G. Grasmick

2003 "Self-control and crime/deviance: Cognitive vs. behavioral measures," Journal of Quantitative Criminology 19:333–365.

Tittle, Charles R. and Wayne J. Villemez

1977 "Social class and criminality," Social Forces 56:474–503.

Tittle, Charles R., Wayne J. Villemez, and Douglas A. Smith

1978 "The myth of social class and criminality: An empirical assessment of the empirical evidence," American Sociological Review 43:643–656.

Toby, Jackson

1957 "Social disorganization and stake in conformity: Complementary factors in the predatory behavior of hoodlums," Journal of Criminal Law, Criminology, and Police Science 48:12–17.

1964 "Is punishment necessary?" Journal of Criminal Law, Criminology, and Police Science 55:332–337.

Tobler, Nancy S.

1986 "Meta-analysis of 143 adolescent drug prevention programs: Quantitative outcome results of program participants compared to a control or comparison group," Journal of Drug Issues 16:537–567.

Tong, Rosemarie

1989 Feminist Thought. Boulder, CO: Westview.

Topalli, Volkan

2005 "When being good is bad: An expansion of neutralization theory," Criminology 43:797–835.

Trevino, A. Javier

1996 The Sociology of Law: Classical and Contemporary Perspectives. New York: St. Martin's Press.

Triplett, Ruth and Roger Jarjoura

1994 "Theoretical and empirical specification of a model of informal labeling," Journal of Quantitative Criminology 10:241–276.

Triplett, Ruth and Brian Payne

2004 "Problem solving as reinforcement in adolescent drug use: Implications for theory and policy," Journal of Criminal Justice 32:617–630.

Troyer, Ronald J. and Gerald F. Markle

1983 Cigarettes: The Battle Over Smoking. New Brunswick, NJ: Rutgers University Press.

Tunnell, Kenneth D.

1990 "Choosing crime: Close your eyes and take your chances," Justice Quarterly 7:673–690.

1992 Choosing Crime: The Criminal Calculus of Property Offenders. Chicago: Nelson Hall.

Turk, Austin T.

1964 "Prospects for theories of criminal behavior," Journal of Criminal Law, Criminology, and Police Science 55:454–461.

1966 "Conflict and criminality," American Sociological Review 31:338–352.

1969a Criminality and the Legal Order. Chicago: Rand McNally.

1969b "Introduction" to Willem A. Bonger, Criminality and Economic Conditions. Bloomington: Indiana University Press.

1976 "Law as a weapon in social conflict," Social Problems 23:276-291.

1977 "Class, conflict, and criminalization," Sociological Focus 10:209–220.

1979 "Analyzing official deviance: For non partisan conflict analyses in criminology," Criminology 16:459–476.

1995 "Transformation versus revolution and reformism: Policy implications of conflict theory," pp. 15–27 in Hugh Barlow (ed.), Crime and Public Policy: Putting Theory to Work. Boulder, CO: Westview.

Turner, M. G. and Alex R. Piquero

2002 "The stability of self-control," Journal of Criminal Justice 30:457–471.

Udry, J. Richard

1988 "Biological predisposition and social control in adolescent sexual behavior," American Sociological Review 53:709–722.

Uggen, Christopher

2000a "Class, gender, and arrest: An intergenerational analysis of workplace power and control," Criminology 38:835–862.

2000b "Work as a turning point in the life course of criminals: A duration model of age, employment, and recidivism," American Sociological Review 65:529–546.

van Bemmelen, J. M.

1972 "Willem Adrian Bonger," pp. 443–457 in Hermann Mannheim (ed.), Pioneers in Criminology. Second Edition Enlarged. Montclair, NJ: Patterson Smith.

Van Ness, Daniel and Karen Heetderks Strong
2006 Restoring Justice: An Introduction to Restorative Justice. Cincinnati, OH: Anderson.

Vazsonyi, Alexander, Lloyd E. Pickering, Marianne Junger, and Dick Hessing
2001 "An empirical test of general theory of crime: A four-nation comparative study of self-control and the prediction of deviance," Journal of Research in Crime and Delinquency 38:91–131.

Vega, William A. and Andres G. Gil
1998 Drug Use and Ethnicity in Early Adolescence. New York: Plenum.

Vold, George B.
1958 Theoretical Criminology. New York: Oxford University Press.

Vold, George B. and Thomas J. Bernard
1986 Theoretical Criminology. Third Edition. New York: Oxford University Press.

Vold, George B., Thomas J. Bernard, and Jeffrey B. Snipes
2002 Theoretical Criminology. Fifth Edition. New York: Oxford University Press.

Voss, Harwin L. and David M. Petersen, eds.
1971 Ecology, Crime, and Delinquency. New York: Appleton-Century-Crofts.

Waldo, Gordon P. and Theodore G. Chiricos
1972 "Perceived penal sanction and self reported criminality: A neglected approach to deterrence research," Social Problems 19:522–540.

Waldo, Gordon and Simon Dinitz
1967 "Personality attributes of the criminal: An analysis of research studies, 1950–1965," Journal of Research in Crime and Delinquency 4:185–202.

Walker, Samuel, Cassia Spohn, and Miriam DeLone
2007 The Color of Justice. Fourth Edition. Belmont, CA: Wadsworth.

Walklate, Sandra
1995 Gender and Crime: An Introduction. London: Prentice Hall.

Walsh, Anthony
2000 "Behavior genetics and anomie/strain theory," Criminology 38:1075–1108.
2002 Biosocial Criminology: Introduction and Integration. Cincinnati, OH: Anderson.

Walsh, Anthony and Lee Ellis
1999 "Political ideology and American criminologists' explanation for criminal behavior," The Criminologist 24(6):1, 14.

Walters, Glenn D.
1992 "A meta analysis of the gene crime relationship," Criminology 30:595–613.

Walters, Glenn D. and Thomas W. White
1989 "Heredity and crime: Bad genes or bad research," Criminology 27:455–486.

Wang, Shu-Neu and Gary F. Jensen
2003 "Explaining delinquency in Taiwan: A test of social learning theory," pp. 65–84 in Ronald L. Akers and Gary F. Jensen (eds.), Social Learning Theory and the Explanation of Crime: A Guide for the New Century. Advances in Criminological Theory. Volume 11. New Brunswick, NJ: Transaction.

Warner, Barbara D.
2007 "Directly intervene or call the authorities? A study of forms of neighborhood social control within a social disorganization framework," Criminology 45:99–128.

Warner, Barbara D. and Glenn L. Pierce

1993 "Reexamining social disorganization theory using calls to the police as a measure of crime," Criminology 31:493–518.

Warr, Mark

1993a "Parents, peers, and delinquency," Social Forces 72:247–264.

1993b "Age, peers, and delinquency," Criminology 31:17–40.

1996 "Organization and instigation in delinquent groups," Criminology 34:11–38.

1998 "Life course transitions and desistance from crime," Criminology 36:183–216.

2002 Companions in Crime: The Social Aspects of Criminal Conduct. Cambridge, England: Cambridge University Press.

2005 "Making delinquent friends: Adult supervision and children's affiliations," Criminology 43:77–106.

Warr, Mark and Mark Stafford

1991 "The influence of delinquent peers: What they think or what they do?" Criminology 4:851–866.

Warren, Marguerite A.

1970 "The Case for Differential Treatment of Delinquents," pp. 419–428 in Harwin L. Voss (ed.), Society, Delinquency, and Delinquent Behavior. Boston: Little, Brown.

Weber, Max

1921/1954 Max Weber on Law in Economy and Society. Edited by Max Rheinstein. Translated by Edward Shils and Max Rheinstein. Cambridge, MA: Harvard University Press.

Webster, Cheryl Marie, Anthony N. Doob, and Franklin E. Zimring

2006 "Proposition 8 and crime rates in California: The case of the disappearing deterrent," Criminology & Public Policy 5:417–448

Weeks, H. Ashley

1958 Youthful Offenders at Highfields. Ann Arbor: University of Michigan Press.

Weerman, Frank M. and Wilma H. Smeenk

2005 "Peer similarity in delinquency for different types of friends: A comparison using two measurement methods," Criminology 43:499–523.

Weis, Joseph G. and J. David Hawkins

1981 "Preventing delinquency: The social development model," Preventing Delinquency. Washington, DC: U.S. Government Printing Office.

Weisburd, David

1997 Reorienting Crime Prevention Research and Policy: From the Causes of Criminality to the Context of Crime. National Insitute of Justice Research Report, U.S. Department of Justice. Washington, DC: U.S. Government Printing Office.

Weisburd, David, Elin Waring, and Ellen Chayet

1995 "Specific deterrence in a sample of offenders convicted of white collar crimes," Criminology 587–607.

Weisner, Margit, Deborah M. Capaldi, and Gerald Patterson

2003 "Development of antisocial behavior and crime across the life-span from a social interactional perspective: The coercion model," pp. 317–338 in Ronald L. Akers and Gary F. Jensen (eds.), Social Learning Theory and the Explanation of Crime: A Guide for the New Century. Advances in Criminological Theory. Volume 11. New Brunswick, NJ: Transaction.

Weiss, Robert P.
2001 "'Repatriating' low-wage work: The political economy of prison labor reprivatization in the postindustrial United States," Criminology 39:253–291.

Welch, Michael R. Charles R. Tittle, and Harold G. Grasmick
2006 "Christian religiosity, self-control, and social conformity," Social Forces 84:1605–1624.

Wellford, Charles
1975 "Labeling theory and criminology," Social Problems 22:313–32.
1989 "Towards an integrated theory of criminal behavior," pp. 119–128 in Steven F. Messner, Marvin D. Krohn, and Allen E. Liska (eds.), Theoretical Integration in the Study of Deviance and Crime. Albany: State University of New York Press.

West, Candace and Sarah Fenstermaker
1993 "Power, inequality, and the accomplishment of gender: An ethnomethodological view," pp. 151–174 in Paula England (ed.), Theory on Gender/Feminism on Theory. New York: Aldine.

West, Candace and Don Zimmerman
1987 "Doing gender," Gender and Society 1:125–151.

White, Helene Raskin, Marsha E. Bates, and Valerie Johnson
1991 "Learning to drink: Familial, peer, and media influences," pp. 177–197 in David J. Pittman and Helene Raskin White (eds.), Society, Culture, and Drinking Patterns Reconsidered. New Brunswick, NJ: Rutgers Center of Alcohol Studies.

White, Helene Raskin, Robert J. Pandina, and Randy L. LaGrange
1987 "Longitudinal predictors of serious substance use and delinquency," Criminology 25:715–740.

Widom, Cathy S. and Michael G. Maxfield
2001 An Update on the "Cycle of Violence." Washington, DC: U.S. National Institute of Justice.

Wiebe, Richard P.
2003 "Reconciling psychopathy and low self-control," Justice Quarterly 20:297–335.

Wikstrom, Per-Olof H. and Rolf Loeber
2000 "Do disadvantaged neighborhoods cause well-adjusted children to become adolescent delinquents? A study of male juvenile serious offending, individual risk and protective factors, and neighborhood context," Criminology 38: 1109–1142.

Wilbanks, William
1987 The Myth of a Racist Criminal Justice System. Monterey, CA: Brooks/Cole.

Wilcox, Pamela, Kenneth C. Land, and Scott A. Hunt
2003 Criminal Circumstance: A Dynamic, Multicontextual Criminal Opportunity Theory. Chicago and New York: Aldine/de Gruyter.

Wilkins, Leslie
1964 Social Deviance: Social Policy, Action, and Research. Englewood Cliffs, NJ: Prentice Hall.

Williams, Franklin P. III and Marilyn D. McShane
2004 Criminological Theory. Upper Saddle River, NJ: Prentice Hall.

Williams, Franklin P. III and Marilyn D. McShane, eds.
1998 Criminology Theory: Selected Classic Readings. Second Edition. Cincinnati, OH: Anderson.

Williams, Kirk R. and Richard Hawkins
1989 "The meaning of arrest for wife assault," Criminology 27: 163–181.

Wilson, James Q. and Richard J. Herrnstein
1985 Crime and Human Nature. New York: Simon & Schuster.

Wilson, William Julius
1987 The Truly Disadvantaged: The Inner City, the Underclass and Public Policy. Chicago: University of Chicago Press.

Winfree, L. Thomas, Jr., Curt T. Griffiths, and Christine S. Sellers
1989 "Social learning theory, drug use, and American Indian youths: A cross cultural test," Justice Quarterly 6:395–417.

Winfree, L. Thomas, Jr., Teresa Vigil-Backstrom, and G. Larry Mays
1994a, "Social learning theory, self reported delinquency, and youth gangs: A new twist on a general theory of crime and delinquency," Youth and Society 26:147–177.

Winfree, L. Thomas, Jr., G. Larry Mays, and Teresa Vigil–Backstrom
1994b "Youth gangs and incarcerated delinquents: Exploring the ties between gang membership, delinquency, and social learning theory," Justice Quarterly 1:229–256.

Winfree, L. Thomas, Christine Sellers, and Dennis L. Clason
1993 "Social learning and adolescent deviance abstention: Toward understanding reasons for initiating, quitting, and avoiding drugs," Journal of Quantitative Criminology 9:101–125.

Winfree, L. Thomas, Terrance J. Taylor, Ni He, and Finn-Aage Esbensen
2006 "Self-control and variability over time: multivariate results using a 5-year multi-site panel of youths," Crime and Delinquency 52:253–286.

Withrow, Brian L.
2006 Racial Profiling: From Rhetoric to reason. Upper Saddle River, NJ: Prentice Hall.

Wolfgang, Marvin E.
1972 "Cesare Lombroso (1835–1909)," pp. 232–291 in Hermann Mannheim (ed.), Pioneers in Criminology. Second Edition Enlarged. Montclair, NJ: Patterson Smith.

Wolfgang, Marvin E. and Franco Ferracuti
1982 The Subculture of Violence. Beverly Hills, CA: Sage.

Wolfgang, Marvin E., Robert M. Figlio, and Thorsten Sellin
1972 Delinquency in a Birth Cohort. Chicago: University of Chicago Press.

Wolfgang, Marvin E, Robert M. Figlio, Paul E. Tracy, and Simon I. Singer
1985 The National Survey of Crime Severity. Bureau of Justice Statistics. Washington, DC: U.S. Government Printing Office.

Wolfgang, Marvin E., Terence P. Thornberry, and Robert M. Figlio
1987 From Boy to Man, from Delinquency to Crime. Chicago: University of Chicago Press.

Wood, Peter B., John K. Cochran, Betty Pfefferbaum, and Bruce J. Arneklev
1995 "Sensation seeking and delinquent substance use: An extension of learning theory," Journal of Drug Issues 25:173–193.

Worden, Robert E. and Robin L. Shepard
1996 "Demeanor, crime, and police behavior: A reexamination of the police services study data," Criminology 34:83–106.

Wortley, Richard

1997 "Reconsidering the role of opportunity in situational crime prevention," pp. 65–81 in Graeme Newman, Ronald V. Clarke, and S. Giora Shoham (eds.), Rational Choice and Situational Crime Prevention: Theoretical Foundations. Aldershot, England: Ashgate Dartmouth.

Wright, Bradley R. Entner, Avshalom Caspi, Terrie E. Moffitt, and Phil A. Silva

1999 "Low self-control, social bonds, and crime: Social causation, social selection, or both?" Criminology 37:479–514.

Wright, John Paul, Francis T. Cullen, Robert S. Agnew, and Timothy Brezina

2001 "'The root of all evil?' An exploratory study of money and delinquent involvement," Justice Quarterly 18:239–268.

Wright, John Paul and Kevin M. Beaver

2005 "Do parents matter in creating self-control in their children? A genetically informed test of Gottfredson and Hirschi's theory of low self-control," Criminology 43: 1169–1202

Wright, Richard A.

1993a "A socially sensitive criminal justice system," pp. 141–160 in John W. Murphy and Dennis L. Peck (eds.), Open Institutions: The Hope for Democracy. Westport, CT: Praeger.

1993b In Defense of Prisons. Westport, CT: Greenwood.

Wright, Richard A. and J. Mitchell Miller

1998 "Taboo until today? The coverage of biological arguments in criminology textbooks, 1961 to 1970 and 1987 to 1996," Journal of Criminal Justice 26:1–19.

Wright, William E. and Michael C. Dixon

1978 "Community prevention and treatment of delinquency," Journal of Research of Crime and Delinquency 14:35–67.

Young, Jock

1987 "The tasks facing a realist criminology," Contemporary Crises 11:337–356.

Zatz, Marjorie

2000 "The convergence of race, ethnicity, gender, and class on court decisionmaking: Looking toward the 21st century," pp. 503–552 in Julie Horney (ed.), Policies, Processes, and Decisions of the Criminal Justice System: Criminal Justice 2000. Volume 3. Washington, DC: National Institute of Justice.

Zetterberg, Hans L.

1962. Social Theory and Social Practice. New York: Bedminster Press.

Zhang, Lening and Steven F. Messner

1995 "Family deviance and delinquency in China," Criminology 33:359–388.

Zhang, S. X.

2000 An Evaluation of the Los Angeles County Probation Juvenile Drug Treatment Boot Camp. San Marcos: CA: California State University.

Zigler, Edward, Cara Tausig, and Kathryn Black

1996 "Early childhood intervention," pp. 144–149 in Joseph G. Weis, Robert D. Crutchfield, and George S. Bridges (eds.), Juvenile Delinquency. Volume 2. Crime and Society. Thousand Oaks, CA: Pine Forge Press.

Zimring, Franklin E.

1971 "Perspectives on deterrence." NIMH Monograph Series on Crime and Delinquency Issues. Washington, DC: U.S. Government Printing Office.

Zimring, Franklin and Gordon Hawkins

1968 "Deterrence and marginal groups," Journal of Research in Crime and Delinquency 5:100–115.

1973 Deterrence. Chicago: University of Chicago Press.

Author Index

Subject Index

CPSIA information can be obtained at www.ICGtesting.com
Printed in the USA
BVOW010407200912

300942BV00001B/3/P